# Nation and Classical Music

# Music in Society and Culture

ISSN 2047-2773

*Series Editors*

VANESSA AGNEW, KATHARINE ELLIS,
JONATHAN GLIXON, & DAVID GRAMIT

*Consulting Editor*

TIM BLANNING

This series brings history and musicology together in ways that will embed social and cultural questions into the very fabric of music-history writing. Music in *Society and Culture* approaches music not as a discipline, but as a subject that can be discussed in myriad ways. Those ways are cross-disciplinary, requiring a mastery of more than one mode of enquiry. This series therefore invites research on art and popular music in the Western tradition and in cross-cultural encounters involving Western music, from the early modern period to the twenty-first century. Books in the series will demonstrate how music operates within a particular historical, social, political or institutional context; how and why society and its constituent groups choose their music; how historical, cultural and musical change interrelate; and how, for whom, and why music's value undergoes critical reassessment.

*Proposals or queries should be sent in the first instance to the series editors or Boydell & Brewer at the addresses shown below.*

Dr Vanessa Agnew, University of Duisburg-Essen,
Department of Anglophone Studies, R12 S04 H,
Universitaetsstr. 12, 45141 Essen, Germany
*email:* vanessa.agnew@uni-due.de

Professor Katharine Ellis, Department of Music, University of Bristol,
Victoria Rooms, Queen's Road, Clifton, BS8 1SA, UK
*email:* katharine.ellis@bristol.ac.uk

Professor Jonathan Glixon, School of Music, 105 Fine Arts Building,
University of Kentucky, Lexington, KY 40506–0022, USA
*e-mail:* jonathan.glixon@uky.edu

Professor David Gramit, Department of Music, University of Alberta,
3–82 Fine Arts Building, Edmonton, Alberta, T6G 2C9, Canada
*e-mail:* dgramit@ualberta.ca

Boydell & Brewer, PO Box 9, Woodbridge, Suffolk, IP12 3DF, UK
*email:* editorial@boydell.co.uk

*Previously published titles in the series are listed at the back of this volume.*

# Nation and Classical Music

## From Handel to Copland

*Matthew Riley and Anthony D. Smith*

THE BOYDELL PRESS

First published 2016
The Boydell Press, Woodbridge

ISBN  978 1 78327 142 9

The Boydell Press is an imprint of Boydell & Brewer Ltd
PO Box 9, Woodbridge, Suffolk IP12 3DF, UK
and of Boydell & Brewer Inc.
668 Mt Hope Avenue, Rochester, NY 14620–2731, USA
website: www.boydellandbrewer.com

A catalogue record for this book is available from the British Library

This publication is printed on acid-free paper

Designed and typeset in Adobe Warnock Pro by
David Roberts, Pershore, Worcestershire

Printed and bound in Great Britain by
TJ International Ltd, Padstow, Cornwall

MIX
Paper from
responsible sources
FSC
www.fsc.org    FSC® C013056

# Contents

# Illustrations

# Music Examples

# Preface

ANTHONY Smith died shortly after this book went into production, after a long illness that was physically, though not intellectually, debilitating. He was a lifelong lover of classical music, enjoyed attending concerts, owned a sizeable CD collection, and practised the piano into his seventies. His interest in national music went back at least to his experience as an undergraduate of university performances of Mussorgsky's *Khovanshchina*. *Nation and Classical Music* is the last of his many and distinguished publications on aspects of nations and nationalism, and, along with his earlier book *The Nation Made Real: Art and National Identity in Western Europe, 1600–1850* (Oxford University Press, 2013), constitutes a sustained application of earlier, more theoretical, writings that placed culture and symbolism at the centre of our understanding of nationalism.

Matthew Riley
August 2016

# Introduction

THIS book develops a comparative analysis of the relationship between Western art music and the phenomena of nations and nationalisms. On the one side, it explores the influence of emergent nations and nationalism on the development of classical music in Europe and North America. On the other, it considers the more or less distinctive themes, sounds and resonances to be found in the repertory of each of the nations, which helped to give shape and meaning to the abstract concept of the nation. This will allow us to assess the contribution of classical music to the potency and dissemination of the national ideal, and at the same time help us determine how far that ideal encouraged the rise of a special category of 'national music'. Our primary focus is the inner world of national feeling and sentiment, the development of its aural symbolism, and the way musicians, above all composers, participated in shaping it, engaging deeply and extensively in nation-making work.

The time is ripe to bring together the insights of nationalism studies, cultural history and musicology. The study of nations and nationalism, which at one time restricted its focus to questions of economics and politics in modern industrial societies, has in the last few decades turned to matters of culture and identity and now takes an historical long view. English-language musicology meanwhile has embraced the study of nationalism along with a wider interest in the politics of culture, moving away from its old 'centre/periphery' model – itself paradoxically a legacy of German nationalism – which presented the history of music from Germany, France and Italy as a universal tradition, while composers from other countries were liable to be considered 'nationalists'. The Romantic notion that national music directly expresses the 'spirit of the people', and that an audience of co-nationals will resonate with it instinctively, has been replaced by a model of creative action by composers, critics and historians.

The work of Richard Taruskin on Russian music was an early example of these trends.[1] Taruskin took a critical stance towards the music and the history of its reception, resisting its national 'ghettoization' by both Western and Soviet historians, and combining historical approaches with close analyses of the music. Three further studies of Russian music come from the same stable, by Francis

---

[1] Richard Taruskin, *Musorgsky: Eight Essays and an Epilogue* (Princeton and Chichester: Princeton University Press, 1993); *Defining Russia Musically: Historical and Hermeneutical Essays* (Princeton and Chichester: Princeton University Press, 1997); *On Russian Music* (Berkeley and Los Angeles: University of California Press, 2009).

Maes, Marina Frolova-Walker and Rutger Helmers.[2] Various monographs on music by individual composers or single national schools have likewise taken a critical line: the cultural historians Robert Stradling and Meirion Hughes on the 'English Musical Renaissance'; Taruskin on Stravinsky; Steven Huebner on French opera; Stephen Meyer on Weber; David E. Schneider on Bartók and Lynn M. Hooker on Hungarian music more generally; Daniel M. Grimley on Grieg and Nielsen; Tomi Mäkelä and Glenda Dawn Goss on Sibelius; and Alexandra Wilson on the reception of Puccini.[3] To these studies can be added revisionist works of cultural history, mainly on the former 'centre', often by non-musicologists: Celia Applegate, Cecilia Hopkins Porter, Hannu Salmi and Barbara Eichner on Germany; Jane Fulcher and Barbara Kelly on France, and Philipp Ther on central Europe.[4] Benjamin Curtis takes a comparative approach to nineteenth-century

[2] Francis Maes, *A History of Russian Music: From Kamarinskaya to Babi Yar* (Berkeley and London: University of California Press, 2002); Marina Frolova-Walker, *Russian Music and Nationalism: From Glinka to Stalin* (New Haven and London: Yale University Press, 2007); Rutger Helmers, *Not Russian Enough?: Nationalism and Cosmopolitanism in Nineteenth-Century Russian Opera* (Rochester: University of Rochester Press, 2014).

[3] Meirion Hughes and Robert Stradling, *The English Musical Renaissance, 1840–1940: Constructing a National Music*, 2nd edn (Manchester: Manchester University Press, 2001); Richard Taruskin, *Stravinsky and the Russian Traditions: A Biography of the Works through Mavra*, 2 vols (Berkeley: University of California Press, 1996); Steven Huebner, *French Opera at the fin de siècle: Wagnerism, Nationalism, and Style* (Oxford: Oxford University Press, 1999); Stephen C. Meyer, *Carl Maria von Weber and the Search for a German Opera* (Bloomington: Indiana University Press, 2003); David E. Schneider, *Bartók, Hungary, and the Renewal of Tradition: Case Studies in the Intersection of Modernity and Nationality* (Berkeley: University of California Press, 2006); Lynn M. Hooker, *Redefining Hungarian Music from Liszt to Bartók* (New York: Oxford University Press, 2013); Daniel M. Grimley, *Grieg: Music, Landscape and Norwegian Identity* (Woodbridge: Boydell Press, 2006); Daniel M. Grimley, *Carl Nielsen and the Idea of Modernism* (Woodbridge: Boydell Press, 2010); Tomi Mäkelä, *Jean Sibelius*, trans. Steven Lindberg (Woodbridge: Boydell Press, 2011); Glenda Dawn Goss, *Sibelius: A Composer's Life and the Awakening of Finland* (Chicago and London: University of Chicago Press, 2009); Alexandra Wilson, *The Puccini Problem: Opera, Nationalism and Modernity* (Cambridge: Cambridge University Press, 2007).

[4] Celia Applegate and Pamela M. Potter, *Music and German National Identity* (Chicago: University of Chicago Press, 2002); Celia Applegate, *Bach in Berlin: Nation and Culture in Mendelssohn's Revival of the St. Matthew Passion* (Ithaca and London: Cornell University Press, 2005); see also 'What is German Music? Reflections on the Role of Art in the Creation of the Nation', *German Studies Review* 15 (1992), pp. 21–32; 'How German is It? Nationalism and the Idea of Serious Music in the Early Nineteenth Century', *19th-Century Music* 21/3 (1998), pp. 274–96; Cecilia Hopkins Porter, *The Rhine as Musical Metaphor: Cultural Identity in German Romantic Music* (Boston: Northeastern University Press, 1996); Hannu Salmi, *Imagined Germany: Richard Wagner's National Utopia* (New

musical nationalism that encompasses both so-called centre (Wagner) and periphery (Smetana, Grieg).[5] He gives much background in political and cultural nationalism and discussion of the composers' writings as 'discourse', although little analysis of their music. There are many shorter studies of single composers, works or national traditions, including three collections of essays and four journal special issues.[6] Overviews of the subject of music, nations and nationalism include those by Jim Samson, Richard Taruskin and Philip V. Bohlman, who has a more 'bottom-up', ethnomusicological orientation.[7]

Our book draws on this work for its comparative analysis. But it also offers a distinctive, broader perspective. In the musicological literature there tends to be a strong focus on the period 1848–1914, with a few composers included from before, such as Weber, Glinka and Chopin. This was, to be sure, the high tide of

York: Peter Lang, 1999); Barbara Eichner, *History in Mighty Sounds: Musical Constructions of German National Identity, 1848–1914* (Woodbridge: Boydell Press, 2013); Jane Fulcher, *French Cultural Politics and Music: From the Dreyfus Affair to the First World War* (New York: Oxford University Press, 1999); Jane Fulcher, *The Composer as Intellectual: Music and Ideology in France 1914–1940* (New York: Oxford University Press, 2005); Barbara L. Kelly (ed.), *French Music, Culture, and National Identity, 1870–1939* (Woodbridge: Boydell Press, 2008); Philipp Ther, *Center Stage: Operatic Culture and Nation Building in Nineteenth-Century Central Europe*, trans. Charlotte Hughes-Kreutzmüller (West Lafayette: Purdue University Press, 2014).

[5] Benjamin W. Curtis, *Music Makes the Nation: Nationalist Composers and Nation Building in Nineteenth-Century Europe* (Amherst: Cambria, 2008).

[6] Tomi Mäkelä (ed.), *Music and Nationalism in 20th-Century Great Britain and Finland* (Hamburg: Bockel, 1997); Helmut Loos and Stefan Keym (eds), *Nationale Musik im 20. Jahrhundert: kompositorische und soziokulturelle Aspekte der Musikgeschichte zwischen Ost- und Westeuropa: Konferenzbericht Leipzig 2002* (Leipzig: Gundrun Schröder, 2004); Michael Murphy and Harry White (eds), *Musical Constructions of Nationalism: Essays on the History and Ideology of European Musical Culture, 1800–1945* (Cork: Cork University Press, 2001); *Journal of Modern European History* 5/1 (2007) on the nineteenth century; *Studia musicologica* 52 (2011) on national opera; *Journal of Modern Italian Studies* 17/4 (2012) on Italian opera; and *Nations and Nationalism* 20/4 (2014) on selected topics.

[7] Jim Samson, 'Nations and Nationalism', in Samson (ed.), *The Cambridge History of Nineteenth-Century Music* (Cambridge and New York: Cambridge University Press, 2001), pp. 568–600; Jim Samson, 'Music and Nationalism: Five Historical Moments', in *Nationalism and Ethnosymbolism: History, Culture and Ethnicity in the Formation of Nations*, ed. Athena S. Leoussi and Steven Grosby (Edinburgh: Edinburgh University Press, 2007), pp. 55–67; Richard Taruskin, 'Nationalism', in *The New Grove Dictionary of Music and Musicians*, 29 vols, 2nd edn (London: Macmillan, 2001), ed. Stanley Sadie, vol. 17, pp. 689–706; Philip V. Bohlman, *Focus: Music, Nationalism, and the Making of the New Europe*, 2nd edn (New York and London: Routledge, 2011).

'national music': an era of choral societies, grand operas and symphonic poems, and of burgeoning nationalist movements in central and Eastern Europe. National identity became a preoccupation of many musicians, and composers attempted to express it through particular modes, dance rhythms and textures borrowed from vernacular sources ('folk music'), special effects to evoke homeland landscapes, and by musical illustration of tales borrowed from national history and legend.

Although we too draw our examples of national music primarily from this period, we are at pains not to perpetuate the view that treats national music – like all national cultural phenomena – as purely reflective, even 'decorative', of political changes, and that associates it too closely with particular nationalist movements. Moreover, a too-narrow focus on the later nineteenth century calls to mind the restricted definition of the nation as a mass, inclusive, and therefore modern, political community of citizens.[8] This overlooks a much longer and earlier history of the language and symbolism of elite nations going back to the Middle Ages (among, for example, court officials and humanists), a period which was subsequently to provide a good deal of the subject matter for a 'national' – and 'nationalist' – music.[9] In fact the interplay of music and nation encompasses the oratorios of Handel, the open-air music of the French Revolution by Gossec, Cherubini and Méhul, and the orchestral works of Beethoven and Mendelssohn, and it stretches on in art music at least to the mid twentieth century in Prokofiev, Shostakovich, Copland and others. Not all of this repertory is tied to the expression of national identity as such or to the employment of vernacular sources; much of it refers to 'the nation' in a more abstract sense.

As a result, we feel the need for a broader, comparative approach. But, rather than providing a general survey of 'the nation in music' and 'music in the nation' from Monteverdi to Shostakovich – a truly multi-volume enterprise – let alone delving into the archives to uncover the music of now-forgotten figures, we have opted for a more concise, thematic approach, a probing investigation into a variety of cultural themes that constitute the key aspects of this two-way relationship. We address each of the main cultural themes of nationhood in turn with reference to well-known classical music from various countries in Europe and North America. Our selection of repertory is intended to engage a general classical music audience familiar with the works from the concert hall and recordings. It is inevitably partial, and indeed partly reflects the process of 'canonization' of national music that we describe in Chapter 6, a legacy that we choose to work with, rather than against, for the sake of our present purposes.

---

[8]  Eric J. Hobsbawm, *Nations and Nationalism since 1780: Programme, Myth, Reality* (Cambridge: Cambridge University Press, 1990), ch. 1.

[9]  Adrian Hastings, *The Construction of Nationhood: Ethnicity, Religion, and Nationalism* (Cambridge: Cambridge University Press, 1997); Caspar Hirschi, *The Origins of Nationalism: An Alternative History from Ancient Rome to Early Modern Germany* (Cambridge: Cambridge University Press, 2012).

In terms of method, this approach requires, first, some clear working definitions of the key terms: 'nation', 'national identity', 'nationalism', 'national music' and 'nationalist music'. This will permit the exploration of key cultural themes which illuminate aspects of the multi-stranded concept of the nation and which have elicited a powerful response from a variety of musicians and audiences. A second requirement is to frame the cultural themes in such a way as to facilitate large-scale comparative analysis across Europe and North America, which is necessary if we are to assess their relative influence. Finally, the ensuing framework will enable us to pursue some general arguments about the meaning and role of 'national music', and its two-way relationship, in the Western tradition.

These arguments operate on two levels: conceptual and historical. On the one hand, music, like the other arts, can be analysed as a semiotic medium, but one that, uniquely, requires rhythm and time and pitch intervals to produce its aural, intellectual and emotional effects. However, in terms of symbolic subject matter, music may be coupled with other arts (usually drama and literature) to enhance its effects or to encompass social, political and historical themes. On the other hand, music is a performance art: it requires one or more interpreters and some kind of audience for a discrete time-limited event. On that level, music becomes enmeshed with technological and social developments, notably changes in resources, especially musical instruments, and the emergence of a musical public increasingly accustomed to attend and respond to scheduled and timed musical performances on a range of instruments, including the human voice, in private and public buildings.

Prior to the eighteenth century, music was dominated by the Church and the aristocracy with their court orchestras. With the exception of England – and Handel – it was not until the end of that century that a new secular public began to attend concerts put on by 'impresarios' (for example, Salomon) and large orchestras with soloists playing works often specially commissioned for these events, such as Haydn's Paris and London symphonies. It was largely through such public performances that the themes which form the main aspects of the concept of the nation were unfolded and widely disseminated, and helped to mobilize and unify the educated middle-class members of the nation. So, from a historical standpoint, the 'nation in music' and 'music in the nation' appear only with the rise, first of a national cultural elite, and then of the middle-class citizen nation with its public audience for performance events, and with it the growing need of musicians for ever larger audiences in specially sited milieux.

# Definitions

Perhaps the greatest problem in the field is the lack of agreement on definitions of basic terms like 'nation', 'nationalism' and 'national music'; there are as many definitions as there are scholars. We are first confronted in the literature with a range of 'nationalisms': ethnic, territorial, traditionalist, progressive, racial, religious, secular, anti-colonial, and many others. That the historical record shows all these different kinds is not in doubt. The question is what unites them sufficiently for us to call them all 'nationalist'. The question is further complicated by the fact that the term 'nationalism' itself is used to refer to different kinds of phenomena, in particular:

1 an ideology or ideologies of the nation, its unity, identity and autonomy;

2 a movement consisting usually of one or more organizations espousing these ideologies;

3 a 'language' and symbolism of the nation and its elements;

4 a sentiment ('national sentiment' or 'consciousness') of belonging to a nation and desirous of its welfare;

5 the 'growth of nations', an historical process which saw the emergence of nations.

For our purposes, the term 'nationalism' needs to be restricted to the first two of the above usages, with the term 'national' referring to usages 3 and 4, national language and national sentiment, the more complex fifth usage being largely irrelevant to our concerns. In this spirit, we define 'nationalism' as an ideological movement for the attainment and maintenance of autonomy, unity and identity for a human population deemed by some of its members to constitute an actual or potential 'nation'.

The ideology in question constitutes a 'core doctrine' of nationalism, the chief propositions of which may be summarized as follows:

1 the world is divided into nations, each having its own character, history and destiny;

2 the nation is the sole source of political power;

3 loyalty to the nation overrides all other loyalties;

4 to be free, an individual must belong to a nation;

5 nations must attain autonomy and full self-expression,

6 peace and justice in the world can only be built on a plurality of free nations.[10]

---

[10] See Walker Connor, *Ethnonationalism: The Quest for Understanding* (Princeton: Princeton University Press, 1994), ch. 4; Anthony D. Smith, *National Identity* (London: Penguin, 1991), ch. 4.

National autonomy, national unity and national identity: these constitute the principal goals of nationalism everywhere, but to these we may add such end values as national dignity, continuity, authenticity and the national homeland. Apart perhaps from this last, these are all high-level abstractions, and in practice nationalists have found it necessary to supplement or embody them in secondary, lower-level and more concrete notions and ideas – for example, the idea that Poland was a crucified and resurrected Christ, found in the writings of Polish exiles like the poet Adam Mickiewicz, or the belief in Japan that the Emperor, the 'father' of the nation, was descended from the Sun-goddess.

In addition to this political version of nationalism, there is also a cultural nationalism that emphasizes identity and includes propositions 1, 3, 4 and 5 but not 2 and 6. On our terms, cultural nationalists do 'national' rather than 'nationalist' work. As an example, Johann Gottfried Herder, the father of cultural nationalism, was not fond of the state but felt it crucial that each nation should have its own distinctive culture and hence its own identity.[11]

But, as if the problems of defining 'nationalism' were not serious enough, they pale before those surrounding the definition of the concept of the 'nation', the object of every nationalism. This has proved to be perhaps the most vexed question in the field of nationalism studies, with almost as many definitions proposed as scholars in the field. However, most of them would concur with the proposition that the 'nation' is a form of human community – unlike the state, which is best defined in terms of institutional authority, especially over the means of violence and extraction. And the fact that most (but not all) nationalisms seek to attain sovereign statehood for their nations – to turn themselves into 'national states' (or even 'nation-states', if the population happens to be mono-ethnic) – should not obscure the gulf between nations and states.[12]

The term 'nation' possesses two quite different uses. On the one hand, as a general analytic category, it serves to differentiate a particular type of cultural community and collective identity from other related categories of cultural community and collective identity, such as ethnic communities, religious communities and caste systems. On the other hand, as a descriptive term, 'nation' enumerates the features of an historical type of cultural and/or political community, one which can be defined as a named and self-defined human community whose members cultivate shared memories, myths, symbols, values and traditions, reside in and are attached to a perceived historic homeland, create and disseminate a distinctive public culture, and observe shared customs and common laws. This in turn allows us to define the concept of 'national identity' as the continuous reproduction and reinterpretation of the pattern of memories,

---

[11] On cultural nationalism see John Hutchinson, *The Dynamics of Cultural Nationalism: The Gaelic Revival and the Creation of the Irish Nation State* (London: Allen & Unwin, 1987).

[12] See Montserrat Guibernau, *Nations without States: Political Communities in a Global Age* (Malden, Mass.: Blackwell, 1999).

myths, symbols, values and traditions composing the distinctive heritage of the nation, and the variable identification of communal members with that heritage.[13]

How do these definitions help us to explain what is meant by 'national music'? The boundaries that define a specifically 'national music' are hard to locate. Certainly, the idea of the nation may exist in the minds of some intellectuals prior to its modern realization, but even then it is usually based on (1) some pre-existing cultural features of the dominant grouping among the designated population – for example, some shared linguistic, ethnic or religious ties; and (2) some external model of the nation – for example, nationalisms in Eastern Europe often looked to France and England as their models. In this view, modern nations are neither 'pre-formed' nor wholly 'invented'; they are usually created on the basis of a variably extant culture of the dominant 'ethnie' (ethnic community) and an historical model of nationhood from outside. In this process of national creation, artists of all kinds often help to 'rediscover' elements of earlier cultures (heroes, landscapes, customs, etc.) in the designated area or areas, and use them to popularize a desired image of the nation.[14]

Western art music is no exception. Typically, composers have taken tales from the poets, heroes from the historians, and landscapes from the geographers and painters, to forge a composite portrait of the nation as they see it and as they desire their audience to feel it. In the later nineteenth and early twentieth centuries this is often the basis for 'national music', a type of music that induces positive ideas of a nation and produces powerful national sentiments in an audience, especially – though not necessarily solely – of co-nationals. The effect may also occur without the composer's intending it: audiences, and hearers generally, may over time come to 'feel the nation', as it were, through particular musical works which seem to evoke powerful national feelings, that is, feelings pertaining to a named, territorialized human community whose members share common myths, symbols, memories, values and traditions, create a distinctive public culture and observe common laws and customs. Such evocation can occur with the minimum of literary programme, as in Sibelius's last tone poem, *Tapiola* (1926), which uses the legend of the god Tapio to evoke the mystery and terror of the Finnish forests. National music is essentially a form of cultural nationalism, and is to be distinguished in our vocabulary from 'nationalist music', the aim of which is purely political and which intends to arouse its listeners to political action.

This approach to national music is clearly preferable to that of simply denoting as national every composer who is a member of a particular national community,

---

[13] See Anthony D. Smith, *Nationalism: Theory, Ideology, History* (Cambridge: Polity, 2010), ch. 1.

[14] See Peter F. Sugar, *Ethnic Diversity and Conflict in Eastern Europe* (Santa Barbara: ABC-Clio, 1980), esp. essays by Hofer, Fishman and Petrovich; for pre-existing ethnic ties, see Anthony D. Smith, *The Ethnic Origins of Nations* (Oxford: Blackwell, 1986).

irrespective of his or her intentions or residence, audience responses to, or the nature of, his or her work; with the result that works like Tchaikovsky's Fourth Symphony and Brahms's Violin Concerto become, respectively, Russian and German national works, in the same category as, say, Mussorgsky's *Pictures at an Exhibition* and Wagner's *Lohengrin*. This is to empty the category of the national of its ideological or cultural content. It is also preferable to treating national music as a deviation from a universal or classical norm, with some countries – those with relatively recent native institutions of secular music pedagogy or without them at all – producing national music, and others with longer pedagogical traditions producing universal music.

The next question concerns the distinction between 'national' and 'nationalist' music. Philip Bohlman argues that 'national music' emphasizes internal characteristics such as national landscape, language and historical experiences, national culture being generated from within and from below, and its folk music being represented by local groups and individuals. 'Nationalist music', per contra, stresses external characteristics, because its practitioners feel that their national culture is threatened from without; as a result the culture becomes competitive and possessive, and its folk music is characterized by large-scale staged events. As Bohlman puts it: 'Nationalist music serves a nation-state in its competition with other nation-states, and in this fundamental way it differs from national music.'[15] Bohlman is surely right to stress the ways in which a 'national' music serves to lend definition to abstract, and often inchoate, ideas of the nation. On the other hand, it would be hard to show, at least for Western art music, that this was a purely internal, 'bottom up' process, given the considerable cross-fertilization and competitive virtuosity in eighteenth- and nineteenth-century European music. Besides, what shall we say of Smetana and Grieg, two nationalist composers, according to Benjamin Curtis, both of them members of small nations which lacked their own states but much of whose music was, and is, widely felt to 'breathe the nation' (of Czechs and Norwegians)?[16] Even if we omit the reference to the 'nation-state' – itself a problematic term – in what way is Grieg's *Peer Gynt* music 'national' and Vaughan Williams's *Fantasia on a Theme by Thomas Tallis* 'nationalist', because the latter composed in a sovereign 'nation-state', and Grieg did not? Can Grieg's music be said consistently to emphasize internal national definition and that of Vaughan Williams external comparison and competition?

It would appear that hard-and-fast distinctions cannot be maintained. We are dealing rather with a continuum from implicitly national to overtly (and often officially) nationalist music such as Tchaikovsky's *1812 Overture* or Sibelius's *Finlandia*, where the composer's and/or patron's nationalist intentions are clear and well known. That is, we find at one end of the spectrum an evocation and definition of national elements (nature, history, community, language); at the

---

[15] Bohlman, *Music, Nationalism, and the Making of the New Europe*, p. 86.
[16] Curtis, *Music Makes the Nation*.

other the didactic imparting of a political 'morality' of nationhood; and in between considerable overlap between evocative and didactic modes of musical expression. In terms of the definitions of nation and nationalism employed here, we might say that national music is more concerned with the myths, memories, symbols and traditions of the community, its homeland and its culture, while nationalist music tends to proclaim the autonomy, unity and identity of the political nation, often in emotionally charged music. Once again, however, while the polar points of the continuum are clear enough, many works in between display both sets of characteristics simultaneously.

In this book we avoid the phrase 'nationalist composer' that is often found in the older musicological literature, taking the view that one and the same composer may write national music one day and some other music the next. Moreover there is no sense that Italian, French and German composers wrote 'universal' music while those from the geographical 'periphery' were 'nationalist composers'. Indeed, as later chapters will show, in many respects composers from Italy, France and Germany pioneered national music. 'Nationalist' is used here as an adjective in the sense just described, but also substantively to refer to an intellectual who espouses the ideology of nationalism. As regards music, such intellectuals – whose nationalism was mainly of the cultural type – may include the composers of national music themselves, such as Balakirev, Wagner, Smetana, Grieg and Vaughan Williams, who developed programmes of activity for promoting the cause of the nation through music. But, more often, 'nationalists' in music were not primarily composing or performing musicians, but folksong collectors such as Ludwig Erk (Germany), Ludvig Mathias Lindeman (Norway), Julien Tiersot (France) and Cecil Sharp (England); or critics, writers and historians who encouraged composers to write national music and explained it to its audiences, such as Franz Brendel and A. B. Marx (Germany), Zdeněk Nejedlý (Czech lands), Vladimir Stasov (Russia), and J. A. Fuller Maitland, H. C. Colles and Frank Howes in England. National music often inhabits a space opened by these cultural nationalists, and realizes their programmes.

## Comparison and time frame

Despite these caveats, the polar points of this continuum can help in the task of cross-national comparison, which is essential to a thematic approach to the relationship between 'music' and 'nation'. Here, the aim is to compare a variety of musical evocations and narratives of the key elements of nationhood, and thereby reveal the powerful musical dimensions of nation formation and persistence, as well as the influence of nations and nationalism on the development of music. The variety is part musical, part cultural. On the one hand, different musical genres are suited to respective elements and sources of nationhood. Certain genres of instrumental music can best convey community dances, like Chopin's piano mazurkas, while orchestral tone poems from Smetana to Sibelius were most suited to evoking national landscapes, with opera appearing as the optimal medium for narrating national historical episodes (though also serving different national ends).

On the other hand, different ethnic cultures and national histories provide the framework, content and colour for particular elements and forms of nationhood. For example, a self-consciously national Russian musical school emerged in the 1860s – later it was much consolidated conceptually – marked by a variable mixture of Russian literature (usually Pushkin), Orthodox church music, folklore and folk music, and sometimes an exotic Orientalism, all of which mark off this music as distinct from the German or French traditions.[17] The German tradition from Bach to Brahms was formed within a German literary and cultural framework and Lutheran or Catholic religious traditions, which helped to shape the disposition to 'serious' music and rigorous musical forms like the symphony, quartet and sonata, and the elevation of abstract music.[18]

As these examples indicate, in this study we shall be concerned with the development of the Western tradition of music and the concomitant emergence of the modern nation in Europe. Here, we shall, for the most part, have to ignore the evidence for other earlier forms of nation in antiquity and the medieval epoch, as well as for non-Western forms of the nation, and the debates around these vexed issues, if only for reasons of space.[19] For our purposes, we can speak of the development of Western music in relation to the rise of nations from the sixteenth century onwards, when 'national schools' of music began to emerge in some national states like England, France and Spain. But, at this stage, it is difficult to gauge the influence of the nation on music, or vice versa, except in the dances of different ethnic communities. From the seventeenth century, we can discern increasingly national elements in orchestral and especially vocal compositions such as Purcell's *King Arthur* (1691) with its prophecies of English glory. As for an end date, nations and nationalism remained a potent force in classical music at least until World War II. For Bohlman, recent folksong and popular competitions like the Eurovision Song Contest have become power-houses of nationalist competition even today, although these repertoires do not come within our remit. As for the extent of the Western tradition, we include not only Europe, from Ireland and Scandinavia to Russia, but also North and South America, where composers like Charles Ives, Samuel Barber, George Gershwin, Aaron Copland, Leonard Bernstein and Heitor Villa-Lobos, all working in the classical tradition, have contributed works to the canon of national music.

---

[17] Maes, *A History of Russian Music*, ch. 5.

[18] Applegate, *Bach in Berlin*, ch. 2.

[19] But see Stein Tonnesson and Hans Antlov, *Asian Forms of the Nation* (Richmond: Curzon Press, 1996), esp. introduction; and Anthony D. Smith, *Nationalism and Modernism: A Critical Survey of Recent Theories of Nations and Nationalism* (London: Routledge, 1998), ch. 8.

# Dimensions of nationhood

What, then, are the chief cultural dimensions of nationhood, which will facilitate comparison of the relations between nation and music across Europe and America? From our definition, the first is the dimension of community itself, the perception that 'the people' of the nation constitute a bonded community of social relations, shared sentiments, myths and memories, and common values and purposes. These find periodic expression in the rites and ceremonies, symbols and traditions of a distinctive public culture with its celebratory festivals. Music plays an integral part in these rites and ceremonies and the public festivals of which they form the central elements. This was evident in the *fêtes* of the French Revolution, and in all the national festivals that took the French examples as their models. Here we may include the national anthems that proliferated across Europe and the Americas from the later eighteenth century onwards, as well as the 'heroic' responses of some classical composers from Beethoven to Verdi and Tchaikovsky, as well as the increasing use of folksongs and folk dances in classical works, and the compilation of books of folksongs from almost all European countries.

A second dimension of nationhood is formed around the actual or putative territory of the nation, its perceived historic homeland. The idea that to each national community there belongs an historic homeland is, of course, of great antiquity; the biblical record of the 'land of Israel' is only the best-known and most influential example from the ancient world, many more being vividly presented in the pages of Herodotus. However, it was only in the later Middle Ages that national homelands became wedded to national states in Western Europe, and only from the eighteenth century, under the influence of the cult of authenticity and, later, Romanticism, that the special qualities of their landscapes were singled out and invested with almost mystical properties. Hence, though we encounter musical works that clearly describe the land and its people in earlier periods, it was not until the nineteenth century that musical works began to evoke the sense of particular homelands for co-nationals.

Alongside landscape, national history formed the other main axis of nationhood. This reflects the conception of nations as temporal categories having their own trajectories, starting from primitive origins, moving forwards in richness and complexity to a heroic or golden age (or ages), then declining for many generations, and only reviving through the efforts of the nationalist 'awakeners'. Central to this ethno-history – a tale of the community told and retold by the members through successive generations – is the belief in heroes and heroines, historical and legendary, models of heroism and virtue to be emulated by later generations. Such *exempla virtutis* became increasingly popular in Western art from c.1750, and we find similar examples in eighteenth- and nineteenth-century music, especially in tone poems (Glazunov's *Stenka Razin*, Sibelius's *Four Lemminkäinen Legends*), operas (*Aida, Siegfried*), and oratorios from Handel to Mendelssohn. The musical drama helps imaginatively to recreate a heroic personality in his or her period, irrespective of historical evidence. Here a poetic authenticity – one that evokes an assumed national epoch – is sought and represented.

As nations are presumed to have a past (or pasts), so are they also endowed with a future. This is not just any future, but one that is foreordained, the national destiny to which history is driving the community. It is a destiny that can only be achieved through struggle and sacrifice, the sacrifices that, as the nineteenth-century historian Ernest Renan put it, one has made in the past and that one is prepared to continue to make in the future.[20] It is these sacrifices that must be commemorated and these exploits that must be celebrated in the rites and ceremonies conducted before the memorials and monuments to the fallen. Music, once again, is integral to these rituals of the nation, often in the form of funeral laments, as in Purcell's *Dido and Aeneas*, the funeral march in Wagner's *Götterdämmerung* and the lament in Prokofiev's *Alexander Nevsky*. The rites of the nation are often accompanied by solemn marches, which may also appear in more abstract works like the second movement of Beethoven's 'Eroica' Symphony.

These constitute the main dimensions of nationhood, and will serve in this book to order the great variety of relations between music and nation and the many kinds of musical composition that express these relations. After a chapter considering the musical expressions of the dimensions of nationhood in general, we pursue in detail the range of musical themes as follows. Chapter 2 considers the national community expressed through art music that incorporates 'folk music' for the purpose of defining national identity. Chapters 3 and 4 deal with the homeland and ethno-history respectively. Chapter 5 returns to the national community, but now from the perspective of commemorative practices. These dimensions do not exhaust the manifold relations between music and nation, let alone the many kinds of musical works that in some way contain a national element. Some compositions, moreover, may articulate more than one theme, or even all of them. Chapter 6 stands back from these themes and addresses broader questions of national musical traditions and the canonization of national music in various countries. This thematic and comparative approach, based on the four dimensions, illuminates the impact of nations and nationalism on Western art music, while at the same time revealing the ways in which the various genres of music have helped to define the properties of nations and in some cases furthered the goals of nationalism. At the same time, the comparative and thematic approach will help to explore and test more general arguments about the rise and role of a 'national music' in the Western tradition.

---

[20] Ernest Renan, *Qu'est-ce qu'une nation?* (Paris: Calmann-Levy, 1882); translated in John Hutchinson and Anthony D. Smith, *Nationalism* (Oxford and New York: Oxford University Press, 1994).

## Essentialism and constructivism

Generations of listeners have attributed national qualities to certain repertoires of European and American art music of the nineteenth and twentieth centuries. They perceive, or believe they perceive, the expression of nationality through the medium of sound, and speak of musical 'Russianness', 'Czechness', 'Englishness' and so on (see Chapter 6). This impression can be very powerful, and may arouse strong, shared feelings of identification among groups of listeners. How can it be explained? On the one hand, nationalists themselves have an account at the ready: national music captures an essential national quality – Herder called it *Volksgeist* (spirit of the people) – which is duly recognized by co-nationals as their own. This account attributes a spiritual content to the music and is, essentially, incorrigible. It is generally rejected by modern scholars, who are sceptical about idealizing treatments of nationality, not least because of the disastrous consequences of nationalism in twentieth-century wars and ethnic conflicts. Instead they emphasize the 'construction' of nationality in music at certain historical moments by certain individuals with certain interests, and the 'invention of tradition' in music. The terms 'invention' and 'construction' appear in the titles of numerous musicological articles on musical nationalism, reflecting two wider intellectual trends. One is the 'modernist' position in the history of nations and nationalism, according to which the emergence of nations is the result of the modernization of economic systems, while national cultures are secondary phenomena. The second is the understanding of language and 'text' in structuralism and poststructuralism in the Humanities, which posits structures of differences rather than essential content. This concept of 'difference' deeply informs Joep Leerssen's recent history of 'national thought' in Europe. He finds the roots of national thought in ancient ways of thinking about self and other, and about society and the wilderness beyond. The very concept of 'ethnie' is understood not just as 'belonging together' but as 'being distinct from others'.[21]

In his book on nation building and nationalist composers (Wagner, Smetana and Grieg), Benjamin Curtis has a chapter entitled 'Constructing "Difference" in the National Culture', about the creation of national boundaries around music, the 'discursive production of difference' and the 'fetishization of difference'. There are two levels in this production: the definition of characteristics to differentiate the music of a nation, and the 'Othering' of separate musical traditions, making them the opposite of one's 'own' music, with, implicitly or explicitly, a negative value judgement. Nations are defined musically through exclusion, although Curtis admits that the boundaries may be 'hard' or 'soft'. He does not discuss the three composers' music as such, only their 'discursive formations'. To take another example, in the view of the influential German musicologist Carl Dahlhaus, 'folklorism' in nineteenth-century music – not the same as

---

[21] Joep Leerssen, *National Thought in Europe: A Cultural History* (Amsterdam: Amsterdam University Press, 2006), sec. 1, p. 17.

nationalism but closely connected with it – is, at the level of compositional technique, essentially the same as 'exoticism': the musical depiction of a remote or alien culture, such as was found in operas for the French stage on Egyptian and Asian subjects. In both cases the original authenticity of the musical materials is irrelevant to their effect. '[T]he key issue is not the original ethnic substance of these phenomena so much as the fact that they differ from European art music, and the function they serve as deviations from the European norm.' That function is the same in a piano piece by Grieg, a song by Balakirev, or episodes in exoticist operas by Gounod, Saint-Saëns or Bizet. Likewise, 'landscape painting' in music – another key element of national music – 'runs against the mainstream of compositional evolution' and has its effect primarily through the negation of standard processes of modern European music.[22]

To question this way of thinking about national music is not to resurrect the *Volksgeist* hypothesis. After all, the early stages of national music often specify no particular national identity or evoke several, while celebratory and commemorative festivals and ceremonies, as we shall see in Chapters 1 and 5, place more emphasis on national form than content. Here it is the sense of a community with shared memories and a public culture, rather than the contents of those memories or the distinctiveness of the culture, that is uppermost. Even music that does project a distinctive 'local colour' or speaks in a strong national 'accent' that sounds different from the norm often incorporates the forms of the celebratory and commemorative traditions, filling them out, as it were, with a particular national content.

Moreover, nationalist historians and musicologists, despite their idealizing tendencies, may possess 'literacy' within their own musical traditions – an informed way of hearing and understanding – that outsiders should take seriously. The semiotics of national music is not determined solely by differences from a perceived 'universal' language, still less a 'mainstream of compositional evolution' running through Austrian and German composers from Bach to Schoenberg, but by internal developments and dialogues within traditions. Such traditions have a starting point, to be sure, and later may be reinvented, but at the same time national music has more ways of communicating than negation. At the aesthetic level, national music is better conceived as a play of similarities and differences within a distinct tradition along with the differences from the perceived universal tradition. Contrary to Dahlhaus, then, folklorism in music may be much more than exoticism. The model is one of multiple, interrelated traditions, which differentiate themselves from one another but also interweave, and share their basic syntax: harmonic tonality, regular phrase structures and homophonic textures. Transnational exchange between traditions is common,

---

[22] Curtis, *Music Makes the Nation*, pp. 146, 147; Carl Dahlhaus, *Nineteenth-Century Music*, trans. J. Bradford Robinson (Berkeley and Los Angeles: University of California Press, 1989), p. 306; see also Ralph P. Locke, *Musical Exoticism: Images and Reflections* (Cambridge: Cambridge University Press, 2009), ch. 4.

especially in musical forms and compositional techniques. Examples include the influences of Brahms on Dvořák; Wagner on Smetana, d'Indy and Elgar; Stravinsky on Szymanowski and Copland; Borodin, Rimsky-Korsakov and Tchaikovsky on Sibelius; and Sibelius on Vaughan Williams and Harris. 'Othering' of non-native musical traditions in fact applies to only one of Curtis's three composers – Wagner (on French music) – and is generally found quite rarely among composers, who, if they were nationalists, tended to espouse a Herderian cultural pluralism (see Chapter 6).

National music often works like a 'contract', in which the composer agrees to use certain conventions and the listener to interpret them in a certain way. Communication takes place on the terms established by the contract and in this way meaning is recognized. The contract of national music is not immemorial: it comes into force over the course of history. Existing indigenous musical traditions may be 'nationalized' through new associations or uses, while cultural phenomena of long-standing duration such as myths or legends may be revived and given new meanings (Chapter 4). A contract may evolve over time, and be 'renegotiated', especially at or following times of crisis: at these moments creativity may be required. An example is Manuel de Falla's turn from *andalucismo* to Castilian neoclassicism in the 1920s, which was soon recognized as a 'true' Spanish idiom by sympathetic listeners (Chapter 3). This is the point at which golden ages may be posited (see Chapter 6) in an effort to erase more recent or received compositional traditions. Processes of cultural reception play an important role too in the negotiation of contracts, certain compositions being selected and preferred over others as instances of the national style, and certain pieces coming to be heard as national that were not intended as such by their composers, such as Bach's *St Matthew Passion*, Glinka's *Kamarinskaya* and Elgar's 'Nimrod' (Chapter 6 again).

Stephen Meyer essentially arrives at the contractual understanding in his study of Weber's *Der Freischütz*, a work that certainly marked a moment of cultural crisis and the premiere of which later acquired mythic status as the inauguration of German national music. The 'national character' of the opera, he suggests, is

> both the topic and the result of a dialogue between 'acts of composition' and 'acts of interpretation and perception' … Weber adopted pre-existing signifiers of national style, but through 'acts of composition' he changed and developed these signifiers. After the premiere of *Freischütz*, certain of its features were themselves adopted, though 'acts of interpretation and perception', as preconditions of the national style, and, perhaps, as elements in the ever-changing definition of the nation itself. This recursive relationship is always fluid and continually redefining its terms, Still, in order for a 'national style' to become a reality … there must be a certain continuity of expectation and convention.[23]

---

[23] Meyer, *Carl Maria von Weber*, p. 115.

We can see this recursive relationship not just in Wagner's compositional response to Weber, but in the responses of Mendelssohn to Beethoven and Bach; Balakirev, Rimsky-Korsakov and Borodin to Glinka; Glazunov and Rachmaninov to them in turn; Vaughan Williams to Parry and Elgar, and so on. In this book, therefore, we avoid the extremes of both essentialism and constructivism. We pay attention to the historical origins of nationality in music, but we do not view it merely as a mass delusion conjured by nationalists. At the same time, we highlight the complex processes of transnational exchange often to be found in these repertoires.

# 1

# Music and the National Community: From Monarchs to Citizens

T‍HE first cultural theme of nationhood is the idea of community, that is, the unity of a 'people' through mutual obligations and shared memories and values. The broadest context for our account of the rise of national music and its role in the development of nations and nationalism is the attempt by 'national educators' to realize the national community by mobilizing its citizens in vernacular mode. Music was drawn into their efforts to arouse national sentiment and make the nation appear real, self-evident and accessible to its people by appeal to language, customs, memories, history and destiny. This chapter sketches the main developments and outlines some key themes in these attempts to realize the national community, focusing especially on political and intellectual developments of the late eighteenth century and their legacies. For it was only when national ideas were conjoined with a notion of 'the people' rather than a monarch or aristocracy, that the sustained development of national music become possible and that music could enter the fabric of the nation.

## Trajectories of 'music' and 'nation'

Western art music, though it had important forebears in ancient Jewish (Temple) and Greco-Roman musical traditions, developed initially from Gregorian chant in Rome and Italy into a rich and complex polyphonic tradition across much of Western and central Europe by the time of Tallis, Vittoria and Palestrina. The dominant influence was Catholic – and subsequently Protestant – liturgical requirements. But, by the sixteenth century, secular music had become prominent at the courts of kings and princes in Italy, France, Spain and England. In the following century, both sacred and secular music, especially opera, were developed by Monteverdi in Mantua and Venice, and secular music, including instrumental works, masques and dances, flourished in Italy and at the court of Louis XIV, which became the model for the princely courts in Germany, Austria, Bohemia and elsewhere. With musical patronage so embedded in supra-national institutions, or monopolized by aristocratic, often non-national, elites, there was little trace of national, let alone nationalist, influence, on musical developments, certainly before the seventeenth century. It is even harder to gauge the contribution of various kinds of music to the formation of modern nations in the late medieval and early modern periods. But there may have been an indirect influence in the various fanfares and processionals of the monarchs and their courts, perhaps linked to the Church as in Gabrieli's Venice, or in marches and songs on the battlefield, such as the Swiss pikemen from each canton sang.[1]

The development of nations is perhaps harder to trace. This is partly a matter of lack of agreed evidence, partly of disputes over the definition of the concept of the nation. A case can, however, be made for a form of nationhood in the ancient world, especially among ancient Egyptians, Jews and Armenians, one that is based not on the centrality of civic ideals and citizenship (except in a limited way in ancient Athens), but rather on the religiously defined membership of an ethno-political community. The subsequent history of the ideal of nationhood, after the fall of the Western Roman empire, is obscure, and many would say non-existent. On the other hand, by the eleventh century, there are clear signs of national differentiation in mainly cultural and territorial terms, though the evidence is literary rather than musical or artistic. In a few cases, notably in the British isles, some kind of elite defensive national sentiment emerged, for example in the wars with the Viking Danes.[2]

By the fourteenth century, we find intellectuals like Petrarch giving vent to vivid expressions of cultural-national ethnic antagonism, but these were only rarely linked to political objectives. However, the latter became all too apparent in the debates at the Council of Constance (1415–20), where political-territorial conflicts between territorially and linguistically defined ecclesiastical delegations, often acting on behalf of their secular patrons, foreshadowed the disintegration of 'Christendom' as a unifying European political concept. By the sixteenth century, the power of west European territorial monarchical states based on dominant *ethnies* (ethnic communities) – and with it a 'crown-centred patriotism' – had largely superseded those of the Papacy, the Holy Roman empire and the city-states, paving the way for growing elite national identification in these states.[3]

This is the point at which the development of Western music and the formation of modern nations begin to intersect. But only to a very limited degree: these are not citizen nations (the Dutch and possibly the Swiss are partial exceptions); and, as we observed, most public music was sacred and ecclesiastical, though courtly dances often had an 'ethnic' character. Even in the following century, there are few examples of the mutual influence of secular music and elite

---

[1] Ulrich Im Hof, *Mythos Schweiz: Identität, Nation, Geschichte, 1291–1991* (Zürich: Neue Zürcher Zeitung, 1991), ch. 1.

[2] Hastings, *The Construction of Nationhood*, ch. 2; Leonard Scales, 'Identifying "France" and "Germany": Medieval Nation-Making in Some Recent Publications', *Bulletin of International Medieval Research* 6 (2000), pp. 23–46.

[3] Scales, 'Identifying "France" and "Germany"'; Leonard Scales, 'Late Medieval Germany: An Under-Stated Nation?', in *Power and the Nation in European History*, ed. Leonard Scales and Oliver Zimmer (Cambridge: Cambridge University Press, 2005), pp. 166–91; Hirschi, *The Origins of Nationalism*; Anders Toftgaard, 'Letters and Arms: Literary Language, Power and Nation in Renaissance Italy and France, 1300–1600', Ph.D. thesis, University of Copenhagen, 2005.

nations, though one exception, as we shall see, was Restoration England. On the Continent, only after the Treaty of Westphalia (1648), which concluded the Thirty Years War, could the subsequent wars of absolutist states over the Spanish and Austrian successions encourage the production of marches and songs glorifying the monarch and his state, which, in retrospect, paved the way for the anthems (in Austria, as in Britain) which in turn served as models for the later republican hymns of citizen nations.[4]

Hence we need to take account of two kinds of nation in the early modern and modern epochs. The first is hierarchical and elite-led, if not monarchical: a paternal, 'subject–master nation', as in Sweden, but also elsewhere.[5] This type of nation emerged in the Middle Ages, but becomes prominent in the sixteenth to nineteenth centuries. The second type is republican, theoretically egalitarian and bourgeois-led, emerging first in the Netherlands and England (where it became diluted by the first kind of elite-led nation after the Restoration), and later and more radically in the United States and France. This latter type is often taken to be the sole genuine kind of nation (mainly because of its strong democratic component); but this is to view Western history in teleological terms, as moving progressively towards an inclusive, rational, liberal and ultimately cosmopolitan endpoint. In fact, throughout the nineteenth and even into the twentieth century, we find emergent modern nations, that is, modern nations created on the basis of much older *ethnies* or ethnic ties, such as Spain, Russia, Poland, Japan and Ethiopia, led by hereditary elites, if not by monarchs. (There are also mixed cases, such as Britain, Denmark and Italy.)[6]

Perhaps even more important has been the influence of a third type of cultural tradition of political legitimation, which we may term 'covenantalism'. Originating in the Mosaic Covenant on Mount Sinai, the idea of a covenant between God and His people entered into the mainstream of Christianity, with the result that the claim to constitute a covenanted and 'chosen' people on the model of biblical Israel was replicated across Europe and America from the early Middle Ages to the Dutch Revolt and the English Glorious Revolution. In its modern, secular expression, this often took the form of a political contract among the members of the dominant *ethnie* to create and maintain a sacred communion of the people in an emerging national state, such as we find in oath-swearing republics like France and the United States to this day.[7]

---

[4] Bohlman, *Music, Nationalism, and the Making of the New Europe*, pp. 109–17.

[5] Bo Strath, 'The Swedish Path to National Identity in the Nineteenth Century', in *Nordic Paths to National Identity in the Nineteenth Century*, ed. Øystein Sørensen (Oslo: Research Council of Norway, 1994), pp. 55–63.

[6] Anthony D. Smith, *The Cultural Foundations of Nations: Hierarchy, Covenant, and Republic* (Oxford: Blackwell, 2008), chs 4 and 5.

[7] See Hastings, *The Construction of Nationhood*, ch. 8; Anthony D. Smith, *Chosen Peoples: Sacred Sources of National Identity* (Oxford: Oxford University Press, 2003), chs 3–5.

Unlike the hierarchical and republican traditions, covenantalism has been too unstable a type of cultural tradition of legitimation to create nations exclusively in its own image, except for short, revolutionary periods. Nevertheless, as Max Weber remarked of charisma, the gift of grace, the dynamic thrust of a covenantal movement such as nationalism can be, and often is, sufficient to destroy or reshape existing hierarchical and republican structures and replace them with others more adapted to the circumstances and needs of the population. Even more important, a covenantal movement, religious or secular, has been a major factor in creating the myth of ethnic election, which in secular guise has to this day proved a potent and durable cultural dynamic for the modern nation.[8]

## The role of the arts

Even today modern nations in Europe and the Americas manifest differing combinations of hierarchical, republican and covenantal traditions of political legitimation; but it is to polities and *ethnies*, and often a combination of both, that we must look for their long-term material and cultural frameworks. However, when we turn to the routes by which different nations emerged, we need to supplement these underlying structural factors with consideration of the dimensions of culture and human agency. In this context, the part played by 'national educators' has been paramount, operating alongside and, in some cases, in lieu of political leaders. Theirs has been a pivotal role. Social philosophers, philologists, historians and folklorists from Rousseau, Herder and Fichte to Mazzini, Palacky and Karamzin, have often taken the lead, providing a national, if not nationalist, education for successive generations of co-nationals, imprinting their visions of the nation on the minds and hearts of the young.

But concepts like the nation, national identity and nationalism are high-level and novel abstractions, unfamiliar to the vast majority of those whom the national educators deem to be members of the nation-to-be and whom they wish to mobilize. As Mazzini and Fichte, among others, found, their national visions are likely to fall on deaf ears, and seem irrelevant to the concerns of the majority of the educated elites, let alone to illiterate lower classes. Hence the need for sensual means of rousing, and educating, both elites and lower classes, and therefore the appeal for support and enthusiastic dedication of all manner of artists – literary, musical and visual – in the task of making the nation appear natural and real. This is the project of 'vernacular mobilization', through which national educators and artists sought to rouse their co-nationals and make the nation tangible and accessible by an appeal to a common civic language and customs, national landscapes, ethnic history and national destiny. And if the national educators turned for help to artists to realize their dream, so equally

---

[8] Max Weber, *From Max Weber: Essays in Sociology*, ed. H. Gerth and C. W. Mills (London: Routledge & Kegan Paul, 1948), ch. 9.

many artists were drawn to the ideal of nationhood and its national institutions in which they might hope to play a formative role and achieve a degree of national prestige.[9]

The creation of a 'national music', one which can arouse national ideas and sentiments in its hearers and inspire a love of the nation among its members, must be placed in the context of 'realizing' the nation and mobilizing its citizens in a vernacular mode. The themes of this kind of music echo those of the project of vernacular national mobilization. As we saw, these are the themes of celebration of community and citizenship, evocation of landscape and homeland, recreation of heroic histories, and commemoration of national sacrifice and destiny. In the rest of this chapter, we look more closely at the first of these themes of a national music: the celebration of community and citizenship.

## Massed Protestant 'unisonance'

Communities of the scale and complexity of 'modern nations', even when they dominated sovereign states and could boast a long, if presumed, ethnic pedigree, required considerable political and cultural work, not to mention socio-economic resources, if they were to survive and prosper in a modern setting. National institutions had to be established, national political processes organized, and legal and educational standards and practices agreed, even in the absence of independent statehood, as in Catalonia and Scotland. But equally important was the cultural work needed to create the nation and make its members 'national'. As the Risorgimento leader Massimo d'Azeglio was alleged to have said: 'We have made Italy, now we must make Italians.' To 'realize the nation', and imbue the mass of the designated population with national feeling, when most of their loyalties were still directed to family, village, town or province, required a long and determined process of education and indoctrination in the significance and benefits of nationhood and the overriding need for national community and solidarity. Hence, the oft-repeated cry for unity and the ceaseless drive for fraternity and solidarity in the history of modern nations and nationalism.

This is where artists, and particularly musicians, played a crucial role. After all, nothing so exemplifies unity and fraternity as the 'unisonance' of massed choirs, and the solidarity created by rousing choral songs of liberty from oppression. We see this in eighteenth-century England and during the French Revolution. Already, after the Glorious Revolution, Purcell's *King Arthur* (1691) with words by John Dryden, an opera in the tradition of the masque, written for the Queen's Theatre, retold the legendary history of King Arthur: how he defeated the forces of darkness and the invading Saxons and through Merlin's prophecies looked

---

[9] See Leerssen, *National Thought in Europe*, pp. 186–203; Anthony D. Smith, 'National Identity and Vernacular Mobilisation in Europe', *Nations and Nationalism* 17/2 (2011), pp. 223–56.

forward to the Glorious Revolution, invoking the aid of the Almighty for his chosen people and their virtues, which the chorus of peasants celebrate. This was also the underlying theme of another, even more successful masque, Thomas Arne's *King Alfred*, first performed in 1740, with a libretto by James Thomson and David Mallet. It retold the tale of Alfred's rise from fugitive to conqueror of the Danes, but its real message was a British nationalism, which dated British rights to the Glorious Revolution and issued a call to arms, especially in the celebrated closing chorus, 'Rule Britannia'. The latter's six four-line verses managed to cover the gamut of eighteenth-century British nationalism, from providential aid and a conviction of liberty to global naval supremacy, cultural excellence and the natural beauty of the 'Blest isle', and it remains to this day a powerful evocation of British resistance and grandeur.[10]

It was in this buoyant climate that Handel's *Judas Maccabeus*, dedicated to the Duke of Cumberland, the victor of Culloden over the Scots, made its appearance in 1747. Its great song of triumph, 'See the Conquering Hero Comes', perfectly expressed the temper of the times, which veered from despair at the Jacobite victory of Prestonpans to triumph at the subsequent victory at Culloden. Handel's oratorio succeeded not just in pleasing London's Jews but more especially its Protestants who saw the British as a latter-day chosen people like the ancient Israelites, who by arming 'In defence of your nation, religion, and laws, The Almighty Jehovah will strengthen your hands', and whose British homeland is a place where 'fleecy flocks the hills adorn, / And valleys smile with wavy corn' (Morell 1746).

*Judas Maccabeus* was one of several biblical (and in this case Apocryphal) oratorios with which Handel revived his flagging career in London, along with *Saul* (1739), *Samson* (1743), *Joseph* (1743), *Belshazzar* (1744), *Joshua* (1747), *Solomon* (1748) and *Jephtha* (1752), to name only the works based on the Old Testament. Indeed, the majority of his oratorios were drawn from the Hebrew Bible and the Apocrypha, with the exception of *Messiah* (1742) which was also drawn from New Testament texts. In several of these oratorios, a hard-pressed tragic hero is placed within the framework of an almost messianic providentialism working on behalf of a chosen people, a theme that would have appealed to the eighteenth-century Protestant British in their struggle with the Catholic French. The exception is *Israel in Egypt* (1739), where the enslavement and oppression of the whole people of Israel and its miraculous deliverance by an all-powerful Deity struck a particularly powerful chord in the hearts and minds of many Britons confronted with hostile Catholic powers on the Continent. Here it is the chorus that expresses the emotions of the Jewish (British) people, as it was to do on so many occasions in later decades and centuries.[11]

---

[10] T. C. W. Blanning, *The Triumph of Music: Composers, Musicians and Their Audiences, 1700 to the Present* (London: Penguin, 2008), pp. 241–5.

[11] Linda Colley, *Britons: Forging the Nation, 1707–1837* (New Haven: Yale University Press, 1992), pp. 31–3; on the contribution of the visual arts see also the essays in

But this was perhaps no more than a harbinger of popular national sentiment, for many of Handel's other works such as the Anthems and Te Deums composed for the Duke of Chandos (*c.* 1718), the *Water Music* (1716), and the later *Music for the Royal Fireworks* (1749), were tied to the British monarchy, often a source of musical patronage. Nevertheless, the turn to biblical oratorio with its emphasis on the divine fate of a chosen people was significant in underscoring the crucial role of ethnic election and the accompanying conviction of British chosenness under its ancient monarchy. That was also the theme of what became the British national anthem, 'God save the King', whose tune was first written down by John Bull in 1619, but only published in 1744, and sung in public the following year after the defeat of the royal army by the Jacobites at Prestonpans. Arranged by Thomas Arne, it was at first an appeal for divine aid against the Scottish rebels; but final victory in this war secured its place in the national consciousness, with constant iteration establishing the national unisonance of massed choirs which became instrumental in 'nationalizing' the British people.[12]

## Hymns of the secular republic

The French counterpart to a Protestant British providentialism was, of course, revolutionary republicanism clad in secular classical garb, but for all that it incorporated a messianic 'covenantalism' every bit as thoroughgoing and profound as its British rival. Here, too, the underlying concept of a chosen people – the enlightened, republican (later imperial) French *ethnie*, so vividly expressed in the oath-swearing ceremonies of the Revolution – was embodied through the arts, notably the visual and musical dimensions of the dramatic revolutionary spectacles. Musically, what mattered was not so much the involvement of a Gossec or a Méhul, but the agency of popular song. From the time of Louis XIV, with the celebrated song of triumph, 'Marlbrough s'en va-t-en guerre' (1709), through the later victory song, 'Battle of Fontenoy' (1745), the high point of the Bourbon dynasty in the eighteenth century, to the early revolutionary 'Ça ira', sung by people everywhere in 1790, marching and street songs provided the popular counterpart to the aristocratic cult of the Opera. These songs culminated in the 'Battle Song of the Rhine Army', later known as the 'Marseillaise', composed in Strasbourg by Claude-Joseph Rouget de l'Isle in 1792. After a first performance there, copies of the hymn were sent to Paris, including to Rouget's mentor, André Grétry. But it was when it was taken up by some four hundred volunteers from Marseilles, who repeatedly sang the Battle Hymn along the way and in the capital just before the 10 August assault

*Conflicting Visions: War and Visual Culture in Britain and France, c. 1700–1830*, ed. John Bonehill and Geoff Quilley (Aldershot: Ashgate, 2005).

[12] Blanning, *The Triumph of Music*, pp. 246–7.

on the Tuileries, that it acquired its undisputed status as France's premier battle hymn. How far it helped to turn the tide of war in 1792–93 remains unclear. Certainly, many witnesses at Jemappes in November 1792 and Cambrai in July 1793 attested to its national potency; and its bloodthirsty language and sacralization of the nation assured its prominence within France and its influence outside.[13]

This suggests that only when national ideas and national language were married to the belief in 'the people' rather than in a monarch or aristocracy, did a sustained interplay of music and nation become possible. Though there were significant exceptions, as the example of Britain illustrates, the experiences of the French Revolution and all the revolutions, attempted or successful, that followed, lend support to this thesis. It is only with the demise of *anciens régimes*, and the rise of the citizen nation, that music enters into the fabric of the nation, first and foremost through the unisonance of massed choirs and national hymns of battle and celebration.

In one sense, the ground for this transformation had been well prepared in the arts. Quite apart from the radical thinkers of the Enlightenment, notably Voltaire and Rousseau, plays, paintings and musical dramas in France had rejected Rococo styles and concerns and had looked to the past, often of classical antiquity, for heroic exempla of the virtue and patriotism that from the 1750s began to exercise the hearts and minds of the educated classes. These culminated in David's great series of paintings in the 1780s on ancient Greek and Roman episodes – *Belisarius* (1781), *Hector and Andromache* (1783), *The Oath of the Horatii* (1785), *The Death of Socrates* (1787) and *Brutus* (1789) – which so manifestly exemplify civic virtue, austerity and patriotic self-sacrifice. In music, too, a new spare style of harmony brought to Paris by Gluck after 1774 had been applied to heroic themes from Greek mythology, and had won many followers in Paris; Gluck's operas, *Iphigénie en Aulide*, *Iphigénie en Tauride*, *Orphée et Eurydice* and *Armide*, remained popular during the Revolution.[14]

This was very much in line with the cult of sensibility and Rousseau's call for music to convey the 'truth and simplicity of nature', which was encouraged by the influx of German and Italian composers brought in by Marie-Antoinette after 1774. Especially important were the role of the opéra comique and the operas of Grétry (1741–1813). From *Le Huron* (1768) to *L'épreuve villageoise* (1784), Grétry

---

[13] Blanning, *The Triumph of Music*, pp. 248–60; Michel Vovelle, 'La Marseillaise: War or Peace', in *Realms of Memory: The Construction of the French Past under the Direction of Pierre Nora*, ed. Lawrence D. Kritzman, trans. Arthur Goldhammer, vol. 3, *Symbols* (New York and Chichester: Columbia University Press, 1998), pp. 29–74; see also Simon Schama, *Citizens: A Chronicle of the French Revolution* (New York and London: Knopf and Penguin, 1989), pp. 597–9.

[14] Emmet Kennedy, *A Cultural History of the French Revolution* (New Haven and London: Yale University Press, 1989), pp. 116–18; Robert Rosenblum, *Transformations in Late Eighteenth Century Art* (Princeton: Princeton University Press, 1967), ch. 2.

aimed for naturalness and fidelity to one's feelings. The songs of his troubadour opera *Richard Cœur de Lion* (1784) became particularly popular, especially its 'O Richard!, O mon Roi', which was taken up by the bodyguard of the Versailles garrison in October 1789. His *Guillaume Tell* (1791), an opera full of local 'Swiss' colour, used cowhorns and storms to communicate 'tumult and violence'. In the same year, the Italian Luigi Cherubini produced his *Lodoïska*, a 'rescue opera', which featured a medieval Polish castle and a captive damsel waiting for her rescuer, Floreski, along with choruses and orchestral colour, using instruments like the clarinet and French horn, all of which anticipated Romantic opera and, more distantly, Beethoven's *Fidelio*.[15]

But it was in the various revolutionary festivals (*fêtes*) that music played so important a part in the spirit of the Revolution. For it was here, as David understood so well, that the ideal of fraternity could be achieved through the unisonality of massed choirs singing hymns to the Republic. Through the music of François-Joseph Gossec, Luigi Cherubini and Étienne Nicolas Méhul, the poetry of Marie-Joseph Chenier and the scenic art and choreography of Jacques-Louis David, the revolutionary *fête* attempted to create, and give expression to, a new sovereign nation of equals unlike any other heretofore. Thus, at the *Fête de la Fédération* in July 1790 (see Fig. 5.1), in addition to a sacred drama (*hierodrame*) by Marc-Antoine Desaugiers commemorating the storming of the Bastille, a Te Deum composed specially for the occasion by Gossec was sung at the main celebration, one which, despite its many debts to his earlier religious works, sought to draw in a crowd of some 400,000 (plus 50,000 National Guards) on the wide open space of the Champs de Mars. Gossec later composed an 'Offrande à la Liberté, scène religieuse', an adaptation of liturgy for the theatre to sanctify liberty, which was performed 130 times during the Revolution; and went on to compose 'Hymn to Equality' (1793), 'Hymn to Humanity' (1795) and 'Martial Song for the Festival of Victory' (1796), while Cherubini wrote hymns to Fraternity and to the Pantheon in 1794, and to Victory in 1796. In the great festivals of August 1793 (*Fête de la Réunion*) and June 1794 (*Fête de l'Être Suprême*), choral music by Gossec played an important part in the procession from the Place de la Bastille to the Champ de Mars, with the choir being divided by age and gender, singing antiphonally and in unison. But, despite his many collaborations with the revolutionary poet Chenier, Gossec's music failed to be politically effective: his works were more like motets than secular hymns with their excessive ornamentation and difficult instrumental sections, which prevented the Parisian crowds from joining in the singing, as was the expectation. The exceptions here were his 'Hymn to the Supreme Being' (1794) and 'Hymn to Jean-Jacques Rousseau' (1794). At the Festival of the Supreme Being, on 8 June 1794, which Robespierre and David organized, 2400 delegates from the Paris sections, divided into old men, mothers, young girls, boys and small children, sang antiphonal choruses with

---

[15] Kennedy, *A Cultural History of the French Revolution*, pp. 119–21.

the audience, and thereafter in unison for the 'Hymn to the Supreme Being', before Robespierre appeared, to burn the statue of Atheism and reveal the statue of Wisdom.[16]

The French Revolution revealed the importance of both music and choreography for creating a sense of national unity and solidarity. The key to this relationship was the relatively new concept of citizenship in the nation, the fount of sovereignty. Music had as a result to become 'popular' and 'national', and to elevate and sanctify the nation and all its members, creating a sacred community of citizens. Here we can see the continuity with older religious ideas of divine 'covenant' and ethnic 'chosenness', which became secularized and politicized in the ritual of oath-swearing ceremonies by the citizens on behalf of the *patrie*, and in the principle of the 'liberty of the people' who form a national community. Like the flags and anthems of the Revolution, its festival music not only reflected but encouraged the transfer of authority from monarch to citizens, hailing their deliverance from both internal (aristocratic) and (after 1792) external (Austrian, British) oppression.[17]

## German successors

Where the French republicans had led, German liberals followed fitfully over the next few decades. Napoleon's defeat of Prussia in 1806–7 had stimulated a movement of political reform in Prussia, which coincided with the first flowering of the Romantic movement. In the War of Liberation in 1813–15, German youth had played a small but significant part in volunteer regiments, among them the poet Theodor Körner, leaving behind a myth of national liberation through heroism in war. In the period of state repression that ensued, particularly in Prussia, the German intelligentsia, especially the students and their *Burschenschaften*, attempted to keep the revolutionary nationalist spirit alive. To this end they organized two major festivals, the first in 1817 at the Wartburg Castle, the site of Luther's translation of the Bible, the second at Hambach in 1832.

---

[16] David Charlton, 'Introduction: Exploring the Revolution', in *Music and the French Revolution*, ed. Malcolm Boyd (Cambridge: Cambridge University Press, 1992), pp. 1–11; Robert Herbert, *David, Voltaire 'Brutus' and the French Revolution: An Essay in Art and Politics* (London: Allen Lane, 1972); Jean-Louis Jam, 'Marie-Joseph Chénier and François-Joseph Gossec: Two Artists in the Service of Revolutionary Propaganda', in Boyd (ed.), *Music and the French Revolution*, pp. 221–35; Kennedy, *A Cultural History of the French Revolution*, pp. 239–41, 337, 343.

[17] Aviel Roshwald, *The Endurance of Nationalism: Ancient Roots and Modern Dilemmas* (Cambridge: Cambridge University Press, 2006), ch. 4; M. Elisabeth C. Bartlet, 'The New Repertory at the Opera During the Reign of Terror: Revolutionary Rhetoric and Operatic Consequences', in Boyd (ed.), *Music and the French Revolution*, pp. 107–56.

The Wartburg festival was devised by the student and gymnastic associations, many of whose members were disciples of Friedrich Ludwig Jahn. Central to this festival was the singing of Protestant hymns as the students, carrying oak leaves, marched up to the castle by torchlight. Having listened to speeches about justice and a sermon, they joined hands and swore to uphold the *Bund*, and concluded with a Lutheran church service. The Hambach gathering was a more motley affair, but it too centred on a procession to the castle ruins, with everyone wearing red, black and gold emblems and ancient Germanic dress, singing patriotic songs and waving flags, and sporting fasces and wreaths of oak leaves. Here, too, there were speeches, fires on the hills and a midday meal, but there was less unity in the crowd and the symbols were more secular and revolutionary.[18]

How was this new spirit of freedom embodied in German music in this period? Already before the Revolution, Mozart had set Da Ponte's version of Beaumarchais's play *Le mariage de Figaro* (1785) the following year as *Le nozze di Figaro*. Its critique of the nobility, as Danton recognized, paved the way for the overthrow of the ancien régime and the birth of new freedoms, but this was social, not national liberty. Even Beethoven's symphonies and his opera, *Fidelio*, with its debts to the music of the Revolution, notably Cherubini and Méhul, spoke to a general conception of universal freedom, not any particular, let alone a national, freedom. The last movement of his Fifth Symphony and second movement of his Seventh Symphony became extraordinarily popular in France in the early nineteenth century, perhaps for that very reason. The exception to this rule is his incidental music for the Viennese revival of Goethe's play *Egmont* in 1810, which tells of the life and persecution of a patriotic freedom fighter in the sixteenth-century Netherlands. Egmont's vision in his prison cell, just before his execution, of a Dutch uprising and its triumph over the Spanish oppressors had obvious political significance for Austria during the Napoleonic Wars.[19]

By this time, a conception of German national identity had taken hold of sections of the German intelligentsia. But this was an exclusively cultural identity, and over the course of the eighteenth century, as Celia Applegate has demonstrated, it had made not only German literature, but German, especially Protestant north German, instrumental and choral music, central to its self-conception and sense of cultural self-worth, in contradistinction to 'lighter' Italian vocal music, especially opera, and 'frivolous' French music. Advanced and spread by German music critics, scholars and journalists, this cultural national identity and sentiment centred on a separate musical heritage over the century from the late seventeenth century. This in turn had prepared the way for Mendelssohn's 'rediscovery' of Bach and his revelatory performance of the latter's *St Matthew*

---

[18] George L. Mosse, *The Nationalization of the Masses: Political Symbolism and Mass Movements in Germany from the Napoleonic Wars through the Third Reich* (Ithaca and London: Cornell University Press, 1975), pp. 77–9, 83–5.

[19] Beate Angelika Kraus, 'Beethoven and the Revolution: The View of the French Musical Press', in Boyd (ed.), *Music and the French Revolution*, pp. 300–14.

*Passion* in 1829 in Berlin before the royal family and assembled notables. In many ways, this was a conservative cultural national sentiment, which sought to uphold the monarchy and aristocratic order, not to be confused with Herder's Enlightenment cultural nationalism with its interest in 'the people' and folksong, nor with the later political nationalism, loudly trumpeted by Fichte in French-occupied Berlin, in his *Addresses to the German Nation* of 1807–8, as well as by the Romantic writers and the German propagandists like 'Turnvater' Jahn and Ernst Moritz Arndt in the 1810s. What it did supply for both cultural identity and a Romantic cultural national sentiment was the collective enthusiasm of the massed choir, which, modelled on the Berlin *Singakademie* and the Hamburg *Gesangverein*, spread to many towns and cities across the German-speaking lands in the mid nineteenth century.[20]

The Bach revival also fed into that fusion of Protestant religion and German cultural identity which some of Mendelssohn's own works, notably his Symphony No. 2 ('Lobgesang'), Op. 52 (1840), exemplify. The link with German identity in that work is contextual: the celebration in the Leipzig Marktplatz in June 1840 of the four-hundredth anniversary of the 'German patriot' Johannes Gutenberg's invention of printing and especially the Gutenberg Bible, which, according to the nineteenth-century liberals, had disseminated spiritual enlightenment to all the German-speaking lands and prepared the way for Luther's Reformation. For this occasion, Mendelssohn composed a *Festgesang* for male chorus and double brass band (one of whose movements took on a new afterlife from 1861 as a Christmas carol, 'Hark! The herald angels sing'). On the next day, Mendelssohn gave the first performance of his 'Lobgesang' Symphony, which linked three instrumental movements to a cantata of nine movements, based chiefly on the Psalms, in a general hymn of praise for the victory of light over darkness, spiritual knowledge over ignorance. For Larry Todd, the textless symphony 'impresses as an instrumental composition aspiring towards imaginary church music, while the cantata, with the addition of sacred texts, in turn approaches the condition of liturgical music'. The chorus stands implicitly for the German people celebrating their own religious and cultural heritage.[21]

This is, of course, not the same as a purely German national sentiment, let alone German nationalism. But, both by its immediate context and by its aspiration to combine specifically Lutheran religion with the German tradition of

---

[20] Applegate, *Bach in Berlin*; Celia Applegate and Pamela M. Potter, 'Germans as the "People of Music": Genealogy of an Identity', in Applegate and Potter (eds), *Music and German National Identity*, pp. 1–35.

[21] R. Larry Todd, 'On Mendelssohn's Sacred Music, Real and Imaginary', in *The Cambridge Companion to Mendelssohn*, ed. Peter Mercer-Taylor (Cambridge: Cambridge University Press, 2004), pp. 167–88; see also Mark Evan Bonds, *After Beethoven: Imperatives of Originality in the Symphony* (Cambridge, Mass.: Harvard University Press, 1996), ch. 3; Ryan Minor, *Choral Fantasies: Music, Festivity, and Nationhood in Nineteenth-Century Germany* (Cambridge: Cambridge University Press, 2012), ch. 2; and further discussion in Chapter 6 below.

Fig. 1.1 *Sängerfahrt* on the occasion of the Wartburg Song Festival, August 1847 (litho), German School (nineteenth century)

symphonic music of Beethoven and Schubert, Mendelssohn's symphony-cantata built on the (north) German tradition of national cultural identity. It fed the great choral movement of nineteenth-century Germany, which from the 1840s mobilized large numbers of middle-class Germans with a mission of musical participation, social harmony and patriotism. As well as concert performances, choirs gathered for competitive festivals at locations such as the Wartburg (Fig. 1.1), the site of a legendary medieval song contest, at which patriotism was the overriding theme. In this context, it comes as little surprise that in 1841, the writer August Heinrich Hoffmann von Fallersleben, then in exile in British Helgoland, composed the words of the 'Deutschlandlied', with its opening words 'Deutschland, Deutschland, über alles', and set it to the tune by Haydn known in Austria as the *Kaiserhymne* ('Gott erhalte Franz den Kaiser'). It was later adopted as the German national anthem, because its wholehearted celebration of Germany and the German people was widely preferred above other popular songs.[22]

In the 1848 revolutions, freedom and unity became the main political goals of the liberals, radicals and democrats at the Frankfurt Assembly. After the latter's break-up and the partial failure of the nationalist freedom movements, Robert Schumann took up the ideals of German unity, freedom and fatherland, which echoed those of the French Revolution, in his later choral works. Many of the settings for his part-songs for male choir of 1848 (the *Drei Gesänge*, Op. 62, and the three *Freiheitsgesänge*, WoO 13–15), as well as the motet of 1849 for male double chorus, 'Verzweifle nicht im Schmerzensthal', the 'Adventlied' Op. 71 of 1848 and the 'Neujahrslied', Op. 144, of 1850 (based on the poetry of Rückert), all project the hope for future joy out of present woes. Some of these pieces have a decidedly militaristic tone, mixed with religious yearnings, but all proclaim the hope for republican triumph, as do the last four Ballades for solo voice, chorus and orchestra (1851–3), composed in Düsseldorf.[23]

## Staging the people

A number of mid-century operas focus directly on the celebration of the nation through its 'people', and the idea of a national community defined by mutual obligations or shared values. The libretti are in the vernacular, not Italian, and in most cases there is an aspiration to ethnic authenticity in musical style and sometimes in the original costumes and sets as well. The onstage chorus usually plays a crucial role. These works do not, however, advance republican or revolutionary political sentiments: either the social classes are shown coexisting in harmony, or no systemic social divisions are presented at all. It is the musical approach that places a new emphasis on 'the people'.

The premiere of Mikhail Glinka's *A Life for the Tsar* (1836) was supported by Tsar Nicholas I and the imperial court and presented as an important state occasion. It portrays the self-sacrifice of a seventeenth-century Russian peasant to save the life of the tsar as a heroic deed, and links monarch and subject in a hierarchical vision of the nation. Glinka even represented the unity of God, tsar and people in a recurrent motif, rather like a Wagnerian leitmotiv. The grand final choral 'Slav'sya' is a hymn-like march in which Russian peasants and nobles are united as a single nation in the glory of the Orthodox religion. But Glinka drew deeply on the style of Russian folk music, at least as this was understood

---

[22] Eichner, *History in Mighty Sounds*, p. 163; Bohlman, *Music, Nationalism, and the Making of the New Europe*, pp. 35–7; Leerssen, *National Thought in Europe*, pp. 148–9.

[23] John Daverio, 'Einheit-Freiheit-Vaterland: Intimations of Utopia in Robert Schumann's Late Choral Music', in Applegate and Potter (eds), *Music and German National Identity*, pp. 59–77.

by the educated classes at the time, and 'Russian style' is integral to the opera, not just local colour. For the first time a peasant is the hero of a grand, all-sung, tragic opera, and he and his family are the focus of the action. For this reason *A Life for the Tsar* appealed to Russian liberals as well as monarchists, who welcomed the use of folklore for cultural self-definition.[24] Glinka's second opera, *Ruslan and Lyudmila* (1842), again combines monarchism and folklore, but now with additional elements of magical epic and fairy tale. It opens with the celebrations in Kiev before the marriage of Ruslan to Lyudmila, and it closes with the wedding feast: long-standing symbols of Russian peasant culture. Maes distinguishes four kinds of national idiom: a Russo-Italian style for the music of Ruslan and Lyudmila, Finnish folk music for the magician Finn, an Italian buffo part for the boastful Farlaf, and 'Oriental' styles for Ratmir, Naina and Chernomor. The latter are not related to Eastern styles of music, but simply depict a languorous sensuality, particularly in the music by which Naina seduces her male heroes.[25] This corresponds to Glinka's intention, particularly in the finale, of encompassing various regions and peoples within a Slavic Russia. Marina Frolova-Walker calls the finale an 'imperial-epic conception', in which Russia's historical enemies are united under its influence in preparation for a glorious future.[26]

A similar concern with the peasantry pervades Stanisław Moniuszko's *Halka* (1848, premiered in Warsaw 1858). Like Glinka, Moniuszko combines folklore with the tragic story of a peasant, transferring the national dances that had been used, in Poland as in Russia, for early nineteenth-century *Singspiele*, to the context of a tragic opera with the aim of establishing a national operatic style. From the opening bars of the overture, *Halka* owes a good deal to French grand opera, and the peasant heroine sings in a conventionally noble style. She falls in love with a nobleman, who eventually abandons her to marry someone of his own class. When Halka is told of the deception by her peasant suitor, she goes mad, but instead of burning down the church in which the noble couple are being married, she throws herself off a precipice. The tragic episode of her suicide, according to Michael Murphy, is framed by a pervasive revolutionary and religious sentiment, with the peasant choir singing a Polish folksong in which Halka joins as she forgives her master for betraying her, in a spirit of Romantic redemptive Messianism, of the kind preached by the Polish nationalists Juliusz Słowacki and Adam Mickiewicz. Nevertheless, for all its social critique of the nobility and tacit support for the peasant uprising in Galicia in 1846, the opera ends abruptly with the peasants being forced to sing a happy song in celebration of the newly-wed nobles. Hence, to grand tragedy, Moniuszko has added both a celebration of the peasantry as the true representatives of the nation and an

---

[24] Taruskin, *Defining Russia Musically*, ch. 2; Frolova-Walker, *Russian Music and Nationalism*, pp. 58–61.

[25] Maes, *A History of Russian Music*, pp. 24–5

[26] Frolova-Walker, *Russian Music and Nationalism*, pp. 119–27

enveloping Messianic nationalism.[27] The popularity of *Halka* was the result less of its melodramatic plot than of its many Polish dances: polonaises for the nobility and the mazurkas that were ascribed to the peasantry, especially of the Mazur region. It was these that expressed the 'national spirit' of Poland and, as the publicity posters suggested, accounted for its great popularity.

Several operas of the 1860s reveal an enhanced cultural nationalism, with monarchs and aristocrats dropping out altogether. Now 'the people' alone are on stage, and the plots are depoliticized, at least ostensibly. A straightforward celebration of the Czech peasantry is found in the ever-popular comic opera by Bedřich Smetana, *Prodaná nevěsta* (*The Bartered Bride*, 1866–70), with a libretto by Karel Sabina, a leading figure in the Czech nationalist movement. The opera's setting is an autonomous and egalitarian village community, realistically portrayed in both its ideal and its mercenary aspects (it boasts no aristocrats, unlike Mozart's *The Marriage of Figaro*, on which Smetana modelled his opera). What made the opera so popular was the addition of the celebrated folk dances, and the portrayal of the distinctive national customs and everyday life of Czech peasants, a central concern for cultural nationalists everywhere whose quest for 'authenticity' is exemplified by the purpose and content of *The Bartered Bride*.[28] The fact that Smetana did not quote any actual folk tunes and that his sources were dances from the towns rather than the countryside did not prevent *The Bartered Bride* defining the sound of 'Czechness' in music.[29]

Wagner's *Die Meistersinger von Nürnberg* (1867) was conceived and composed on the eve of German political unification, yet, ironically, its message was one of German greatness through culture. The belatedness of German political unity in comparison with its industrial, commercial and administrative modernity, meant that German nationalism earlier in the nineteenth century had always come with a strong cultural component, and *Die Meistersinger* is the culmination of that trend. Nevertheless, folklore plays little role here, even in the music. The setting, sixteenth-century Nuremberg, is urban, not rural, and 'the people' are bourgeois townsfolk, not peasants, bound together by trade guilds, not their work on the land. Wagner took up an idealized, nostalgic image of Nuremberg as a *Volksgemeinschaft* that had been promoted by the Romantics, who regarded the city as an ancient seat of German greatness and freedom, situated at the geographical heart of Germany, and renowned for the glory of its artists and craftsmen. 'The people' are thus defined neither through monarchy nor through republican citizenship, but through values and culture. In the language of the German historian Friedrich Meinecke, Wagner imagines Germany as

---

[27] Michael Murphy, 'Moniuszko and Musical Nationalism in Poland', in Murphy and White (eds), *Musical Constructions of Nationalism*, pp. 163–80.

[28] Anthony Arblaster, *Viva La Libertà!: Politics in Opera* (New York and London: Verso, 1992), pp. 212–13, 215–17.

[29] John Tyrrell, *Czech Opera* (Cambridge: Cambridge University Press, 1988), pp. 215–17, 226–32.

a *Kulturnation* in heightened terms just as, in reality, it is about to turn into a *Staatsnation*. The opera gives no evidence of commerce taking place in the city, and the civic authorities are barely visible. On the other hand, German culture is connected with religion. As the cobbler-poet Hans Sachs says in his final speech to the people of Nuremberg, 'Were the Holy Roman Empire / To dissolve into mist / We still would have / Holy German Art!' Here culture replaces the monarch in the definition of the nation, and acquires a religious aura.[30]

The chorus is crucial in conveying this message. Act I opens with the singing of an imitation Lutheran chorale in St Katharine's church, while the opera ends with choral affirmation on the 'festival meadow' outside the city at the end of the song competition. Indeed the final scene distinctly recalls the historicizing festival culture of nineteenth-century Germany, a mass movement which, as Arthur Groos puts it, 'approximated the liturgy of a secular religion'. Deriving from the Wartburg festival of 1817 and the Hambach festival of 1832, the *Volksfest* movement spread through German societies and clubs, which held processions with historical costumes and flags representing ancient crafts, to a national or sacred location, where they would typically hear speeches or sermons and sing hymns. These mass celebrations became increasingly nationalized. Nuremberg itself celebrated such a festival in 1861, when the town was turned into an historical stage set, and thousands of German men from 260 music clubs gathered for parades, assemblies and singing. Relative to sixteenth-century Nuremberg these activities were largely anachronistic, but they gave Wagner a model for the celebration of German culture through the voices of the people. Hans Sachs defends the musical judgement of the ordinary people to the sceptical mastersingers, and at the end of the opera the people and the mastersingers sing together as the art of the guild is identified with national culture. Thus *Die Meistersinger* stages both 'the people' and the very process of vernacular mobilization itself.[31]

The definition of the nation through the people's culture is reinforced near the end of the festival-meadow finale by Hans Sachs's warning of foreign threats to German life. He exhorts his compatriots to 'honour your German masters' of the mastersingers' guild, for

[30] Stephen Brockmann, *Nuremberg: The Imaginary Capital* (Rochester: Camden House, 2006), ch. 2, pp. 102–3).

[31] Arthur Groos, 'Constructing Nuremberg: Typological and Proleptic Communities in *Die Meistersinger*', *19th-Century Music* 16/1 (1992), pp. 26–32; Stewart Spencer, 'Wagner's Nuremberg', *Cambridge Opera Journal* 4/1 (1992), pp. 31–2; Brockman, *The Imaginary Capital*, pp. 52–5; Stephen C. McClatchie, 'Performing Germany in Wagner's *Die Meistersinger von Nürnberg*', in *The Cambridge Companion to Wagner*, ed. Thomas S. Grey (Cambridge: Cambridge University Press, 2008), p. 142.

> if foreign airs and foreign vanities
> should infiltrate our German land;
> then none would know what's German and true,
> were it not to survive through the honour of German masters.

This is, literally speaking, a prophecy of the detachment of rulers and people that would follow the imposition of absolutist rule on a fragmented Germany after the Thirty Years War, and the development of a Frenchified culture at the courts. But it was understood by later generations, quite consistently with Wagner's chauvinistic prose writings of the 1860s, to refer to a contemporary threat from corrosive French or Jewish influences. Although this passage became notorious in later German history, the theme of foreign infiltration was a familiar and even logical aspect of national opera at the time, for instance in Smetana's *The Brandenburgers in Bohemia* (1862–3).

## Folk music and the nation

While the French Revolution was promoting and realizing the ideal of citizenship and national community, with music as a force in its vernacular mobilization, a new intellectual movement looked to culture and the arts for the very definition of national community, proposing that one might almost 'sense' the nation in the aesthetic experience of seeing, reading or listening. The themes and style of a work of art would reflect the heritage of a particular nation, appealing – supposedly – to deep-seated instincts among co-nationals or arousing them when dormant. This view went along with an interest in folklore, mythology, locality and national history in the arts, and ultimately a move away from the universalism of the Enlightenment and, more generally, of aristocratic traditions of patronage. In music, particular emphasis was laid on so-called 'folk music', especially 'folksong', and its incorporation into professionally composed art music. The strategies adopted by composers in this regard were often quite pragmatic and the authenticity of their sources open to question, but there is no doubt of the efficacy and long-lasting impact of their endeavours: the cultural definition of the nation through music has had an international legacy and to this day affects listeners' reactions, concert programmes, CD production, music reviews and books.

The eighteenth century witnessed a growing interest in ethnic musics amongst European intellectuals and publics, beginning around 1720 with the publication and promotion of Scottish songs and tunes in anthologies and on the English stage. Lowland Scots initiated the process as a form of cultural self-definition within the Union with England, and the music appealed to them and to the English as a mode of benign primitivism, the Highlanders being portrayed as wild and rude but also innocent and picturesque. The poet Allan Ramsay led the publication of 'Scots songs' and urged Scottish musicians to 'own' and 'refine' them in their compositions, so joining Highland and Lowland music in a single national music. This aim was at least partly accomplished in the 'Scots Drawing Room Style' in which the tunes were harmonized, endowed with features of the fashionable, pan-European 'galant style', and published for middle-class consumption in Scotland and London.[32] The cult of Ossian in Germany helped to endow these tunes with the allure of a bygone, heroic age. Demand for arrangements of Scottish songs suitable for amateur performance was met by Haydn, Koželuch and Pleyel and, later, Beethoven, Weber and Hummel.

The concept of 'folk music' as such was first advanced by non-musician scholars of the generation of the 1760s and 1770s, and was soon established as an object of primary research. Now circles of the intelligentsia in Europe, led by Herder and the German Romantics, displayed increasing interest in the 'authentic' music of 'the people' of every region and ethnicity – their ballads, dances, music and instruments – as 'rediscovered' by scholars in their 'original' rustic settings. Already in the 1750s, Jean-Jacques Rousseau had drawn attention to the influence of different speech patterns on national variations in music. In his *Dictionnaire de la Musique* (English version 1779), he pointed to Italian, French and German repertoires of music, and claimed that language, more than any other factor, determined particular sound shapes and melodic patterns, and that these had become, to a large extent, national. But it was Johann Gottfried Herder who not only coined the term 'folksong' (*Volkslied*) for the songs of the rural populations in *Von deutscher Art und Kunst* (1773) but stressed the centrality of music, dance and, above all, song for national distinctiveness and cultural diversity. His anthologies *Stimmen der Völker in Liedern* (1778) and *Volkslieder* (1778–9) claimed that the 'voices of the people' in various nations could be heard in their songs, along with their poetry and dance. Although he focused on the texts of the songs, most of them published without melodies, he did name their ethnicity or nation of origin (including those like Ireland and Estonia that had yet to achieve independence). As a man of the Enlightenment, Herder thought folksongs had both a universal quality, as they could represent all of human culture, and a particular dimension, because they could also give voice to distinctive cultures in their specific forms, of which the national was the most common, and God-given, form.[33] Herder was not alone in giving a name to this musical phenomenon; in other countries phrases were used such as 'canzoni populari' and 'canzoni traditionali'; 'narodnaya pesnya'; 'national song' and 'popular song'. These terms reflect a growing awareness of the music of traditional peasant societies, rooted in work and fixed customs; anthropological thought about pre-modern

[32] Matthew Gelbart, *The Invention of 'Folk Music' and 'Art Music': Emerging Categories from Ossian to Wagner* (Cambridge: Cambridge University Press, 2007), pp. 28–31; Graham Johnson, *Berlioz and the Romantic Imagination* (London: Arts Council, 1969), p. 34.

[33] Bohlman, *Music, Nationalism, and the Making of the New Europe*, pp. 28–9; F. M. Barnard, 'Culture and Political Development: Herder's Suggestive Insights', *American Political Science Review* 62 (1969), pp. 379–97.

communities, including the primitivist ideas of Rousseau; the growth of exotic tourism; and the reception of the poetry of James Macpherson that he attributed to an ancient Gaelic bard called 'Ossian'.[34] Herder's *Von deutscher Art und Kunst*, for instance, is really an essay about Macpherson's writings.

The nineteenth century saw the spread, systematization and, above all, the nationalization of folk-music research. In the early days, 'folk music' was almost synonymous with Scottish music. Herder's first folksong collection (1774; he soon withdrew it from publication) comprised only German and British material, and Scottish songs loomed large in his discussions of folk music.[35] Herder's later collections (1778, 1779), however, covered many more European traditions as well, including France, Spain, Italy, Scandinavia, the Baltics, and even Lapland, Greenland and Peru. The next steps were again taken in Germany, with Clemens Brentano's and Achim von Arnim's two-part anthology, *Des Knaben Wunderhorn* (1806, 1808), which emphasized the German language, and which was re-edited and adapted throughout the century, accruing ever-greater national resonance. This was followed by *Deutsche Lied für Jung und Alt* (1818), edited by Bernhard Klein and Karl August Groos, whose texts were predominantly by leading German poets like Goethe, Friedrich Schlegel and Ludwig Uhland, writing in the style of folksong, but this time with music appended; and the landmark publication of Ludwig Erk and Franz Magnus Böhme, *Deutscher Liederhort* (1893–4), which included 2175 songs. It was primarily through the German example and German ideas that the study, publication and aesthetic of folk music spread across Europe, first in the Celtic countries, Scandinavia and the Slavic regions – Herder's ideas were especially influential in Eastern Europe – and then, in the later nineteenth century, in Italy, France and England as well. In Russia, folksongs had been printed since the 1770s, but the famous collection by Nikolai Lvov (1790) was a response to Herder. Examples of national folk music and folklore scholarship include those by Ludvig Mathias Lindeman (1840) for Norway; Oskar Kolberg (1857–90) for Poland; Karel Jaromír Erben for the Czechs (1842–45); and Julien Tiersot (1889) for France. A policeman in Chicago, Francis O'Neill, collected over 2500 Irish melodies, which he published in nine volumes in the early twentieth century; as a product of the Irish diaspora, it served to unify the different local traditions of folk music in Ireland. At the other end of Europe, Shaul Ginsburg and Pesach Marek published the first comprehensive anthology of 376 Jewish folksongs in their *Jewish Folk Songs of Russia* (1901), both Yiddish and other. This enterprise was supported by the St Petersburg Society for Jewish Folk Song, and proclaimed the clear nationalist ideological motivations of the editors, who followed the model of Erk and Böhme's *Deutscher Liederhort*, seeking to rescue an essential part of its history for the Jewish people.[36]

---

[34] Gelbart, *The Invention of 'Folk Music' and 'Art Music'*, pp. 106–7.

[35] Ibid., p. 102.

[36] Bohlman, *Music, Nationalism, and the Making of the New Europe*, pp. 75–82.

Interest in folk music was from the outset coordinated with an implicit critique of modern European societies undergoing industrialization and bureaucratic rationalization. The idea that different peoples expressed their differences through their culture and music was a vital aspect of the cult of authenticity that became increasingly widespread in Europe during the nineteenth century, in which the many meanings of the term 'the people' were narrowed down to an equation with the peasantry in its original rural setting. Here, the followers of Herder hoped to find the authentic nation and its true and genuine culture in the dialects, dances, ballads and music of supposedly uncorrupted peasants, even if, like most artisans, they continued to remain outside the circumscribed bond of citizenship. Folk music became a means by which a newly urbanized middle class could, and in some cases did, reconnect with what they felt to be their authentic ethnicity and their lost rural past. At the same time, national educators distinguished folk music from other popular musics, especially urban popular song, which was deemed impure, kitsch or commercial. Collectors such as Arnim and Brentano aimed not just to preserve a record of vanishing customs, but, as they saw it, to educate and improve the taste of the urban lower classes who had forgotten their peasant roots. By the early twentieth century, the folk-music aesthetic was drawn away from the earlier citizenship ideology to serve instead the various movements for national regeneration that sprang up at the time. These movements, echoing the *völkisch* conservatism first enunciated in nineteenth-century Germany by Fichte and others, proposed a model of organic community in opposition to modern, urban, 'cosmopolitan' society, and sought to reverse the processes of cultural and even racial miscegenation to bring the nation back to its true 'type'.

## Incorporating folk music

As Chapter 2 will show, the eighteenth century witnessed a growing interest in ethnic idioms in music, particularly songs from Scotland; effects of 'local colour' on the musical stage, especially in comedies; and the emergence of a 'folksy' style in German songs for domestic performance. But none of these forms of music was presented or perceived as 'national music' in our sense – arousing positive ideas of a nation and national sentiments in its listeners. And they hardly served the purpose of vernacular mobilization. The nationalization of ethnic idioms and folk-like styles occurred in concept in the late eighteenth century and then in practice in the nineteenth, as they were drawn into nationalist programmes and ideologies, and combined with other potent cultural resources such as the idea of the homeland and national history and myth. This firmer intellectual background accompanied an elevation of the quality and aspirations of compositions based around folk music. The important composers to take this path were Weber, Chopin and Glinka in the 1820s and 1830s; they were followed later in the nineteenth century by Liszt, Smetana, Balakirev, Borodin, Mussorgsky, Rimsky-Korsakov, Grieg, d'Indy, Dvořák and others; and by Albéniz,

Vaughan Williams and others in the early twentieth century. Some composers themselves collected and published folk music and then incorporated it in their own music, notably Balakirev, Janáček, Vaughan Williams, Holst, Bartók and Kodály. To some extent one can detect an increasing accuracy of reproduction that reflects the professionalization of folk-music research. Mussorgsky and Janáček were interested in speech rhythms along with folk music, and in their work these influences went along with an overarching aesthetic of realism and gritty compositional styles that stood against bourgeois prettification. But the results do not always amount to national music: greater ethnographic accuracy does not in itself imply greater nationality in art music. By the 1900s and 1910s some folk-music-influenced composition was no longer strictly national music in our sense but an ethnically coloured modernism concerned with problems of communication, artistic individuality and the renewal of the musical language through alternative structuring principles.

A good example of the incorporation of folk music is found in four of the Russian composers of the so-called *moguchaya kuchka* ('mighty little heap'): Mily Balakirev, Alexander Borodin, Nikolai Rimsky-Korsakov and Modest Mussorgsky. Here it is combined with an explicitly nationalist cultural programme and occasional original ethnographic research as well. The *kuchka* was formed during a period of liberalization in Russia under Alexander II, and was motivated by opposition to Anton Rubinstein and his organizations: the Russian Musical Society and the St Petersburg Conservatory (founded 1862). Rubinstein's project was international and professional in outlook, his staff imported from overseas, his aim being to spread musical culture and technique from Germany to Russia, where, in his view, composition was left to dilettantes. The *kuchka* were musical autodidacts, all of whom at some time held professional jobs outside music. As well as resentment of Rubinstein's new musical establishment, the *kuchka* were united by the nationalist ideas of their mentor, the critic Vladimir Stasov (who coined the name for the group), along with Balakirev, the intellectual leader amongst the composers, who encouraged and oversaw a number of compositions by the others. The *kuchka* styled themselves musical progressives, opposing academicism and favouring programme music, bright orchestral colours, sharp contrasts and a pseudo-oriental style derived from Glinka's opera *Ruslan and Lyudmilla*. They were not in agreement about the use of folksong: Stasov and the fifth composer of the group, César Cui, felt that it failed the test of realism. Balakirev however went on a folksong collecting trip along the Volga in summer 1860, the results issued in a volume of forty arrangements (1866). He listened carefully to Caucasian folk music, developed a new harmonic style based on the modality of Russian folk tunes, and advocated the use of folksong in orchestral compositions along with alternative structuring principles to those found in conventional – thus principally German – symphonic music. In this respect he was able to found a school of orchestral composition (explored in Chapter 2). Mussorgsky and Rimsky-Korsakov, meanwhile, used folksong in their operas with a wide range of dramatic functions. By the 1870s the *kuchka* had effectively broken up as a coherent group – Rimsky-Korsakov joined the St Petersburg

Conservatory as a professor, Balakirev suffered a nervous breakdown, Mussorgsky joined reactionary circles, while Cui found more success as critic than composer – but their collective style and their mode of folksong stylization remained touchstones for later Russian composers who wanted to evoke nationality.

In England the folksong revival began in the late 1880s – later than in most of Europe – and from the outset was strongly tinged by anti-urbanism and anti-industrialism. It provided a focus for middle-class disaffection with Victorian utilitarianism and the cultural outcomes of political economy. In his inaugural address to the newly founded Folksong Society in 1898, the composer Hubert Parry, widely regarded as the leader of the musical profession in England, recommended that English composers study folksong, since 'style is ultimately national' and it could provide a wholesome alternative to 'the sordid vulgarity of our great city populations'.[37] Folk traditions in England were dying out as urbanization drew ever greater numbers of rural workers to the expanding towns, and the first concern of these national folk revivalists was to save as much of the folk heritage as possible. At the same time, musical life in England, including professional composition, was undergoing a 'Renaissance', as it was termed by its advocates, cultivated people from middle-class professional backgrounds and from the high-minded Radical families of the English 'intellectual aristocracy'.[38] They aimed to revive the great English musical traditions of the Tudor and Jacobean periods as well as drawing on the possibilities of folksong, and opposed what they saw as a long-standing tendency of the English to import music from abroad rather than creating their own.

The concerns of these two movements intersect in the figure of Ralph Vaughan Williams, the most successful English composer of the generation after Elgar, who was at the same time dedicated to collecting, arranging and editing folksong, and publicizing and lecturing on the subject. He was joined in his fieldwork by his friends and fellow composers Gustav Holst and George Butterworth. Vaughan Williams's interest was not just ethnographic but cultural and philanthropic, as befitted a gentleman of leisure with Radical family traditions and a strong ethical outlook. His musical project was a fine example of vernacular mobilization, for he wanted to build a musical culture from the grass roots, acquainting ordinary people with traditional English music and uniting professional composition with everyday amateur music-making in a belief that art must grow out of the community. Vaughan Williams included the tunes of folksongs in his edition

---

[37] Hubert Parry, 'Inaugural Address', *Journal of the Folksong Society* 1/1 (1889), p. 3.

[38] Noel Annan, 'The Intellectual Aristocracy', in *Studies in Social History: A Tribute to G. M. Trevelyan*, ed. J. H. Plumb (London: Longman, Green & Co., 1955), pp. 241–87; Julian Onderdonk, 'Ralph Vaughan Williams' Folksong Collecting: English Nationalism and the Rise of Professional Society' (Ph.D. dissertation, New York University, 1998), pp. 79–140; and 'The Composer and Society: Family, Politics, Nation', in *The Cambridge Companion to Vaughan Williams*, ed. Alain Frogley and Aidan J. Thomson (Cambridge: Cambridge University Press, 2013), pp. 9–28.

of the *English Hymnal* (1906), an attempt to reform the music of the Anglican Church from below. He and Holst were ostensibly socialists, but of the middle-class variety of William Morris and the Fabian Society.[39] Vaughan Williams called folksong the 'spiritual life-blood of a people'.[40] Among his original instrumental music, the *Norfolk Rhapsody* No. 1 (1906), the *Fantasia on English Folk Song* (1910) and the *Five Variants on Dives and Lazarus* (1939) are based on folksongs he collected. The operas *Hugh the Drover* (1911–14; first performed 1924) and *Sir John in Love* (1924–29) draw on folksong extensively. Nevertheless, direct allusions to folksong are relatively uncommon in Vaughan Williams's artistically ambitious compositions, belying his reputation as a 'folksong composer'. In his early years Vaughan Williams was searching for an individual compositional voice and he found it by absorbing some of the rhythms and contours of English folksong into his style, which he blended with other influences, such as Debussy and Ravel, along with his interests in landscape, Tudor music, and the visionary literature and religion of the English Radical tradition. In the 1920s his music explored themes such as religion (*Sancta Civitas*, 1925, *The Pilgrim's Progress*, 1921–51), sexuality (*Flos Campi*, 1925), mortality (*Riders to the Sea*, 1936), and modern life and music (Symphony Nos. 4 and 6, 1934, 1947, Piano Concerto, 1931). He returned to folksong and landscape imagery only by necessity during and immediately after World War II, writing scores for government propaganda films and one, *The People's Land* (1943), for the newly formed National Trust. Vaughan Williams's interest in folksong was a single component within a powerful artistic synthesis that resonated with the anti-industrial, communitarian redefinition of English nationality from 1880 in the era of industrial contraction, economic competition from Germany and the United States, and imperial challenge overseas.

The first major composer to pursue a parallel career as a professional ethnomusicologist was Béla Bartók, who from 1905 collected material in Hungary with his fellow composer Zoltán Kodály, who was writing a doctorate on Hungarian folk music. Later Bartók broadened his remit, first to other ethnic groups within the Hungarian political sphere in today's Slovakia and Romania, then to North Africa, and finally to Turkey. He developed his own method of comparative ethnomusicology, expressed in essays and then in his book *The Folk Music of Hungary and of the Neighbouring Peoples* (1934). Bartók's earliest original compositions, such as the symphonic poem *Kossuth* (1903), stand in a nineteenth-century tradition of Hungarian style derived from Liszt and Brahms and heavily dependent on the 'verbunkos' idioms that came to be associated with the performances of the Hungarian Roma. This 'gypsy

---

[39] Paul Harrington, 'Holst and Vaughan Williams: Radical Pastoral', in *Music and the Politics of Culture*, ed. Christopher Norris (London: Lawrence & Wishart, 1989), pp. 106–27.

[40] Ralph Vaughan Williams, *National Music and Other Essays* (Oxford: Oxford University Press, 1987), p. 23.

music' was favoured by the Budapest nobility and gentry, and it was popularized internationally as a Hungarian national style by Liszt in his Hungarian Rhapsodies. The initial impetus of Bartók's folksong research was the realization that authentic Hungarian folk music, as he saw it – the music of the peasants in the countryside – was something quite different. His mission was to protect the little-known, true Hungarian music from the encroachment of the false, and at first he hoped build a new national compositional style upon it. Soon, however, he began to combine different ethnic influences and use them to alter his musical language in fundamental ways that placed his style in the company of an international group of modernist composers including Stravinsky, Scriabin and Schoenberg. Bartók was a Hungarian patriot who wanted to draw attention to Magyar folk music, but he promoted other ethnic musics as well, recognized the cross-fertilization between them, and in his works of the 1910s and 1920s developed a challenging modernist idiom aimed at connoisseurs that had none of the popular touches of nineteenth-century national music and was unlikely to mobilize citizens for the national cause. However, in the late 1930s Bartók allowed the verbunkos style back into his language in works such as *Contrasts*, the String Quartet No. 6 and the Violin Concerto.[41] In general his works reflect a notion of a multi-ethnic imperial Hungary that after the Great War no longer existed.

The practice of incorporating folk music in art-music compositions was not associated with a single political stance and could serve monarchical, republican and organicist concepts of the nation. In the case of relatively small communities fighting for independence, such as the Czech lands, Finland and Norway, the cultural definition of the nation through music and the distinctive accents and themes of national music fostered a model of the nation based on citizenship. Smetana, for instance, identified with the liberal 'young Czech' party, while Sibelius was associated with 'Young Finland' in the 1890s. Music served the process of vernacular mobilization and the national education of future free citizens. In well-developed nation states the situation was sometimes rather different. In post-Napoleonic Russia, nationalism was state policy, and the folklore movement was accommodated and even promoted by the state, as illustrated by Glinka's *A Life for the Tsar*. Tchaikovsky, who enjoyed extensive imperial patronage, never drew more on folksong than in his opera *Vakula the Smith* (1874), which was a court commission and reflected state propaganda against Ukrainian separatism. Mussorgsky's *Sorochintsï Fair* (1874–81), in the same officially approved genre of 'Little Russian comedy', uses more authentic folksongs than ever, but reflects the composer's associations with reactionary aristocrats such as the folksong expert Tertiy Ivanovich Filippov.[42] Even Balakirev changed the programme associated with his folksong-based second Overture on Russian Themes from a revolutionary one reflecting the political mood of the early 1860s to an anti-liberal, Slavophile celebration of Russian history, showing

---

[41] Schneider, *Bartók, Hungary, and the Renewal of Tradition*, introduction and p. 263.

[42] Maes, *A History of Russian Music*, pp. 124–6, 129.

that the same piece of music could support politically progressive and reactionary programmes.[43] In France, folksong-influenced composition was encouraged at the Schola Cantorum, an educational institution established in 1894 in opposition to the state Conservatoire, which reflected the regenerationist objectives of its founder, the composer Vincent d'Indy, a fierce and articulate opponent of the liberalism of the Third Republic. (D'Indy's *Symphony on a French Mountain Air* and its cultural background are discussed in Chapter 2.) D'Indy's student Joseph Canteloube, who devoted a lifetime to the collection and arrangement of French folksong, was a member of the counter-revolutionary monarchist movement *Action française* and took a position in the Vichy government. The remarks of Hubert Parry, a committed social Darwinist and believer in Germanic racial supremacy, to the English Folksong Society (quoted earlier) reveal his fears of urban degeneration. Bartók's writings on music are full of the vocabulary of race, degeneration and cultural contamination. He feared the influence of Jews and Roma on Hungarian cultural life, and wanted to reverse the cosmopolitanism of the Austro-Hungarian empire in order to preserve the ethnic musics of the countryside, since those musics, although hybrids themselves, were acceptable, peasant hybrids.[44] The Australian composer, pianist and folksong collector Percy Grainger held a lifelong belief in Nordic racial supremacy that was to him like a religion. He regarded Australia as a southern repository of Nordic racial purity.[45] These conceptions still appeal to 'the people', but do so with a view to biology and ancestry as much as any republican ideal of citizenship.

[43] Taruskin, *Defining Russia Musically*, pp. 145–9.

[44] David Cooper, 'Béla Bartók and the Question of Race Purity in Music', in Murphy and White (eds), *Musical Constructions of Nationalism*, pp. 16–32; Katie Trumpener, 'Béla Bartók and the Rise of Comparative Ethnomusicology: Nationalism, Race Purity and the Legacy of the Austro-Hungarian Empire', in *Music and the Racial Imagination*, ed. Ronald Radano and Philip V. Bohlman (Chicago: University of Chicago Press, 2000), pp. 403–34; Julie Brown, 'Bartók, the Gypsies and Hybridity in Music', in *Western Music and its Others: Difference, Representation and Appropriation in Music*, ed. Georgina Born and David Hesmondhalgh (Berkeley: University of California Press, 2000), pp. 119–42.

[45] Malcolm Gillies and David Pear, 'Percy Grainger and American Nordicism', in Julie Brown (ed.), *Western Music and Race*, pp. 115–24.

# 2

# Folk Music into Art Music

As we have seen, national educators of the nineteenth and early twentieth centuries who hoped to realize the national community turned their attention to 'the people'. Those who followed Herder's way of thinking sought the essence of the nation in the people's indigenous culture. Folklore research became central to their project, and they disseminated their findings widely to alert co-nationals to their own national culture. In particular, nationalist thinkers urged composers to build their high-status art music upon this foundation in the hope that nationality would be recognized and spread through the culture of the educated classes. Scholarly interest in folk music first arose in Germany, before spreading first to countries that lacked long-standing professional, literate traditions of musical composition, and later in part to those that did possess them (France and Italy). Now there was an intellectual tradition that made a deep connection between the everyday music of rural populations and the art music of European 'high culture'. The project of vernacular mobilization would be supported by the creation of new semi-vernacular idioms within the art-music tradition.

The nationalist programme was successful, insofar as, to this day, thousands of listeners to classical music hear national character in art music that alludes to vernacular ethnic sources, starting with Chopin and Glinka and continuing with Smetana, Dvořák, Grieg, the Russian *kuchka* and, in the early twentieth century, Vaughan Williams, Albéniz and Falla. It would seem at first glance that an influence from folk music is a prerequisite for national music and definitive of it. This impression is however partly deceptive. Despite considerable overlap, not all national music draws on vernacular ethnic music and, conversely, not all art music that draws on it can, by our definition, be called national music. Wagner's *Der Ring des Nibelungen* depends on non-musical folklore – literary sources, mythology and Wagner's pseudo-antique alliterative *Stabreim* – but not on folksong or dance. Yet it was undoubtedly intended and perceived as a contribution to German national culture. Elgar's cantata *Caractacus* and his 'symphonic study' *Falstaff* are not concerned with folklore at all, yet both were intended and understood to portray English national characteristics and arouse national sentiments. On the other hand, the careful folklore researches of Janáček and Bartók and the absorption of particular modality, rhythmic structures and melodic inflections into their compositional idioms by no means restricted them to national music in their later works. At the same time, the authenticity of a composer's sources does not determine the national element in the music. Weber's *Der Freischütz* was the foundation for German Romantic opera and a theatrical institution in German-speaking central Europe, but its folksy melodies sung by German peasants in an idyllic rural setting were Weber's own invention, even if they were soon taken up on the streets outside the opera houses. At the level of compositional technique, transnational exchange was fundamental to these repertoires, composers looking across borders for models in favoured genres such as rhapsody, overture, symphony and piano dance collection.

Composers employed many degrees of stylistic assimilation, imitation and transformation of ethnic materials, not just literal quotation, and they combined these musical elements with literary themes in national culture, history and landscape to create music that would be perceived as national by their urban audiences. But nationalism was not the only reason they were drawn to folk music. A second set of cultural forces – related to nationalism but distinct from it – urged them to seek expressive authenticity, individuality and originality. The Romantic artist maintained an ambivalent relationship with historical traditions, and sensed a widening division between urban popular culture and the art of the 'poetic'. One solution to Romantic alienation was to evoke the spirit of a naive human collective (the folk) whose cultural productions were thought to be simple, bold, primitive and non-bourgeois. Ethnic music offered a source of authenticity for the newly valorized creative artist and a way to reintegrate the individual within a reformed society. The aims of nationalist movements overlapped with those of Romanticism through their shared quest for origins and authenticity and their simultaneous articulation by Herder. But at times it is important to separate them conceptually, especially since, in the early decades of the twentieth century, the legacy of Romanticism, intensified in the guise of artistic modernism, replaced nationalism as the motivation for many compositions that absorbed ethnic influences.

Music of the countryside had long been absorbed into the professionally composed music of the courts and towns – Georg Philipp Telemann (1681–1767) often drew on Polish tunes, for instance – without it being conceived by its creators or perceived by its patrons as 'national music'. Satirical 'ballad operas' such as John Gay's *The Beggar's Opera* (1728) incorporated popular tunes, ballads and hymns. The process was eased by the change of taste within urban communities against the florid, interwoven styles of the 'Baroque' in favour of homophonic textures (melody/accompaniment), short, symmetrical phrases, simple harmony and easy lyricism, along with a 'galant' aesthetic that valued 'the natural' and 'the simple'. Elements from peasant music were easy to accommodate within this framework. Moreover, sophisticated composers could play off rustic idioms against learned, civilized styles in a deliberate contrast. A conventionalized vocabulary grew up to signify peasant music: short conjunct phrases, fiddle effects and bagpipe-style drones. This vocabulary can be heard in the trios within Haydn and Mozart's minuet movements (the very term 'trio' derives from the make-up of a rustic ensemble). Haydn wrote countless finales in 'contradance' rhythm and introduced perky tunes into otherwise grand and serious movements for humorous effect. He may have used Croatian folk tunes too, although the matter has long been disputed. But this idiom was still conceived as the music of the countryside as such. It reflects a hierarchical and differentiated view of human society in which different styles and the rhythmic gestures of certain dances stood for different social strata in a universal, transnational order. Local colour was possible in music, such as Mozart's 'Turkish' style, but was part of a standard eighteenth-century vocabulary of exoticism. Along with the rustic styles, this 'Turkish' music contributed to a world-view based around typologies of characters and styles and defined them in terms of their use rather than their origins.[1]

Likewise there had long been concepts of 'national styles' in music, reflected especially in music theorists' distinctions between French, German and Italian styles. But these styles were associated with the traditions and tastes of the courts and urban publics, not the music of rural or other lower-class peoples. The styles were sometimes not even defined by internal features: the German style, for instance, was thought to be a mixture of the others. Composers from any country could adopt these national styles. The Italian Giovanni Battista Lulli was accepted as the master composer in the French style (as Jean-Baptiste Lully), to whom later composers of French serious opera looked as an authority. J. S. Bach wrote an 'Italian Concerto' BWV 971, so-named simply because it uses ritornello form, and Mozart prided himself on his professional ability to imitate the style favoured in whichever country he visited. The French encyclopaedists advocated Italian music over French in the famous *querelle des bouffons*, but only because they thought it was better music. Rousseau, despite his primarily Francophone heritage and domicile, passionately attacked French opera and defended the style of modern Italian opera, arguing that the Italian style was more 'natural', more human and more universal, and recommending it to the French public.

Perhaps the first step towards a national music based on vernacular idioms was taken in Berlin, where the earliest German art songs in the modern sense (*Lieder*) were composed. These were ersatz folksongs with simple melodies, symmetrical phrase structures, and simple, optional accompaniments for domestic performance. The principles behind this repertoire were first expressed by Christian Gottfried Krause (*Von der musikalischen Poesie*, 1752), and contributors to the genre included C. P. E. Bach, Johan Adolf Peter Schultz and Johann Friedrich Reichardt. The style encouraged sensitive personal expression on the part of the performer but not individuality on the part of the composer; it was thus personal as well as notionally collective – a theme that would later appeal to the Romantics. Display, melodic embellishment, and anything redolent of virtuosity and the modern public sphere were avoided. At this stage the boundary between what was borrowed from a popular source and what was composed was very blurred, as the common phrase 'im Volkston' ('in the folk style') indicates. Composers were taking advantage of a Rousseauian trend, an aesthetic of the 'natural', meaning something simple and unaffected but still universal. Like later national music, the early *Lieder* were supposed to appeal across social classes. The repertoire expanded in the nineteenth century with more explicit German

---

[1] Gelbart, *The Invention of 'Folk Music' and 'Art Music'*, pp. 14–15.

national associations, especially in settings for male chorus. Brahms continued the tradition in his *Lieder*, which are sometimes entitled 'Volkslied' even though they are clearly his own compositions.[2]

The south Germans had their version of this folk style too. Mozart's German *Singspiel Die Zauberflöte* (1791) was written for the middle-class audience of the bourgeois Freihaus-Theater auf der Wieden in the Viennese suburbs, and is full of down-to-earth melodies, waltzes, *Ländler* and contradances. Nevertheless, in its combination of these elements with learned styles (for Sarastro and the priests) and classical forms, *Die Zauberflöte* is the culmination of eighteenth-century principles of synthesis and universality: in its music just as in its intellectual themes it aims for reconciliation and a common language.[3] Haydn continued this approach in his late oratorios *Die Schöpfung* (1798) and *Die Jahreszeiten* (1801). In the latter, rustic musical idioms are associated with ancient pastoral tropes and stock peasant characters to celebrate the passing of the seasons: hardly the stuff of national music. By contrast, Haydn's famous *Kaiserhymne* is an early instance of the *Volkston* as national music. Haydn celebrated the Habsburg monarchy, but the national feeling the hymn embodies is supposed to appeal to all social classes. It was used as the national anthem of Austria and, later, Germany. Beethoven developed a version of the celebratory folk-like tune, most famously the Ninth Symphony's 'Ode to Joy', but also in the Choral Fantasy Op. 80 and the finales of the Fourth Piano Concerto Op. 58 and the String Quartet in E flat Op. 127. All are diatonic and symmetrically phrased with mostly even note values. Nevertheless these examples preserve a good deal of the spirit of Enlightenment universalism: no nation is specified by either text or tunes. The non-specificity of the Ninth Symphony melody aided its late twentieth-century adoption as the supranational anthem of the European Union.

The aesthetic of the *Volkston* in Viennese music was perfected by Schubert, who built on the legacy of the Berlin song school but took the *Lied* to a much higher artistic level and incorporated touches of Romantic irony, distance and longing. Many of Schubert's folk-like *Lieder* are framed or inflected in sophisticated ways that suggest a lost innocence or unreachable perfection, or the recollection of buried memories. In his first song cycle to poems of Wilhelm Müller, *Die schöne Müllerin* (1824), Schubert's strophic, folk-like settings disguise a tragic tale and convey bitter irony beneath their guileless surface. 'Der Lindenbaum', from *Winterreise* (1827), Schubert's second Müller cycle, was later treated as a genuine folksong in German schools, even though its turn to the tonic minor at the start of the second stanza and the finely graded accompaniment of the original setting are artistic touches that would never be

---

[2] Richard Taruskin, *The Oxford History of Western Music*, vol. 3, *Music in the Nineteenth Century*, 2nd edn (New York and Oxford: Oxford University Press, 2010), pp. 119–23; Natasha Loges, 'How to Make a "Volkslied": Early Models in the Songs of Johannes Brahms', *Music & Letters* 93/3 (2012), pp. 318–19.

[3] Dahlhaus, *Nineteenth-Century Music*, p. 35.

found in a real folksong. Schubert put the style to use in instrumental music too. In the String Quartet in A minor D. 804 (1824), two bars of introductory accompaniment precede the entrance of the melancholy, folk-like main theme, which is played three times, the third in a transfigured version in the tonic major mode. The third movement of the quartet is a minor-key *Ländler* that is interrupted by some of Schubert's boldest tonal shifts to remote keys. Here the contrast of the 'tuning up' effects of the imaginary village band and the magical changes of tonal colour turn the focus to the subjective responses of the band's cultured listeners rather than the musicians themselves. There is no overt national element in Schubert, but his Romantic treatment of the *Volkston* anticipates the rhetoric of later national music.

The first successful expression of the nation using the *Volkston* in a large-scale work was Weber's opera *Der Freischütz* (1821). Weber used the folk style for peasant choruses and dances, bridal songs and a hunting chorus, as well as some arias and ensembles. The audience is invited to identify with the peasant characters in their forest setting. *Der Freischütz* became understood retrospectively as the first German Romantic opera and the foundation of a tradition. Weber was held in high esteem by Wagner, who admired this work in particular. In reality it draws heavily on French *opéra comique* and on stage traditions of melodrama, and includes no actual folksongs: Weber composed the melodies himself.[4] But even though Weber's folklore is not authentic, *Der Freischütz* has the ingredients of later national music based around folk music, the sources that, for cultural nationalists, were to shape the musical style of each nation.

## Folk music and art music: aesthetics and poetics

The writings of the polymath Herder offered an alternative conception of truth and value to the eighteenth-century universalism and the classical tradition in literature, turning to culture rather than reason, and finding multiple human truths that existed relative to communities and periods of history. Herder located the essence of the individual human being in language, which was in turn unique to and defined by a community and its culture. Community, through language, determines what is expressed in human utterances. The 'spirit of the people' (*Volksgeist*) is embodied in communal activities and culture. From Herder's perspective, folklore is thus of crucial importance. Research into the culture and traditions of a people serves not merely to uncover the songs and tales of untutored rural labourers, but to establish a unique and precious heritage that is at the same time essentially human and thus of universal significance.

---

[4] Ludwig Finscher, 'Weber's "Freischütz": Conceptions and Misconceptions', *Proceedings of the Royal Musical Association* 110 (1983–84), pp. 79–90; Dahlhaus, *Nineteenth-Century Music*, pp. 64–75.

Music was no less significant for Herder than language since the very origins of language lay in music. Herder categorized folksongs in his collections by nation, not locality, and, under his influence, later nationalists presented folk music, like folklore in general, as the common property of all classes within the nation. At the same time, like Herder they sought the *Volksgeist* in the music of rural communities. These were thought to preserve national culture because they stood outside history, largely untouched by modernity and industrialization. Nationalists presented folk music, unlike urban popular songs, as the record of an ancient, vibrant people that offered a firm foundation for building a nation.[5]

Herder's ideas also influenced the way folk music was assimilated into art music in practice, and the way that process was understood. In this field the concerns of Romanticism press closely upon those of nationalism. The literary generation of the 1760s and 1770s, including Edward Young, Rousseau, Goethe and Schiller along with Herder, promoted the idea of 'genius' as a creative force and as a challenge to the mimetic conception of the arts in French classical theory, replacing its concern with universal rules, genres and styles with an interest in the origins of the individual artwork and the process of its production. They conceived art not as the imitation of nature but as the expression of nature as a deep human drive. Artistic genius makes its own rules rather than following the procedures of craft and training. In these and later Romantic conceptions, art was thereby separated from science, rationality and mechanical production. The coherence of an artwork of genius was like that of a living organism, growing like vegetation, and spontaneously ordering itself without fully conscious control. The fiery, natural, creative genius of the artist, independent of rules and the classical tradition, thus runs parallel with the spirit of Scottish folk music as it had been described even earlier in the eighteenth century (see Chapter 1). By the late 1770s Herder had dropped the old distinction of nature and art, inherited from his eighteenth-century predecessors, even when referring to Scottish music, in favour of a dynamic and organic conception of artistic creation, and indeed of the whole universe. In line with his generation's concern with holism, he conceived art as a reconciliation of human artifice and nature. In the Preface to his 1779 volume of folksongs, 'Volkslied' still stood for nature, but was conceived not as the opposite of art, but rather as 'material for poetic art'.[6] The people too represented a form of genius, pure and authentic, and Herder blurred the line between it and the individual genius of the artist. In this way individuality and originality could coexist in the same music with universality and inter-subjective validity. 'Art could now claim to be both individual and national in its original genius.'[7]

By bringing together the two types of genius – folk genius and artistic genius – Herder appealed to his own and later generations of nationalists and Romantics alike. Nationalists seized on the thought that the individual genius of a great

[5] Dahlhaus, *Nineteenth-Century Music*, p. 107.

[6] Gelbart, *The Invention of 'Folk Music' and 'Art Music'*, pp. 198–9.

[7] Ibid., p. 203.

composer writing for a bourgeois/aristocratic audience in a concert hall or opera house was in fact an expression of the collective genius of the folk, and even determined by it. Herder had shown that folk music was not something merely exotic and primitive, but the point of origin for all musical activity, however sophisticated. For Romantics it was the reconciliation of opposites that appealed. Their concerns were the composer's personal style, originality, independence from rules and relationship to tradition. The dangers faced by the Romantic artist were the prospects of total subjectivity, alienation of the popular audience and dissolution of shared culture. The linkage of art music to folk music offered a solution to these difficulties by locating the subjective origin of the artwork in the collective origin of the people. In the typical nineteenth-century conception, 'original nationality' should work 'from the inside outwards', in contrast to the eighteenth-century idea of national styles.[8]

The first signs of these ideas coming together in practice are to be found in Beethoven's 140 or so settings of British folksongs, mainly Scottish, made for the Edinburgh publisher George Thomson between 1809 and 1820 (he also wrote sixteen sets of variations on folksongs for flute and piano Opp. 105 and 107, again for Thomson). Thomson had previously commissioned settings from other well-known continental composers, who doubtless brought a measure of prestige to his commercial enterprise. Haydn contributed more than 400. Thomson thoroughly refashioned the songs, commissioning new verses for many of them from poets including Robert Burns. He offered his composers melodies without texts and asked them to provide piano, violin and cello parts and a purely instrumental introduction and postlude for each song. In effect Thomson polished and prettified the original folksongs, making them acceptable for domestic performance by the bourgeois young ladies who purchased his editions. But his approach left leeway for bold compositional decisions that displayed 'genius' and 'originality' that, on Romantic terms, matched the primitive genius of the folk source. Leopold Koželuch's first reaction was to return the melodies to Thomson, complaining that they were 'une musique barbare'. Haydn's response was to bring to his settings the full technical resources of the classical style.[9] Beethoven's approach was more in keeping with the 'wildness' that Romantics perceived in the melodies. His harmonic palette is wider than Haydn's, his choice of chords is sometimes odd, with 'primitive' effects and harmonies that contradict the obvious interpretation of a melody. Beethoven did not blanch at aspects of the melodies that sit uneasily within the major/minor tonal system, such as modality, double tonics and non-tonic endings, instead treating them as invitations for

---

[8] Carl Dahlhaus, *Between Romanticism and Modernism: Four Studies in the Music of the Later Nineteenth Century*, trans. Mary Whittall (Berkeley and Los Angeles: University of California Press, 1980), p. 91.

[9] Richard Will, 'Haydn Invents Scotland', in *Engaging Haydn: Culture, Context and Criticism*, ed. Mary Hunter and Richard Will (Cambridge: Cambridge University Press, 2012), pp. 44–74.

bold harmonization. In the introductions and postludes he took the opportunity to introduce motivic development, building up the introduction from fragments of the melody; avoiding full closure at the end of the introduction, thereby integrating instrumental and vocal sections; and treating the final postlude (after the last stanza) as though it were a coda in a sonata movement, functioning to resolve any remaining tensions with further motivic development and climax.[10] In 'Sunset', for instance (Ex. 2.1; text by Walter Scott), Beethoven accentuates the melody's tonal ambivalence between relative major and minor keys (A minor and C major). Although the tonic is A minor, the music spends much time on the dominant or tonic chords of C major, moving there indeed after only one bar. The high prolonged E in the melody in bar 27 cries out for a harmonization with a dominant chord of A minor, yet Beethoven uses a root-position tonic chord of C major instead. In the final bars of the tune he avoids a dominant chord of A minor altogether, or any cadence in the tonic, at the last moment slipping back discreetly from C major to an A minor chord. The setting has an introduction based on motifs of the melody, while the long postlude recomposes the melody with a melancholy, hypnotic effect. By this stage of his career Beethoven's reputation for untrammelled 'genius' was well known to a European audience, and in a sense he returned the Scottish folk tunes to their primitive origins as these were understood at the time. Beethoven prepared the way for a tradition of stylistically progressive and even modernist responses to folk music, including Chopin, Balakirev, Mussorgsky, Grieg, Stravinsky and Bartók, all of whom at times distanced themselves from the easy assimilation of peasant music to bourgeois culture.

Adolf Bernhard Marx, the influential nineteenth-century pedagogue and theorist, regarded Beethoven's settings of Scottish melodies as the finest examples of this type of music. As Matthew Gelbart points out, learning to set folk tunes became a component of the pedagogical programme for future composers that Marx set out in his writings of the 1840s, but was conceived as a step towards the goal of writing fully original works. For Marx, Beethoven's originality lay in his 'constant fidelity to himself and his object'; he was original even when using folk tunes as he made them his own.[11] But Marx and the later Romantics reserved their highest praise for original works in which folk music is assimilated at a deeper, 'organic' level, without any literal quotation. Marx thought the composer should use folksongs to 'penetrate more profoundly into the soul of his art'.[12]

From today's perspective, the ideas of the intellectuals and educators who first collected and discussed folk music often seem dubious. Peasant musicians themselves had no concept of folk music and did not think of their music as national. Aside from remote locations, the music of rural communities was

---

[10] Barry Cooper, *Beethoven's Folksong Settings: Chronology, Sources, Style* (Oxford: Clarendon Press, 1994), pp. 149–68, 171–9.

[11] Gelbart, *The Invention of 'Folk Music' and 'Art Music'*, p. 217.

[12] Ibid., p. 220.

Ex. 2.1 Beethoven, 'Sunset', 25 *Schottische Lieder*, Op. 108,
for violin, cello, voice and piano, bars 12–31

Ex. 2.1 *continued*

seldom unique and purely indigenous but was mingled with urban, popular or even art-music idioms. This music did not stand outside history, pouring from the *Volksgeist* like a fresh spring, but was affected by wars, conquests, the movements of peoples and, latterly, industrialization and new means of transportation. Musicians have always travelled in search of work, and since the great European empires encompassed many peoples, there was much overlap and exchange. Much of the music the early collectors found could best be described as regional or subnational traditions, and there were stylistic features, such as bagpipe drones, that spread far across borders, and were thus supranational.[13] Moreover, by transcribing folk music into Western music notation and making it available for harmonization, collectors may have ironed out the expressive individuality of

[13] Curtis, *Music Makes the Nation*, p. 94.

peasant musicians, falsely standardizing them in the service of their conception of national cultural unity. Historians of the English folksong revival informed by Marxism and cultural studies have complained that bourgeois folksong collectors distinguished too sharply between 'true' folk music and the music of the urban working classes, focused on modal tunes for the sake of their exotic sound relative to art music, and bowdlerized the often bawdy lyrics of rural songs for the sake of domestic consumption.[14] Whatever the case, most nineteenth-century composers took a pragmatic attitude to their vernacular sources anyway: some were filtered through the traditions of the salons and popular theatre (Chopin, Glinka); some came from professional musicians as much as peasants (Liszt, Albéniz); and some originated in towns rather than the countryside (Smetana).

Herder and the early collectors of folksong were literary men, who – astonishingly, given their elaborately developed theories – published only the texts of the songs, not the tunes. Herder's concept of the *Volksgeist* works better for language than for music, as the former is more closely tied to a community and functions as an independent system. In art music there was a historically developed language of tonality that was shared internationally and traditionally spoken as a 'first language' by trained European musicians. In the later nineteenth century, the use of folk sources in art music often relies on various semiotically 'marked' features of musical syntax that distinguish the style from the universal norm. These include unusual scales with 'altered' notes relative to the major/minor norms, especially the raised fourth and lowered seventh degrees; 'modal' pitch collections akin to those used by professional composers of the medieval and Renaissance periods, especially 'Dorian', 'Lydian' and 'Mixolydian', again departing from the major and minor scales; the pentatonic scale; drone basses with 'open' intervals of fifths like bagpipe effects; repetitive rhythmic effects (ostinato); harmonic 'pedal points' (sustained notes in a texture); rhythmic 'snaps' (short-long patterns with the short note falling on the beat) and so on. Many of these features are shared by different regional traditions and, in nineteenth-century art music, often overlap with exotic effects found in operatic music that portrays African and Asian settings. Like the wider category of musical exoticism, indeed, this type of national music portrays a culture that is actually quite different, even remote, from that of its audience.[15] Both styles represent 'integratable irregularity' relative to the standard language of Western art music,[16] and they share a tendency to downplay the sense of progressive

---

[14] Vic Gammon, 'Folk Song Collecting in Sussex and Surrey, 1843–1914', *History Workshop Journal* 10/1 (1980), pp. 61–89; David Harker, *Fakesong: The Manufacture of British 'Folksong' 1700 to the Present Day* (Milton Keynes: Open University Press, 1985), chs 6 and 8; Georgina Boyes, *The Imagined Village: Culture, Ideology, and the English Folk Revival* (Manchester: Manchester University Press, 1993), chs 1 and 3.

[15] Locke, *Musical Exoticism*, ch. 4.

[16] Dahlhaus, *Nineteenth-Century Music*, 306.

temporality characteristic of tonal harmony with its logic of dominant-to-tonic harmonic progression and semitone steps ('leading notes') to underpin harmonic implication.

What is genuinely distinctive in the various regional idioms is rhythm, especially dance rhythms. A mazurka has a different rhythm from a Highland reel, which is different in turn from a tarantella or a polka. For nineteenth-century professional composers, the knack of writing national music with folk sources was to combine these characteristic rhythms with the vocabulary of modal, rhythmic, harmonic and timbral aspects that were marked relative to the pan-European norm, and to surround them with suitable ideas such as national myths, history, community and thoughts of the homeland. The success of such music in representing the nation and arousing national sentiments in its audience was not directly related to its ethnographic authenticity.

## Piano music: national dances

Piano music was central to the dissemination of national music in folk-music idioms. The main form was the short piece or collection of short pieces with a dance title and a characteristic dance rhythm. Although this may seem a humble kind of music in comparison to national operas or symphonic poems, the piano dance piece was a most effective way to represent the nation by means of folk music. The problem of the integration of folk sources into large forms was avoided, and collections of dance pieces could suggest a kaleidoscopic overview of national life, perhaps with fragments of the cultures of various peoples and regions, moods, times and festivals brought together in an overarching unity.

The most important contributions to this type of music are the more than fifty mazurkas of Frédéric Chopin (1810–49). Aside from their fascinating variety, originality, expressive depths and influence on later composers, the mazurkas are among the earliest pieces of instrumental music to embody the ideas of nineteenth-century nationalism. Chopin began his main series of mazurkas in earnest in the aftermath of the Warsaw uprising of 1830, the latest chapter in Poland's tragic history, which led, after its failure, to the confirmation of the partition of 1815 between Russia, Prussia and Austria. By this time Chopin had left Poland – for good, as it turned out – and the seriousness of purpose with which he evidently approached his task and the melancholy tone of so many of the mazurkas, despite their lively folk-dance rhythms, captures the nostalgia and recollections of the emigrant. Chopin elevated the peasant mazurka to the authentic national dance of Poland, overtaking even the polonaise, a ballroom dance of the Polish aristocracy that had been a staple of eighteenth-century instrumental music by composers from all parts of Europe. The mazurkas span the whole of his career, and he returned to the mazurka more often than to any of the other genres he favoured such as nocturne, étude, prelude and ballade. Despite the fixed triple metre, relatively schematic phrase structures and repetitive motivic and formal structures of Chopin's mazurkas, they allow a wide expressive range, including some of Chopin's most intimate thoughts, and are full of dazzling harmonic shifts, supple rhythmic patterns, contrapuntal textures and surprise events. In these pieces Chopin combined the styles of three rather contrasted dances of central Poland: mazur, oberek and kujawiak. The resulting range of expression, character and rhythmic forms, all gathered under a single generic title, parallels at an abstract level the nationalist effort to unite a people as a nation. Chopin's efforts match the ideas developed by Warsaw intellectuals in the 1820s – the time of his youth in Warsaw – on folklore and nationalism. Chopin did not articulate such ideas himself, but his composition teacher Józef Elsner was a published writer in the field. Herder was an especially strong influence on the Warsaw nationalist movement. In a pamphlet *O tańcach* (*On Dances*, 1829), the Romantic poet Kazimierz Brodziński explored, in Herderian fashion, the question of Polish national character, the rhythms of national dances and the role of such dances in art. As the hopes for Polish political definition faded, Chopin's mazurkas marked the emergence of Polish nationalism in culture instead.[17]

Chopin's personal stance on Polish nationalism was ambivalent. He was hardly a 'national artist' in the mould of his compatriot and fellow Parisian exile Adam Mickiewicz, or even, in music, Franz Liszt. Although he moved in radical society in Warsaw in the 1820s and amongst Polish exiles in Paris in the 1830s, and clearly sympathized with the Polish cause, Chopin's politics were not revolutionary and he did not participate in any political action. In Warsaw he associated with the moderate aristocracy and even with the Polish–Russian government, including the commander-in-chief, Grand Duke Constantin, brother of Tsar Alexander I. In Paris he associated mainly with the wealthy bourgeoisie and the cosmopolitan aristocracy, in whose salons he found a congenial atmosphere and a source of income, rather than the exiled Polish aristocracy, from whose society he gradually withdrew. These society patrons were not associated with the Polish cause, which was well known in France but supported by the middle and lower classes. Chopin avoided public concert performances after his first few years in Paris and was only indirectly connected with Polish intellectuals such as Mickiewicz. He did not respond to Elsner's repeated exhortations to compose a national opera. According to one eyewitness account, Chopin was once berated at length by Mickiewicz for wasting his talents on the amusement of the aristocracy rather than influencing the sympathies of the broader public for the Polish cause.[18] The mazurka was a genre for the salon, not for public occasions, and Chopin used his mazurkas for teaching and private performance. There is little evidence of national feelings in the public reception of the mazurkas in Chopin's lifetime, in Poland or elsewhere. Before he left Warsaw his compositions with a national flavour were of an entirely

---

[17] Jim Samson, *Chopin* (Oxford and New York: Oxford University Press, 1996), pp. 44, 56, 74; 'Music and Nationalism', pp. 55–6.

[18] Jolanta T. Pekacz, 'Deconstructing a "National Composer": Chopin and Polish Exiles in Paris, 1831–49', *19th-Century Music* 24/2 (2000), pp. 166–71.

different type: public virtuoso pieces such as *Rondo à la Mazur* Op. 5, *Rondo à la Krakowiak* Op. 14, *Fantasy on Polish Airs* Op. 13, *Introduction and Polonaise Brillante* Op. 3 for cello and piano, and *Andante Spianato and Grand Polonaise Brillante* Op. 22 for piano and orchestra. Chopin also played improvisations on Polish songs in his concerts at that time. Had he been able to return to a free Warsaw, Chopin said that at his first concert he would have performed his *Allegro de Concert* Op. 46, a grand virtuosic public gesture in concerto style, but one without any folklore dimension and to modern ears hardly one of his finest pieces.[19] The intricate mazurkas, then, were at first appreciated mainly by musicians. Still, as a mode of vernacular mobilization they were significant in Poland, where practically all Chopin's music was heard as carrying a national quality.[20]

Chopin undertook no folklore research, and the mazurkas should not be regarded as authentic transcriptions of vernacular music. Extensive musicological efforts in the late nineteenth and twentieth centuries to identify specific sources have proved unconvincing. He did spend two summer holidays in his teenage years on a country estate near his birthplace at Żelazowa Wola, where he heard folk music and described it in letters to his family. Perhaps he remembered something of its spirit and energy in his mature mazurkas, although they also stand in more immediate Warsaw traditions of dances for productions on the comic stage and keyboard music for the salons: mazur, oberek, kujawiak, polonaise and krakowiak. Some of these pieces from the 1820s anticipate the characteristic features of Chopin's mazurkas: repetitive rhythmic patterns and motifs, accents on the second or third beat of the bar in triple metre, sharpened fourths and drones.[21] Despite a good deal of theory, the collection of Polish folk music was in its infancy in Chopin's lifetime, and he was aware that the published collections with composed accompaniments were adapted for urban consumption. 'A future genius will one day arrive at the truth and restore it to its full value and beauty. Until then, folksongs will remain hidden under all that paint.'[22] Chopin's achievement was not to give voice to an authentic type of folk music but to revolutionize the musical quality and expressive significance of a professionally composed genre, which now conveyed far more than local colour.

A description of the compositional strategies and expressive subtleties of the Chopin mazurkas could fill a book of their own, so two examples must suffice. The expressive effects of these pieces reflect Chopin's coordination of folk-derived

---

[19] John Rink, *Chopin, the Piano Concertos* (Cambridge: Cambridge University Press, 1997), p. 92.

[20] Zofia Chechlińska, 'Chopin Reception in Nineteenth-Century Poland', in *The Cambridge Companion to Chopin*, ed. Jim Samson (Cambridge: Cambridge University Press, 1994), pp. 206–21.

[21] Barbara Milewski, 'Chopin's Mazurkas and the Myth of the Folk', *19th-Century Music* 23/2 (1999), pp. 131–5.

[22] Samson, *Chopin*, p. 17.

Ex. 2.2  Chopin, Mazurka in B major Op. 56 No. 1, bars 1–14

elements with innovations in tonal and formal structure and the disruption of conventional expectations in ways redolent of literary and musical Romanticism. Just as the Romantic critic Friedrich Schlegel thought that only the aesthetic 'fragment' could point beyond itself to an ideal 'whole', Chopin's mazurkas, both individually and collectively, suggest an original wholeness, now presented to the listener as 'lost' and recoverable only in the imagination. Op. 56 No. 1 in B (1844; Ex. 2.2) is a 'fragment' of this kind. It begins with non-tonic harmony and swiftly moves away from the tonic key by means of a 'real sequence', that is, a sequence that transposes its model exactly, without respect for its original key. Before the 1840s such techniques would normally be reserved for developmental sections, and certainly avoided at the openings of pieces, where tonal stability is usually established. By bar 6 Chopin arrives at G major, a key only distantly related to the tonic and seldom introduced as early as here. The music settles on an open-fifth drone in G: an indicator of a rustic peasant band, and thus carrying implications of simplicity and wholesomeness, yet, paradoxically, a disruptive force in this mazurka, underlining and stabilizing at a very early stage a key only obliquely related to the tonic. The rest of the piece explores distant key relationships even further, the two central, waltz-like episodes being in E flat major and G major. Op. 59 No. 1 in A minor (1845; Ex. 2.3) is melancholy but highly fluid in mood and tonality, continually leaving the minor mode for short periods in related major keys, at which point the dance rhythms enter more assertively (bars 9–10 and 17–21), before the music slips back to the minor for subdued cadences or the start of new sections. Later the main theme returns uncannily in the distant key of G sharp minor, pitched one semitone away from the tonic A minor, but far away in terms of conventional tonality. It is hard not to hear in this piece the elusive

Ex. 2.3  Chopin, Mazurka in A minor Op. 59 No. 1, bars 1–22

workings of memory in the mind of the solitary exile. The lively dance rhythms fade in and out in the middle of sections, outside the tonic key, and never reach a climactic statement that would confirm their present reality.

In the second half of the nineteenth century, sets of national dances became commercially successful and tremendously popular. Brahms produced four sets of *Hungarian Dances* (1869) based on gypsy music for the amateur piano-duet market. Dvořák followed suit with his first book of *Slavonic Dances* (1878; a second followed in 1886), which made his name famous in Germany and Austria almost overnight. The dances were issued both for piano duet and in an orchestral version, and within a few months they had been performed in Dresden, Hamburg, Berlin, Nice, London and New York. As a result Dvořák emerged from obscurity into international musical consciousness; other compositions of his were taken up and he was besieged by commissions from the leading German musicians of the day.

Whether any of the Brahms or Dvořák dance sets can truly be called 'national music' on our definition is questionable. Brahms was not Hungarian and was not writing for Hungarians, and the gypsy style was only indirectly Hungarian (see below on Liszt's Hungarian Rhapsodies), while Dvořák was writing for an international market, specifically serving up an attractive dish from the provinces of the Austrian empire for consumption in the German-speaking cultural 'centre'. Dvořák later maintained that his music was Slavic rather than Czech; Czech music he attributed to Smetana. Indeed Smetana conceived the second set of his own *Czech Dances* (1879) for piano as an answer to Dvořák's first set of *Slavonic Dances* (1878), showing what, in his view, genuine Czech dance music should be like. A virtuoso concert pianist himself, Smetana's national dance music for piano began without folklore associations with his patriotic marches in the revolutionary year of 1848. He continued with a large number of polkas for piano. The famous national dances in his opera *Prodaná nevěsta* (*The Bartered Bride*, 1866–70) do not quote authentic tunes, but established a code for Czechness in music. Those associations are confirmed by the frontispiece of a piano arrangement of the march from the opera, which is illustrated with images of dancing peasants in national costume (Fig. 2.1). The two sets of *Czech Dances* are, significantly, for piano solo rather than duet, and are conceived in the traditions of progressive Romantic solo keyboard music begun by Chopin, Schumann and Liszt, as befits a composer who associated himself with the 'New German School' of Wagner and Liszt. According to the composer's diary, they are composed 'in the manner of Chopin's mazurkas'. The first two polkas in the first set are in minor keys and moderate tempi, belying the impression given by *The Bartered Bride* that Czech national dances are essentially cheerful. The first begins with non-tonic harmony and chromatic chord progressions, in the manner of a Romantic 'fragment'. For the second set Smetana used materials from *Prostonárodní české písně a říkadla* (*Czech Folk Songs and Rhymes*, 1864) edited by Karel Jaromír Erben, but his treatment drew on the power and techniques of modern virtuoso piano music in the manner of Liszt to create a heroic public monument to Czech music. The dances are dramatic and varied, each resembling a tone poem in itself. In a sense Smetana upheld the 'authentic' approach of Chopin over the 'Hausmusik' of Dvořák's *Slavonic Dances*, but in terms of artistic values as much as folklore. Like the Chopin mazurkas, the *Czech Dances* are quite in line with Herder's call for the intermingling of artistic genius and folk genius. In his œuvre as a whole, Smetana was instrumental in realizing Erben's vision of the polka as a Czech national dance. However, he rejected the call for authenticity in folksong-based music promoted by some Czech nationalists, along with their anti-German stance. He preferred to compose his own national dances, and he imitated the musical styles of the towns rather than the countryside.[23]

National dances (and some songs) for piano span the whole career of Edvard Grieg (1843–1907), starting in the mid 1860s, when he took up the cause of Norwegian cultural nationalism. Grieg was acquainted with the internationally famous Norwegian violinist Ole Bull, who had been performing Norwegian folk music in his European concerts for some time. As a composer he is best known for his piano miniatures, especially the sixty-six *Lyric Pieces* in ten books published between 1866 and 1901. These are a mixture: some pieces are Norwegian folk dances, some claim to be settings of folksongs, and some

---

[23] Curtis, *Music Makes the Nation*, pp. 121–9.

Fig. 2.1 Bedřich Smetana (1824–84), frontispiece of the March from *The Bartered Bride* (*Prodaná nevěsta*), piano transcription

have other folklore elements or portray scenes from peasant life or mythology such as 'Bell Ringing', 'Elves' Dance' and 'Wedding Day at Troldhaugen'. Other pieces however have no obvious national significance, or suggest a general Romantic atmosphere that could be heard as national if desired. Clearer cases can be found in the 23 *Norwegian Folk Songs and Dances* Op. 17 (1869) and the 19 *Norwegian Folk Tunes* Op. 66 (1896), and even the *Pictures from Country Life* Op. 19 (1874). Grieg collected folk music himself and spent much time in the mountains of western Norway, but for his compositions relied heavily on Ludvig Mathias Lindeman's collection *Aeldre og nyere norske fjeldmelodier* (*Older and Newer Mountain Melodies*, 1840). Grieg's settings are notable for his individual and innovative harmonic style – an advanced chromaticism parallel to, but independent of, Wagner's – and the folk-music arrangements include some of his most experimental pieces. In his writings Grieg spoke a Herderian language of cultural nationalism, extolling the 'folk-soul', and claiming that 'the folk song reflects musically the inner life of the people'.[24]

Grieg's boldest approach is found in a late work: the seventeen *Slåtter* Op. 72 (1903), based on Hardanger-fiddle tunes transcribed from the playing of Knut Dahle. The peculiar style of Hardanger-fiddle music arises from its sympathetic strings, which create harmonic resonance in response to two-part double stopping by the player on an open-string drone and a stopped string. Hardanger-fiddle music is structured in short units of one, two or three bars and is distinguished by unusual tuning and melodic ornamentation, sharp dissonance and a lack of vibrato. Grieg could not transcribe this idiom directly for the piano, but compensated by inventing strange, percussive and dissonant chords to convey the effect of the fiddle's sympathetic resonance, and stressing cross rhythms and off-beat accents (Ex. 2.4). Just like Beethoven in his settings of Scottish folksong, Grieg added preludes, interludes, postludes and motivic development. Grieg thus arrived at a Romantic mode of authenticity in a way that recalls Herder's logic once again: the raw genius of the folk meets the original genius of the creative artist. The *Slåtter* represent a primitivist aesthetic and take the innovations in the musical language so far that they can be called modernist. They were well received by advanced musicians in Paris, and probably influenced Bartók. At the same time, like much modernist music that adapted folk idioms, their status as national music is questionable. The *Slåtter* do not offer themselves for popular consumption and were not taken up by pianists. Their effectiveness in spreading national sentiment is limited, and they were one of the few works of Grieg that did not take on national significance in his later popular reception.[25]

In the twentieth century, perhaps the worthiest successor to Chopin's mazurkas is *Iberia* (1906–8) by Isaac Albéniz: a kind of suite of twelve piano

---

[24] Cited in ibid., p. 131.

[25] Ståle Kleiberg, 'Grieg's "Slåtter", Op. 72: Change of Musical Style or New Concept of Nationality?', *Journal of the Royal Musical Association* 121/1 (1996), pp. 46–57; Curtis, *Music Makes the Nation*, pp. 130–5; Grimley, *Grieg*, pp. 147–91.

Ex. 2.4  Grieg, 'Knut Luråsens halling I', Op. 72 No. 10, bars 25–38

pieces of monumental scale, extreme harmonic and rhythmic complexity and great technical difficulty, grouped systematically into four books. *Iberia* is not really a single work, however, and is seldom performed complete. The pieces span a wide range of dances and moods, many of them, despite their titles, combining references to several dances or idioms in highly stylized ways. The title suggests that the whole peninsula is covered, although in practice southern Spain, specifically Andalusia, is disproportionately represented. Some pieces portray particular locations or yearly festivals, and together they suggest a panorama of Spanish life through a collection of fragments and fantastic visions. In contrast to Chopin and most other national dance pieces for piano, *Iberia* has a focus on urban settings and the noisy bustle of the street. For instance, 'El puerto' portrays a busy seaport town, El Puerto de Santa María near Cádiz, with a *zapateado* dance, while the programmatic 'Fête-Dieu à Séville' describes a Corpus Christi Day procession, combining lively dances with the sounds of religious chant and church bells. Albéniz had mastered Spanish popular idioms, and manipulated them deftly along with techniques learned from recent French piano music, especially Debussy, and narrative effects derived from programme music. In the first piece, *Evocación*, for instance, it is unclear which dance or dances, or what combination, is referenced, and the slow tempo confuses matters further. Albéniz here creates a nostalgic reflection on his sources, a sublimation of Spanish popular music that suggests a stream of memories passing through consciousness. Many of the pieces end in stillness, as though the dance has finished and the streets are cleared, with only memories remaining. In this expressive depth as well as the progressive compositional technique and monumentality of the four books overall, *Iberia* marks an advance over Albéniz's many earlier salon pieces in Spanish dance forms, which offer a picture-postcard exoticism.[26]

## Overtures and symphonies

From a nationalist perspective, the integration of folk music into symphonic forms meant the absorption of the *Volksgeist* into one of the highest forms of art music and a perfect vehicle for the mobilization of the nation's educated citizens through culture. By the mid nineteenth century the symphony, epitomized by the nine works of Beethoven, especially the heroic odd-numbered symphonies, had acquired tremendous prestige among high-minded musicians and critics, and embodied the values of liberal humanism. His semi-programmatic overtures on heroic themes (*Egmont, Coriolan, Leonore*), were held in similarly high regard. By the late nineteenth century, symphony halls and symphonic societies were springing up all over Europe and the United States, with subscription-paying audiences and a stable repertoire. Still, to import folk music into the abstract genre of the symphony steered into a conflict with its dynamic style, goal-directed structures, flexible phrase lengths and characteristic processes of 'motivic development'. Folk music occupies a different temporality from the Beethovenian symphonic style, being based on regular stanzas, bardic intonation, ostinato rhythms and other repetitive processes. If a folk melody is fragmented and subjected to motivic development by a process of professional compositional manipulation, the link with the *Volksgeist* is severed. As the English composer Constant Lambert quipped in his polemical *Music Ho!* (1934), 'the whole trouble with a folk song is that once you have played it through there is nothing much you can do except play it over again and play it rather louder'.[27]

Many composers who drew deeply on folk music largely avoided symphonic forms, some deliberately because they thought they had to be transcended or rejected (Liszt, Smetana, Bartók), some because of lack of interest or perceived incapacity (Chopin, Glinka, Grieg). At the same time not all 'national' overtures and symphonies directly quote vernacular sources. The practice was most common in Russian works from the 1860s and 1870s inspired by Glinka's orchestral piece *Kamarinskaya* (1848) as interpreted by Balakirev. By contrast, despite his lifelong engagement with the English folksong movement and his use of folksong in vocal works, the nine symphonies of Ralph Vaughan Williams (1872–1958) do not allude to any known folksongs. *A London Symphony* (No. 2) quotes urban songs and cries, while some of the others foreground modality and

---

[26]  Walter Aaron Clark, *Isaac Albéniz: Portrait of a Romantic* (New York and Oxford: Oxford University Press, 1998), pp. 220–48.

[27]  Constant Lambert, *Music Ho! A Study of Music in Decline* (London: Faber & Faber, 1934), p. 164; from the section 'On the conflict of nationalism and form'.

what Vaughan Williams interpreted as the general melodic contours of English folksong.

An early example of folk idioms within symphonic forms is found in Niels Gade's (1817–90) Overture *Nachklänge von Ossian* (*Echoes of Ossian*, 1841), and it illustrates some of the complexities of this kind of music. Danish music historians have heard in the overture a 'national tone' and indeed it uses a folksong, 'Ramund va sig en bedre mand', with suggestions of modality in the harmonization. Gade, who collaborated with Hans Christian Andersen, was interested in folklore and wrote some overtly national pieces, but was also dependent on Germany for his musical career, becoming Director of the Leipzig Gewandhaus in the 1840s and a friend of Mendelssohn and Schumann. The overture was composed for a competition organized by the Copenhagen Music Society. The judges for the competition were German, and originally were to have included Mendelssohn, whose recent Overture 'The Hebrides' ('Fingal's Cave'; 1832) was a model for Gade. The German title for the work is thus significant, as is a Romantic inscription from Ludwig Uhland's poem 'Freie Kunst'. Ossian of course had nothing to do with Denmark, and the short fashion for Ossian in Denmark had passed by the 1840s; in Germany, by contrast, Ossian was regarded by some as a national hero and, paradoxically, the father of German literature. The overture does possess what the Danish historians would call a 'national tone' (the archaic atmosphere, the harping of a bard, the ballad-like folk melody and its modality), but which nation is being represented – Scotland, Denmark or Germany – is less clear.[28]

The best-known attempt to incorporate folk sources into symphonic music was made in Russia by the composers of the so-called *kuchka*, and was inspired by Balakirev's example, encouragement and theories. The number of literal folksong quotations in Russian symphonies is not large,[29] although there is a good deal of imitation of folk idioms: modal inflections, pedals, short repeated units, changing metrical groupings, and an emphasis on melodic integrity over motivic fragmentation. Russian composers turned this last feature into a characteristic gesture, favouring the presentation of musical ideas over their development. Nevertheless, *kuchka* symphonies are always in four movements; sonata-form schemes are often apparent; the standard tonal 'narrative' of tonic minor to tonic major, originating in Beethoven's Symphonies No. 5 and 9, is common; and there are allusions to symphonic music by German composers, especially Schumann.

Balakirev attempted to define a style of Russian orchestral music based on folk materials with a new emphasis on colour and rhythmic and melodic inflection and a new approach to large-scale structure. His model was Glinka's

---

[28] Anna Harwell Celenza, *The Early Works of Niels W. Gade: In Search of the Poetic* (Aldershot: Ashgate, 2001), pp. 121–36.

[29] A. Peter Brown, *The Symphonic Repertoire*, vol. 3, Part B, *The European Symphony from ca. 1800 to ca. 1930. Great Britain, Russia and France* (Bloomington: Indiana University Press, 2008), pp. 521–3.

*Kamarinskaya* (1848), a 'Fantasia for Orchestra on the Themes of a Wedding Song and a Dance Song' that used two folk melodies in alternation, one slow, one fast, constructed as rhythmic ostinatos and as 'variations' with changing accompaniment rather than altered melody. The avoidance of conventional motivic fragmentation or varied phrase structures, and the use of orchestral colour to shape the piece as a whole seemed to offer a welcome alternative method of musical construction to the academic programme being introduced to Russia at Anton Rubinstein's St Petersburg Conservatory. Glinka himself had no nationalist agenda with *Kamarinskaya*: he aimed for local colour just as in his two *Spanish Overtures* (1848, 1851). Balakirev, though, backed up by the critic Vladimir Stasov, aimed to establish a school of Russian symphonic composition with his two *Overtures on Russian Themes* (1858, 1862), closely modelled on Glinka, but now cast in modified sonata form. The first Overture has the same slow–fast contrast between its first two folk melodies and similar key relationships, while the three-bar phrase lengths of the two fast themes resemble one of the *Kamarinskaya* tunes. In the second Overture, later to become the symphonic poem *Russia*, Balakirev found an innovative way of harmonizing a modal folksong that emphasized its alternative tonic note and avoided dominant harmony and authentic cadences in favour of the subdominant. This approach to tonality, which became known as the 'Russian minor', was taken up by many later Russian composers as an element of national style even when no folk material was involved. At the same time Balakirev favoured radical modulations and key relationships of the kind associated at the time with progressive Romanticism, especially Liszt. In this respect Balakirev's treatment parallels and intensifies Beethoven's response to Scottish folksongs. Rimsky-Korsakov followed up with his *Overture on Russian Themes* Op. 28 (1866), *Fantasia on Serbian Themes* (1867) and *Russian Easter Festival Overture* (1888).[30] Many non-symphonic Russian compositions make local reference to 'changing-background variation', folksong, and sharp contrasts of slow and fast sections.

The repetitive, changing-background approach to symphonic form may be said to encode in musical structure an aspect of the Slavophile ideology of the *kuchka* composers. Russian peasant life, rooted in the eternal seasonal cycles and in Orthodox religion, was held to be superior to modern Western liberal society, which had unfortunately been foisted on Russia by Peter the Great. The static, repetitive forms of the Russians and their interest in timbre and innovative orchestral scoring can likewise be contrasted with the forward-pressing developmental processes of the Beethovenian symphony.[31] Yet, for all their Slavophile rhetoric, the *kuchka* composers never severed their links with the language of the German musical 'centre'. Indeed their musical project depended on a sense of partial displacement from a universal idiom. Their symphonic

---

[30] Taruskin, *Defining Russia Musically*, pp. 113–51.

[31] Benedict Taylor, 'Temporality in Nineteenth-Century Russian Music and the Notion of Development', *Music & Letters* 94/1 (2013), pp. 79–80.

writing had its own logic, which included drawing out links between seemingly contrasted themes (present already in *Kamarinskaya*) and the positioning of sonata-form movements within an 'introduction-coda frame'.[32] In the first movement of his Symphony No. 1 in C (1864, 1897) Balakirev combines repetitive thematic presentation with traditional motivic manipulation and phrase contraction to build up and reduce tension in ways closely related to conventional symphonic writing.[33]

Rimsky-Korsakov used Russian folksongs in two movements of his Symphony No. 1 in E flat minor (1865; revised 1884), partly under Balakirev's supervision. Changing-background variations are found in the slow movement. The same applies, more freely, to the introduction to the first movement of his Symphony No. 3 in C (1873, 1886). In other ways, however, these works stand firmly in the symphonic tradition, with debts to Schumann. The transition between the themes in the first movement of No. 3 is smooth and highly polished, indicating an aspiration to conventional symphonic mastery rather than juxtaposition and sharp contrast. Rimsky-Korsakov's Symphony No. 2 is national music of another kind: it follows an Arabian story by Osip Ivanovich Senkovsky (1800–58) and uses Arabian melodies from Salvator Daniel's *Album de chansons arabes, mauresques et kabyles* (1863) and Alexander Christianovich's *Esquisse historique de la musique arabe* (1863). The composer made four versions between 1868 and 1903 and eventually renamed it *Symphonic Suite: Antar*, on the grounds that there was nothing symphonic about it save the number of movements (four). In doing so, however, he abandoned *kuchka* ideals and appealed to a traditional conception of the symphony of which Rubinstein would have approved, in relation to which the work represents a licence.[34]

Borodin's Symphony No. 2 in B minor was once popular with Western concert audiences, who heard in it a strong Russian flavour. Stasov called it the 'Heroic' Symphony and maintained that Borodin had a programme for three of the four movements: the first describes a gathering of Russian warriors, the third the ancient bard Bayan, and the fourth a scene of heroes feasting. Only the scherzo uses actual folk material, but the others project a similar sense of heroic and even primitive force. The finale is a set of Slavic dances with mixed triple and duple metres and heavy use of percussion – a 'primitive' touch – but also cast in a structure similar to sonata form, illustrating the tangential but very real relationship to the German symphonic tradition. César Cui spoke in a review in 1885 of the symphony's 'unconquerable, elemental power. The symphony is permeated by traits of Russian nationality, but the nationality of remote times; Rus' is perceptible in this symphony, but primitive pagan Rus'.' He spoke also of a 'harshness of thought and expression' coexisting with 'custom-hallowed

---

[32] On this term see James A. Hepokoski, *Sibelius, Symphony No. 5* (Cambridge: Cambridge University Press, 1993), p. 6.

[33] Taylor, 'Temporality in Nineteenth-Century Russian Music', pp. 94–9.

[34] Brown, *The Symphonic Repertoire*, vol. 3, pp. 254–301, 433–61.

western forms', the basic paradox on which the symphonic project of the *kuchka* thrived. Finally Cui dwelled on the composer's originality. The critic's themes of primitiveness and original genius recall the Romantic reception of Scottish folk music and the agenda for art music laid out by Herder.[35]

Pyotr Illych Tchaikovsky (1840–93) steered a course between Rubinstein and the *kuchka*; he was one of the first graduates of the St Petersburg Conservatory, from his youth possessed an accomplished technique and managed to create a career as a professional composer, but he drew on *kuchka* principles at times, for a while worked closely with Balakirev and was later a friend of Rimsky-Korsakov. Tchaikovsky's traditionalist aesthetic meant that he tended to reserve folksongs for the finales of instrumental compositions and the trios of scherzo movements, following the same pattern as Haydn, and observing rhetorical 'decorum' (choosing the right style for the task at hand). His First Symphony (1866, revised 1874) begins with a theme structured in three-bar units like those of *Kamarinskaya* and Balakirev's first Overture; the theme of the second movement is a stylization of a typical 'drawn-out' Russian folksong with variations; the finale quotes a Russian folksong in its finale, which is treated in the 'changing-background' style. His Third Symphony is known widely as the 'Polish' on account of the polonaise finale, but the title is not the composer's and the symphony inhabits the world of Tchaikovsky's orchestral suites, which were composed in what Richard Taruskin, following George Balanchine, calls Tchaikovsky's 'imperial style', in which the polonaise featured centrally.[36] If this is national music, then Russia, not Poland, is represented, through a hierarchical conception of the nation. Tchaikovsky's main symphonic contribution to national music is his Symphony No. 2 in C minor, subtitled 'Little Russian' (that is, Ukrainian; 1872–81). Here Tchaikovsky is at his closest to the *kuchka*, above all in the finale, where a fast Ukrainian dance tune is repeated against a changing background. This technique appears briefly also in the first movement's slow introduction, accompanying a folksong-like theme played with characteristic Russian subdominant emphasis at the ends of phrases. The return of this horn melody at the end of the movement follows the structure of the two Balakirev Overtures, but also evokes memories of the Austro-German tradition and the majestic horn theme of Schubert's 'Great' C major Symphony. The theme is drawn into the development section too: a further synthesis of symphonic process and folklore. In the third movement the elements are kept separate; the outer sections are in a sonata form, and only the trio has a folksong.[37]

The first two symphonies of Alexander Glazunov (1865–1936) were written as a prodigious teenager and draw on *kuchka* techniques and folk materials. The first is subtitled 'Slavonian'. Thereafter, however, Glazunov abandoned any pretence of an anti-Western stance, and in his next six symphonies integrated

---

[35] Ibid., pp. 313–30.

[36] Taruskin, *Defining Russia Musically*, pp. 276–90; *On Russian Music*, pp. 131–2.

[37] Maes, *A History of Russian Music*, p. 77; Taruskin, *On Russian Music*, pp. 129–30.

Russian and German approaches. No. 3 is dedicated to Tchaikovsky and No. 4 to Anton Rubinstein. A similar rapprochement can be found in the symphonies of Vasily Kalinnikov (1876–1901) and even, from the opposite direction, Rubinstein himself.[38] By the early twentieth century, folk-music materials were almost never used in Russian symphonies; rather the direction is towards religious sources, with Rachmaninov at the forefront, evoking bells and Orthodox chant, especially in his Second Symphony (1907).

Outside Russia, one of the most successful symphonies to incorporate folk music is Vincent d'Indy's (1851–1931) *Symphonie sur un chant montagnard français* (*Symphony on a French Mountain Air*, 1886), sometimes called *Symphonie cévenole*. As an educator d'Indy had a profound influence on the next generation of composers of national music. D'Indy came from an aristocratic family with deep roots in the Ardèche region of southern France. He was fiercely patriotic and strongly opposed to the secular, bourgeois Third Republic, campaigning for social and cultural reform and promoting Catholic regionalism over the official state republicanism. To reform French music he looked to the universality of the modern German tradition for inspiration, especially Beethoven and Wagner. His musical mentor César Franck offered ways to reconcile the technical innovations of Liszt and Wagner with the tradition of abstract instrumental music, including the use of 'cyclic' themes that recur in different movements. To d'Indy, music was an ethical and ennobling art. He regarded the symphony as the greatest compositional challenge, and attempted to overcome French traditions of lightweight orchestral music and in some ways to Germanize French music so that it would speak for a regenerated French nation. Thus, although his ultimate aim was to bring France back to its destiny as a universal culture, he temporarily turned it into a musical 'periphery' relative to Germany, which may have facilitated the use of folksong in a symphony. With the *Symphonie cévenole*, d'Indy 'transplanted' the abstract symphony from its German home to the French countryside.

The folklore movement came to France in the second half of the nineteenth century, and d'Indy was a friend of the musicologist and folklorist Julien Tiersot, author of *Histoire de la chanson populaire en France* (1889). D'Indy himself published *Chansons populaires du Vivarais* (1892). The theme of the symphony is a mountain song heard and notated by d'Indy in the Cévennes in 1885 while on a mountain walk. An out-of-doors mood is conveyed by the opening cor anglais presentation of the theme, the landscape painting of the slow movement, the evocation of clangorous bells at the end of the first movement's development, and the suggestion of village festivities in the finale.[39] The *Symphonie cévenole* is a generic hybrid: the inclusion of a prominent solo piano part and the restriction to three rather than four movements means that it resembles a concerto. However,

---

[38] Taylor, 'Temporality in Nineteenth-Century Russian Music', p. 100.

[39] Andrew Thomson, *Vincent d'Indy and his World* (Oxford: Clarendon Press, 1996), pp. 50, 66–8.

this is not a conventional virtuoso concerto, as the piano part, although difficult, is primarily accompanimental, participating in highly inventive textures, often in combination with the harp. The work draws on up-to-date symphonic techniques. There are two cyclic themes, one being the mountain air, the basis for the main themes of all three movements, which is treated to thematic transformation rather in the manner of Liszt, but is also recollected in its original guise at hushed moments. The original, complete version of the mountain air stands outside the sonata-form portion of the first movement, forming another 'introduction-coda frame'. The theme itself is metrically complex, beginning with pairs of bars of three and two beats respectively, thus essentially two bars of five beats each (Ex. 2.5(i), bars 3–4, 5–6 and 9–10, counting dotted-crotchet beats). When the main theme of the sonata-form portion of the first movement enters, it is cast in a more regular triple metre, despite the melody (in the lower orchestral instruments) being based on the folksong (Ex. 2.5(ii)). In the finale the implicit quintuple metre is realized more fully. These subtle metrical processes substitute to some degree for conventionally symphonic motivic development.[40]

D'Indy's later pedagogical and literary activities involved him in the politics of culture and he developed a compositional school of sorts, with some orientation to national music and folksong, albeit multinational in its members. In 1894 d'Indy co-founded a new conservatoire, the Schola Cantorum, which challenged the establishment Conservatoire Nationale de Musique, a state institution that controlled musical education in France and focused on training composers of contemporary opera. D'Indy established a 'code' that linked his new cultural values to certain genres, styles and repertoires, creating a nationalist symbolism that drew together art, politics and religion and laid out a cultural programme in opposition to the state.[41] The Schola's syllabus emphasized counterpoint and historical studies for composition and drew on d'Indy's revival of Gregorian chant and music of the sixteenth and seventeenth centuries. The Schola invited its students to participate in a long European tradition, establishing a canon of great works of the past on which to build. D'Indy developed his approach in a treatise, *Cours de composition musicale* (1903–50), in which he described the symphony in analogy to a Gothic cathedral. The symphony conveyed a moral message and had the power to improve society.[42]

By the first decade of the twentieth century, in the wake of the Dreyfus affair, the arts were becoming highly politicized in France, with right-wing nationalist leagues such as the *Ligue de la Patrie Française* and *Action Française* taking a deep interest in culture as a way to advance their programmes for national renewal.[43] D'Indy was a member of the *Ligue* and took advantage of its resources to promote his educational programme. He was fiercely anti-Semitic, following

---

[40] For further analysis see Brown, *The Symphonic Repertoire*, vol. 3, pp. 640–54.

[41] Fulcher, *French Cultural Politics and Music*, p. 6.

[42] Ibid., p. 31.

[43] Ibid., p. 5.

Ex. 2.5  D'Indy, *Symphonie cévenole*, first movement (reduction):
(i) bars 1–10; (ii) bars 27–30

up on Wagner in his attacks on Jewish composers, although not all the Schola students were anti-Dreyfusard.

Many of d'Indy's circle of students and colleagues were interested in folk music and French regional culture as well as early music. The Breton Guy Ropartz (1864–1955) used folksong in his Franckian *Symphonie sur un thème Breton* (1894–95), and Déodat de Séverac (1872–1921) brought the music of his native Languedoc into his Piano Sonata (1898–99). Joseph Canteloube (1879–1957) had in some ways a similar background to d'Indy. Again, although born in Paris, generations of his family had come from one region of southern France, in his case the Auvergne. From the early years of the century until the end of his life Canteloube undertook expeditions into the French countryside for research into folksong, publishing them in anthologies for solo voice and accompaniment or for choir. Canteloube is best known for the five volumes of *Chants d'Auvergne* (1923–54), of which by far the most famous is the luxuriantly scored 'Baïlèro'. He was a typical product of the Schola insofar as his interest in folksong collection was encouraged in combination with a firmly grounded technique. D'Indy also had a legacy in southern Europe, Latin America and beyond, especially for composers from those countries who incorporated folksong within sonata forms and symphonic design such as Joaquín Turina (1882–1949; Spain), and Ahmed Adnan Saygun (1907–91; Turkey).

Perhaps the most famous symphony to draw on folk materials is Dvořák's Symphony No. 9 in E minor, 'From the New World' (1893). This work, though, is full of ironies. Dvořák lived in America between 1892 and 1895 having been recruited to head the new National Conservatory of Music by the philanthropist Jeanette Thurber, who wanted a high-profile European musician to establish the institution and create a school of American music. His appointment was accompanied by much publicity. Dvořák was in close contact with American music critics and journalists, and the national dimension of the symphony was trailed in advance of its premiere and dominated its early reception. The music was drawn into ongoing debates about American cultural identity, its degree of independence from European culture and its ethnic diversity. Dvořák learned about Southern plantation music at first hand through his black student Henry Burleigh, and studied Amerindian melodies. He gave his views in a *New York Herald* article 'The real value of Negro melodies'. The style Dvořák arrived at in his works composed in America such as the 'New World' Symphony, the 'American' Quartet Op. 96, the 'American' Suite Op. 98 and the Biblical Songs Op. 99 is characterized by alternate lyricism and rhythmic energy, syncopated rhythms, plagal (subdominant) harmony, a characteristic 'snap' rhythmic figure with a short note on the downbeat, the pentatonic scale and passages of harmonic stasis that suggest landscape. Multi-movement works have programmatic bases and there are cyclic recollections between movements. Vivid thematic character and contrast is foregrounded over thematic development. In the symphony, there are real or apparent quotations from African American songs (including 'Swing Low, Sweet Chariot') and a programme for the inner movements based on

Longfellow's *The Song of Hiawatha*, both of which were made public.[44] This style was one of several that Dvořák the composer had learned to switch between on occasion, moving from Brahmsian abstraction in his chamber music written for Germans and Viennese, flexible 'Slavonic' idioms in his dances, Czech national music in the manner of Smetana in the 'Hussite' Overture, and oratorio style for his choral commissions for the English provincial festivals. The American musicians who hired and discussed Dvořák's music wanted an accommodation between art music and popular styles; in this respect his American music is the first step in a process that went much further in later American art music. At this stage, though, his patrons wanted a European to do it for them. Dvořák produced a symphony that sounded the way 'national music' was by then meant to sound, whatever its sources. At the same time the piece is classically symphonic: the forms of the movements are traditional and clear, and in the first movement a transition links the contrasting themes of the exposition no less smoothly than in Rimsky-Korsakov's Third.

Dvořák's prescription for American music was put into practice by the next generation of American composers, including Arthur Nevin (1871–1943), Charles Wakefield Cadman (1881–1946) and Henry F. Gilbert (1868–1928), all of whom collected African American or Amerindian songs and built them into their classical compositions. This repertoire has not survived in performance, and has met with the predictable objections. The conservative composer and critic Daniel Gregory Mason called it 'the music of indigestion', while the historian Barbara Tischler speaks disparagingly of 'American musical nationalism by quotation'.[45]

## Rhapsodies

The rhapsody – its title suggesting the improvisatory freedom of the Romantic artist – presented fewer complexities than the symphony for composers of folk-inspired national music. Here the composer, who was sometimes also the performer, need not worry about motivic development but could act like an ancient bard, evoking the *Volksgeist* and the nation, at first in misty antiquity, then presently and heroically, in forms that varied from one piece to the next. The term 'rhapsody' was first used as a generic title in music for late eighteenth-century songs, and then, in the early nineteenth century, for keyboard pieces aimed at amateurs that imitated in accessible form the expressive extremes of famous contemporary keyboard virtuosos. Only in the second half of the century did the rhapsody transform into a heroic piece for orchestra with national associations. This was largely the work of Liszt, who first turned the rhapsody

---

[44] Michael Beckerman, *New Worlds of Dvořák: Searching in America for the Composer's Inner Life* (New York and London: Norton, 2003), pp. 18–19.

[45] Barbara L. Tischler, *An American Music: The Search for an American Musical Identity* (New York and Oxford: Oxford University Press, 1986), pp. 6, 33–8.

into a virtuoso piano piece with his nineteen Hungarian Rhapsodies for piano (Nos. 1–15, 1846–47, published 1851–53; Nos. 16–19 published 1882–85), originally conceived as *Magyar dallok/Ungarische National-Melodien* (1839–40) and their successors, six *Magyar rhapsodiák/Rhapsodies hongroises*.[46]

In November 1839 Liszt returned to Hungary for the first time since his childhood, now an international celebrity and the best-known living Hungarian. At the time Hungary was engaged in a political struggle for independence from Austria. Liszt was hailed as a national hero, honoured at a ceremony at the National Theatre, and made a habit of playing in public his arrangement of the Rákóczy March, a melody that was banned by the authorities. However, if judged on his published works, Liszt was not at this stage a national composer, and he resolved to become one. Liszt had been aware of Roma music since his youth, but he now took it more seriously, listening carefully to 'gypsy' bands and writing an account of their playing. The Hungarian Rhapsodies are sectional pieces with sharp tempo variations between sections, evoking melancholy and ecstasy, and working to a feverish climax. They evoke the *verbunkos* style (the word meaning 'recruiting', as the music was associated with recruitment by the Austrian army) played by Roma bands, including the cimbalom effects, the 'gypsy scale' with the melancholy interval of the augmented second and a host of other rhythmic, melodic and harmonic traits. The question of whether Liszt used genuine folk materials is complex. The Roma who played this music were professional musicians, not peasants, and they were not perceived as Hungarian either by themselves or by the Hungarian educated classes for whom they performed. Some of the tunes Liszt used were originally composed by upper-class Hungarians before being taken up by the Roma. The style of the rhapsodies, although heightened, was not new in the European tradition: the *style hongrois* went back to the eighteenth century and had become a characteristic musical dialect in Haydn, Beethoven and, above all, Schubert. This style did have roots in Hungarian songs and dances, but was filtered first through the performance and interpretative traditions of the Roma and then through compositional traditions.[47] Liszt himself ironically identified with the Roma at least as much as with Hungarian peasants, being attracted by their instrumental virtuosity and their homelessness. He mistook the origins of some of the music and confused matters further in his verbose and controversial book *Des Bohémiens et de leur musique en Hongrie* (1859), where he attributed the style entirely to the Roma, leading to accusations of betrayal from Hungarian nationalists. This all applied to the first fifteen rhapsodies: the last four, from thirty years later, reveal a new, highly chromatic style that Liszt cultivated from the 1860s onwards, in which 'gypsy' elements are minimized.[48]

---

[46] John Rink, 'Rhapsody', in Sadie (ed.), *New Grove*, vol. 21, pp. 254–5.

[47] Jonathan Bellman, *The Style Hongrois in the Music of Western Europe* (Boston: Northeastern University Press, 1993), pp. 12, 47–68.

[48] Ibid., p. 189.

Liszt probably underestimated the traces of genuine Hungarian folk music – the music of the Magyar peasants – preserved in his Hungarian Rhapsodies. But the historical significance of these pieces is separate from questions of their authenticity. Liszt elevated a genre (rhapsody) and a distinctive, exotic style (*style hongrois*) to the status of public virtuoso concert music, and gave it airs of the heroic and the epic. His example was followed by composers of national rhapsodies such as Svendsen (four *Norwegian Rhapsodies* for orchestra, 1876–77); Dvořák (three *Slavonic Rhapsodies*, 1878–79); Lalo (*Rapsodie norvégienne*, 1879); Mackenzie (*Rhapsodie écossaise*; *Burns: Scotch Rhapsody No. 2*, 1779–1880); Chabrier (*España, rapsodie pour orchestra*, 1883); Albéniz (*Rapsodia española* for piano and orchestra, 1887); Saint-Saëns (*Rapsodie d'Auvergne*, piano solo, 1884, *Rapsodie Breton*, 1891); Rachmaninov (*Russian Rhapsody*, 1891, two pianos); Enescu (two *Romanian Rhapsodies*, 1901); Stanford (six *Irish Rhapsodies*, 1902–22); Vaughan Williams (three *Norfolk Rhapsodies*, 1905–6); Delius (*Brigg Fair: An English Rhapsody*, 1907); Ravel (*Rapsodie espagnole*, 1908); Casella (*Italia: Rhapsody for Orchestra*, 1909); Finzi (*A Severn Rhapsody*, 1923); and Bloch (*America: An Epic Rhapsody for Orchestra*, 1926). Gershwin's *Rhapsody in Blue* (1924) stands in this tradition too. Most of these pieces allude to vernacular music in one way or another. They are highly varied in form and scoring – most are orchestral but some include solo instruments, while others have programmes like a symphonic poem – although an intense mood and improvisatory touches in the tradition of Liszt are quite common. Most national rhapsodies refer to nations of the musical 'periphery', even when the composer comes from the 'centre', as with the Spanish rhapsodies of French composers. 'German rhapsodies' are extremely rare, if they exist at all.

## Fantasia

For much of the nineteenth century, the musical fantasia or fantasy was closely related to the rhapsody in its freedom of form and improvisatory tendencies: it would be difficult to pin down any consistent differences between the genres. In the early twentieth century, however, there was a move in England to define a type of 'phantasy' on the model of the Jacobean viol fantasia. The wealthy amateur Walter Willson Cobbett ran competitions in 1905 and 1907 to encourage modern English composers to write fantasias for chamber ensemble and directly commissioned twelve compositions thereafter, although, beyond the scoring, little about the genre was specified. Nearly seventy submissions were received for both competitions. These competitions reflected a wider Tudor revival in English culture between 1890 and 1914, in music as well as other fields such as architecture and design. In music it was part of a self-conscious English 'Renaissance'. A return to the spirit of Tudor and Jacobean music, it was felt, would bypass the intervening centuries of commercial and colonial expansion, which also happened to be a period when English composition did not flourish and the English imported most of their music. Between 1910 and 1912 Vaughan

Williams composed four pieces entitled fantasia: *Fantasia on English Folk Songs* for orchestra (1910), *Fantasia on a Theme by Thomas Tallis* for double string orchestra and string quartet (1910; revised 1913, 1919), *Phantasy Quintet*, commissioned by Cobbett, for two violins, two violas and cello (1912) and *Fantasia on Christmas Carols* for baritone, mixed chorus and orchestra (1912). The *Tallis Fantasia*, although not written for Cobbett, is one of the most famous pieces by any English composer and is still heard by listeners today as uniquely 'English' in sound. The success of this evocative piece lies in its modern synthesis of historical elements: the Jacobean genre transformed into a string orchestra piece; various traditions of sacred choral music, including the theme by the Tudor composer Thomas Tallis (1505–85) from his psalm setting 'Why fum'th in fight the Gentiles spite'; the spatial conception of the work and the imaginative scoring for the double string orchestra and soloists, with antiphonal effects that suggest choral singing and seem to match the Tudor-period English Perpendicular style of architecture of Gloucester Cathedral where it was first performed at the Three Choirs Festival; the status of that festival as a great English musical tradition; the hints of 'landscape painting' in musical terms; and, last but not least, the use of English folksong idioms – though not, as far as is known, direct quotation.

Vaughan Williams believed in the influence of folksong on church music, both plainchant and especially Tudor sacred music, which, he argued some years later, arose out of indigenous English practices rather than compositional traditions and for this reason seemed to music historians to come 'from nowhere'.[49] The first motivic material presented in the *Tallis Fantasia* consists of fragments of Tallis's theme in the bass instruments; it is followed directly by an imitation of the ancient ecclesiastical 'organum' style (a way of harmonizing a melody with parallel voices in medieval music). There follow two presentations of Tallis's theme in the Phrygian mode, the second an ecstatic apotheosis that seems designed to fill the architectural space. The very opening of the work suggests a broad landscape with its slow-moving, widely spaced chords. This way of evoking vast spaces was already a staple of national music, and had been used by Vaughan Williams himself in his *Norfolk Rhapsody* No. 1. The introduction of folksong is delayed until the other signifiers of English identity have been presented and the atmosphere established.[50] Out of the silence that follows the apotheosis, the solo viola presents a folksong-like melody in rhapsodic fashion; it is then joined by a solo violin in a duet. At this point the music moves from grand historical and mystical gestures to a human scale and, at the same time, refers to the Jacobean genre of the viol fantasia. The *Tallis Fantasia* thus evokes an air of antiquity and the grand sweep of English musical and cultural history. Vaughan Williams's synthesis conspicuously excludes certain musical elements (sonata

---

[49] Vaughan Williams, *National Music and Other Essays*, p. 50.

[50] Anthony Pople, 'Vaughan Williams, Tallis, and the Phantasy Principle', in Alain Frogley (ed.), *Vaughan Williams Studies* (Cambridge: Cambridge University Press, 1996), pp. 47–80.

form, Wagnerian chromaticism) and combines themes from religion, architecture, landscape, chamber music and folksong in order to project a certain conception of the English nation and its identity and destiny, both embedded in tradition and looking forward to a renewed culture.

## Folk music and modernism

Folk music became a subject of intense interest for composers of the modernist generation of the early twentieth century such as Janáček, Bartók, Stravinsky, Falla and Szymanowski. At this time ethnographers were undertaking more systematic research than ever before, and truth to the sources became a central theme for the modernists. Bartók disparaged the national efforts of Chopin and Liszt, finding too little genuine folklore, too much exoticism and too much 'banality' in the compositional crafting. Perceptions of the raw, uncultivated quality of folk music played into the modernists' aesthetic of primitivism and their desire to overcome what they saw as the stale conventions of nineteenth-century bourgeois culture. It is no longer useful to classify the modernists' compositions by genre, as increasingly each work was regarded as sui generis, either transcending generic classification or blending genres in an unrepeatable way. Yet the function of folk music in their compositions in many ways reflected the old imperatives of Romanticism, and they invested more than ever in the original genius of the artist and the authenticity bestowed by the common people. Folk music became a basis for reforming and renewing the musical language itself, facing compositional problems and finding a 'style', not just a way of adding an exotic flavour or invoking the *Volkston*. The rhythmic and modal structures of the folk sources were of special interest. Stravinsky, Bartók and Falla found ways of transforming those modal structures into chromatic structures. This system would bypass the tonal language of German late Romanticism (Wagner and Richard Strauss) with a new kind of chromaticism no longer based on major/minor harmonic tonality. But more scientific ethnography and more systematic assimilation did not lead directly to greater nationality in art music, for the modernists' efforts often fail to fit the category of national music in the sense developed in this book. Some produced deliberate ethnic or cultural hybrids, some eschewed broad popular appeal in their home countries, while some drew on folk music only intermittently.

Igor Stravinsky's (1812–1971) best-known national music was composed for Sergei Diaghilev's Ballets Russes: the three great ballets *L'oiseau de feu* (*The Firebird*, 1910), *Petrushka* (1911) and *Le sacre du printemps* (*The Rite of Spring*, 1913) and the generic hybrid *Les noces* (*The Wedding*; begun 1914; first performance 1923). The ballets stand to varying degrees in the shadow of Stravinsky's teacher Rimsky-Korsakov, and extend the vocabulary of Russian nationalist art music. Diaghilev was aiming at a Parisian audience strongly guided by the tastes of an international aristocracy that looked to the *kuchka* for 'authentic' – which to that group meant exotic – Russian music. The innovations of *L'oiseau* are mainly at the level of designs and sets, which, as Richard Taruskin points out, reflect Russian 'neo-nationalism', an applied arts movement akin to the English 'arts-and-crafts', which had some of the same aims as the musical modernists in its search for 'style' and looked for it in folklore.[51] In the music for *Petrushka*, despite residual debts to Rimsky-Korsakov, Stravinsky offends against a principle of the *kuchka* by drawing on urban rather than rural sources: concertina and music-box effects, barrel-organ tunes and street cries. Earlier Russian nationalists regarded such music as degenerate. Taruskin argues that the first coincidence of folklorism and modernism in Stravinsky is found in the first 'tableau', where Stravinsky attempts an accurate portrayal of the 'Carnaval barker', a traditional figure whose task is to attract a crowd to a showman's booth with improvised jingles (*pribautki*) on a high-pitched monotone with rhyming couplets of unequal lengths. Stravinsky writes static, additive rhythmic periods of varying length that begin and end unpredictably, a technique that became fundamental to his later music.[52] *Le sacre* is famous for its deliberate barbarism, but along with its brutal accents, harsh dissonances and theme of human sacrifice (not in fact documented as a Russian prehistoric practice) go structural innovations in rhythm and pitch organization that were derived from Russian and East European folk music. *Le sacre* intensified and extended the rhythmic processes of *Petrushka* and thematized them in the ritual context of the ballet, so that ostinato and irregularity are fundamental to the entire rhythmic structure. Moreover, Taruskin shows that Stravinsky combined short, modal, folksong-derived units to generate 'octatonic' pitch collections. This eight-note chromatic pitch structure, which alternates whole- and half-steps, had been popular with Russian composers since Glinka, especially Rimsky-Korsakov, but it had always been kept separate from the major/minor diatonic 'default' language as an effect reserved for supernatural characters or events. Allusions to folk music in the same scores had also been distinct from the octatonic passages. Stravinsky thus synthesized two Russian traditions – folklore and nineteenth-century art-music techniques – but in a quite new way that transformed the musical language in typically modernist fashion.[53]

*Le sacre* was the culmination of a new interest in Russian folklore in the 1900s among scholars, historians and nationalist artists that was tinged with the mysticism and occultism of the era. Ancient pagan peoples were thought to have lived in harmony with nature, and the revival of their customs, including songs, dances, rituals and spells, was deemed a remedy for modern over-civilization. Stravinsky's collaborator on the *Rite* was Nicolai Roerich (1874–1947), painter and expert in the art of Russian antiquity, whose work had already foregrounded

---

[51] Taruskin, *Stravinsky and the Russian Traditions*, pp. 502–18.

[52] Simon Karlinsky, 'Stravinsky and Russian Pre-Literate Theater', *19th-Century Music* 6/3 (1983), pp. 232–40; Taruskin, *Stravinsky and the Russian Traditions*, pp. 710–17.

[53] Taruskin, *Stravinsky and the Russian Traditions*, p. 937.

idols, ritual dances and sacred sites – precisely the subjects of the *Rite*. He and Stravinsky tried to create a new kind of ballet by omitting mime and all attempts at narrative. Roerich aimed for ethnographic authenticity in his sets and costumes, and Stravinsky's choice of folk sources was fairly authentic too, even corresponding to the stages of the action in the ritual. He used so-called 'ceremonial songs', and in particular seasonal or 'calendar' songs that were associated with the festivals on which Roerich based the action of the ritual. But it is not clear exactly what is authentic folk material and what is Stravinsky's invention or transformation: folklore has been transformed into modern style.[54]

Between 1914 and 1920, the years of Stravinsky's exile in Switzerland, he wrote eight compositions on Russian folk texts, utilizing recently published musical sources by Slavophile collectors, much of it provincial and humble in origin. At this time Stravinsky was continuing his search for alternatives to traditional compositional norms, and developed a radical, abrasive style. The sources for his wartime works include the Russian peasant wedding ritual, prose folk tales, jingles and children's rhymes. In his songs from this period the texts are sung to short, simple melodic formulae (*popevki*) that are repeated with irregular metre, as for instance in the four songs published as *Pribaoutki* ('Rhymes' or 'Jingles'; 1914), scored for voice, flute, oboe, clarinet, bassoon, violin, viola, cello and double bass. *Renard* (1916; 'The Fable of the Fox, the Cock, the Cat and the Ram'; 'A merry performance') is Stravinsky's appropriation of the traditions of the *skomorokhi* (itinerant Russian minstrels who gave satirical performances), a farmyard morality tale that requires acrobatic dance as well as singing.[55]

*Les noces*, premiered again by Diaghilev's Ballets Russes, is scored for four soloists, mixed chorus, four pianos and percussion and subtitled 'choreographic scenes', being neither an opera, cantata nor ballet, and lacking any conventional plot. Unlike the rituals of *Le sacre*, the Russian peasant wedding ritual was a living Christian tradition rather than prehistoric pagan folklore. The long, formalized peasant wedding rituals had come to represent Russian peasant life in 'high' culture long before Stravinsky, and can be found in operas by Glinka and Rimsky-Korsakov. Stravinsky's main source was more recent and accurate: a collection of over 1000 peasant wedding songs published in 1911.[56] But he continued his flexible compositional approach to the sources, avoiding a one-to-one correspondence of texts and melodies, generating his own flexible *popevki* in folk style but without specific reference to a single original source, and allowing them to combine in ways determined by octatonic collections.[57] In later years Stravinsky covered his tracks, maintaining that his ethnographic studies were either non-existent or extremely casual, presumably in order to distance himself from Bolshevism and, later, Stalin's nationalist cultural policies.

[54] Ibid., pp. 891–3.
[55] Ibid., pp. 1244–6.
[56] Ibid., pp. 1330–7.
[57] Ibid., pp. 1363–72, 1386–403.

Against all the Russianness explored by Taruskin, however, must be set a distinct pan-Slavic dimension to Stravinsky's music. His family was Polish, and the name Strawinski, relating to the area of the Strawa river, is common in Poland. Stravinsky spent childhood summers at the town of Ustulig, now on the border between the Ukraine and Poland, but for centuries well within Polish territory, which before partition at the end of the eighteenth century covered today's Belarus, Ukraine, Lithuania and parts of Russia. Some of the melodies in the *Rite* resemble tunes from the region around Ustulig, which are better classified as Ukrainian or Polish than Russian. Elsewhere in the *Rite*, for instance in the famous opening bassoon melody, Stravinsky draws on Lithuanian folk tunes that he found in an anthology of 1900 by the Polish priest Anton Juszkiewicz. These decisions are significant: Poland was of course Catholic, not Orthodox – a deep cultural difference – and had been the dominant power in Eastern Europe for centuries. Poland was portrayed as Russia's enemy in many nineteenth-century nationalist operas.[58]

In contrast to Stravinsky, Béla Bartók (1881–1945) never tried to cover up his folk sources; as well as a composer he was an ethnomusicologist, critic and musical writer who wanted to publicize the deep distinction, as he saw it, between modern popular music traditions, especially what stood for Hungarian 'national music' composed by the gentry and performed by Roma musicians, and genuine folk music of the rural peasants. Hungarian peasant music, Bartók argued, was built on quite different, modal principles, either diatonic or pentatonic. Soon after he began investigating Hungarian folk culture with his friend Zoltán Kodály in 1905, he started to use the modes as the basis for the structures of his own compositions. Modal pitch collections can undermine the harmonic functions of the dominant chord that is so vital to the sense of logical direction in tonal music, as well as the 'leading notes' whose semitone melodic steps create the impression of yearning and striving in the chromatic harmony of nineteenth-century composers. But Bartók pushed further, using chordal formations derived from the modes such as seventh chords and chords built from perfect fourths, and repeating them for their sonority rather than their function in a logical progression. The results are sometimes static and 'non-developmental' in parallel with Stravinsky, and may be atonal or produce alternative means of pitch centricity through repetition and rhetorical emphasis. Bartók was also attracted to 'symmetrical' pitch structures that are identical when reversed around a single pitch 'axis'. In this way he could generate chromatic structures, including the octatonic collection, out of modal folk materials in a similar way to Stravinsky. These techniques can be found first and most obviously in folksong harmonizations such as the *Fourteen Bagatelles* for piano Op. 6 (1908) and the *Eight Hungarian Folk Songs* for solo voice and piano Op. 47 (1905, 1917), but also in more ambitious and famous works such as *Duke Bluebeard's Castle* (1911–17),

---

[58] Luke B. Howard, 'Pan-Slavic Parallels in the Music of Stravinsky and Szymanowski', *Context* 13 (1997), pp. 15–19.

*Music for Strings, Percussion and Celesta* (1936), *Concerto for Orchestra* (1943) and the six String Quartets.[59]

But is Bartók's music 'national music' according to our definition? In 1906 Bartók and Kodály appealed to the people of Hungary to support a complete, scholarly collection of authentic folksongs, and his sustained efforts in fieldwork might make the question seem settled. Later, however, while Kodály concentrated on Hungarian folklore, Bartók's interests, both ethnographic and compositional, became more catholic. Bartók collected folk materials in many parts of the Austro-Hungarian empire in its last years, including Hungary and what are now Slovakia and Romania. He later travelled to Turkey and North Africa. He was equally interested in all of these ethnic sources, as an ethnographer but also as a composer. From 1908 much of his music is based on a 'fusion' of ethnic idioms.[60] Bartók proposed his own ethnically hybrid music as a replacement for the 'bad' hybrid Hungarian national music of the nineteenth century (urban gentry and gypsy).[61] In the *Dance Suite* (1923) he went further and combined even Arab dances with the other sources, all linked together by a ritornello in Hungarian style.[62]

Bartók's approach leaps back and forth between the untouched peasants on the one hand and the compositional problems of the modernist art-music composer on the other, omitting the urban middle classes and the Hungarian gentry. In an essay of 1921 entitled 'The relation of folk song to the development of the art music of our time' he maintained that

> artistic perfection can only be achieved by one of the two extremes: on the
> one hand by peasant folk in the mass, completely devoid of the culture of
> the town-dweller, on the other by creative power of an individual genius.
> The creative power of anyone who has the misfortune to be born between
> these two extremes leads only to barren, pointless and misshapen works.[63]

He was in search of 'authenticity', both ethnographic and artistic, and this meant that the particular ethnic identity of the peasants was not of critical importance. Although Stravinsky and Kodály, he says,

> gave themselves up to the folk music of a particular country ... I wish
> especially to emphasize that this exclusiveness is not important. The
> personality of the composer must be strong enough to synthesize the

[59] Elliott Antokoletz, *The Music of Béla Bartók: A Study of Tonality and Progression in Twentieth-Century Music* (Berkeley and London: University of California Press, 1984), pp. 26–50.

[60] Benjamin Suchoff, 'Fusion of National Styles: Piano Literature, 1908–11', in Malcolm Gillies (ed.), *The Bartók Companion* (London: Faber, 1993), pp. 124–45.

[61] Brown, 'Bartók, the Gypsies and Hybridity in Music', pp. 122–3.

[62] Schneider, *Bartók, Hungary, and the Renewal of Tradition*, pp. 4–5, 216.

[63] Béla Bartók, *Essays*, ed. Benjamin Suchoff (London: Faber, 1976), p. 322; cited in Cooper, 'Béla Bartók and the Question of Race Purity in Music', pp. 21–2.

results of his reactions to most widely divergent types of folk music. He
will, of course, probably react only to a folk music in harmony with his
personality. It would be stupid to force a selection for exterior reasons such
as a wrongly conceived patriotism.[64]

At the same time Bartók the modernist artist was adopting a 'primitivist' idiom,
many of his works being aimed at an elite international audience, not a popular
Hungarian one. Despite his anti-Romantic rhetoric, then, Bartók's appropriation
of folk music ultimately reveals a Romantic agenda more than a nationalist one
in his alienation from urban society and his search for expressive authenticity.
Bartók's best candidates for national music are his earliest major works: the
Lisztian symphonic poem *Kossuth* (1903), on a hero of the Hungarian Revolution
of 1848, and the *Rhapsody* (1905) and *Scherzo burlesque* (1904), both for piano
and orchestra, which draw on influences from Liszt and Brahms and deploy
nineteenth-century Hungarian signifiers, including *verbunkos*, *csárdás* and
popular art songs. All these were written before Bartók began his ethnographic
researches, and represented, as he came to see it, his lack of a coherent style. In
general the music of his colleague Kodály is more straightforward Hungarian
national music. His great choral/orchestral work *Psalmus Hungaricus* (1923), for
instance, although quoting no Hungarian folk music, uses pentatonic collections
and the Lydian mode, along with references to historical styles from the medieval,
Renaissance and Baroque periods as well as modern harmony to express
Hungary's present and past suffering. It has always been heard as a national work
by Hungarians.

Leoš Janáček (1854–1928) presents a comparable case insofar as he drew on
folk sources for their rhythmic possibilities and modality in order to fashion
a new musical language. Again, though, Janáček's contributions to 'national
music' come from relatively early in his career and do not include most of his
best-known compositions. Like Bartók, Janáček was closely involved in folklore
research, working with the philologist and folklorist František Bartoš (1837–
1906) at the Czech Gymnasium in Brno from 1886. They edited two volumes of
Moravian folk music (1980, 1899–1901), the second comprising 2057 songs and
dances. Janáček drew on his own research for his *Valašské tance* (*Valachian
Dances*; 1889–91), the Suite for Orchestra (1891), the ballet *Rákoš Rákoczy* (1891)
and the one-act opera *Počátek románu* (*The Beginning of a Romance*; 1894). The
two stage works consist largely of orchestrated folk dances. But the famous *Její
pastorkyňa* (*Her Stepdaughter*, 1904; known outside the Czech lands as *Jenůfa*),
an adaptation of a play by Gabriela Preissová, appears not to contain any original
folk material, despite a few folk-like set pieces. In this opera Janáček instead
adapted the characteristic rhythms and inflections of Moravian folk music and
speech, combining it with a gruesome realist scenario and modern compositional
idioms. He then took forward a compositional style based on the speech patterns
of Moravian Czech, which he applied in later operas that had no Czech themes,

---

[64] Bartók, *Essays*, p. 326.

including adaptations from the Russian authors Ostrovsky (*Kát'a Kabanová*; 1921) and Dostoyevsky (*Z mrtvého domu*; *From the House of the Dead*; 1928) with Russian characters and settings. Janáček's political stance was consistently anti-German, and he welcomed the new Czechoslovakia, but he also had strong subnational loyalties to Moravia, and, like Dvořák, pan-Slavic sympathies that make him an unlikely Czech nationalist. *Taras Bulba* (1918), subtitled 'Rhapsody for Orchestra' and dedicated to the Czech army, appears at first glance to be national music, yet the subject is a Russian Cossack warrior from a novel by Gogol. The *Glagolitic Mass* (1927) sets the Catholic text in Old Church Slavonic, not Czech. Moravian folk music has much in common with Bartók's Hungarian and Slovakian sources, so Janáček's brand of musical folklore is rather different from those of his Bohemian predecessors, Smetana and Dvořák. *Jenůfa* is set on the Moravian/Slovakian border, and would have seemed almost as exotic and distant to Prague audiences as to those in Germany. Indeed Preissová's original play was regarded as unsuitable when it was produced at the Prague National Theatre, and Janáček's opera did not reach Prague until 1915, when it was performed with cuts and revised orchestration. His late-career international success occurred only when his operas were taken up by German and Austrian theatres in German translation. As with Bartók, Janáček's interest in folk music was in the end a means of freeing himself as an artist from the perceived fetters of tradition.

Karol Szymanowski (1882–1937) turned to national music in the 1920s when he was in his forties. He had long held that Polish music of the late nineteenth century failed to live up to the standards set by Chopin, but had seen the problem as provincial stagnation and addressed it by engaging with wider European musical developments. At the same time, Szymanowski felt that post-Chopin Polish national dances, along with folklore-based music from other countries, merely inserted exotic elements into standard forms. This music reminded him of 'European wild birds imprisoned in an academic cage of elaborate design and forced to forget their songs of fields and forests'. Stravinsky's Russian works of the 1910s changed his perspective. The first result was *Słopiewnie* (1921), setting poems by Julian Tuwim written in an experimental, Slavonic-style semi-nonsense language with assonance, alliteration and internal rhyme. Stravinsky's *Pribaoutki* is the obvious precursor for both text and music.[65]

In 1922 Szymanowski settled in Zakopane, a tourist town at the foot of the Tatra mountains on the southern border of Poland where artists and folklorists had developed a special community devoted to the preservation of Tatra culture. Here he studied Tatra folk music, which is more similar to the music of the Slavic highlander groups spread across the borders of Poland and (by then) northern and eastern Czechoslovakia than lowland Polish folk music. The twenty mazurkas composed in 1924–25 were intended as worthy successors to Chopin's

[65] Jim Samson, *The Music of Szymanowski* (London: White Plains and New York: Kahn & Averill, 1980), pp. 156–62.

mazurkas on the grounds that they imitated neither him nor his nineteenth-century imitators. The special modes and melodic gestures of Tatra folk music are combined with traditional mazurka rhythms in another ethnic hybrid. At the same time these mazurkas are modernist in idiom, with prominent bitonality, irregular phrase lengths and the dissonant interval of the minor second. The ballet *Harnasie*, written between 1923 and 1931, takes this approach further. The influence of Stravinsky's Russian music is apparent, and *Les noces* is a model for the scenario, which centres on a Goral peasant wedding.[66] These pieces could be regarded as a grand Polish synthesis, although there are pan-Slavic overtones as well.[67]

Spanish folk music and a modernist aesthetic came briefly into alignment in Manuel de Falla's (1876–1946) *El sombrero de tres picos* (*The Three-Cornered Hat*, 1919) written for Diaghilev's Ballets Russes, which by the late 1910s were touring Spain. Picasso designed the sets, costumes and curtain in Cubist style, while Massine's choreography was equally untraditional. Falla's well-known finale is a 'Jota', part of the vocabulary of Spanish dance music for Spanish and non-Spanish composers alike for much of the nineteenth century. But the stage action it accompanies is ironic: grotesque characters and peasants throw around an effigy of a magistrate in imitation of a painting of midsummer misbehaviour by Goya, *El pelele*. This ironic treatment of folklore divided opinion in Spain: conservative critics hated it, finding the music and imagery disrespectful to national culture.[68] Falla's later piano piece *Fantasía bética* has roots in his gypsy- and flamenco-influenced 'andalucismo' style, with swirling figuration, Phrygian mode, grace notes of sevenths and ninths, hemiola rhythms, and suggestions of flamenco singing, but these are now absorbed into a modernist idiom: aggressive, percussive and dissonant.[69] In the 1920s Falla developed a neoclassical modernism that drew on Spanish history, literature, art songs, and medieval and Renaissance heritage, but purged of the musical vocabulary of 'andalucismo': a national modernism without folk music.

To an extent, the coexistence of modernism and national music was more straightforward in America than Europe, as the experience of cross-fertilization was familiar in the post-colonial societies of the New World. Aaron Copland, who devised the most influential American national style, made this point in one of his Norton Lectures at Harvard of 1951–52, entitled 'The Musical Imagination of the Americas'. At the same time, Copland asserted a Pan-American solidarity between composers from north and south who were engaged in similar syntheses of immigrant and indigenous cultures, standing against the European legacy of art music and concert culture. No less than in Europe, then, there was a pronounced

[66] Ibid., pp. 166–80.

[67] Howard, 'Pan-Slavic Parallels in the Music of Stravinsky and Szymanowski'.

[68] Carol A. Hess, *Sacred Passions: The Life and Music of Manuel de Falla* (Oxford: Oxford University Press, 2005), pp. 114–20.

[69] Ibid., pp. 122–3.

supranational dimension to the absorption of ethnic musics in art music in the twentieth century.[70]

Copland's own style was shaped by European modernist influences, from Stravinsky to Webern, but he maintained a lifelong interest in vernacular sources and the expression of American identity. It first appears in his jazz- and blues-influenced modernist works of the 1920s such as *Music for the Theater* (1925) and the *Piano Concerto* (1926), complex and acerbic pieces that did not go down well with mainstream concert audiences. Copland later undertook a deliberate simplification of his idiom that he termed an 'imposed simplicity', an attempt to engage with 'the people' as understood by the leftist Popular Front at the time, while still drawing on the technical resources of musical modernism. The culmination of this stylistic change was the three famous ballets scores – *Billy the Kid* (1938), *Rodeo* (1942) and *Appalachian Spring* (1944) – that use vernacular melodies of Anglo-Celtic settlers: cowboy songs in the first two ballets and the Shaker hymn 'Simple Gifts' in the third. However, Copland's first step in this newly simplified vernacular style, *El Salón México* (1937), underlines the Pan-American significance of the move. It is a brilliant, single-movement orchestral fantasy inspired by a dance hall in Mexico City, combining rural and urban Mexican melodies and rhythms, although subjecting them to modernist distortion and fragmentation. Later Copland wrote a two-piano piece *Danzón Cubano* (1942) based on music he heard in a dance hall on a visit to Havana. He made three government-sponsored tours of Latin and South America between 1941 and 1963 as a musical ambassador, giving concerts, making radio appearances and meeting musicians, along with many visits of his own to Mexico. At the Boston Symphony Orchestra's Tanglewood summer school he taught many younger Latin American composers.[71]

From 1928 Copland maintained an important friendship with the Mexican composer Carlos Chávez (1899–1978), whom he regarded as an exemplar of modern national music and one of the few American musicians to be free from European dominance. The two had very similar goals, aesthetically and stylistically, and Chávez conducted the premiere of *El Salón México*. Chávez was familiar from an early age with Mexican Indian culture, and his public image was shaped by the Mexican Revolution of 1921, which brought an official nationalist cultural programme through state patronage of the arts. His early Aztec ballets *El fuego nuevo* (composed in 1921) and *Los cuatro soles* (1925) presented the country's pre-colonial heritage. Chávez studied the musical instruments of the ethnic culture and the accounts of early Spanish historians and attempted to capture its spirit in *Xochipilli* (1940), 'An Imagined Aztec Music' for four wind

---

[70] Martin Brody, 'Founding Sons: Copland, Sessions and Berger on Genealogy and Hybridity', in *Aaron Copland and his World*, ed. Carol J. Oja and Judith Tick (Princeton and Oxford: Princeton University Press, 2005), pp. 21–6.

[71] Elizabeth Bergman Crist, *Music for the Common Man: Aaron Copland during the Depression and War* (New York: Oxford University Press, 2005), ch. 2.

instruments and six percussion players. Chávez's reactions to European musical life were negative, but from 1923 he began a long association with the United States, meeting the experimental musicians Henry Cowell and Edgard Varèse as well as Copland and joining the International Composers' Guild and the Pan American Association of Composers. Chávez represents another eclectic mix of neoclassicist modernism, avant-gardism and nationalism. Thus the leading American composers of the 1920s and 1930s who took an interest in ethnic sources and national music were at the same time engaged with modernism and Pan-Americanism.[72]

# Conclusion

The compositional use of ethnic vernacular sources in art music was motivated by two interrelated forces: nationalism and Romanticism. In the late eighteenth century an aesthetic of mock-folksong composition grew up around a Rousseauian type of early Romanticism that valued simplicity and emotional directness. Another type of Romanticism encouraged boldly individual treatments of vernacular sources, an approach pioneered by Beethoven and later taken up by Chopin, Liszt, Smetana, Grieg and the *kuchka* composers. They treated the modality and characteristic rhythms as starting points for original compositional strategies. In the 1820s the agenda of cultural nationalism entered opera and instrumental music, with Weber, Chopin and Glinka the leading figures to use literal or stylized vernacular idioms. The simple and direct folk style remained available to later nineteenth-century composers such as Brahms, but the post-Beethoven emphasis on originality outweighed it in larger-scale compositions. The project of vernacular mobilization was best served by spectacular rhapsodies and grandiose, aspirational symphonies, whereas the nationalizing effects of piano dance collections spread more slowly, at first through musicians' circles. In the early twentieth century, nationalism receded once again as the prime motivation for folk-music assimilation in art music, as an intensified form of Romantic thinking, took hold in the first modernist generation. Now the transnational dimension, earlier restricted to the exchange of musical forms and genres, spread to the ethnic sources, literary programmes and theatrical scenarios. The strongest candidate for modernist national music is that of Stravinsky in the 1910s. On the basis of our (admittedly selective) sample, it seems clear that in Europe, the histories of national music and 'folk'-influenced art music run parallel, intersecting for a period of about a century, before separating once again.

---

[72] Robert Parker, 'Chávez (y Ramírez), Carlos (Antonio de Padua)', in Sadie (ed.), *New Grove*, vol. 5, pp. 544–8; Alejandro L. Madrid, *Sounds of the Modern Nation: Music, Culture, and Ideas in Post-Revolutionary Mexico* (Philadelphia: Temple University Press, 2008).

# 3

# Music of the Homeland

THE idea of a national homeland has deep roots, but only with the advent of nationalism has it become commonplace and taken-for-granted. On the one hand, attachment to 'home', as opposed to 'abroad', can be found in many cultures. The object of such attachment may be the homestead, village, district, region or province. On the other hand, only rarely can we find a sense of belonging to what we would call a nation or national state in pre-modern epochs. Exceptions include the ancient Egyptians on the banks of the Nile, early Christian Armenia caught between Rome and Sassanian Persia, and the kingdom of Judah, hemmed in by Assyria and Egypt, and later under the Maccabees by Seleucid Syria and Ptolemaic Egypt. But it was not until the early modern period that, in both Europe and Asia, a sense of homeland was identified with something like national kingdoms from England and France to Safavid Iran and Tokugawa Japan. For example, in medieval Italy, divided as it was into so many city-states and duchies, there was no political sense of 'Italia', as there had been in the Rome of Horace and Virgil, only an Italian cultural identity embraced by Dante, Petrarch and the humanists, despite the later lone call by Machiavelli for Italians to unite against the invading French. It was not, again, until the late eighteenth century that the ideal of a national homeland began to gain favour, in Italy and in Europe generally, and still later outside, as the ideology of nationalism took hold.[1]

## The cult of nature

In what did this ideal consist? Here we need to distinguish 'natural' features, including factors of geography, ecology and economics; historical contexts, largely ethno-history and geopolitics; and social and cultural contents, notably folklore, and popular customs, myths and symbols. For the nationalists, the ideal of the homeland includes:

1  The delimitation of territory as a collective possession of a part of nature by a people or ethnic community, and hence an ethnoscape.

2  A sense of beautiful or sublime landscapes and poetic spaces pertaining to this territory.

---

[1] See Steven Grosby, 'Religion and Nationality in Antiquity: The Worship of Yahweh and Ancient Israel', *European Journal of Sociology* 32/2 (1991), pp. 229–65; Toftgaard, 'Letters and Arms'.

3 A sense of belonging to this territory and attachment to these ethnoscapes on the part of a designated population who are normally resident there.

4 A belief in the deep historicity of this homeland through a process of the historization of landscape, by which collective history shapes the ethnoscapes.

5 A sense of the homeland as both 'ancestral' and 'natural', through a process of naturalization of history, where the history of a people is shaped by its ethnoscape.

Hence, the nationalists' homeland is always delimited, historical and natural. At the same time, it is populated by autochthons, by an authentic ethnic 'us' who originate in and are expressions of the land: in short, 'the land and its people'. It was the early Romantics – poets, artists and philosophers – who gave the homeland ideal a theoretical basis. They argued that the homeland was a necessary element of the concept of the nation, for every nation needs a homeland, preferably its 'own', or at least needs to have had one, just as every homeland needs, or at least needed to be populated by its 'own' people, along with a (preferably deep) ethnic past and a collective destiny forged through struggle and sacrifice.

As far as the homeland was concerned, the key figure in this ideological transformation was Jean-Jacques Rousseau. His call for a return to nature and his evocation of an authentic life of rural simplicity and freedom, in contrast to the sophistication and corruption of urban and court life, struck a deep chord among the European educated classes and inspired a wide variety of artistic responses. Building on earlier topographical, pastoral and picturesque traditions, we find the Romantic poets in England, as well as artists like Turner and Constable, exemplifying this spirit of rural simplicity and freedom with its novel approach to nature. An important aspect of this approach was a new valuation of landscape in and for itself, and the concomitant rise of landscape painting in its own right, presaged as it often was by a new kind of 'nature' poetry, such as that of Thomson and Gray. In Germany, too, the Romantic poets, artists and philosophers like Schelling turned a sharper light on the mysteries of nature, endowing its landscapes with an almost mystic quality, particularly in the paintings of Caspar David Friedrich. Inevitably, such increased attention to 'nature' led to a growing self-identification with the artist's own natural environment, such as we find in Constable's many vistas of his native Suffolk.[2]

While this did not automatically induce a love of country, let alone any kind of political nationalism, it provided a strong incentive for the cultivation of a homeland ideal. In many ways, the new cult of nature can be seen as a precondition of the homeland ideal, as it directed attention to the beauty

---

[2] Anthony D. Smith, *The Nation Made Real: Art and National Identity in Western Europe, 1600–1815* (Oxford: Oxford University Press, 2013), ch. 4.

and sublimity of nature as well as its changing moods, but equally to the life of the countryside, its patterns of settlement and labour, and its distinctive mores and customs. This growth of interest in territory and nature and the novel appreciation of 'poetic landscapes' marked a critical new stage in the development of national attachments. More generally, we can understand this phenomenon as part of the wider quest for authenticity which was to gain such a following in nineteenth-century Europe, a quest realized in both time, as 'our ethno-history', and space, as 'our territory and landscapes', populated by 'our own' rural folk, which for the nationalists constituted the primary expressions on the ground of a distinctive national spirit.

## Language differentiation

While the 'return to nature' was a vital precondition, two other factors worked simultaneously to historicize and delimit territory and landscapes, thereby turning them into national 'homelands'. The first was linguistic differentiation, which both enabled communication within a community and set it off against those outside who were ignorant of the language, a phenomenon that goes back to the ancient Greek sense of 'Hellene' and 'barbaros' (someone of 'unintelligible' speech). The Bible, too, remarks on peoples of strange language (Psalm 114), as did the Romans for whom distant tribes speaking unintelligible languages were termed 'nationes' (the term only much later being transferred to 'one's own people'). Words and phrases of particular languages may act as 'border guards', to use John Armstrong's term, thereby creating bounded language communities, even without the benefit of state-policed frontiers. At the same time, language boundaries are often permeable, with considerable overlap in border zones. This permeability was something over which many early modern German intellectuals agonized, given the political fragmentation of the German-speaking lands, and the fact that Habsburg Austria possessed a long-established dynastic state with a quite separate jurisdiction from the other German states. Perhaps for this reason, there developed in Germany a new understanding of the role of language, first enunciated by Herder. He argued that we think in language, which is the distinguishing mark of the human species. Language is not just a means of communication, but also has an expressive function both for individuals and for groups; indeed, language is the sign and means of the intimate relationship between the individual and the group. For Herder, we can become expressive individuals only within a shared culture, whose distinctive 'spirit' (*Geist*) we inevitably share and which acts as a repository of our collective memories and shared history. Hence, it is through literature, philology and the cultivation of a national literary canon that language exercises its binding power, as the brothers Grimm were among the first to demonstrate. To this end, cultural nationalisms, especially those of the Romantics in Germany and Eastern Europe, stimulated the creation of vernacular literatures and competing literary canons, which became so influential for the other arts. The national homeland became, therefore, as much a sanctuary of linguistic culture and a source of cultural identity as of any poetic landscapes and delimited territories.[3]

## The state at war

The second factor tending to the creation of national homelands after the 'return to nature' was the growing power and intrusiveness of the bureaucratic state. The model in this respect was the dynastic, and later the revolutionary, state in France. Its origins can be traced back to at least the thirteenth century, but its drive for centralization reached a climax first under Louis XIV and later under the Jacobins, the Directory and Napoleon. It was the state, in alliance with the Gallican Church, which sought to unify a linguistically and historically diverse population, making the language and culture of Paris and the Île de France the cultural standard for the regions of France, whether by example or by force. During the Revolution and the ensuing wars, Danton among others encouraged the idea of France's 'natural frontiers', an important stage in the diffusion of a sense of a national homeland based on the territorial jurisdiction of the French state. We find similar models in England (and later Britain) and Spain, despite the latter's deep regional and linguistic cleavages, and later in Denmark and Sweden. In all these cases, the idea of a sacred homeland, propagated by the state and ultimately modelled on the original 'holy land' of ancient Israel, took hold and provided the basis for the homeland ideal.[4]

But perhaps more compelling than state intervention was the effect of the many wars in which European states so frequently found themselves involved. Not only was war a determinant of state frontiers, as in the case of the Dutch Republic after its long wars with Habsburg Spain, it was also, as Charles Tilly showed, a creator (or destroyer) of states. Equally important was its role as mobilizer of men and creator of territorial attachments to the land for which so many had sacrificed their lives. George Mosse reminds us of the power of the myth of the war experience and its camaraderie, but even more important were the facts of mass loss and the myths of blood sacrifice on behalf of country, especially in defeat, myths that go back to the epitaphs for ancient Greeks who fought and died in the wars against Persia, and to the record of the sacrifices of the Maccabees in the Jewish uprising against the Seleucids. In the modern epoch,

[3] John Alexander Armstrong, *Nations before Nationalism* (Chapel Hill: University of North Carolina Press, 1982), ch. 1; Isaiah Berlin, *Vico and Herder: Two Studies in the History of Ideas* (London: Hogarth Press, 1976), pp. 145–52; Barnard, 'Herder's Suggestive Insights'; Leerssen, *National Thought in Europe*, 93–102.

[4] Armstrong, *Nations before Nationalism*, ch. 8; Geoffrey Hously, 'Holy Land or Holy Lands? Palestine and the Catholic West in the Late Middle Ages and the Renaissance', in *The Holy Land, Holy Lands and Christian History*, ed. Robert Swanson (Ecclesiastical History Society, Woodbridge: Boydell Press, 2002), pp. 234–49.

all these effects of war became visible on a mass scale in the Revolutionary and Napoleonic Wars.[5]

Still, wars are often divisive and their effects may be temporary, whereas the homeland ideal generally persists through long periods of peace. As for the state, it may provide a shell for the nation, but it attracts no affection and directs no attachments to the homeland and its landscapes, except in moments of grave crisis. Moreover, what of the many cases of deep attachments to homelands among *ethnies* without states and unmobilized by wars, like the Czechs, Norwegians and Finns, or those divided into several states like the Germans and Italians? Among all these, the homeland ideal flourished after 1800 and fed on myths of legendary or historic golden ages in ancestral territories and pristine landscapes. Besides, war and the state are not intrinsic to the modern epoch: we find them in the ancient as well as in medieval epochs. The homeland ideal, by contrast, though it had its pre-modern precursors, really only flourished widely in the early modern and modern epochs. It was only from the Renaissance onwards that scientific curiosity about nature began to become acceptable, and only somewhat later that a new attitude to the beauty and variety of landscapes became prevalent. And it was not until the eighteenth century that the cult of authenticity directed attention to the distinctiveness and individuality of national territories and ethnoscapes in terms, not only of their geographies and topographies, but also their ethnic resources and symbolisms, so paving the way for the emergence of the ideal of the national homeland.

## Music and landscape

What part does classical music play in reflecting or encouraging these changes in attitudes and perceptions? Can we trace a parallel trajectory in what we might term 'nature music', that is, music that evokes and depicts the natural environment, at least from the late seventeenth century? And, if so, at what point in time can we discern distinctive soundscapes of the nation and its homeland, soundscapes that help to fix the dominant images of the nation in the minds and hearts of both co-nationals and outsiders?

By the eighteenth century, a long European tradition had established a vocabulary of musical 'pastoral' based around the imitation of shepherds' piping. The typical signs are melodies for woodwind instruments, especially flutes, often in pairs and doubled in thirds; a lilting 6/8 or 12/8 metre; regular rhythms and conjunct melodies; and slow-moving harmony or even static pedal points

---

[5] Charles Tilly, *The Formation of National States in Western Europe* (Princeton: Princeton University Press, 1975); Michael Mann, *The Sources of Social Power*, vol. 2, *The Rise of Classes and Nation-States* (Cambridge: Cambridge University Press, 1993), pp. 4ff.; George L. Mosse, *Fallen Soldiers: Reshaping the Memory of the World Wars* (New York: Oxford University Press, 1990), esp. chs 2 and 3.

with 'drone' harmony like a bagpipe. Famous examples can be found in Corelli's 'Christmas Concerto' Op. 6 No. 8, the 'Pifa' from Handel's *Messiah* and the nativity scene from J. S. Bach's *Christmas Oratorio*. In French opera there was a tradition of storm scenes accompanied by spectacular orchestral sound effects.[6] In the second half of the century, 'characteristic' symphonies portrayed pastoral idylls and storms.[7] Direct depiction of nature is to be found in Vivaldi's *The Four Seasons* (1712), four violin concertos describing aspects of the countryside and rural life in, respectively, spring, summer, autumn and winter. But in these pieces, as in Handel's 'Pastoral Symphony' from *The Messiah* (1742), or in Haydn's much later *The Seasons* (1801), there is no sense of place, of a specific, let alone delimited, terrain and particular landscapes. They are vivid but generalized descriptions, even though it is an Italian spring and summer that Vivaldi portrays. Even Beethoven's more direct portrayal of 'emotions experienced in encountering nature' in his 'Pastoral' Symphony (1808), the composer warns us, is not to be taken as a description of specific landscapes and particular peasant scenes, although, in fact, we know it was the woods around Vienna in which the composer loved to walk that formed the material basis of his imaginative encounters. At the same time, this is very far from imagining a national homeland; any other woods and brooks would have served as well.

In German Romanticism, music and landscape became intricately connected through the poetry of nature and memory, especially in the great song cycles of Beethoven (*An die ferne Geliebte*, 1816), Schubert (*Die schöne Müllerin*, 1823; *Winterreise*, 1827) and Schumann (the Eichendorff cycle *Liederkreis*, 1840). Here the emphasis is on landscape as a subjective experience, mediating dream and reality, humanity and nature. Nature becomes quasi-animate to the imaginative mind, seeming to speak to the poet. The experience is unique, but not necessarily the landscape itself, which is described in a conventional vocabulary of forests, meadows, fields and babbling brooks.[8] In fact the sense of a national homeland and its soundscapes in music comes almost half a century behind its evocation in literature and visual art, and even longer in Britain and France, where already in the late eighteenth century insular geography in the one case, and a strong tradition of centralized monarchy in the other, had encouraged the rural imagery and political ideal respectively of the national homeland, so clearly absent in Germany and Italy. The singular exception is the Netherlands after 1579, where both in literature and in painting the imagery of a separate, embattled and later prosperous homeland flourished, although, again, not in music.

---

[6] Caroline Wood, 'Orchestra and Spectacle in the *Tragédie en musique* 1673–1715: Oracle, Sommeil and Tempête', *Proceedings of the Royal Musical Association* 108 (1981–82), pp. 40–6.

[7] Richard Will, *The Characteristic Symphony in the Age of Haydn and Beethoven* (Cambridge: Cambridge University Press, 2002).

[8] Charles Rosen, *The Romantic Generation* (Cambridge, Mass.: Harvard University Press, 1995), ch. 3.

In terms of musical technique, the localization of landscape in music went along with a new technique that Carl Dahlhaus has called 'sound-sheet' (*Klangfläche*), 'outwardly static but inwardly in constant motion'. Rapid 'surface rhythm' – perhaps representing the rustling of leaves, the babbling of a brook or even a lashing storm – takes place over static harmony and without the presentation of distinctive melodic ideas. The music stands outside normal time, minimizing any sense of harmonic progression towards a goal, the logic of motivic ideas, regular phrase structure or form as process. The fast surface may present unresolved dissonances, transcending the intervallic functions of consonance and dissonance in tonal music, as in the 'Waldweben' ('forest murmurs') in Wagner's *Siegfried*.[9] The listener is invited to value the sound-sheet's distinctive sonic quality and timbre, like a particular state of being. The possibility is opened for a wide range of such states, all of them equally static and equally outside normal musical temporality, and suggestive of a particular, rather than a generic, landscape. Against the sound-sheet, certain 'foreground' details may emerge, such as imitation birdcalls, horn calls, folksong or thematic fragments, which can give still further specificity to the musical landscape. Sibelius especially favoured this technique. More generally, sometimes composers relied on nothing more than a single note or octave in the high strings to suggest 'background' behind these foreground gestures, as in the opening bars of Balakirev's two Overtures on Russian Themes, Borodin's *In the Steppes of Central Asia* (Ex. 3.1) and Vaughan Williams's *First Norfolk Rhapsody* and *Fantasia on a Theme by Thomas Tallis*. As so often in national music, these techniques were shared by composers from different countries, even though they served the purpose of localization.

But music, like the other arts, had to contend with two problems in representing the homeland. The first, as we have seen, was overgeneralization, nature bereft of political anchorage; the second, its converse, was excessive specificity of place, or localism. As far as the first is concerned, later examples of musical landscape generalization might include, first, a generic 'Nordic' landscape music, though it could equally be read as a purely Danish (Nielsen), Norwegian (Grieg) or Finnish (Sibelius) landscape, related in the latter case to the Finnish epic, the *Kalevala*; and, second, the exotic 'Oriental' landscape music of works like Borodin's *Prince Igor* (1869–87) and Rimsky-Korsakov's *Sheherazade* (1888) and *Le coq d'or* (1906–7). Here, there is little sense of place or attachment to a specific land or even landscape. The cult of the North or the Orient is all pervasive, divorced from any particular human collectivity, recording only general soundscapes and their individual human (or magical) activities.[10]

More common, perhaps, was the problem of localism. In the visual arts, which, unlike music, can embrace only a single viewpoint and landscape, this could be a major stumbling-block for a landscape painter who wished to delineate

---

[9] Dahlhaus, *Nineteenth-Century Music*, pp. 307–8.
[10] Maes, *A History of Russian Music*, pp. 80–3.

Ex. 3.1 Borodin, *In the Steppes of Central Asia* (reduction), bars 1–27

the essence of England, France or Germany. There were several ways round the problem. One was to draw or paint a whole series of scenes of England or France, highlighting unity in diversity; that was Turner's chosen procedure, and it proved immensely popular through the resulting prints and engravings of Britain.[11] Another was to resort to symbolism, especially the depiction of monuments, ruins and the like, as in Constable's dramatic watercolour of Stonehenge (1836), or one of Friedrich's chosen historic sites, the *Abbey of Eldena* (1824–25), which for the artist stood for the 'real Germany', or as with Schinkel's *Cathedral by the River* (1815), to conjure a vision of medieval Germany and contrast it with her modern decline.[12] Perhaps the most common method of dealing with the problem of localism, though, was to accept and even exalt it. We see this particularly in Constable's vision of an Arcadian England, depicted in so many of his Suffolk landscapes. Even though the Suffolk of his day was undergoing early industrialization and attendant class conflicts, particularly around modern technology, Constable portrayed his birthplace and the river Stour through the prism of the eighteenth-century 'nature' poets – Thomson, Gray and Cowper – whom he loved, thereby attaining to a wider vision of southern England, in which

[11] See James Hamilton, *Turner's Britain* (London: Merrell, 2003), ch. 3.

[12] William Vaughan, *German Romantic Painting* (New Haven: Yale University Press, 1994), pp. 101–2, 193–9.

the local stood as one potent image of the national, and one that over the course of the nineteenth century was to achieve immense popularity in middle-class circles.[13]

Several composers adopted similar procedures. One can readily see the 'series' method in cycles of symphonic poems, pre-eminently Smetana's cycle of six pieces on Czech history entitled *Ma Vlast* (*My Homeland*; 1874–76), and Albéniz's evocation of various places in Spain in his piano collection *Iberia* (1905–8; see Chapter 2). Symbolism in nature can be found in Dvořák's fairy-tale symphonic poems like the *Golden Spinning Wheel* and *The Noonday Witch* (both 1896), and in Rimsky-Korsakov's syncretic (Christian–pagan) *Russian Easter Festival Overture* (1888), not to mention the whole Russian vogue of 'Orientalism', of which his violent and sensuous *Sheherazade* (1888), and Borodin's haunting *In the Steppes of Central Asia* (1880–81), with its languorous depiction of an 'Oriental' merchant caravan in endless open plains, are perhaps the best-known examples. Here 'place' is defined primarily by native history, mythology and ideological contrasts with a (usually negatively defined) 'Other' of both land and people.[14]

But, like the painters, some composers preferred to treat the particular area and specific place, perhaps the place in which they resided, as the representation, sometimes the very epitome, of the national homeland. For Carl Nielsen, for instance, this was the Danish island of Funen, a place remote from Zealand and the capital Copenhagen, but for him capturing the essence of Danishness.[15] This could be called a musical 'synecdoche': the part standing for the whole. In his cantata *Caractacus* (1898), Elgar portrayed a tribe of ancient Britons living, worshipping and fighting the invading Romans beneath the Malvern Hills in Worcestershire, a landscape not far from his home, and a source of inspiration for his compositions. Elgar overcame the problem of localism in two ways. The work was dedicated to Queen Victoria and ends with a rousing – and chauvinistic – choral hymn of praise to the contemporary British empire. More subtly, Elgar's musical landscapes in his cantata transfer and synthesize in sound two iconographic traditions in English art stretching back to the eighteenth century: a landscape tradition portraying the Malvern Hills and a tradition of heroic history painting that showed Caractacus before the emperor Claudius. It thus unmistakably associates national images with local ones.[16] In the

---

[13] Stephen Daniels, *Fields of Vision: Landscape Imagery and National Identity in England and the United States* (Princeton: Princeton University Press, 1993), ch. 7; Michael Rosenthal, *Constable: The Painter and his Landscape* (New Haven: Yale University Press, 1989), ch. 3.

[14] Maes, *A History of Russian Music*, p. 81.

[15] Daniel M. Grimley, 'Horn Calls and Flattened Sevenths: Nielsen and Danish Musical Style', in Murphy and White (eds), *Musical Constructions of Nationalism*, p. 135.

[16] Matthew Riley, *Edward Elgar and the Nostalgic Imagination* (Cambridge: Cambridge University Press, 2007), pp. 161–2.

terms of the visual arts, the pictorial aspect of *Caractacus* represents a 'mixed genre', combining landscape and history. Many nineteenth-century homeland landscapes, especially in instrumental music, work this way too, sometimes with a degree of deliberate vagueness and suggestiveness, just as in the popular Romantic genre of the landscape with ruin. The audience is invited to repopulate the landscape with historical, heroic figures to create the sense of historicity, ancestral and natural belonging.[17] For landscapes on the Grand Tour, tourists and audiences carried with them a stock of ideas and images; for new, local landscapes – those that were to be imagined as homelands – composers had to create their own or rely on the work of their immediate nationalist forebears.

In their different ways, these artistic methods and procedures were all directed to one overriding aim: to evoke the distinctiveness and the beauty or sublimity of particular landscapes deemed to reveal both an unspoilt nature and an historic ethnoscape, as authentically as possible, thereby combining the return to nature and the ideal of the homeland. The quest for authenticity, in particular, requiring as it did the use of a range of musical forms and instruments to capture nature's moods and the specific features of the homeland, exercised a compelling power of outside identification and inward self-identification on the part of the composer or artist.

But how was this quest for authenticity in evoking the homeland to be realized? Three processes are involved. The first is 'differentiation': the distinguishing of particular ethnic soundscapes in terms of their *differentia specifica*, in musical terms such things as their habitual rhythms, textures and instruments, or particular types of sound-sheet. The second is 'characterization': delineating the profile and character of ethnic soundscapes in terms of binary adjectives like hot and cold, peopled and desolate, land and sea, modern and ancient, everyday and exotic. The third is 'identification': an attachment and identity of self with a named ethnic soundscape in its historical context, giving rise to an expressive intimacy with 'the land and its people' which can sometimes exclude those deemed unable to so identify.

The first two processes – differentiation and characterization – can already be found in some of the partly programmatic music of Mendelssohn, whose musical landscapes at the same time remained within the bounds of contemporary tourist trails. Two visits on his walking tour of Scotland and Wales with his friend Carl Klingemann in 1829 proved musically fruitful, revealing the composer to be at the forefront of those attempting to characterize 'the land and its people' in terms of an ethnic soundscape. In both cases, 'the people' proved to be historical or legendary, thereby linking the ethnic soundscape to a putative national past. In the first case, in the overture *The Hebrides* (1830) to which Mendelssohn gave various titles, including *Fingal's Cave* and *Overture to the Lonely Islands*,

---

[17] Thomas S. Grey, 'Tableaux Vivants: Landscape, History Painting, and the Visual Imagination in Mendelssohn's Orchestral Music', *19th-Century Music* 21/1 (1997), p. 56.

it appears that Mendelssohn had already drafted in some detail the opening of the overture when he arrived at the west coast of Scotland, but before he had visited the celebrated cave on Staffa associated with Fingal, a hero in the Ossianic cycle of poems. It seems, too, according to Douglass Seaton, that Mendelssohn's reading of James Macpherson's 'translations' of 'Ossian' had already influenced his view of the Scottish ethnoscape, as it must have done for his German audiences. Mendelssohn translated two visual genres into music: the sublime Ossianic landscapes that were popular in early nineteenth-century painting, and the tourist tradition of sketching picturesque scenes in the Scottish Highlands and islands. The overture also reflects the composer's own discomfort on the choppy sea journey he undertook to visit the cave; the periodic repetition of its initial descending theme strongly suggests a seascape which, near the end, is engulfed in a storm, before subsiding into the opening motif. When he revised the work, Mendelssohn sought to include a stronger sense of the differentiated environment, 'of train oil, sea gulls and salt fish'; but the sequence of harmonies also suggests a sense of remoteness in time and space, as befits an ancient epic.[18]

Differentiation and characterization also pervade Mendelssohn's 'Scottish' Symphony (1842; Mendelssohn suppressed the title on publication). This took its inception from a visit to Holyroodhouse in Edinburgh, where the ruins of the royal chapel recalled to the composer the tale of the doomed love of Mary Queen of Scots and David Rizzio – a typical Romantic act of imaginative repopulation of a ruin – and set off the composition of the symphony. The chapel had already been the subject of Romantic paintings and dioramas.[19] A ballad-like theme that Mendelssohn claimed to have noted down on that visit begins the symphony and returns in fragmentary form in the first movement's coda, functioning as a frame around the main, sonata-form part of the movement, a structure found in many later symphonies with folksong elements (see Chapter 2). Here the introduction and coda seem to represent the modern viewer's contemplation of the ruins, while that viewer's imaginative repopulation of the landscape takes place in the dramatic and passionate fast section within the frame.[20] The second movement is a lively scherzo with 'Scotch snap' rhythms. The slow third movement contains a funeral march. The finale is even more agitated than the first movement, but a triumphant hymn-like transformation of the first movement's ballad-like opening theme, repeated three times, brings the symphony to a close. Should we characterize the symphony as a 'historical epic' in the manner of the novels of Walter Scott, or as an 'ethnic soundscape'? For Mendelssohn, the line between the two was blurred, since the Romantic Scottish history was stimulated by the royal chapel in Edinburgh. In effect, they appear to be closely related forms of ethnic

---

[18] Douglass Seaton, 'Symphony and Overture', in *The Cambridge Companion to Mendelssohn*, ed. Peter Mercer-Taylor (Cambridge: Cambridge University Press, 2004), pp. 91–111; Grey, 'Tableaux Vivants', p. 41.

[19] Grey, 'Tableaux Vivants', pp. 57–8.

[20] Ibid., pp. 56–7.

characterization sited on Scottish soil recalling the Scottish past and transmitted through a distinctive ethnic soundscape. Like contemporary history painting, especially images inspired by Scott, the 'Scottish' Symphony stands in a mixed genre, which 'imbues its imaginative sites with a sense of historical event'.[21]

A further excursion took Mendelssohn to Italy, especially Rome, where he witnessed the carnival season in early 1831. An echo of this experience can perhaps be heard in the joyous and high-spirited opening movement of his 'Italian' Symphony (1833–34, subsequently revised). The second and fourth movements draw implicitly on a stock of visual images common in genre paintings of the period such as processions of silent pilgrims and groups of shepherds and dancing peasants in the countryside around Rome. Mendelssohn called the finale a 'Saltarello', although it actually comes closer to a Neapolitan tarantella with its exceptional speed and compound metre, as well as the imitation of tambourines and tamburo drums and the flute duet. At the end, the music fades into the distance, again recalling aspects of the visual tradition. Thomas Grey associates Mendelssohn's national landscapes with new technologies and entertainments such as *tableaux vivants*, magic lantern shows, dioramas and theatrical special effects, which 'sought to animate landscape and historical scenes'.[22]

Mendelssohn's work does not yet amount to national music, but rather a pioneering 'ethnic characterization'. Identification is lacking, both by composer and by audience. Mendelssohn was writing primarily for German and English audiences, not Scottish or Italian ones, just as German artists in Rome sold their Italian landscapes to German tourists who had absorbed Goethe's *Italienische Reise*. For early nineteenth-century Germans, Scotland was romantic and exotic. Nevertheless we have here the beginnings in classical music of imaginative recreations through ethnic evocation of the land and its people, in terms of interwoven soundscapes of nature and ethno-history. Mendelssohn's approach would later be taken further in Max Bruch's *Scottish Fantasy*, as well as the ethnic evocations of Spain by Glinka, Rimsky-Korsakov, Chabrier and Ravel. The Saltarello finale of the 'Italian' Symphony initiated an exotic symphonic tradition of its own by French composers such as Saint-Saëns, Lalo and d'Indy.[23]

Self-identification with the native land is added to Mendelssohn's ingredients in Schumann's 'Rhenish' Symphony No. 3 in E flat (1850). The title was not released by Schumann on the first performance and publication of the work, but it reflects his intentions and the original titles of the five movements. Schumann said he aimed to express 'national elements' as well as 'local colour' at the premiere in Düsseldorf, a combination that makes sense because German nationalism found a focus on the river Rhine after the Rhineland crisis of 1840 when France threatened to invade. The first movement is supposed to be 'a bit of

---

[21] Ibid., p. 41.

[22] Ibid., pp. 40–55.

[23] Locke, *Musical Exoticism*, p. 73.

life on the Rhine'; the second, a Ländler, was originally entitled 'Morning on the Rhine'; and the fourth 'An accompaniment to a solemn ceremony'. According to Schumann's biographer Joseph Wilhelm von Wasielewski, the latter describes a ceremony at Cologne Cathedral, another focus for nationalist sentiments, which, after standing half-built since the Middle Ages, was being completed at the time with funding from Prussia as a national monument to rival the great cathedral at Strasbourg. Schumann responds with a unique movement full of ecclesiastical touches such as the solemn sound of trombones and *stile antico* counterpoint like a grand motet. The finale continues these associations by introducing a chorale-like theme near the end, perhaps following the model of Mendelssohn's 'Scottish' Symphony. Finally, the choice of key, E flat, inevitably recalls Beethoven's 'Eroica' Symphony, especially as the first movement is a fast, triple-metre dance. Schumann's symphonic project as a whole was an attempt to build on Beethoven's formidable legacy and continue a tradition now conceived as both universal and German.[24]

## Genres of homeland soundscape

The genre most favoured for homeland soundscapes by composers of all countries was the symphonic poem. The genre was invented by Liszt in the 1850s for the purpose of renewing musical tradition by investing instrumental music with content. Liszt occasionally used national styles in his symphonic poems, such as the gypsy music in his patriotic *Hungaria* – essentially a Hungarian Rhapsody for orchestra – but soundscapes were not his main concern. Nevertheless his style and techniques proved to be of great use to later composers of national music who adapted the vehicle of the symphonic poem to characterize and identify with particular ethnoscapes and homelands. As Keith Johns points out, in his symphonic poems Liszt developed a collection of 'topics' – conventional styles or gestures that stand for an idea such as a class of people, mood, dance or place – such as lament or funeral march; martial triumph; pastoral or lullaby; pensiveness (instrumental recitative); transcendence or immortality (chorale); awakening (horn call); idealism, beauty or love. Moreover, Liszt developed his famous process of thematic transformation, through which he could change a single motif or idea from one 'topic' to another or into something quite different, facilitating narrative effects in orchestral music. Finally, Liszt favoured programmes with plots culminating in apotheosis, which could be combined with thematic transformation. Thus in *Tasso*, the gondolier's song is transformed into a funeral march and a love song and then given a final

---

[24] A. Peter Brown, *The Symphonic Repertoire*, vol. 3, *The European Symphony from ca. 1800 to ca. 1930, Part A, Germany and the Nordic Countries* (Bloomington: Indiana University Press, 2008), p. 278.

apotheosis.[25] Later composers adapted these narrative techniques to national programmes and materials, and added such ingredients as sound-sheets; bardic harping and incantation; introduction / coda frames, setting the framed 'events' in a pre-modern or legendary time; and repetitive, non-developmental structures such as ballad-like strophes, incantation effects or feverish dance repetitions. Symphonic poems could characterize the national homeland without reliance on a text, and were thus especially useful to composers of small nations who aimed for international, as well as national, recognition. Closely related to the symphonic poem was the programmatic overture, which emerged earlier (many of Liszt's own symphonic poems originated as theatrical overtures). Balakirev's Second *Overture on Russian Themes* later became his symphonic poem *Russia*. The orchestral rhapsodies discussed in Chapter 2 are also hard to distinguish from symphonic poems. In opera, orchestral preludes or interludes were the most common location for soundscapes, such as the prelude to Wagner's *Das Rheingold*, the forest murmurs from *Siegfried* or the chiming of the bells of St Basil's Cathedral in Mussorgsky's *Boris Godunov*.

Similar adaptation applies to other genres, symphonic, instrumental and vocal. We find references to national homelands, if only indirectly, in movements of symphonies (d'Indy, Dvořák, Bruckner, Sibelius, Vaughan Williams), concertos (Sibelius's Violin Concerto, Rachmaninov's Piano Concertos Nos. 2 and 3), song cycles (Grieg's *Haugtussa*, Vaughan Williams's *On Wenlock Edge*) and piano music (Chopin's mazurkas, some of Grieg's *Lyric Pieces*, Albéniz's *Iberia*). In chamber music, soundscapes and homelands are rarer, perhaps reflecting the genre's traditionally abstract status and contrapuntal textures, and its relation to aristocratic forms of taste and judgement. Dvořák's chamber music is ethnically coloured, but the colour is often as much Slavic or even American as Czech.

Musical compositions expressing an attachment to the homeland overlap both with the folk-influenced repertoires discussed in Chapter 2 and with the ethno-historical and mythological inspiration which we consider in more detail in Chapter 4. It could hardly be otherwise, since we are at all times dealing with the wide category of 'the land and its people', their songs and dances, their myths and legends, their forests, valleys and mountains. This is ultimately because a homeland is a site of attachment, because it is perceived to be an ethno-historical territory in which the inhabitants tell each other and their children the tales of themselves and their forebears as these unfolded within an ethnoscape with its unique profile and character. Hence the importance of relics and monuments of the land embodying the shared memories, myths and symbols of the inhabitants of the homeland and their cultures, the people whose home it is or is felt to be.[26]

[25] Keith T. Johns, *The Symphonic Poems of Franz Liszt*, ed. Michael Saffle (Stuyvesant: Pendragon Press, 1996), pp. 17–45.

[26] See Anthony D. Smith, *Myths and Memories of the Nation* (Oxford: Oxford University Press, 1999), ch. 5; all the essays in David J. Hooson (ed.), *Geography and National Identity* (Oxford: Blackwell, 1994).

## Music of eight homelands

In the rest of this chapter, the focus is on the poetic spaces of the national homeland, including those of its natural features that are felt to possess ethnic and ethno-historical significance, and on the process of the naturalization of history, as opposed to the historicization of nature, which we address in Chapter 4. The creation of a homeland soundscape can be traced through a host of European and American examples. But the various national musicians differed in their starting points and resources for achieving their musical goals. Our first example, the German soundscape, was defined in the first half of the nineteenth century when Germany possessed a strong musical tradition and a growing sense of nationhood but no political state. The next three examples portray the homelands of small, poorly resourced and previously submerged peoples, relatively lacking in art-music traditions of their own, yet whose members were beginning to assert their cultures and territories as expressions of their 'old-new' communities. These peoples are the Czechs, the Norwegians and the Finns. In these cases the homeland soundscape is mainly the work of a single influential composer, whose music has resonated with his peers to become the defining sonic counterpart of the visual and literary imagining of the national homeland. Three further examples are based in large, historic national states – Russia, England and Spain – with concomitant resources and musical traditions, the members of whose dominant *ethnies* were undergoing a musical renewal, or renaissance, of their own. The final example, the United States, stands in the tradition of European musical soundscapes, but takes on a new guise on account of the very lack of history – at least, settlers' history – in the landscape, which gives it a different cultural significance. In each case, the ultimate effect of the creation of a homeland soundscape is to imprint on the hearts and minds of many members of the community a uniquely memorable national sound-world.

## The German homeland

In music the German homeland was associated above all with two landscapes: the German forest and the river Rhine. Their national significance was tinged with pantheism of a peculiarly German kind, stemming from an intellectual reaction of the late eighteenth and early nineteenth centuries against the determinism and materialism that some German intellectuals found in Enlightenment rationalism, which, they thought, irrevocably divided humanity and nature. Herder and Goethe, for instance, were interested in organicism, holism and natural processes; the Idealist philosopher Friedrich Schelling argued that consciousness is generated from nature and still resides in it. He and his sometime neighbour and fellow student in Jena Friedrich von Hardenberg ('Novalis') imagined humanity and nature united in a single mighty organism, and their friend Friedrich Schlegel found in nature the hieroglyphic language of God. The German Romantics proposed the unity of physical and psychological phenomena and cultivated an interest in dreams, unconscious processes and artistic genius. From this perspective, landscape could provide a glimpse of a more-than-human wholeness, and this spiritual understanding, combined with religious visual motifs, can be found in the paintings of Caspar David Friedrich. In the prose and poetry of Novalis and the lyrics of Eichendorff, nature is reanimated; thus the German Romantics became 'topographers of the sacred'.[27] In music a vocabulary for nature emerged: distant horn calls, birdcalls, rustling leaves and babbling brooks, along with static effects suggesting rapt attention and solemn stillness, like a poem by Eichendorff realized in sound.

Forests were common themes in the folk poetry collected by Arnim and Brentano and the folk tales collected by the Grimm brothers, and these could easily be viewed retrospectively through a modern, pantheist lens. Their national significance dates back to the Renaissance reception of the Roman historian Tacitus, who described the destruction of Roman legions by the ancient warrior Arminius (Hermann) in a forest ambush in AD 9. Tacitus held up the primitive but tough, virtuous and republican Germans as a lesson for decadent, imperial Rome. Friedrich Gottlieb Klopstock wrote an epic trilogy of plays on Arminius in the 1760s and Heinrich von Kleist a play, *Die Hermannschlacht*, in 1808, which carried obvious anti-Napoleonic symbolism. Long-standing proposals for a monument to Arminius were finally realized in 1875 when the *Hermannsdenkmal* was completed in the Teutoburg forest near Detmold, which was also the occasion for celebration of the new Kaiser Wilhelm I. In Friedrich's painting *'Chasseur' in the Forest* (1814), a symbol of the war of liberation, a single French soldier wanders into a dark, menacing pine forest, observed ominously by a raven from a tree stump.[28]

Weber's *Der Freischütz* gave the German forest its first great musical realization, even though it is set in Bohemia. The characters are all woodlanders and the action takes place in the forest and in a forester's house. In the Act II aria of the heroine Agathe, she draws the curtain from her room to reveal the starlit landscape outside, and she praises nature between her prayers. The final scene is set in a beautiful landscape, but the Wolf's Glen scene in Act II takes place in 'a fearsome gorge, for the most part overgrown with dark wood, surrounded by high mountains'.[29] Here, amidst hair-raising shrieks and startling harmonies and orchestral effects, seven magic bullets are forged by the demon Samiel, which the hero Max is to use at a shooting contest. Even the famous soft passage for four horns in the overture, which launched the association of the instrument with nature mysticism for German composers (the very name for the instrument in

---

[27] Kate E. Rigby, *Topographies of the Sacred: The Poetics of Place in European Romanticism* (Charlottesville: University of Virginia Press, 2004), p. 53.

[28] Simon Schama, *Landscape and Memory* (London: Fontana, 1996), ch. 2; Leerssen, *National Thought in Europe*, pp. 36–51.

[29] Meyer, *Carl Maria von Weber*, p. 94.

German is *Waldhorn*), is soon interrupted by darker scoring, ominous tremolandi and a turn to the minor mode. For Wagner the libretto of *Der Freischütz* seemed to have been written by the Bohemian forest itself, and he claimed that its German character lay in its feeling for nature. The composer Hans Pfitzner thought the forest was the real leading character of the opera.[30]

In Wagner's *Der Ring des Nibelungen*, the German forest is the setting for the actions of the Wälsungs, the race of human beings created by Wotan to recover Alberich's ring freely from the dragon Fafner and set the world to rights. The first act of *Die Walküre* is set in a forest hut, but is represented in the Prelude by a tumultuous sound-sheet that represents Siegmund's desperate flight from his enemies. The forest enters the drama later in the act when the door of the hut swings open to reveal a moonlit spring night, and Siegmund breaks into an ecstatic love song ('Winterstürme wichen dem Wonnemond') with rustling orchestral accompaniment. The Prelude to *Siegfried* brings out the brooding menace of the forest, which in Act II will hold the dragon and two scheming Nibelungs. Act II has an idyllic sound-sheet for the forest murmurs; bird calls, which Siegfried manages to understand once he has tasted the dragon's blood; Siegfried's horn; and the lurking dragon in his cave. Nevertheless, the forest of Act II remains in the end picturesque and harmless, as befits the overall comic register of the drama. Siegfried is protected by Wotan and cannot fail.

The fairy-tale forest is found again in Engelbert Humperdinck's children's opera *Hänsel und Gretel* (1893), and also in his lesser-known *Königskinder* (1910). The forest in *Hänsel und Gretel* of course hides a witch, but Humperdinck strongly brings out its benevolent aspect in Act II, when the children are lulled to sleep by the kindly Sandman and angels come to guard their sleep to the accompaniment of a Wagnerian orchestral interlude. The prelude to the opera opens with the music for the children's prayer played by four horns, evoking both the overture to *Der Freischütz* and the tradition of the four-part Lutheran chorale. Another post-Wagnerian contribution is Anton Bruckner's Symphony No. 4 in E flat ('Romantic'), in which, according to a programme that the composer told his friend Theodor Helm, the first movement portrays a medieval town at dawn, when from the towers the morning call is sounded by a horn; the gates open and knights go forth on horseback; they encounter the magic of the forest, the rustle of the leaves and birdsong. The call of the blue tit is heard in the second theme group.[31] The scherzo is based on stylized hunting horn calls, with all the brass, especially horns, to the fore. Sound-sheets are prominent, especially at the opening of the work as a backdrop to the distant call on a single horn, and at the end of the finale, where a vast, harmonically static coda builds from *pp* to a momentous climax. The symphony is 'romantic' in the sense of Wagner's

---

[30] Ibid., p. 105.

[31] Edward Laufer, 'Continuity in the Fourth Symphony (First Movement)', in *Perspectives on Anton Bruckner*, ed. Crawford Howie, Paul Hawkshaw and Timothy Jackson (Aldershot: Ashgate, 2001), p. 143.

*Lohengrin* or *Tannhäuser*, that is, a celebration of the German Middle Ages. This historic homeland is for Bruckner naturally connected with the forest, and the symphony is in the key most associated with horns, E flat.

The Prelude to Wagner's *Das Rheingold* is another vast sound-sheet on an E flat major triad, starting from a low E flat and building ever-greater waves of sound over four minutes. A revolutionary musical concept, the Prelude nevertheless stands firmly in the German tradition of landscape as transcendent whole. It portrays the Rhine as the amoral origin of the world and life, standing prior to any of the creatures in Wagner's universe, including the gods. The Rhinemaidens are the personification of nature at an early stage of becoming conscious, a concept that would have appealed to Schelling and his Romantic successors and to German nationalists who understood the nation as natural and organic, and for whom the Rhine was the emblem of its totality. At the end of *Götterdämmerung*, and thus of the whole *Ring* cycle, the Rhine overspills its banks and the Rhinemaidens reclaim the ring that Alberich forged from the gold he stole from them. Despite the active, implicitly national, Wälsung heroes, however, no institutions flourish in the historicized homeland landscape of the *Ring*. The court of the Gibichungs holds nothing but treachery and vanity, and value can be located only in the transcendent power of love. In this respect the Ring differs from Wagner's *Die Meistersinger von Nürnberg*, in which individual and society, the free artist and the mastersingers' guild, are finally reintegrated through the mediation of Hans Sachs, and Nuremberg is reaffirmed as the ancient geographical and cultural centre of the homeland (see Chapter 1).

The *Ring* was conceived in the late 1840s at a time when the Rhine was at the centre of German cultural politics because of the Rhineland crisis of 1840. For centuries the river had marked a boundary between Germanic and Latin civilizations, going back to the era of Varus and Arminius. Schumann's 'Rhenish' Symphony (yet another E flat major German landscape piece) stands at the end of the decade, and during it a host of patriotic and Romantic poems were published celebrating the Rhine, while more than 400 songs for voice and piano or guitar or for male chorus were published. The early phase of Rhine Romanticism belongs to the Heidelberg Romantics, including Arnim, Brentano, Eichendorff and Hölderlin, who were simultaneously discovering German folklore. Later Friedrich Schlegel saw the Rhine as alive with consciousness and at the same time a symbol of the German nation.[32] The texts of the *Rheinlieder* cover the usual German Romantic themes of longing, wandering, the mystery of the cosmos, and organic developmental process, and feature the Lorelei – the more common version of Wagner's Rhinemaidens – and the Nibelungs. Some texts mix national and pantheistic sentiments. Most of the musical settings are in a direct and simple folksong style (*Volkston*; see Chapter 2) and are of limited aesthetic value, although there are nine by Schumann and a few by Mendelssohn and Liszt.[33]

---

[32] Porter, *The Rhine as Musical Metaphor*, pp. 35–6.

[33] Ibid., ch. 3.

'Auf einer Burg' from Schumann's Eichendorff *Liederkreis* Op. 39 describes an old knight who has been sleeping for hundreds of years in a ruined castle above the Rhine, possibly representing Frederick Barbarossa, who, according to legend, will one day awaken and save Germany. Below him on the river a wedding passes by, but the bride – possibly modern Germany – is weeping. 'Im Rhein' (Heine), from *Dichterliebe* Op. 48 No. 6, has the 'holy city' of Cologne mirrored in the 'holy stream' of the Rhine, with landscape and German culture brought into a sacred unity. Both of Schumann's settings adopt a subdued, deliberately archaic style in a minor key, just like the Cologne Cathedral movement of the 'Rhenish' Symphony, the first with constant dotted rhythms in the style of a Baroque 'French overture'. Neither attempts to 'paint' the landscape in tones, but instead reflects the antiquity of German culture in the landscape.

## The Czech homeland

It is, above all, to one composer, Bedřich Smetana, and to one work in particular, his six tone poems comprising *Má Vlast* (*My Homeland*) (1874–79), that the soundscape of a Czech national homeland is indebted. Others contributed, notably Zdeněk Fibich, Antonín Dvořák and Josef Suk. But Smetana's contribution amounts to a programmatic nationalism, which created a sound world and a set of associations that defined the parameters and contents of the Czech homeland ideal. This is largely because in his works, and especially in *Má Vlast*, history, mythology, folklore and nature are so closely intertwined that episodes in Czech history are naturalized in an ethnoscape replete with relics and monuments of the events of its history, real or imagined. By the late twentieth century a performance of *Má Vlast* always opened the annual international Prague Spring Festival on 12 May, the date of Smetana's death, and this event has become a national ritual.

The Czechs were among the earliest to promote a distinctive cultural nationalism, predominantly in the sphere of language and literature, both of which had been repressed after the defeat of the Czech nobles by the Catholic Habsburgs in 1618, at the start of the Thirty Years War. However, following the rise of a merchant and artisan class in the later eighteenth century, and the reforms of the Emperor Joseph II promoting German as the language of central administration, but tolerating minority languages at the provincial level, a language movement emerged among the small Czech intelligentsia, led by the Catholic priest Josef Dobrovsky and the teacher Josef Jungmann. Both published their researches on Czech grammar, language and literature in the early nineteenth century, the former embracing all the Slav languages, the latter focusing specifically on Czech language and literature, a distinction that was to find an echo in Czech music nearly fifty years later in the figures of Dvořák and Smetana. The most celebrated Czech nationalist intellectual was František Palacky, archivist, journal editor, co-founder of the Czech Museum from 1822 and historian, his foundational history of Bohemia appearing in several volumes from

1836 onwards. Palacky also entered the political fray, affirming in a famous letter of 1848 in reply to an invitation to join the Frankfurt Assembly that the Czechs were not Germans; they were linked to the German empire only through dynastic ties.[34]

The emergence of a Czech national music surfaced on the back of the movement to build a Czech National Theatre to rival the German-language theatres in Prague. The building itself was at last opened in 1881, only to burn down a few weeks later, requiring a second long campaign of public subscription (it reopened in 1883). The leading musical figure in this movement was Smetana, who, after training in Prague in the 1840s and moving to Sweden following the repression of Czech nationalism in Prague in the 1850s, returned in 1864, to find the state of Czech music and theatre, in his view, deplorable. Opera, in particular, was purveyed almost wholly in poor translations of Italian and French originals, and could not meet European artistic standards or cultivate a true national taste. As for the current teaching in the music conservatories, it was outmoded because it failed to incorporate the most 'progressive' innovations of composers like Berlioz, Liszt and Wagner, all of whom Smetana admired. And this highlights the peculiar position of Smetana as founder of the Czech 'national school of music', as he came to be seen: on the one hand, the zealous promoter of Czech nationalism in music, on the other hand, the devotee of progressive European music, which was seen as mainly the New German School of Liszt and Wagner. Little wonder that Smetana, who dismissed the idea that folk music could form the basis of a national style in opera, which he felt would result in a 'pot-pourri, and not a unified artistic whole', was attacked by Czech nationalist critics for being too Wagnerian.[35]

Yet it was Smetana who laid down the matrix of a Czech school of national music, with his heroic and comic operas and his symphonic poems. Though he may not have been the first to think about a specifically Czech style, Smetana, according to Michael Beckerman, was the first to articulate it in a strongly nationalist manner, such that subsequent Czech composers had to deal with his musical presence and his mode of reconciling Czech elements with the progressive European musical forms which he prized. For Leoš Janáček, writing in 1924, the 'Czech quality in Smetana's music consisted in three things: "Smetana's love of nature, his concerns for the events of everyday life, and his ability to evoke the deep recesses of Czech history".'[36] In *Má Vlast* Smetana combines all three in a monumental synthesis with a ceremonial and optimistic character, which took the measure of the Czech homeland in both time and space.

---

[34] Hugh Seton-Watson, *Nations and States: An Enquiry into the Origins of Nations and the Politics of Nationalism* (London: Methuen, 1977), pp. 149–5.

[35] Taruskin, *The Oxford History of Western Music*, vol. 3, pp. 448–51; Curtis, *Music Makes the Nation*, pp. 59–61.

[36] Michael Beckerman, 'In Search of Czechness in Music', *19th-Century Music* 10/1 (1986), p. 66.

Smetana systematically engenders the historicity of the Czech landscape, and makes the homeland seem ancestral and natural.

The first four symphonic poems were composed mainly in 1874–75. The first, *Vyšehrad*, evokes the great rock in Prague overlooking the river Vltava, on which stood the proud castle of the ancient Bohemian Přemyslid kings, and whose ruins, according to Smetana's explanatory preface to his score, the ancient bard Lumír now conjures through his harp (heard in the opening bars). The second symphonic poem, *Vltava*, depicts the ever-growing main stream of the river from its springs, through a forest, past dancing peasants, water nymphs in the moonlight, the St John's rapids, into the capital and past the castle rock (the *Vyšehrad* theme returning in triumph at this point). *Šarka* describes a horrific story from the mythological 'maiden's war', a time near the start of the Czech nation when women had declared war on men. *Z Českých luhů a hájů* (*From Bohemia's Woods and Fields*), the fourth symphonic poem, has no precise programme, but represents the sublimity and beauty of the Czech landscape, along with birdcalls, folksong and dance, all tied together with motivic unity and ending with tremendous momentum. Three years later Smetana added two further pieces to the cycle, which stand out as a closely related pair: *Tábor*, the garrison town of the fifteenth-century Hussite warriors, and *Blaník*, the mountain in central Bohemia, beneath which, according to legend, the Hussite warriors retreated after their final defeat, and where they now slumber, awaiting the nation's hour of direst need. Both are based on the Hussite chorale 'Ktož jsú boží bojovníci' ('Ye Who Are Warriors of God'); both gradually generate the complete chorale from fragments presented at the outset; they are in the same key; and the beginning of *Blaník* is so similar to the end of *Tábor* that it sounds like a continuation of the same piece. All this links history with legend, and past with projected future glory, as the cycle ends in triumph with another return of the *Vyšehrad* theme, indicating the future restoration of national sovereignty.[37]

Smetana's differentiation of the Czech homeland is effected with stylistic features such as polkas, melodies doubled in thirds, the repetition of motifs transposed down by the interval of a third, and the modality of the Hussite chorale. Its characterization appears at first quite diverse, covering the brutality of murders and battles, the idyllic countryside, the majesty of Prague and the glory of future Czech triumph, along with a certain dark, even primitive quality that emerges at times in the last four pieces. However, Smetana's Czech homeland is in fact rather specific. It is entirely Bohemian – Moravia is absent – and he focuses on the central region of Bohemia around Prague. Three further subjects for symphonic poems that Smetana discarded confirm this orientation: Říp, the hill north of Prague to which, according to legend, Čech, founder of the nation, led his people and from which, Moses-like, he surveyed the new land; Lipany, the site of a massacre during the Hussite wars to the east of Prague; and Bíla Hora (White Mountain), where the fateful battle in 1620 took place just west of

---

[37] Brian Large, *Smetana* (London: Duckworth, 1970), ch. 11.

Prague that established Habsburg dominance.[38] Since the central theme of *Má Vlast* is sovereignty, the images of the homeland are clustered around the capital. Identification could not be stronger on the part of the composer, the original title of the four-movement cycle (*Vlast*) later accruing the emotive first-person possessive. The cycle is dedicated to the city of Prague, and the historical and legendary events take place at named locations that could be visited by the Czech audience; indeed at the premiere and at any Prague performance some are only a few metres away. The use of the Hussite chorale brings sacred associations to the celebration of the nation, the performance taking on something of the character of a communion service. (The real quarrels about the communion that sparked the Hussite wars are not at issue in *Má Vlast*; the Hussites are portrayed as patriots, not religious sectarians.)

Smetana's approach to programme music is flexible. The depiction of landscape is found throughout *Vltava* and *Z Českých luhů a hájů* and in places in *Vyšehrad* and *Blaník*; narrative techniques are used intensively in *Šarka* but more lightly in most of the other pieces; the grim and monotonous *Tábor* is a psychological portrait of the strong-willed warriors rather than the depiction of a battle; while *Blaník* is a prophetic fantasy of national resurrection and an exhortation to action. *Má Vlast* was conceived just as Smetana was finishing his festival opera *Libuše* (discussed in Chapter 4), which anticipates some of its music, including the *Vyšehrad* theme and the Hussite chorale, has a similarly ceremonial character and, in anticipation of *Blaník*, ends with Queen Libuše's prophetic vision of the future history of the Czech people and the founding of Prague. Both works echo the forward-looking dimension of Wagner's *Die Meistersinger* (see Chapter 1), one of Smetana's models for the opera, in which the audience's present and future are alluded to by an historical character on stage. Smetana avoids stories about individual heroes in a way that typifies the mixed genre of history and landscape in the tradition of Mendelssohn. In *Vyšehrad*, the bard's harp romantically evokes the glorious history of the ruined castle above the river Vltava, asking the audience to repopulate it in their imaginations, just as in Mendelssohn's 'Scottish' Symphony.

Modern international audiences and institutions tend to bracket Dvořák and Janáček with Smetana as composers of Czech national music, but, as Chapter 6 will show, Czech musicians of the late nineteenth and early twentieth centuries by no means perceived them as a single national school. One thing Smetana, Dvořák and Janáček clearly shared, though, was an interest in the landscape of forests. They can be found in *From Bohemia's Woods and Fields* from *Má Vlast*; in the nocturnal forest scene in Smetana's opera *The Kiss*; in Dvořák's operas with Czech rural settings *King and Charcoal Burner* and *The Cunning Peasant* as well as *Rusalka* with its motifs from folk mythology; in Janáček's early opera *Šarka* (composed 1887–88), where it brings forth the best music of the score; and in the pantheistic responses to nature in *The Cunning Little Vixen* (1924) and the

---

[38] John Clapham, *Smetana* (London: Dent, 1972), pp. 75–6.

*Glagolitic Mass*. Dvořák's Overture *V přírodě* (*In Nature's Realm*; 1891) begins with typical 'nature sounds' against a sound-sheet that is followed by a theme closely related to the Czech hymn *Vesele zpívejme, Boha Otce chvalme* ('Let us Sing Joyfully, Praise God the Father'). This reverence for nature can also be found in Josef Suk (*Pohádka léta*; *A Summer's Tale*, 1907–9) and in Vítězslav Novak (*V Tatrách*; *In the Tatras*, 1902) and *Pan* (1910–12).[39]

## Scandinavian homelands

As in the Czech lands, language and historical literature became the dominant concern of a growing cultural nationalism in Norway during the later nineteenth century, which developed alongside its political nationalism. Externally, this cultural nationalism was directed against the Danish cultural influence that remained even after four centuries of Danish political rule was terminated by the forced union with Sweden from 1814, as well as by political opposition to Swedish rule after 1814. Internally, there were two aspects of this cultural nationalism: a burgeoning interest in Norwegian ancient history, and the growing linguistic division between the supporters of 'riksmal' and 'Landsmal'.

The interest in historical literature, evinced already in the late eighteenth century, centred on the translations into Danish by Gerhard Schøning of Snorri Sturlason's Norse sagas. But it was the poet Henrik Wergeland who, in a speech at Eidsvoll in 1834 entitled 'In Memory of the Ancestors', asserted the need to reinstate the medieval royal Norwegian state in modern Norwegian consciousness as the other half-ring, and solder it properly together with a new Norwegian national state. The historians who followed Wergeland, notably P. A. Munch, claimed that the Edda and sagas, and their language, were wholly Norwegian, a position that was immensely influential, not least for writers like Ibsen and Bjørnson; and they contrasted the golden age of the independent medieval Norwegian nation with the immediate past of the 'Danish era', which Ibsen dubbed 'The four hundred year night'. As for the language division, this stemmed from the persistence of a pervasive Danish cultural influence among the Norwegian urban elite, as the literary language ('riksmal') was effectively Danish, the Old Norse literary language having been abandoned. In this situation, the philologist Ivar Aasen produced a Norwegian grammar in 1848, and two years later a Norwegian dictionary, based on the spoken language of the countryside in western Norway, to form an alternative Norwegian language, or 'landsmal', free of Danish influence; and in 1885 the latter was accepted by the Storting (Parliament) as co-equal to the Dano-Norwegian 'riksmal', despite encountering considerable resistance to this day.[40]

---

[39] Tyrrell, *Czech Opera*, pp. 153–5.

[40] Øystein Sørensen, 'The Development of a Norwegian National Identity during the Nineteenth Century', in *Nordic Paths to National Identity in the Nineteenth*

Musicians, too, were inspired by the ancient sagas and folklore. As in Bohemia, there was a similar Norwegian movement for a national theatre, national opera and nationalized folk music, such as was first evident in Waldemar Thrane's comic opera *Fjeldeventyret* (*The Mountain Tale*; 1825). The movement also drew support from Johan Svendsen and the cosmopolitan patriot and violinist Ole Bull. In 1849 Norwegian artists interested in the promotion of national culture organized a set of *tableaux vivants* in the Christiania Theatre that helped to establish the Norwegian landscape as an image of national identity. The pictures were accompanied by music and poetic descriptions of nature and folklore. This event gave the impetus for the composer Halfdan Kjerulf to investigate Norwegian folk music.

However, it fell to Edvard Grieg, who hailed from Bergen in western Norway, to raise his people's international cultural profile from the 1860s onwards through a musical depiction of the western Norwegian landscape, but set within a frame of assimilation to European musical standards. As he put it, 'To paint Norwegian nature, Norwegian folk life, Norwegian history and Norwegian folk poetry in sounds stands for me as the area where I believe I can achieve something.'[41] This would be a musical translation of his practice of drawing the landscape himself, including that of his birthplace (Fig. 3.1). Nevertheless, Grieg was no partisan of 'landsmal', composing songs in both Norwegian languages. He was trained in Leipzig and always had an eye for international, as well as national, approval, especially from Germany. Most of his works are small-scale: he composed only one operatic fragment, *Olav Trygvason* (first performed in 1889), one early symphony and a piano concerto. In his songs and piano pieces Grieg translated into music the emerging Norwegian homeland imagery of folk weddings, mountain pastures, mountain spells and 'troll magic'. The western Norwegian landscape is portrayed in the 'dark wood' of the nostalgic song 'Den Bergtekne' ('The Mountain Thrall'), the mysterious forest in the song 'Langs ei Å' ('Along a Stream'), the evocations of rural life in some of his *Lyric Pieces* and the mountain trolls of Norwegian mythology in the incidental music to Ibsen's famous dramatic poem *Peer Gynt* (1875). The song cycle *Haugtussa* (*The Mountain Maid*, 1898), the text of which was written in 'landsmal' by the novelist and poet Arne Garborg, takes up from Schubert's *Die schöne Müllerin*, but with an emphasis on the supernatural and the heroine's hallucinatory visions of the spirits of the landscape. Grieg extends the style of the Romantic *Lied* with pervasive chromaticism and the flexible use of static effects and natural sounds in an exploration of the psychology of landscape.[42]

Grieg's interest in static sonorities encourages a contemplative attitude from the listener, directing attention to the quality of the sound, not its function

*Century*, ed. Øystein Sørensen (Oslo: Research Council of Norway, 1994), pp. 15–35; Seton-Watson, *Nations and States*, pp. 761–74; Grimley, *Grieg*, p. 34.

[41] Quoted in Curtis, *Music Makes the Nation*, p. 74.

[42] Ibid., pp. 76–7; Grimley, *Grieg*, pp. 26–7, 79–86, 117–146.

Fig. 3.1 View of landscape from Edvard Grieg's (1843–1907) birthplace, from composer's sketchbook

in harmonic/melodic logic, and may have initiated a wider Scandinavian trend, especially evident in Sibelius and Nielsen, which suggests the idea of a supranational, 'Nordic' approach to landscape that is inflected in individual cases. In Grieg's case, the sonorities are often combined with a technically advanced, yearning harmonic chromaticism that places the focus on the Romantic subject in the landscape. Moreover, in pieces like *Gangar* Op. 54 No. 2 and *Klokkeklang* ('bell-ringing') Op. 54 No. 6 Grieg makes great play of folksy open-fifth sonorities and pedal points, extending them from exotic colour into an independent parameter that can structure a complete composition.[43] These pieces arguably stand in a tradition of Nordic diatonicism that stretches back to Franz Berwald (1796–1868) and forward to many of Sibelius's later works, including the Symphonies No. 6 (1923) and 7 (1924). The second movement, 'Andante pastorale', of Nielsen's Symphony No. 3 (*Sinfonia espansiva*, 1912), is, ironically, a version of the static, 'German' E flat major triad (Wagner's *Das Rheingold*; Bruckner's Symphony No. 4); it begins with the usual horn calls and repetitive processes, but soon turns to a sweetly melodic, 'open-air' diatonicism with parts for wordless

---

[43] W. Dean Sutcliffe, 'Grieg's Fifth: The Linguistic Battleground of "Klokkeklang"', *Musical Quarterly* 80/1 (1996), pp. 161–81; Grimley, *Grieg*, pp. 8, 57.

soprano and baritone.[44] One could of course find prominent diatonicism in other national traditions too, including those of England (Elgar, Vaughan Williams) and the United States (Copland), so this effect is not even exclusively Scandinavian.

If anything, the Finns were even more a 'submerged' *ethnie* than the Norwegians had been during the long years of Danish rule. But, in this case, it was Sweden that had incorporated the territory east of the Gulf of Bothnia, and, after it converted to Lutheranism in the sixteenth century, the latter became also the dominant religion of the eastern territory of Finland. Here the majority were Finnish-speaking, but there remained an important minority of Swedes who occupied most of the elite positions. Through the Treaty of Hamina in 1809, approved by Napoleon, the Tsarist empire acquired the eastern territory of Finland, which became a Grand Duchy within Russia until 1917. For all that, the Swedish ruling minority was left in place. Even though many of its members were prepared to assimilate to the majority Finnish language, the Swedish elite became the target of a growing Finnish-language movement among the majority's intelligentsia. The main base of this movement was in the old university of Turku, where Professor Henrik Porthan, a contemporary of Herder, presented his *Dissertatio de poesi fennica* in 1778, which argued the need to present folk poems without alteration, though they might perhaps be restored to 'a more complete and suitable form', as Macpherson had supposedly done with his Ossianic fragments.[45]

When the Treaty of Hamina severed the Finnish intelligentsia's close relations with Sweden, its members found they had no choice but to identify with the unlettered majority of Finland's population and gradually shed their Swedish language for Finnish. To this end, they founded the Finnish Literary Society in Helsinki in 1831, when the university moved there, and, *inter alia*, aimed to achieve a Swedish or German translation of the *Kalevala* and a Finnish translation of Runeberg's poem *The Elk Hunters*, which portrayed the Finns as a harmonious, cheerful people even amidst their poverty. But, to be worthy of European status, the intelligentsia felt it had to supply the Finns with a commensurate history and literature for a people that lacked both. In 1835, the doctor Elias Lönnrot published the first version of his collection of Karelian oral poetry, under the title of *Kalevala*, or *Land of Heroes* (the second and fuller edition was published in 1849). This soon became Finland's national epic, although its editor, Lönnrot, was responsible not just for compiling its contents from original Karelian singers and their ballads, but for arranging and even supplementing them.

---

[44] Grimley, *Grieg*, pp. 135–6.

[45] Lauri Honko, 'The *Kalevala* Process', *Books from Finland* 19/1 (1985), p. 17; see also Seton-Watson, *Nations and States*, pp. 71–3; Matti Klinge, '"Let us be Finns": The Birth of Finland's National Culture', in *The Roots of Nationalism: Studies in Northern Europe*, ed. Rosalind Mitchison (Edinburgh: John Donald Publishers, 1980), pp. 67–75.

Towards the end of the century, when attempted Russification created a strong Finnish political nationalism by way of reaction, a new current of cultural nationalism pervaded literature, the pictorial arts and music. This can be seen in the movement known as Karelianism, the vogue for intellectuals, including folklorists, artists, linguists, ethnographers, photographers and musicians, to visit, and in some cases to reside in, the easternmost province of Finland, which was at the time deemed to be the oldest part of the country and witness to its original Iron Age culture. Karelia had been a disputed territory on the Swedish–Russian border and a battlefield for centuries, but it was in the remote areas of this region that Lönnrot collected his materials for the *Kalevala*. Sibelius's popular *Karelia Suite* originated as the music for a gala evening in 1893 in support of a lottery, a common fund-raising technique of Finnish nationalists. It was held by the Student Association of the ancient and architecturally important Karelian city of Viipuri to enable the founding of an adult education college. An exhibition of Finnish handicrafts, furniture and costumes was organized, and the evening was based around *tableaux vivants* showing Karelian landscapes, especially Viipuri Castle, demonstrating the sweep of Finnish history from ancient to modern times. Sibelius's music accompanied these images. As Glenda Dawn Goss points out, his sources were a mixture: 'Bachlike chorales, Russian-Karelian *runo* song, Swedish folk ballads, Lutheran hymns, Germanic fugues, and Grieglike techniques' (the latter meaning 'open-space music').[46] The famous symphonic poem *Finlandia* was also composed for a *tableaux-vivants* lottery evening, this one in Helsinki in 1899, its images beginning with the mythic ancient history of the *Kalevala* and reaching forward to the age of the steam engine.[47]

Sibelius had already explored the *Kalevala* in his monumental, five-movement *Kullervo Symphony* (1892) for large orchestra, mezzo-soprano and baritone soloists and male chorus. The premiere was presented as a national occasion and is recalled by Finnish historians as the birth of a genuine national music.[48] In terms of musical style, *Kullervo* marks the beginning of Sibelius's distinctive idiom, which he would push much further later. James Hepokoski lists

> modally-tinged ('Finnish') melodies and reiterative accompaniment patterns; obsessive ostinato repetition, long pedal points and epic recyclings of brief melodic ideas; bluntly cut rhythms; broodingly thick, dark and often minor-mode textures, redolent of stern historical burdens and inescapable tragedy; unmediated juxtapositions of utterly contrasting timbre fields; and a favouring of texturally stratified, prolonged sound-images at the expense of traditional, linear-contrapuntal development.[49]

[46] Goss, *Sibelius*, p. 156.

[47] Ibid., chs 8 and 15.

[48] Matti Huttunen, 'The National Composer and the Idea of Finnishness: Sibelius and the Formation of Finnish Musical Style', in Grimley (ed.), *The Cambridge Companion to Sibelius*, p. 15; Goss, *Sibelius*, ch. 7.

[49] James A. Hepokoski, 'Sibelius, Jean', in Sadie (ed.), *New Grove*, vol. 23, pp. 322–3.

In *Kullervo* this style creates a primitivist, doom-laden atmosphere for an oedipal tale of incest and suicide by the eponymous hero. Sibelius later developed and refined it in a series of symphonic poems and symphonies, the former often based on episodes from the *Kalevala*. In some of the symphonic poems and in the Fourth Symphony he did not avoid gloomy endings, against the general drift of symphonic music over the nineteenth century, thereby underlining his characterization of the Finnish landscape as desolate and unforgiving. Sibelius is nevertheless clearly the heir to nineteenth-century traditions of national music and homeland landscapes, and also to the universal symphonic tradition, with which, like the *kuchka* composers, he stayed in touch, perhaps even relying on it to facilitate his expression of the nation in music. Indeed he is especially close to Russian compositional traditions and in (partial) reaction against German ones; this musical situation differs from the political one in which Russia was the alleged oppressor of Finland.[50]

Two techniques in particular were central to Sibelius's evocation of the Finnish homeland in his symphonic music. First, Sibelius explored an extraordinary range of static effects with high surface activity, in particular his own peculiar sound-sheets typified by scurrying strings, chattering woodwind and ominous brass crescendos. *A Saga* (*En Saga*, 1893), for instance, starts with a kaleidoscopic array of static effects, including wide arpeggio figuration on all string instruments at *pp* for the sound-sheets, like a pervasive rustle. Against one of the sound-sheets a solemn theme emerges in the bass instruments with a bardic tone (Ex. 3.2), which returns mournfully on a solo clarinet at the very end of the work. Within this 'introduction/coda frame' the 'action' of the symphonic poem takes place, ending in violence and tragedy. The work thus stands in the traditions of Mendelssohn's 'Scottish' Symphony, the *kuchka* and d'Indy, but is distinctively differentiated and characterized in a way that, aided by programmatic associations and consistency of application in Sibelius's œuvre, audiences have come to hear as specifically 'Finnish'. *The Wood Nymph* (*Skogsrået*, 1895) consists almost entirely of four long sections of stasis; the second, representing the forest in which a hero will be fatefully seduced by the wood nymph, is a five-and-a-half-minute rustling sound-sheet based on a single harmony. The final section is a colossal, harmonically static crescendo, perhaps modelled on the coda to the finale of Bruckner's 'Romantic' Symphony.

A second technique is the use of circular, repetitive structures on several levels. At the local level Sibelius imitates the improvisatory runic recitation of *Kalevala* singers who would deliver the whole of a poem to a particular set of reciting tones. The music invites the listener to step outside linear time into an ahistorical, epic world, and eschews motivic development. This is arguably a distinctively characterized version of the *kuchka* technique of changing-background variation discussed in Chapter 3. Sibelius tends to use it for the second theme groups of

---

[50] Philip Ross Bullock, 'Sibelius and the Russian Traditions', in Grimley (ed.), *Sibelius and his World*, pp. 24–49.

Ex. 3.2 Sibelius, *En Saga*, bars 34–41 (reduction to timpani and strings)

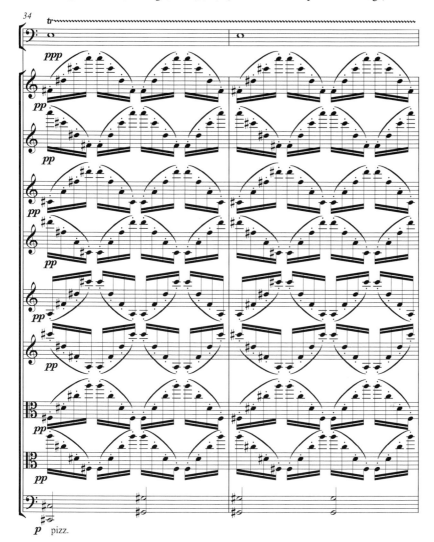

sonata structures (Symphonies No. 1, first movement, No. 2, finale, No. 3, first movement), as did Tchaikovsky before him in finales (Symphonies Nos. 2 and 4, Violin Concerto). The finale of Sibelius's Second Symphony has five iterations in its exposition and eight in its recapitulation, growing to a grandiose climax of implicitly national triumph. By contrast, the second movement of Symphony No. 3 is a subdued version. At broader structural levels, in the later symphonic works the principle takes over from sonata form: instead of the three-fold exposition/development/recapitulation, Sibelius first lays out thematic or sonic materials in a certain order before reiterating that presentation a number of times,

Ex. 3.2 *continued*

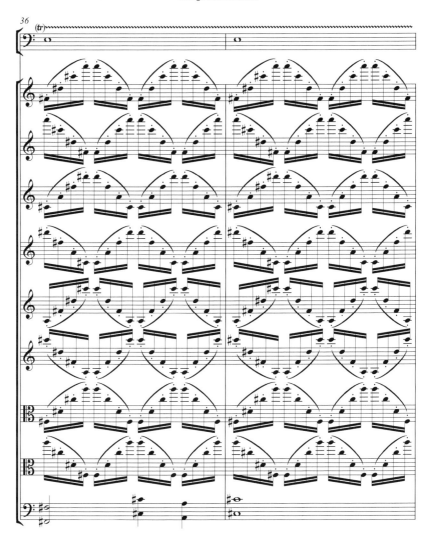

each time with various developments, omissions or additions. The three sonata functions may be blurred or diminished in each of these reiterations.[51]

James Hepokoski has argued that Sibelius links his sonic effects and

---

[51] Hepokoski, *Sibelius, Symphony No. 5*, pp. 23–6. See also James A. Hepokoski, 'The Essence of Sibelius: Creation Myths and Rotational Cycles in *Luonnotar*', in *The Sibelius Companion*, ed. Glenda Dawn Goss (Westport, Conn. and London, 1996), pp. 121–46; and 'Modalities of National Identity: Sibelius Builds a First Symphony', in *The Oxford Handbook of the New Cultural History of Music*, ed. Jane F. Fulcher (New York: Oxford University Press, 2011), pp. 452–83.

Ex. 3.2 *continued*

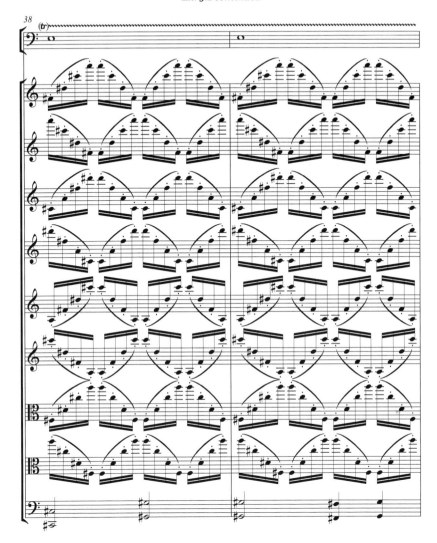

sound-sheets with his circular processes, so that the emergence of 'music as sound' becomes the goal of the 'labour' of multiple reiteration. *Night Ride and Sunrise* (1909) is a work of two contrasted sections, both repetitive and structurally circular, exploring contrasted sonic 'states of being'. The second is a static – not to say ecstatic – apprehension of nature. The transitional, chorale-like thematic material stands in a tradition of chorale-transformations from the end of the finales of Mendelssohn's 'Scottish' Symphony and Schumann's 'Rhenish'. Sibelius's Symphony No. 5 (1915, 1916, 1919) is a complex application of similar principles, again reaching ecstatic states in the finale after cumulative repetitions through the earlier movements. In this way, Sibelius's later landscapes become

Ex. 3.2 *continued*

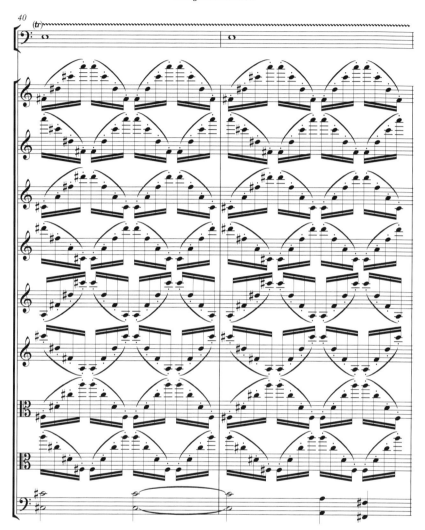

an integral part of symphonic form, not just a background for other action or a framing device. The goal of the whole structure is the subjective perception of a musical object – harmonic/timbral/textural – 'in itself', and implicitly this is like the sense of being in a landscape. One might say that the very process of identification is narrated in Sibelius's symphonic work as the listener learns to become one with the sound-world.[52]

The abstraction of landscape in Sibelius's later music can be partly attributed

---

[52] Hepokoski, *Sibelius, Symphony No. 5*, pp. 26–7, ch. 5; 'Sibelius, Jean', pp. 331–4.

to the symbolist currents that reached Finnish artists from Paris in the late 1890s. Their attention turned to the subjective reactions of the viewer or listener and the exploration of the dark recesses of inner life. The narration of specific events of the *Kalevala* that is found in *Kullervo* is reduced in the four-movement *Lemminkäinen Suite* (1896), with its evocation of the black swan of Tuonela, the land of the dead. Sibelius's last work, *Tapiola* (1926), has no programme beyond the portrayal of the home of the mighty Finnish forest god Tapio. Sibelius's first two symphonies (1899, 1902) are full of heroic endeavour as well as landscape painting, and therefore still broadly match the mixed genre of landscape/history that we have found in Mendelssohn, Smetana and Elgar. The later trend to abstraction means a less explicit historicization of nature. The listener is not invited to populate the landscape with people or their culture, let alone institutions. Just as Sibelius often minimizes any sense of musical theme – an accompanied melody with a regular phrase structure – so he depopulates his homeland landscape, avoiding named heroes or concrete narrative programmes. We are left with the sense of 'being in a place', albeit a place that is richly characterized and invites close identification.

## The Russian homeland

National sentiment, which at times verged on outright nationalism, was also found in large, established states during the nineteenth century, as John Breuilly has demonstrated. Often, it became part of an official doctrine and the rationale for an imperialist 'mission' of conquest and incorporation, if not assimilation. This was the case in Tsarist Russia. The earliest stirrings of a modern Russian national identity can be found, subsequent to the reforms of Peter the Great, among westernizing aristocrats in the latter half of the eighteenth century. Along with admiration for French and German culture, there were serious movements to reform the Russian language, overseen by the Russian Academy, founded in 1783, which published a multi-volume Russian dictionary and a Russian grammar. In the subsequent linguistic dispute, the modernists, led by the historian Karamzin, who opted for the demotic language, won out over the Church Slavonic model of the traditionalists. At the same time, Tsarist Russia under Catherine the Great and subsequently Alexander I established a great-power presence in Europe, culminating in the defeat of Napoleon's invasion of Russia in 1812. Military prowess and political prestige coincided with and strengthened a Romantic cultural efflorescence in the 1820s, which included Karamzin's history of Russia and Pushkin's poetry, permeating even the dominant neoclassical style of paintings. However, the rule of the reactionary Tsar Nicholas I (1825–55) acted as a brake on westernization, and prompted the promulgation of an official doctrine of Autocracy, Orthodoxy and Nationality (*narodnost'*), proposed by Count Uvarov, the Minister for Education, in 1832. If the principles of Autocracy and Orthodoxy were long established, that of *narodnost'* was new, and in the long term it was to inspire strong national sentiments and currents, notably with the Slavophiles among a growing intelligentsia and merchant class.[53]

By the 1860s we can speak of national music in a strong sense, with the formation of the *kuchka* as a coherent group with an ideological agenda articulated by Stasov and Balakirev; an anti-academic stance; Balakirev's investigation and application of Russian folk music; and their canonization of Glinka as the founding father of Russian art music, with his *Ruslan and Lyudmila* and *Kamaryinskaya* as compositional models. From this point we can identify certain recurrent elements that articulate the Russian homeland in music, such as the use of characteristic folk-music idioms; evocations of Orthodox chant, choral music and bell ringing; literary sources from Pushkin, now canonized as a Russian master even more than Glinka, along with Lermontov and Gogol; and the vogue for portrayal of the Orient: fabulous, sensuous and exotic. These four elements are often intertwined, and as such they point to a conception of the national homeland as very much one of 'the land and its people', as opposed to the vast silent spaces of, say, Sibelius's Finland in *Tapiola*. Musorgsky's *Boris Godunov*, for instance, is based on a text by Pushkin, and contains a majestic bell-ringing episode and religious chant in the Coronation scene, along with folksong stylizations.

The use of the Orthodox religion to define the homeland begins with Glinka's *A Life for the Tsar* (see Chapter 1), and can be found also in the finale of Mussorgsky's *Pictures at an Exhibition* (1874) 'The Great Gate of Kiev' (literally 'The Bogatyr Gate'), where sounds of chant and bell ringing evoke the grandeur of an ancient Rus' homeland and its capital. Echoes of Russian Orthodox motifs can be heard in Rimsky-Korsakov's *Russian Easter Festival Overture* (1888), commingled with a prevalent mood which is more folk and pagan than Christian; his aim being, the composer averred, to capture what he called 'pagan merry-making' on Easter morning, as a conspicuous example of the 'double faith' or syncretic religion of pagan Slavic and Christian rites that characterized much of medieval Russia, especially in the countryside.[54] In the twentieth century, the imitation of chant and bell ringing is preserved throughout the œuvre of Rachmaninov, sometimes at an abstract level, even as the other homeland elements drop out.

The oriental element is the single recurrent element in Russian music that could support the expression of a national landscape as such (folksong, Pushkin and the Orthodox liturgy not being directly connected to landscape). The very idea might sound paradoxical at first – how could an exotic cultural 'Other' stand for the nation? – but must be viewed in the light of Russian imperialism. Russian expansion meant that 'the East' became incorporated into the idea of *Rossiya*, the

[53] Seton-Watson, *Nations and States*, pp. 83–5; Edward C. Thaden, *Conservative Nationalism in Nineteenth-Century Russia* (Seattle: University of Washington Press, 1964), pp. 18–20.

[54] Maes, *A History of Russian Music*, p. 188.

Russian state, if not *Rus'*, the ancient land and people of Russia. It thus stood both within Russia and outside. In the same way, from *Ruslan and Lyudmila* onwards, the Orient helped to define the Russian nation indirectly through the glory of its reigning dynasty. The very fact of cultural difference could stand for the greatness of the monarchy and thus the nation. What is absent here is personal identification with the landscape in the sense we find in Weber, Smetana or Grieg.

The landscape aspect of the Orient is most prominent in Borodin's 'musical picture' entitled *In the Steppes of Central Asia* (1880). Starting with a dominant pedal extending almost continuously over ninety bars in the upper register of the violins, it reveals the endless monotony of Russia's eastern steppes, while an oriental theme for cor anglais, languorous and sensual, alternates with a more active, brighter, folksong-like Russian theme. The piece was a tribute to the twenty-fifth anniversary of the reign of Alexander II, the monarch under whom, more than any other, tsarist policy was devoted to the conquest of the East, especially Central Asia.[55] Orientalism is again to the fore in the famous 'Polovtsian Dances' in Borodin's only opera, *Prince Igor* (1869–87, unfinished), which was loosely based on the twelfth-century *Lay of Igor's Campaign*. Igor was captured by Khan Konchak, who, hoping to make an ally of the Russians, sought to seduce his captive host and his son through both the dances and, in the opera, the charms of his daughter, Konchakovna (something only hinted at in the original *Lay*). While the Dances themselves reveal a barbarian splendour, Konchakovna's duet with Vladimir displays a languorous hedonism for the specific purpose of 'entoiling the falconet by means of a fair maiden', as the Khan intended (though there is no mention of Konchakovna in the original *Lay*). By these means, Stasov's scenario for the opera provided a justification for an aggressive Russian nationalism in Central Asia by underlining the superiority of Russia and the 'Russian character' to the inferior hedonistic peoples of the East.[56]

Several of Rimsky-Korsakov's works are imbued with an escapist Oriental hedonism. One of the earliest was his symphonic suite *Antar* (1868, revised 1875 and 1897), a four-movement musical tableau about a poet and a peri, or winged Persian fairy, in whose arms he eventually expires, the music proceeding by variation and repetition around the recurrent main theme representing the poet Antar himself. In the four-movement orchestral suite *Sheherazade* (1888) the strong theme in the brass of Sultan Shakriar is countered by the violin arabesques of his wife, who succeeds in delaying, and ultimately annulling, her execution by her one thousand and one tales. Rimsky-Korsakov later tired of the Oriental complex: his last opera, *The Golden Cockerel* (1907), is a satirical-fantastic tale of the dim-witted King Dodon, an Astrologer and the Queen of Shamakha. Its

---

[55] Taruskin, *Defining Russia Musically*, pp. 149–50, 154, 168; Maes, *A History of Russian Music*, p. 81.

[56] Maes, *A History of Russian Music*, p. 188; Taruskin, *Defining Russia Musically*, ch. 9.

targets include not just the tsarist political system, albeit heavily veiled, but also the nationalist precepts of the *kuchka* and even the esteemed Glinka.[57]

At the end of the nineteenth century, Rimsky-Korsakov found another way of representing the Russian homeland, which was later taken up in new guises by Stravinsky. This approach, which comes under the broad heading of 'neo-nationalism', was in one sense earthy and popular, being derived from the folk traditions favoured by the *kuchka*, but at the same time was concerned with the stylization of those materials for the sake of grand spectacle, fairy tale and even the mystical apprehension of nature. In Rimsky-Korsakov's opera *Snegorouchka* (*The Snow Maiden*, 1881), the attempts to hide the snow maiden from the sun's rays fail when she is freed by the god of love, Lel', and marries, thus freeing the frozen land of the tsar. Essentially an allegory of the transition from winter to spring and then midsummer (*kupala*), when, in ancient Slav mythology, the Sun-god Yarilo takes control of the earth, *Snegorouchka* is also a vehicle for folk traditions, for which the composer used seasonal calendar songs and ceremonial dances. In the later *Christmas Eve* (1894–95), Rimsky-Korsakov kept to Gogol's text, but added Ukrainian Christmas carols and a ballet intermezzo, celebrating the ultimate flight of the demons as the sun returns at the moment of celebration of Christ's birth with an Orthodox Christmas morning hymn. Rimsky-Korsakov's mystical pantheism was fed by the folkloristic studies of books such as *The Slavs' Poetic Outlook on Nature* by Alexander Afanasiyev, also the collector of the folk tale that inspired *Snegorouchka*. *The Legend of the Invisible City of Kitezh and the Maiden Fevroniya* (1903–4), based on the sixteenth-century hagiography of Fevroniya of Murom, is a pantheistic epic opera with folk stylization, using folk church style and wedding songs, to reveal the near-identity of Christian neighbourly love and natural religion, the Christian God being coupled with Sirin and Alkonost, the prophet birds of Slavic mythology.[58]

In many ways, Stravinsky's three great ballets for Diaghilev, *The Firebird* (1910), *Petrushka* (1911) and *The Rite of Spring* (1913), continued this folk neo-nationalism and drew on Rimsky-Korsakov's example in terms of musical technique and subject matter, even if they catered to international, chiefly Parisian, audiences, not Russians. For the *Rite*, Stravinsky and Nikolai Roerich aimed to depict 'a series of images of a holy night among the ancient Slavs'. Originally a celebration of *kupala*, midsummer, these images were later moved to *Semik*, the spring rituals. As Stravinsky put it, 'Throughout the whole composition I give the listener a sense of the closeness of the people to the earth, of the commonality of their lives with the earth, by means of lapidary rhythms.'[59] Some of the elements in the ballet were taken from Herodotus' description of the ancient Scythians, notably the Glorification of the Elders; at the time, the Scythians were seen as

[57] Frolova-Walker, *Russian Music and Nationalism*, pp. 218–25; Maes, *A History of Russian Music*, pp. 70, 175–6.

[58] Maes, *A History of Russian Music*, pp. 187–91.

[59] Cited in ibid., p. 225.

the distant ancestors of the Russians, contributing to their character a barbaric vitality that differentiated Russia from the West. Roerich's sets and costumes followed the style of his archaistic paintings, which he populated with elders, rituals, idols and standing stones.[60] Stravinsky used a considerable amount of folk music throughout the *Rite* (see Chapter 2), notably calendar songs, though they were metamorphosed during composition in true neo-nationalist style, in a manner analogous to that of Gauguin, whose paintings Stravinsky admired; and, closer to home, not unlike the products of Abramtsevo, Savva Mamontov's colony of artists which included Victor Vasnetsov, Vassily Polenov, Ilya Repin and Konstantin Korovin. From the early 1880s they promoted a similar revivalist stylized neo-nationalism, including the decor for operas like *Snegorouchka*. Thus, in the *Rite*, the earlier *kuchka* ethnographic realism was attenuated through an abstract, almost classical, simplification of forms. But, as Taruskin points out, that is to focus solely on 'the music itself', and to forget the extra-musical genesis and the disturbing issues raised by the *Rite*: the celebration of an anti-human mythology of cruelty, biologism, blood sacrifice of the individual to the community, an absence of compassion, attributes that came to characterize totalitarian societies, but which could also be found, albeit unselfconsciously, in the simple, aboriginal societies that Durkheim was researching at this very time, and in which he discerned the seeds of an 'eternal religion', namely, the worship by society of itself, whose modern form, the cult of the nation, has been at the heart of the modern epoch.[61]

## An English homeland at the periphery

In the case of that other great late nineteenth-century empire, Great Britain, we are confronted by a duality and an ambiguity: can we speak of a British or an English nation, a British or an English nationalism? These are not simply academic questions: they have wider ramifications in society and culture, not least in music in *fin-de-siècle* Britain. For some scholars, the matter is relatively straightforward: there was no English nationalism until the end of the nineteenth century, only a preceding British imperialism. In terms of national identity, according to Krishan Kumar, empire trumped nation, until it began to decay and voices critical of empire began to be heard. That was the moment of ideological need, and a specifically English nationalism stepped into the breach. Of course, this relegates other moments of English nationalism, notably that of Milton and Cromwell in the Puritan Commonwealth, and again the anti-French literary and

---

[60] Taruskin, *Stravinsky and the Russian Traditions*, p. 851.

[61] Taruskin, *Defining Russia Musically*, ch. 13, esp. pp. 384–8; Émile Durkheim, *The Elementary Forms of the Religious Life*, trans. J. Swain (London: Allen & Unwin, 1915); see also Camilla Gray, *The Russian Experiment in Art, 1863–1922* (London: Thames and Hudson, 1971), pp. 9–36.

political movement in the eighteenth century associated with Hogarth, Hurd, Smollett and Cowper, which Gerald Newman explored. Kumar dismisses the latter as a kind of moralistic primitivism of uncorrupted virtue, such as Rousseau espoused, and which fed into, but was not exactly, 'nationalism'. It was, he argues, only at the end of the nineteenth century that there was a real need for an ethnic 'Englishness' (hardly a full-blown nationalism), of the kind expressed in the Whig interpretation of English history as cumulative and continuous progress from a base of ancient Saxon liberties. The myth of Anglo-Saxon democracy espoused by historians such as William Stubbs and J. R. Green had a kernel of racial populism, opposing Anglo-Saxons to Celts and foreigners, but it was also expansive, including all white British dominions who partook of the exclusive privilege of being part of the 'chosen people'.[62]

This was also the moment of the English musical revival. After the mid-eighteenth-century flowering of music in England associated with Thomas Arne and William Boyce, and of course Handel, the nineteenth century saw a succession of eminent foreign composers visiting Britain – Mendelssohn, Bruch, Brahms and Dvořák among them. But 'English music' – music composed by English people in England – did not revive until the end of the century, with Stanford and Parry. Their pupils' generation, coming to maturity in the 1900s, presented their own work as national music, a self-conscious 'Renaissance' relative to sixteenth- and seventeenth-century English music that was also closely linked to the contemporaneous folksong revival. A sense of landscape was central to their project, sometimes explicit, sometimes implicit.

One corner of England was extraordinarily popular as a synecdoche for the English nation: the area of the west Midlands from the Severn estuary to Shropshire known to music historians, following a remark by Elgar, as 'Severnside'. A disproportionate number of composers happened to been born in the area (Parry, Elgar, Vaughan Williams, Holst, Howells) or established links there, and it was the home of the Three Choirs Festival held at the cathedrals of Worcester, Gloucester and Hereford, the oldest English music festival, an important event in regional society, and a venue for commissions and performances of new English music such as Vaughan Williams's *Tallis Fantasia*, which received an auspicious premiere in Gloucester Cathedral at the 1910 Festival. But it was above all the poetry of the Classics professor A. E. Housman that set off the cult of Severnside. Born in humdrum Bromsgrove in Worcestershire, and never having visited Shropshire, Housman unexpectedly brought out a volume of pastoral poems in 1896 entitled *A Shropshire Lad*. His straightforward but poignant language and regular verses describe life and work in Shropshire villages and farms peopled by yeoman Englishmen, made real to

---

[62] Krishan Kumar, *The Making of English National Identity* (Cambridge: Cambridge University Press, 2003), pp. 202–7; Gerald Newman, *The Rise of English Nationalism: A Cultural History, 1740–1830* (London: Weidenfeld and Nicolson, 1987), esp. ch. 4.

the reader by frequent reference to named towns, hills and rivers. More than one thousand settings were made in the first half of the twentieth century, including a well-known series of cycles starting with Arthur Butterworth (1904), including two by Vaughan Williams (1909, 1927), two by George Butterworth (1909–11), two by Ivor Gurney (1919), and one by John Ireland (1920–21).[63] Vaughan Williams and Butterworth set Housman in folksong idioms, another contribution to the synthesis of heterogeneous English sources that was noted with regard to Vaughan Williams in Chapters 1 and 2. What especially appealed to composers were the pangs of regret that hung over Housman's imagined Shropshire, a 'land of lost content' which lads left for foreign wars never to return. This aspect – 'et in arcadia ego' – resonated for Edwardian composers because of the Boer War (1898–1901) and did so still more after the Great War. Officers took Housman to the front in 1914 and wrote home in ways that echo his verse. George Butterworth even seemed to live the fate of a Shropshire lad by dying aged thirty-one on the Somme, his great musical talent unfulfilled. Ivor Gurney wrote a book of poetry entitled *Severn and Somme*.

To the Housman settings can be added other Severnside compositions such as Holst's early 'Cotswold' Symphony (1900); Butterworth's evocative orchestral *A Shropshire Lad: Rhapsody* (1911); Finzi's *A Severn Rhapsody* for chamber orchestra (1923); Vaughan Williams's folksong opera *Hugh the Drover* (1910–14, premiered 1924), set in a Cotswold village; Howells's String Quartet *In Gloucestershire* (1922); and his monumental *Missa Sabrinensis* (*Mass of the Severn*; 1954), a work that approaches Bach's B minor Mass and Beethoven's *Missa Solemnis* in scale, projecting the Severnside mood of sorrow and ecstatic mysticism onto a universal plane. Elgar grew up in Worcester and was famously devoted to the countryside of the Severn valley, but, contrary to popular perception, his music seldom attempts to represent it directly, except in *Caractacus*, in one of the 'interludes' from the symphonic poem *Falstaff* (a Gloucestershire orchard) and arguably in the *'Enigma' Variations* (1899), which comprises musical portraits of members of the Severnside society of the rural Worcestershire gentry.[64] The *Introduction and Allegro* for string orchestra and four string soloists (1905) has links with the neighbouring Wye valley in Herefordshire ('that sweet borderland where I have made my home'), but also with the memory of a Welsh folksong heard floating across a Welsh valley while on holiday.

It might seem paradoxical that a region on the western periphery could become the principal site for composers to explore Englishness in microcosm. Broadly, the trend reflects a reconceptualization of Englishness in terms of the geography and territory of the British Isles instead of – or in tension with – any

[63] Robert Stradling, 'England's Glory: Sensibilities of Place in English Music, 1900–1950', in *The Place of Music*, ed. Andrew Leyshon, David Matless and George Revill (New York and London: Guilford Press, 1998), pp. 176–96.

[64] David Cannadine, 'Orchestrating his Own Life: Sir Edward Elgar as a Historical Personality', in Kenyon (ed.), *Elgar*, pp. 11–13.

sense of 'chosenness' or imperial destiny. This new Englishness incorporated a Celtic dimension, albeit understated, since these were the peoples with whom the English shared their islands, and indeed their original inhabitants: the descendants of the ancient Britons of Elgar's *Caractacus*. (The Victorians had much preferred King Alfred and the Anglo-Saxons to the indigenous Britons when it came to ancient historical heroes.) The melancholy and mysticism of the 'Celtic twilight' became part of English identity too. Severnside was the perfect location, as the Severn was the historic boundary between Saxon and Celtic domains. It runs for its first sixty miles in Wales, and the basin it drains covers swathes of both Wales and central England. Housman's Shropshire Lad longs for his 'western playland' beyond the Severn; he does not look eastward down the flow of the Thames to its estuary, which would symbolize metropolis and empire.[65] The Severn is conceived as a river of culture and nature rather than politics. The peripheral location of the region was crucial to its centrality in the new conception of Englishness.

In English literature, advertising and wartime publicity, the typical landscape of England was the South Downs of Surrey, Sussex and Kent. In music however this region never approached Severnside in popularity. The nearest challenger to Severnside was Thomas Hardy's Wessex, a bleaker alternative that inspired fine song cycles from Gerald Finzi, Holst's *Egdon Heath* (1928) and Vaughan Williams's Symphony No. 9 (1958; the programme suppressed by the composer). Later a small area of East Anglia became significant for Benjamin Britten, but the particular works it inspired hardly count as national music. Representations of northern England in music are few, but one is found in Frederick Delius's *North Country Sketches* (1915), one of the more English works of that émigré Yorkshireman (his Englishness or lack of it is discussed in Chapter 6).

More abstract evocations of the English countryside can be found in Vaughan Williams's *The Lark Ascending* (1920), which combines landscape, nature music and folksong style in another powerful synthesis. His ruminative *Pastoral Symphony* (1922) boldly applies this approach to the 'dynamic' symphonic genre, even if Vaughan Williams himself and later commentators have played down the English ruralism and stressed the links with continental modernism and the war-torn landscape of northern France remembered from Vaughan Williams's military service.[66] These two works are not just pastoral but quietist, although

---

[65] David Martin, 'The Sound of England', in *Nationalism and Ethnosymbolism: History, Culture and Ethnicity in the Formation of Nations*, ed. Athena S. Leoussi and Steven Grosby (Edinburgh: Edinburgh University Press, 2007), pp. 68–83; Schama, *Landscape and Memory*, pp. 3–5.

[66] Michael Kennedy, *The Works of Ralph Vaughan Williams* 2nd edn (Oxford: Oxford University Press, 1980), pp. 167–72; Michael Vaillancourt, 'Modal and Thematic Coherence in Vaughan Williams's *Pastoral Symphony*', *Music Review* 52 (1991), pp. 203–17; Eric Saylor, '"It's Not Lambkins Frisking At All": English Pastoral Music and the Great War', *Musical Quarterly* 91/1–2 (2009), pp. 39–59; 'Landscape and Distance: Vaughan Williams, Modernism and the Symphonic

they do not lack drama. Both works feature a soloist: respectively a violin and a wordless soprano voice in the symphony's finale. Both reach states of visionary ecstasy before ending with a single line for the soloist that fades away to nothingness. As in the English Severnside tradition, Vaughan Williams here plays down historical or heroic events that might take place in the landscape, and tilts the 'mixed genre' of the national homeland firmly towards landscape.

After Elgar's *Caractacus*, indeed, English music largely avoided heroic historical subjects; Arnold Bax's *Tintagel* (1921), which evokes the Celtic legends surrounding the ruined Cornish castle and quotes Wagner's *Tristan und Isolde*, is redolent of Bax's adoptive Irish nationalism as much as any English agenda, and sits with his other tone poems such as *Cathaleen-ni-Hoolihan* (1905), *In the Faery Hills* (1909) and *The Garden of Fand* (1920). There was a Celtic/Wagnerian vogue for Arthurian legends in opera led by Hubert Parry (*Guenever*, although never performed) and Rutland Boughton with his Glastonbury Festival – an English answer to Bayreuth – but no English operas on King Alfred, King Harold or Hereward the Wake, and no heroic or tragic operas on Shakespeare.

## Spanish homelands, exotic and otherwise

The specification of place was central to the European tradition of 'Spanish' music by Spanish and non-Spanish composers alike that flourished in the late nineteenth and early twentieth centuries. Towns and gardens were frequent references in the titles of these compositions. For Spanish composers, the image of the homeland was important for building a renewed sense of nationhood after the loss of empire following the Spanish–American War of 1898. The significance of national art music in Spain is however complicated by the tradition of exoticization of Spanish styles by non-Spanish composers, especially from France and Russia, along with the highly contested cultural field within an increasingly divided nation in the early twentieth century. Over the nineteenth century Spain began to turn itself into a tourist destination to compensate for its decline as a world power. Flamenco music emerged as a public genre in the late nineteenth century as café entertainment for foreigners. By the early twentieth century the most recognizably Spanish musical styles (broadly those of flamenco) were primarily associated with an ethnic group (the Roma) that was socially peripheral. For European listeners the Spanish were portrayed as partial outsiders, standing at the periphery of Europe with contacts to Africa and Asia through their Moorish and gypsy traditions. Spanish music was an opportunity for brilliant orchestral showpieces such as Chabrier's *España* (1883), Rimsky-Korsakov's *Capriccio espagnol* (1887) and Ravel's *Rhapsodie espagnole* (1908). The heroine of Bizet's opera *Carmen* encapsulates this exoticized Spain. In Spain itself flamenco met with growing opposition from nationalists who identified it with backwardness and decadence.[67] Spanish composers themselves did not entirely resist the exoticizing impulse, but redirected it to their own purposes. They looked to Paris for cultural leadership, after all, and most studied or even lived there.[68]

The European history of Spanish musical styles goes back to the eighteenth century with dances such as the fandango, bolero and seguidilla. They later served for local colour in operas for the French stage by Cherubini and Méhul, and in the two Spanish Overtures of Glinka, Liszt's *Rhapsodie espagnole*, the piano music of Gottschalk and the operas of Verdi. Folk-music research, professional or casual, provided impetus for the orchestral fireworks of Chabrier and Rimsky-Korsakov. Finally, Ravel and Debussy combined Spanish elements, especially stylized habanera rhythms and keyboard guitar imitation, with modernist effects of harmony, rhythm and texture and a tendency to dreamy subjectivity. Writing concurrently, the Spanish composers Albéniz, Falla and, to an extent, Enriqué Granados, undertook further exploration of flamenco idioms, including Phrygian modality and guitar effects on the keyboard, combining them with the French composers' modernist techniques. Albéniz and Falla transformed Spanish folk modes into more chromatic systems, rather in the manner of Bartók. In Albéniz's *Iberia* there is convergence with Debussy even down to (French) publisher, score layout and some of Debussy's characteristic French performance directions. While he was living in Paris in the years 1907 to 1914, Falla absorbed the romanticized French view of Spain, and his concerto-like *Noches en los jardines de España* (*Nights in the Gardens of Spain*; 1916) for piano and orchestra sounds very much like Debussy in his Spanish mode. It is not obvious to the average ear that the Spanish composers' efforts are more authentic. Some of their pieces suggest, no less than those of Debussy, the perspective of Romantic outsider or tourist, who does not identify with the music makers of the scenes but observes them. James Parakilas regards Falla as 'an exemplary case of auto-exoticism'.[69]

In all this music, the southern province of Andalusia is, predictably, the most prominent region of Spain. One exotic Andalusian location in particular recurs: the Moorish Alhambra palace in Granada and its gardens, especially at night. French Romantic writings on Grenada by Chateaubriand, Hugo and Gautier had portrayed the city as a glimpse of the Orient and the gypsies as modern substitutes for the Spanish Arabs. The Paris Exposition Universelle of 1900 had a display on 'Andalucia at the time of the Moors', which showed the Alhambra palace populated with Spanish gypsies and North Africans accompanied by

[67] Michael Christoforidis, 'Manuel de Falla, Flamenco and Spanish Identity', in Brown (ed.), *Western Music and Race*, p. 242.

[68] James Parakilas, 'How Spain Got a Soul', in Jonathan Bellman (ed.), *The Exotic in Western Music* (Boston: Northeastern University Press, 1998), pp. 137–93; Locke, *Musical Exoticism*, ch. 7.

[69] Parakilas, 'How Spain Got a Soul', p. 189.

dancers and flamenco music: a mixture of ancient and modern exoticism.[70] These themes, if not the musical style of *andalucismo*, go back to Cherubini's opera *Les Abencérages, ou L'étendard de Grenade* (1813). Debussy covered the ground four times, in *Lindaraja* (1901) for two pianos; *La soirée dans Grenade* from *Estampes* (1903); the central section of *Ibéria* from the orchestral *Images* (composed 1903–10); and *La Puerto del Vino* from the second book of *Préludes* (1913). These pieces record the (imagined) impressions of a night in Grenada with a stylized habanera and modernist textural and harmonic effects, the idiom indebted to an earlier habanera by Ravel. Falla's *Noches en los jardines de España* likewise describes two Andalusian gardens, the first the familiar Alhambra. The locations specified in the titles of the pieces in Albéniz's four-volume masterpiece *Iberia* maintains the emphasis on Andalusia, as noted in Chapter 2, even though it mixes and merges Spanish song and dance styles of various regions quite freely. Thus 'Triana' is named after the gypsy quarter in Seville, one of the cradles of flamenco; 'El Albaicín' after the gypsy quarter in Granada; 'Eritaña' is the name of an inn on the outskirts of Seville where flamenco was performed; 'Fête-Dieu à Séville' and 'El puerto' are likewise Andalusian locations.[71]

In the 1920s Falla altered his representation of the Spanish homeland, coming in line with the intellectuals of the 'Generation of 1898', which, following the loss of Spain's empire, espoused modernization and a new Spanish identity oriented culturally to Castile rather than Andalusia, the former now held up at the centre of Spain, both geographically and culturally.[72] Falla now downplayed folklore and *andalucismo* in favour of a severe, modern neoclassicism with pared-down orchestration that paralleled Stravinsky's contemporaneous work, together with historical allusions to seventeenth-century Spanish composers. With this approach he sought to renew modern Spanish music by evoking the courtly culture of Spain's golden age, when it was a leading European power. This was a Spain that the French composers had largely ignored. Falla adapted an episode from Cervantes's *Don Quixote* for his puppet opera *El retablo de maese Pedro* (1923). His Stravinskian Harpsichord Concerto (1926; Ex. 3.3) is really a sextet in three short movements, inspired partly by the eighteenth-century keyboard style of the Spanish-assimilated Domenico Scarlatti. It quotes a Castilian folksong incorporated in a fifteenth-century *villancico* and a melody by the Renaissance polyphonist Tomás Luis de Victoria, which is intended to evoke religious ecstasy and the feast of Corpus Christi. Falla thus shifts the focus from gypsies, Moorish palaces and the outdoors to a world of sovereignty, courts and the Catholic religion, from Romanticism to neoclassicism, from the geographical periphery to the centre, from localism to universalism, and from tourist sites to historical artists, writers and musicians. Contemporary listeners were very alert to these

---

[70] Christoforidis, 'Manuel de Falla, Flamenco and Spanish Identity', p. 232.

[71] Parakilas, 'How Spain Got a Soul', pp. 174–84; Clark, *Isaac Albéniz*, ch. 7.

[72] Christoforidis, 'Manuel de Falla, Flamenco and Spanish Identity', pp. 237, 242.

Ex. 3.3  Falla, Harpsichord Concerto, first movement
(reduction of flute, oboe, clarinet, violin and cello parts), bars 1–10

messages.[73] For Parakilas, 'This move can be seen as an attempt to find beneath the social, political, and regional divisions of Spain – which had been intense throughout his life and were becoming catastrophic – a stratum of history that all Spaniards shared.'[74] But Falla remembered the exoticized image of the Alhambra gardens in pieces such as the song *Psyché* (1924), for mezzo-soprano, flute, harp and string trio, which combines neoclassical evocations of the music of the eighteenth-century Spanish court with flamenco trills, as Queen Isabella Farnese sits in the Alhambra with her courtiers. Another instance of this synthetic trend is the famous *Concierto de Aranjuez* by Joachín Rodrigo, inspired by the gardens of the royal palace of Philip II outside Madrid. The composer pointed out that the palace stood 'on the road to Andalusia', an idea which captures perfectly his blend of courtly, neoclassical and flamenco stylistic elements. The concerto, composed in 1939 in the closing stages of the Spanish civil war, offers an embracing conception of the national homeland.

## American Eden

The best-known attempts to capture the American homeland in art music come from the mid twentieth century, although they can be traced back to Dvořák's 'New World' Symphony, and, half a century earlier still, to the 'Niagara' Symphonies by Anthony Philip Heinrich (1781–1861) and William Henry Fry (1813–64). The movement came to focus in the Depression era and culminated in Aaron Copland's three famous ballet scores, *Billy the Kid* (1938), *Rodeo* (1942) and *Appalachian Spring* (1944). A sense of the homeland is implicit also in some of his patriotic pieces of the time, such as *Fanfare for the Common Man* (1942), *Lincoln Portrait* (1942) and the Third Symphony (1946), and it can be found a little earlier in the works of Roy Harris, Virgil Thomson and others. In the 1930s Copland's music underwent a major stylistic change from his explicit modernism and jazz-influenced compositions of the 1920s to a new diatonicism and what he termed an 'imposed simplicity'. More generally the new interest in landscape records a shift of orientation in American art music, which turned its focus from African American vernacular sources to those of British and Irish origin and its geographical orientation from the energy and bustle of the eastern industrial cities to the wide open spaces of 'the West'. In the wake of the economic collapse, artists associated themselves with progressive politics and sought an engagement with 'the people' through new media such as documentary film (Thomson's *The Plow that Broke the Plains* (1937)), radio (Copland's *Music for Radio: Prairie Journal* (1936)), children's opera (Copland's *The Second Hurricane* (1936)) and cinema. There was a renewed interest in the pioneer spirit and sympathy with

---

[73] Carol A. Hess, *Manuel de Falla and Modernism in Spain, 1898–1936* (Chicago: University of Chicago Press, 2001), chs 7 and 8.

[74] Parakilas, 'How Spain Got a Soul', p. 193.

American farmers dispossessed by the economic system. This was a defining moment in American musical self-definition. Copland's American style later became a code for American pastoral and American heroism in Hollywood and the mass media. The *Fanfare* and excerpts from the ballets can be heard at concerts of American music, political conventions, Fourth of July celebrations, commemorative events and on television commercials. Ironically in 1953 Copland was called before the Senate Permanent Subcommittee on Investigations for questioning by Joseph McCarthy on his 'Un-American' links with the Communist Party, not long after his *Lincoln Portrait* was removed from the inaugural programme of President Eisenhower.[75]

The Depression-era version of the American musical homeland stands in European cultural traditions in terms of its form, even if in its content it establishes dimensions and a sense of expansive possibility that were necessarily absent from most European conceptions. Rousseau is still the father of this movement, with its emphasis on rural simplicity and primitive virtue and the self-conscious simplification of its musical style, although the goal is not to historicize the landscape, since it is conceived as a pristine wilderness. The music strikes a note of nostalgia – still Rousseauian of course – for by this time the frontier had closed; no further expansion could ever occur. The legacy of European national music is felt too. Harris's symphonies build on Sibelius, while Copland had benefitted from his years of study in Paris, admired what he saw as Stravinsky's Russianness, and learned from him the value of vernacular sources in a modern style. In their progressive political context too, Copland's efforts stand in European traditions of national music (if not that of Stravinsky), drawing on vernacular sources to define the nation through 'the people' in a way that recalls Liszt, Grieg and Sibelius. In terms of musical style, the American composers relied a good deal on diatonicism and made use of pedal points and harmonic stasis to indicate landscape, although sound-sheets as such are generally avoided. The American landscape is characterized not by a fast-moving surface ('forest murmurs') but by 'openness' first and foremost, conveyed through sparse textures, wide intervallic spacing and angular melodies with wide leaps, summoning thoughts of the prairie, the western deserts and, more generally, a freedom-loving state of mind. The purest example is perhaps the opening of *Fanfare for the Common Man*, a melody for trumpets in unison moving first by fourths and fifths, and largely by disjunct motion, twice outlining a great arch shape. The second statement is accompanied by unison horns, forming 'open' dyads of fourths, fifths and sixths. A long tradition of music theory and everyday musical speech

---

[75] Neil Lerner, 'Copland's Music of Wide Open Spaces: Surveying the Pastoral Trope in Hollywood', *The Musical Quarterly* 85/3 (2001), pp. 477–515; Denise Von Glahn, *The Sounds of Place: Music and the American Cultural Landscape* (Boston: Northeastern University Press, 2003), ch. 1; Taruskin, *The Oxford History of Western Music*, vol. 3, p. 637; Beth E. Levy, *Frontier Figures: American Music and the Mythology of the American West* (Berkeley: University of California Press, 2012), pp. 2–10.

has termed the sound of the intervals of perfect fourths and fifths 'open', since to an ear accustomed to triadic harmony such dyads seem to lack the interval of third or sixth that would 'fill' the 'gap'. Copland took a crucial step in associating this ingrained metaphor with topological and, ultimately, mental 'openness'. The scoring of the *Fanfare* is for brass and percussion only, and elsewhere Copland likewise places the emphasis on wind instruments, taking his textural bearings from Stravinsky in avoiding the vocal-expressive idiom typical of the orchestral strings and favouring bell-like sonorities. The sense of freshness of this frontier music marks it out from European musical homelands.[76]

The introductory and closing sections of *Billy the Kid*, entitled 'The Open Prairie', accompany a slow, mass procession across the stage that represents a great migration of people. These scenes are modelled on descriptions of westward expansion in Walter Noble Burns's novel *The Saga of Billy the Kid* (1925), the source for the ballet's scenario. Although the choreographer, Eugene Loring, asked Copland for a 'march', the composer wrote music in triple metre, with a weary, offbeat bass figure and Stravinskian touches in the scoring for wind instruments and the ostinato pattern, which distinctly echoes Stravinsky's Russian ballets *Petrushka* and *Le sacre du printemps*. At the opening (Ex. 3.4) the diatonic melody is doubled in 'open' fifths in woodwind instruments, and the scoring is no less sparse when the strings enter (bar 7). The soft opening and gradual crescendo as the line of people wends its way across the plains has a famous precursor in Borodin's *In the Steppes of Central Asia*. This music of the American landscape strikes a heroic note but is by no means blandly optimistic. *Billy the Kid* as a whole could be regarded as pastoral in the literary sense, that is, a representation of the full range of human life, emotions and characters within a simple setting away from the artificial complexities of urban existence. Burns's novel is a sympathetic portrayal of the notorious outlaw, and Copland and Loring underline this interpretation. Billy is a naive, almost victim-like hero, whose eventual death, although necessary for the progress of American civilization, is also tragic.[77]

The opening of *Appalachian Spring* again stands in the tradition of European musical landscape with pedal points and sustained string notes as 'background' and woodwind snatches as 'foreground' figures or nature calls. A major triad is arpeggiated and a dissonant seventh on top is left unresolved, indicating a sense of timelessness and 'pure' sonority requiring no 'in-time' resolution. The music suggests the opening up of a pristine new world, and the scenario at the premiere referred to 'that movement of Pennsylvania spring when there was "a garden eastward of Eden"'. The faster sections are Stravinskian in scoring and sonorities, but incorporate stylized folksongs and dances and a certain diatonic sweetness, culminating in the variations on the Shaker hymn 'Simple Gifts'. This section, which preserves the melody throughout while varying tempo, dynamics,

---

[76] Taruskin, *The Oxford History of Western Music*, vol. 3, pp. 664–8.

[77] Crist, *Music for the Common Man*, pp. 119–32; Levy, *Frontier Figures*, pp. 324–8.

Ex. 3.4  Copland, *Billy the Kid*, 'Introduction: The Open Prairie' (reduction), bars 1–18

texture and scoring, has a pedigree in European national music too, standing in the Russian *kuchka* tradition of variations with 'changing background' accompaniment. Like *Billy the Kid*, *Appalachian Spring* is a genuine pastoral, encompassing American good and evil, although conveying an ultimately optimistic message. Its music is best known from the concert suite, which presents a more idyllic picture than the ballet itself, many of the sorrowful and sinister elements being omitted. The choreographer and commissioner, Martha Graham, was politically, like Copland, aligned with the Popular Front, and the scenario, which underwent many revisions, was initially related to the Civil War. Even the final version, which concerns a newly married couple setting up a home, shows the presence of sin and corruption in the garden, along with biblical allusions ('east of Eden' means the land of Cain's banishment). The precise historical period of the story is ambiguous, and generations shift so that the ballet seems to encompass the whole sweep of American history. Copland and Graham shared a modernist aesthetic, but one that in *Appalachian Spring* was adapted to traditional musical idioms and to some extent conventional ballet choreography in a popular synthesis. The minimalist sets of the original production by Isamu Noguchi conveyed a strong sense of place, matching the studied simplicity of Copland's music and aiming to capture the 'pioneer spirit' in the domestic setting, which included a Shaker rocking chair.[78]

Copland was not the first on the scene during the Depression. For a time during the 1930s Roy Harris had been hailed as the great American composer of art music for whom the nation had been searching. A Harris myth grew up around the composer's origins and background: he was born in Oklahoma and grew up in California, where his father was a farmer. Harris became an emblem of the West in music, and he made much of his rugged persona, his love of home territory and the roots of his creativity in nature. Critics applied these values to his works, which, with a few exceptions such as *A Farewell to Pioneers* (1935), were mainly presented without explicit programmes. Harris favoured asymmetrical, prose-like melodic structures, which grew gradually in widening intervals and great upward-striving spans. He termed them 'autogenetic', a concept not unfamiliar from the history of musical Romanticism, but applied here to capture implicitly the pioneer spirit in symphonic form. His most famous composition is his Third Symphony (1939), an instant success, which, Harris admitted, caught the mood of the time, and has remained in the performed repertoire. In all, Harris composed thirteen symphonies and laid the ground for a mid-century American symphonic school. Howard Hanson, William Schuman, Walter Piston and Copland all composed 'heroic' Third Symphonies in the wake of Harris. In the end Harris's version of the American homeland lost out to that of Copland in the popular imagination. Ironically Copland's polished technique and freely adapted modernist influences gave him an edge over the more rough-hewn Harris in the Rousseauian quest for the American musical homeland. His American idiom was not at all 'autogenetic', but a carefully crafted synthesis that drew deeply and expertly on European compositional traditions.[79]

One of the best-known evocations of the American homeland was also one of the latest in the tradition, and a one-off for its composer. Samuel Barber's 'lyric rhapsody' *Knoxville: Summer of 1915* (1947) for soprano and orchestra was composed after World War II but looks back with the poet James Agee to a childhood before World War I and a state of pastoral innocence. American

---

[78] Lynn Garagola, 'Making an American Dance: *Billy the Kid, Rodeo*, and *Appalachian Spring*', in *Aaron Copland and his World*, ed. Carol J. Oja and Judith Tick (Princeton and Oxford: Princeton University Press, 2005), pp. 135–41; Crist, *Music for the Common Man*, pp. 165–76.

[79] Taruskin, *The Oxford History of Western Music*, vol. 3, pp. 637–49; Levy, *Frontier Figures*, ch. 8.

listeners and singers over several generations have identified with the childhood experience described in *Knoxville*, even those with no connection with Tennessee, as did Barber himself, who was the same age as Agee. The text captures the everyday sights, sounds and tastes of a summer evening in the South, with a Proustian attention to the recollection of sensory detail, and Barber responds with pastoral idioms such as pentatonicism, rocking figuration and a hint of blues, along with musical onomatopoeia. The text is characterized also by repetition and lists: for sensations, recollections of family members, and prayers. Barber creates a rondo-like form based around a rocking refrain. The rural South here substitutes for the rural West as an authentic source of American identity. The idyll is broken, though, by the intrusion of the sounds of trams and cars. *Knoxville* ends with a reference to the closing chord of *Appalachian Spring* as a major triad is given added seventh and ninth degrees.[80]

## Conclusion

The pastoral in music is nothing new, but the harnessing of music to the expression of the homeland ideal and the process of naturalizing the history of a people in its ethnoscape was a novel development in the nineteenth century. It began with locations that have a history of representation in the visual arts, literature or the Grand Tour: the German forests, the Rhine, Rome and its countryside, Scottish ruins and coast. These were translated into music, either with identification (Weber, Schumann, Wagner) or without (Mendelssohn), creating a quasi-pictorial mixed genre of landscape/history. Later composers' attention turned to homeland landscapes with a less distinguished literary or pictorial history, or a history that was itself in the process of creation by nationalists: the countryside around Prague, the mountains of western Norway, the Finnish forests and lakes, the hills and valleys of the English/Welsh marches, the Alhambra palace and the North American prairie. To the examples given in this chapter we could add d'Indy's Ardèche, discussed in Chapter 2, and many others. In all these cases musical differentiation, characterization and identification are stronger. Composers developed traditions of distinctive sound-sheets and foreground/background effects and drew on the traits of their indigenous folk music. At the same time they maintained transnational dialogue with one another in terms of techniques such as sound-sheet and genres such as symphonic poem. Sometimes their musical landscapes originally accompanied visual spectacles such as *tableaux vivants*, in which the ethnoscape was made immediately visible to the audience. Here, and especially at the Finnish lotteries, the music of the homeland served the goal of vernacular mobilization in the most direct way.

---

[80] Benedict Taylor, 'Nostalgia and Cultural Memory in Barber's *Knoxville: Summer of 1915*', *Journal of Musicology* 25/3 (2008), pp. 211–29.

On the other hand, the mixture of genres is sometimes reduced as history and human action are minimized in favour of subjective responses to nature, pantheistic reactions, or existential transformation through intuition of the essence of the natural phenomenon. The preoccupation with characteristic qualities of sounds rather than their discursive function, even to the extent of the vibrating wood and brass of the players' instruments, the very lack of concrete action, detailed programme or even musical theme in any conventional sense in some of Sibelius's later music invites the audience's collective re-engagement with an unspoken world of everyday human life in an ethnic community that must rest in a certain location.

# 4

# Myths and Memories of the Nation

I F a nation is delimited in territorial space, it is equally defined in historical, and prehistorical, time. For nationalists, each nation possesses a unique origin, trajectory and destiny, and each has its share of historical memories, myths and legends. Nationalists of the nineteenth century delved into and recorded the legends, myths and memories that enact their own nation's trajectory and illuminate its aspirations. The contribution of musicians to the imaginative reconstruction of the nation's past was vast, even if much of it is now forgotten. In this chapter, we examine a sample of pieces by well-known nineteenth-century composers that remain in today's performed repertoire, and which illustrate national histories, myths and legends. From this sample alone it is clear that certain musical works became intrinsic to the national vision of the ethnic past, and, conversely, that successive waves of nationalism attracted some of the finest composers and shaped key works in their œuvres.

## The cult of the ancestors

A good place to start is with the 'cult of the ancestors'. This was how Ernest Renan introduced the importance of national history for the differentiation, and the shaping, of nations. Having rejected the many attempts to define the concept of the nation in terms of race, religion, geography, language and economic interests, Renan turned to present collective will and to national history, specifically the cult of the ancestors, as the key constituents of the nation, which he regarded as a 'spiritual principle'. He went on:

> The nation, like the individual, is the culmination of a long past of endeavours, sacrifice, and devotion. Of all cults, that of the ancestors is the most legitimate, for the ancestors have made us what we are. A heroic past, great men, glory (by which I understand genuine glory), this is the social capital upon which one bases a national idea. To have common glories in the past and to have a common will in the present; to have performed great deeds together, to wish to perform still more – these are the essential condition for being a people. One loves in proportion to the sacrifices to which one has consented, and in proportion to the ills one has suffered ... A nation is therefore a large-scale solidarity, constituted by the feeling of the

sacrifices that one has made in the past and of those that one is prepared to make in the future.[1]

Two ideas are linked here, which will soon find a musical voice: sacrifice and heroism, and their union in the self-sacrifice of heroes and heroines. Sacrifice constitutes a powerful social bond, for it places successive generations under an obligation and spurs them to emulation. Equally important are the exploits, sufferings and triumphs of heroes and heroines such as Hector, Siegfried, Joan of Arc and Alexander Nevsky. Identification with the triumph and, even more, the self-sacrifice of the hero or heroine, is an equally potent source of national solidarity and the continuity of generations, for this is felt to inspire and renew the community. As Renan noted, 'suffering in common unifies more than joy does', and he went on to explain that 'Where national memories are concerned, griefs are of more value than triumphs, for they impose duties, and require a common effort'.[2]

Equally important is the idea that the heroic exploits and sufferings disclose not only the exemplary qualities of the exemplary individuals, but the virtues and true inward character of the national community. Nor are the heroes isolated cases. Heroic ancestors and their *exempla virtutis* are most often icons of a golden age of virtue, power, wisdom, faith and creativity, revealed through the epics, art and chronicles of the distant past. Well-known Western examples include Periclean Athens, Davidic Israel, the Roman Republic, Elizabethan England and the *grand siècle* in France. These are golden ages with some historical basis, albeit much embellished. In other cases, we are in the realm of legend, as with the Norse Edda, the heroes of Troy and the ancient Germanic or Finnish heroes, though for artists of all kinds these latter constituted just as promising a field for the uses of evocation and characterization. For it was in the characterization of past epochs, and the evocation of their distinctive atmospheres, that artists, and especially composers, found fertile terrain for their imaginative powers and skills of depiction, above all in the genres of opera, symphonic poem and cantata. Grand opera, with its emphasis on spectacle and its social cachet, was a perfect vehicle for these themes and for the vernacular mobilization of citizens at a cultural level, while cantata was a phenomenon of the patriotic choral movements, especially in Germany and England.

As far as most artists were concerned, the line between legend and history was blurred, and authenticity, a central ideal of nationalism and its devotees, was often interpreted to mean poetic truth rather than historical veracity. What mattered to nationalists, including certain composers, was that each nation should possess its own trajectory and destiny, and hence a set of memories, myths and traditions which witness to and illuminate its past. For Jean Sibelius, for example, the primeval myths of the *Kalevala* not only recalled a distant epoch of Finnish heroism, but defined for Finns their lineage, telling them who

[1] Renan, *Qu'est-ce qu'une nation?*; in Hutchinson and Smith, *Nationalism*, p. 17.
[2] Ibid., p. 19.

they were, where they lived and what their essential qualities were, through the character of specifically Finnish heroes and the northern landscape of lakes and forests. For Grieg, likewise, it was the legends of the Norwegian mountains and fjords and the exploits of Norwegian kings that shaped the Norwegian nation, while for Smetana, the Czech past encompassed both legend and history, locating the community in a specific time and place. In all these cases, it is the most distant past that is most evocative, for it is more unsullied and less assailable by historical research; here the artistic imagination can have freer rein.

Today's musical audiences are aware of only a fraction of these repertoires. Rossini's *Guillaume Tell* (1829), on the subject of a patriotic freedom fighter and set in a sublime homeland landscape (Fig. 4.1), is an early example, even though the composer was Italian, the hero Swiss, the librettists and audience French and the original author of the story (Friedrich Schiller) German. Today the overture is hackneyed, but the complete opera is seldom revived. In France, direct realizations of nationalist themes, such as Auguste Mermet's *Roland à Roncevaux* (1864) and *Jean d'Arc* (1876), did not remain repertoire works, any more than, say, George Macfarren's *Robin Hood* (1860) in England. In Germany, Wagner's *Tannhäuser*, *Lohengrin* and *Der Ring des Nibelungen* are the obvious instances from today's perspective, but in their day they shared their mythological subject matter with lesser-known works recently explored by Barbara Eichner such as Heinrich Dorn's *Die Nibelungen* (1854) and Carl Armand Mangold's *Gudrun* (1851). The historical Hermann (Arminius) and his defeat of the Roman legions was the subject for Carl Heinrich Hofmann's *Armin* (1877) and Grammann's *Thusnelda* (1881). By the same token, the well-known symphonic poems by Smetana and Sibelius coexisted with works such as Siegmund von Haussegger's *Barbarossa* (1900) and Lyadov's *Baba Yaga* (1905), *Kikimora* (1909) and *The Enchanted Lake* (1909). Amongst cantatas, along with Elgar's *Caractacus* (1989) and Prokofiev's *Alexander Nevsky* (1939), no fewer than fifteen oratorios on St Boniface and nine on Luther were composed in late nineteenth-century Germany, along with many cantatas and shorter choral pieces on the theme of Hermann.[3]

In this chapter we investigate the more familiar contributions of Smetana, Sibelius, Mussorgsky, Wagner and Verdi. What emerges here is a diversity of creative vision. These artistically outstanding individuals drew deeply on the symbolic worlds of cultural nationalism of their respective countries but realized them in elaborate, original and highly personal ways, reflecting their own philosophy and aesthetic outlook.

---

[3] Eichner, *History in Mighty Sounds*, ch. 1, ch. 2, pp. 253–72, 164–81.

Fig. 4.1 Scene from *Guillaume Tell* by Gioachino Rossini (1792–1868), engraved by Zincke (coloured engraving), Johann Christian Schoeller (1782–1851) (after)

## Czech history and legend

Smetana's grand and ceremonial fourth opera, *Libuše* (completed 1872, premiered 1881), was in some ways unprecedented in the history of opera: a tribute to the greatness of the Czech nation comprising scenes from Czech legend with the character of a pageant as much as a drama. Smetana thought that *Libuše* made him the 'creator of a new kind of Czech music' and that it was a work of 'unique importance in our history and literature'. '*Libuše* is not an opera of the old type, but a festive tableau – a form of musical and dramatic sustenance.'[4] The libretto is based largely on the account of the early history of the Bohemian state in the eleventh-century *Chronicon Bohemorum* by Cosmas, Canon of Prague, which describes Queen Libuše's reign, a dispute between a pair of noble brothers, Libuše's choice of the farmer Přemysl as her husband and the founding of the city

---

[4] Letters of 20 December 1880 and 17 August 1883, cited in Large, *Smetana*, pp. 215, 212.

of Prague and the first Czech royal dynasty, the Přemyslids. A number of earlier operas had used the story or at least the character of the prophetess queen, by German and Italian composers as well as Bohemian, but Smetana was the first to 'nationalize' the legend for the stage, investing it with symbolic and ritual significance. The opera has a direct contemporary significance too, for the quarrel of the two brothers echoes the modern political disputes of the old and young Czech parties (see Chapter 6), and offers a scene of reconciliation.[5]

The core message of the work is conveyed only at the end of Act III after the dramatic action is complete and Libuše's marriage has taken place. In a dramatic monologue, Libuše has a series of visions of future Czech history, the glory and tragedy of the nation, its heroes and monarchs, the Hussite warriors and the royal castle of Prague. Some of the material for the opera grew out of music Smetana wrote in 1869 on the subject of Libuše's judgement for a fund-raising concert of *tableaux vivants* and poetry reading to support the completion of St Vitus's Cathedral in Prague, which had stood unfinished since the fifteenth century. In the opera, the visual illustrations and Libuše's noble declamation and occasional static poses distinctly recall these origins.[6] In the three preceding acts there are a few traditional operatic situations and some lyrical vocal writing, but throughout Smetana relies heavily on a declamatory vocal idiom, sustained static harmony, cumulative effects, diatonic harmony and stately tempi to convey a sense of formality and monumentality. One of his main musical sources was Wagner's *Die Meistersinger*, the grand prelude of which was a model for Smetana's orchestral introduction, in its key, C major, its ceremonial character and the way its themes are combined simultaneously in polyphonic textures. The antiphonal effects in Smetana's choruses recall *Die Meistersinger* too, while Libuše's prophecy of devastation as well as survival and triumph for the Czechs echoes Hans Sachs's warning about the fate of Germany in the festival meadow scene. However, in *Libuše* there is much greater emphasis on the outward images of nationhood – dynasty, capital city, heroic action – as captured in myth and legend than in Wagner's aestheticizing vision.[7]

Smetana conceived *Libuše* as a tribute to the Czech nation and wanted it reserved for the celebration of great national occasions. At first he hoped it would be played at the coronation of the Emperor Franz Joseph as King of Bohemia, and when the Emperor refused the Czech crown, he withheld it for nine years until the long-delayed opening of the National Theatre in Prague in 1881. After the destruction of the new theatre by fire only a few weeks later, the reopening in 1883 was also celebrated with *Libuše*. The spacious stage and modern technology available at the National Theatre were especially suitable for the production of the opera.[8]

---

[5] Ibid., pp. 218–19; Tyrrell, *Czech Opera*, pp. 3–4, 140–3.

[6] Large, *Smetana*, pp. 211–12.

[7] Clapham, *Smetana*, pp. 100–1; Large, *Smetana*, pp. 224–9.

[8] Large, *Smetana*, p. 220.

Soon after the completion of *Libuše*, Smetana began his cycle of symphonic poems *Má Vlast* (see Chapter 3), and the opera sets the tone for the orchestral work: ceremonial, heroic, pastoral, pictorial and a deliberate mixture of legend and documented history. The music for the fourth tableau in Libuše's vision is the Hussite chorale, the rhythm of which persists until the end of the opera, and which Smetana used again in the two concluding movements of *Má Vlast*: *Tábor* and *Blaník*. The 'Vyšehrad' motif from *Má Vlast* is also anticipated in *Libuše*, and with the same meaning. *Má Vlast* was not intended to offer a historical survey of the Czech lands, but it represented the spirit of creativity and resistance in Czech history. Smetana was close to such Czech nationalists as Palacky and Rieger, and intended his operas, including the tragic and heroic *Dalibor* and the comic *Prodaná nevěsta* (*The Bartered Bride*) as well as *Libuše*, and his great symphonic cycle as a musical contribution to the spirit of his people in their struggle for autonomy. In achieving these goals, he laid the foundations for a Czech school of national composition, not only through his choice of subject matter, but by investing his music with a network of recognizable national symbolism which resonated with his contemporaries and his successors.[9] Since World War II, the annual performance of *Má Vlast* at the opening night of the Prague Spring Festival has cemented its position as the central work of Czech national music.

## The land of heroes

Given the renewed oppression of minorities and nations under Tsar Alexander III (1881–94) and his successor, Nikolas II (1894–1917), it is little wonder that the Finns resorted to a cultural nationalism which took the form, as we saw in the last chapter, of the 'Karelianist' movement in the arts and in lifestyles. At the centre of this movement was the return to a golden age of Finnish culture, as portrayed in the *Kalevala*, the Land of Heroes. This collection of Karelian ballads by Elias Lönnrot (1835, expanded version 1849) experienced a renewed popularity and was treated as ancient Finnish history as much as legend, and later came to be taught as such in Finland's schools.[10]

Musically, episodes in the *Kalevala* had been treated before Sibelius, notably by Filip von Schantz in 1860 and by Robert Kajanus's symphonic poem *Aino* in 1885. Sibelius, however, looked deeper into the character of the epic, having met the Karelian runic singer Larin Paraske, whose inflections and rhythms he carefully noted down. This was not an isolated episode. It must be seen in the context of Sibelius's move away from his former dependence on his Swedish mentor Martin Wegelius, who had adopted a more academic approach to musical composition and teaching, towards Kajanus's more popular approach and his embrace of Finnish culture, and was summed up by Sibelius's statement: 'I see the

[9] Beckerman, 'In Search of Czechness in Music'.
[10] Lauri Honko, 'The *Kalevala* Process'.

pure Finnish elements less realistically than before but, I think, more truthfully.' However, it was during his sojourn in Vienna in 1891–92 that Sibelius addressed the tales of the *Kalevala*, selecting from them the tragic story of Kullervo, which he fashioned into a 'symphonic poem' with chorus, and which received its first performance in Helsinki in 1892. The performance proved to be a great national occasion and a resounding success. It became part of the emerging national myth, arousing, and fulfilling, high national expectations. The critic Oskar Merikanto wrote of it: 'We know these [melodies] as our own, even if we have never heard them as such.'[11] In the same vein, Juho Ranta, a choir member at the premiere on 28 April 1892, remarked: 'Although at a conscious level, I did not hear in the music any fragments of familiar pieces, it was still like something that I had known for a long time and heard before. It was *Finnish* music.'

The tale of Kullervo, as recounted in the *Kalevala*, starts with the hero's clan supposedly being wiped out by his uncle Untamo, and Kullervo sold into slavery as a herdsman to the smith Ilmarinen, from whom he eventually escapes back to his parents. Sent to town to pay the taxes, on his way home Kullervo enters the forest where he attempts to seduce various girls, the last of whom he rapes. But she subsequently turns out, to his consternation, to be his long-lost sister (in the epic she drowns herself). Later, Kullervo goes to war with Untamo and, with the aid of a mighty sword given to him by Ukko, king of the gods, he in turn wipes out Untamo's clan. But, on his return home, he finds his family has died, and he wanders off into the forest. Chancing on the very spot where he raped his sister, Kullervo is consumed by guilt and falls on his sword.

Sibelius's *Kullervo* focuses on the psychological aspect of the tale, the hero's act of rape, incest and ensuing guilt – themes that Glena Dawn Goss traces to the influence of its milieu of composition, *fin-de-siècle* Vienna, and of literary works of erotic realism.[12] The first two movements of this five-part symphony, the *Introduction* and *Kullervo's Youth*, do not follow the storyline, but contrast a more pastoral mode with 'runic style' music, especially in the slow movement's lullaby. It is in the long third movement, *Kullervo and his Sister*, that Sibelius follows the text of the epic and inserts a men's choir to recount Kullervo's journey home through the forest and his encounters with the maidens, whom he attempts to seduce. The climax of this movement is the rape scene, followed by his discovery that the young woman is his sister: this leads to her impassioned recitation, and Kullervo's lament. The fourth movement, *Kullervo goes to War*, a vigorous scherzo *alla marcia*, again departs from the story of the epic, only for choir and orchestra in the final movement, *Kullervo's Death*, to recount Kullervo's chancing on the scene of the rape, his consuming guilt and

---

[11] Matti Huttunen, 'The National Composer and the Idea of Finnishness: Sibelius and the Formation of Finnish Musical Style', in Grimley (ed.), *The Cambridge Companion to Sibelius*, p. 8.

[12] Glenda Dawn Goss, 'Vienna and the Genesis of *Kullervo*: "Durchführung zum Teufel!"', in Grimley (ed.), *The Cambridge Companion to Sibelius*, pp. 22–31.

his self-inflicted death, in music of great cumulative power and inexorable intensity.

In one sense, *Kullervo* was unique in Sibelius's œuvre. Neither a choral symphony nor a symphonic poem, it combined Karelian nationalism with a vivid erotic realism. In another sense, *Kullervo* stood at the head of a succession of Sibelius's symphonic poems, several of whose subjects were drawn from the *Kalevala*. The first, *En Saga* (1892), is part of Sibelius's folkloristic 'Karelian' phase, but it is a generalized tragic-heroic poem, evoking rather than describing the atmosphere of the shamanistic world of the *Kalevala*. To this folkloristic category we must assign the heroic *Karelia Suite* (1893), whose subsequent popularity should not obscure its political origins in a series of national *tableaux vivants* composed for the feast of the Viipuri students' union's campaign to support public education in the region, when it played to a relatively small group of academics. The *Four Lemminkäinen Legends* (1896, subsequently revised) are another fruitful encounter with the legends of the *Kalevela*. If the shamanistic sage Väinämöinen was the presiding spirit of the epic, it was his younger counterpart, Lemminkäinen, a kind of Finnish Achilles who, through his handsome appearance, reckless daring and roguish playfulness, had the greatest popular appeal. The four legends follow the hero's adventures, starting with *Lemminkäinen and the Maidens of the Island* (1895–96) which charts the encounter of the vigorous male hero with seductive virgins of the island, and evokes the irrational, supernatural mood of a midsummer's night, a topos that appealed to many Nordic artists, ending in a glow of self-confidence. This is immediately followed by the slowly unfolding opening A minor chord of *The Swan of Tuonela* (1896, revised 1900) which suggests the dark, vast space of the Finnish underworld. Its haunting cor anglais melody vividly evokes the primordial antiquity of the Finnish epic. *Lemminkäinen in Tuonela* (revised 1935) evokes the hero's ill-fated journey to the dark waters of the Finnish underworld, where he attempts to slay the Swan but is himself slain, and has to be reconstituted, bone by bone, by his lamenting mother. Finally, *Lemminkäinen's Return* (1896, revised 1900) inverts the tragic sequence, to end in a triumphant affirmation of the male hero in an E flat major chorale.[13]

A further attempt to evoke the heroic but dark world of the *Kalevala* produced the symphonic poem *Pohjola's Daughter* (1905–6). Based on Canto 8 of the epic, it describes the efforts of the ancient seer Väinämöinen, the true subject of the poem, to win the hand of the daughter of the north by completing impossible tasks for her, and Sibelius's use of birdsong in the woodwind cadenzas anchors the poem in a Finnish landscape. But, in contrast to the text,

---

[13] Daniel M. Grimley, 'The Tone Poems: Genre, Landscape and Structural Perspective', in Grimley (ed.), *The Cambridge Companion to Sibelius*, pp. 96–9, 101–2; Stephen Downes, 'Pastoral Idylls, Erotic Anxieties and Heroic Subjectivities in Sibelius' *Lemminkäinen and the Maidens of the Island* and First Two Symphonies', in Grimley (ed.), *The Cambridge Companion to Sibelius*, pp. 35–7.

there is no triumphant conclusion, only a sense of desolation. This is a highly symphonic work in which two attempts to establish a secure harmonic centre are undermined, and the music drifts into nothingness. Sibelius returned to the *Kalevala* with his symphonic poem with voice, the enigmatic *Luonnotar* (1913). The text, taken from the first Canto, describes the creation of the world from the pieces of a gull's egg which fell from the knee of the female nature spirit, floating in the waves of a primeval ocean. The music illustrates the birth pangs of the nature spirit in three strophes, with the voice ascending at the end to describe the creation of the stars in the night sky. Sibelius's final *Kalevala*-inspired symphonic poem is the bleak and hair-raising *Tapiola* (1926), which describes in general terms the Finnish forest wilderness, home to the forest god, Tapio.[14]

If his later tone poems take us into the depths of the ancient Finnish world and landscape, and even beyond, Sibelius's most famous work, *Finlandia* (revised 1901), brings us back to the earthly realm of contemporary politics. Conceived at the height of Finnish political agitation against Russian rule as 'Finland awakens', this was the last of six chronological *tableaux*, starting in the 'dark days' of the early nineteenth century and concluding with the broad melody of the hymn of awakening. The music describes this progress, with a minor mode introduction alluding to the powers of darkness, then goes on to illustrate the age of awakening through the educators of the nation, epitomized by the rat-a-tat volleys of rhythm and the call to awaken, before moving ultimately to an episode symbolizing the moment of Finnish self-realization in its own history, language, poetry, education and industrial progress, the latter embodied in the motif of the locomotive. This in turn leads into the hymn which reveals the now triumphant spirit of the Finnish nation, with the past disclosing that spirit in present time. The fact that Sibelius may have taken some of the opening phrases of this hymn from a choral patriotic piece of the 1880s by a Finnish composer, Emil Genetz, only serves to reinforce its national – in this case, national*ist* – connotations. Similarly, the revised 'long' conclusion of the work reveals the full hymn as the bearer of national identity. Here, it is the Finnish people who constitute the hero, a people emerging from and through their history into modernity, in ways analogous to the Hungarians in Liszt's *Hungaria*, the Russians in Balakirev's *Russia* and the Czechs in Smetana's *Má Vlast* – hence the publisher's preferred title, *Finlandia*.[15]

---

[14] Grimley, 'The Tone Poems', pp. 103–5, 111–13.

[15] James A. Hepokoski, '*Finlandia* Awakens', in Grimley (ed.), *The Cambridge Companion to Sibelius*, pp. 81–94.

## A flawed hero

But were other peoples such as the Russians similarly forged, at least musically? Borodin's opera *Prince Igor* (1869–87, unfinished) sets an adaptation by Vladimir Stasov of the medieval *Lay of Igor's Campaign*, telling of the struggle between the Kievan Rus and the nomadic eastern tribe of the Polovtsii. Against *kuchka* theoretical principles, Borodin conceived the work as a traditional grand opera based around set pieces such as choruses, tableaux and arias, giving plentiful opportunity for representation of the people. The original story – a tale of defeat – was transformed by Stasov into triumphalist propaganda for Russia's contemporary eastern campaigns. Stasov and Borodin modelled the opera on Glinka's *Ruslan and Lyudmila*, and the music closely follows its stylistic opposition of Russia and Orient.[16] On the other hand, in 1242, the year of the battle on the ice of Lake Peipus, a Russian army stopped the invading Teutonic Knights, to form the subject of Sergei Prokofiev's dramatic music for Eisenstein's anti-Nazi propaganda film, *Alexander Nevsky* (1938). And as we shall see, the Russians of Pskov emerged as the people in Rimsky-Korsakov's *Pskovityanka* (*The Maid of Pskov*; 1868–72) based on a play by Lev Alexandrovich Mey which recounted the tale of Ivan the Terrible's conquest of Novgorod and Pskov in the 1560s. Nevertheless, for all the involvement of 'the people', these are all tales of kings and aristocrats, and it is they who represent a sense of Russian nationhood.

The same is ultimately the case with Mussorgsky's two great historical operas, *Boris Godunov* and *Khovanshchina*. And it could hardly have been otherwise, for anyone concerned with portraying Russian history authentically, as Mussorgsky was committed to doing. Though his mentor Vladimir Stasov continually urged him to produce a progressive drama of the people, Mussorgsky remained obstinately deaf. For the most part, the people, for him, did not constitute the motor force of history. This is not to say that they are absent from his operas. They appear prominently in the first scene of the first version of *Boris Godunov* (1869), and they give the 'Slava' salute for Boris, but they are revealed as stupid and uninterested in larger events – in this the composer is faithful to the aristocrat Pushkin's text. Mussorgsky himself is more interested in individual members of the people, like Missail and Varlaam, rather than the people as such, in line with the realism he had displayed in his unfinished project on Gogol's *The Marriage*. Even the *Yurodiviy* (the Holy Fool) who accosts and accuses Boris, stands, as Richard Taruskin demonstrates, outside the people.[17]

Mussorgsky based his opera on Pushkin's tragedy of 1825, which was itself indebted to Nicolai Karamzin's great *History of the Russian State* (1818 onwards). For the Romantic Karamzin, Boris's guilt for his crime was the focal point of his reign; and while Pushkin's attitude was more ambiguous, it too formed the pivot of his drama, since that guilt could be, and was, used by others like the Pretender

---

[16] Maes, *A History of Russian Music*, pp. 182–4.

[17] Taruskin, *Defining Russia Musically*, pp. 75–80.

Dmitri (Grigori Otrepev). In fact, there is no evidence that Boris murdered Ivan the Terrible's other son, the boy Dmitri, in Uglich in 1591, and he is unlikely to have felt any guilt if he had done so. But, from the time of the *Smuta* (the anarchic 'Time of Troubles', 1605–13), the story of Boris's guilt became a part of European literature right up to Schiller's fragment *Demetrius* (1805). According to the historical record, Boris Godunov, the brother-in-law and adviser of the reigning son of Ivan the Terrible, Fyodor (1584–98), was crowned Tsar on Fyodor's death and by all accounts he acquitted himself well. However, from 1601 unusual cold, floods and famine brought great suffering to the populace, who blamed the tsar. So, when an ex-monk called Grigori Otrepev fled to Poland and pretended to be the boy Dmitri, he was able to raise an army with Polish support, advance on Moscow and seize the crown after Boris's death in 1605. Mussorgsky followed Pushkin's tragedy closely, but he made Boris and his guilt the focus of his opera. Hence the first version of *Boris Godunov* (1869–72) is a drama about a flawed hero of Russian history, one in which the people play only a background role.[18]

This first version was rejected by the directorate of the Imperial Theatres, mainly because it had no female role, and Mussorgsky immediately and enthusiastically revised it (1872–74), as Richard Taruskin shows in his exposition of the differences between the two versions of the opera. Not only did Mussorgsky introduce a new 'Polish' act with a scheming Polish princess, he added more scenes and gave the people a greater role. In many ways, this second version was more traditional, owing something to Verdi's methods of composition in large blocks, but it retained the focal point of Boris's guilt, and hence the centrality of the scene in the Terem (tsar's private apartments) in the Kremlin, in which Boris, haunted by guilt, has a vision of the murdered child, Dmitri. Essentially, then, Mussorgsky stayed close to the traditional statist history of Karamzin, a history of tsars, boyars and the Church, though shorn of any romanticism of 'love'. There is one exception, and it is a crucial one: the last scene of this second version takes place in the forest near Kromy, and it replaces the St Basil scene. Here we see the people in action, changing their allegiance from Tsar Boris to the imposter Grigori, the false Dmitri. There is some historical justification for this, as bands of hungry serfs roamed the countryside to escape the famine, which they attributed to the hated Muscovite regime, a circumstance central to the more populist writings of Mussorgsky's contemporary, Nikolai Kostomarov. But for the composer there was another source of influence for this scene: the example, mentioned above, of Rimsky-Korsakov's opera, *Pskovityanka*. In the republican *veche* scene in Pskov, the citizens' assembly called to decide how to deal with the military threat from Ivan the Terrible, Rimsky-Korsakov demonstrated how the people could be more than a mere commentator; they could be shown individually, and almost chaotically, discussing the alternatives, with the orchestra providing the continuity. This was an example

[18] Maes, *A History of Russian Music*, pp. 101–7; Taruskin, *Musorgsky*, pp. 244–9.

not lost on Mussorgsky, who, in the final Kromy scene, appears to suggest that the people could decide the fate of rulers. This provides the ground for chaotic declamations by the chorus and the use of folksongs, as when the people mock the boyar Kruschov or in the song of Varlaam and Missail. However, theirs is not the last word. Before the curtain falls, the *Yurodiviy* makes a final pathetic lament for poor, suffering Russia, as if to suggest the futility of all political action.[19]

## A 'national musical drama'

The futility of politics, indeed of all purposive action, is central to Mussorgsky's second, and unfinished, opera, *Khovanshchina* (1874–81, completed by Rimsky-Korsakov). The events of the drama are rooted in well-documented episodes of late seventeenth-century Russian history, which Mussorgsky researched diligently, intermittently reporting the progress of his research to Stasov and others. This period of Russian history was also a Time of Troubles, and one that was even more complex and chaotic than the earlier *Smuta*. It began in 1666, when the Patriarch Nikon sought to return Russian Orthodox ritual and practice to its Greek (Byzantine) origins. This provoked a massive schism in the Church, with the Old (or 'True') Believers seceding and forming their own religious communities, often in the forests. The state reacted with violence; Tsar Alexei (1645–76), and after him his daughter, the Regent Sophia (1682–89), sent out search parties to destroy these communities, who often preferred death by self-immolation in the forests. The year 1682 was one of crisis over the succession. Tsar Fyodor III (1676–82) had just died and there was rivalry between the clans of Tsar Alexei's two wives. In Moscow, where most of the opera's action takes place, Prince Golitsyn, chief minister to Sophia, was seeking to introduce Western-style reforms. He was opposed both by the Old Believers and by the rowdy Streltsii guards (or musketeers), under the protection of Prince Ivan Khovansky. The latter had at first backed the ten-year-old Peter (the future Peter the Great), but then supported Sophia as Regent for the two half-brothers, Peter and the sickly adolescent Ivan V. At least twice, in 1689 and 1698, the Streltsii musketeers rose in rebellion, and they had ultimately to be put down and disbanded by Peter, before he could begin to inaugurate his great reforms of the Russian state.[20]

For Mussorgsky, this proved a fertile period for exploring competing factions and conceptions in 'Old Russia'. It was also highly topical, since the year 1872 was the bicentenary of Peter's birth; for the tsarist state and many of the intelligentsia

---

[19] Maes, *A History of Russian Music*, pp. 107–15; Caryl Emerson, *The Life of Musorgsky* (Cambridge: Cambridge University Press, 1999), pp. 83–8; Taruskin, *Musorgsky*, pp. 249–80.

[20] Maes, *A History of Russian Music*, pp. 118–19; Nicolas Riasanovsky, *A History of Russia* (Oxford: Oxford University Press, 1963), pp. 235–8.

this was a moment for celebration of the progress of Russia, both nationally and on the international stage, with many a eulogy for Peter and the Petrine Russian state. However, such a view had no appeal for Mussorgsky, who did not share the intellectuals' belief in progress. While rejecting nihilism, Mussorgsky's assessment of Russia's development was essentially pessimistic. In an intoxicated letter to Stasov, which combines a populist Russian primitivism with a dour, despairing pessimism, he speaks of trying to plough the 'unfertilized, virgin earth' of Russia, but in a very different way from the westernizers and the 'alien materials' of their tools, repeating time and again that, despite technical and material 'progress', the people 'haven't moved'.[21]

The plot of *Khovanshchina*, such as it is, would appear to illustrate and confirm this overall message. It is a tale of intrigue, denunciation and violence within historical time, ending in a world of faith outside time. Act II reveals a conference between the main protagonists, Prince Golitsyn, Prince Ivan Khovansky and the Old Believer leader, Dosifei, each insisting on their high status, each speaking for Russia. By Act IV we see Golitsyn being sent into exile, and Khovansky assassinated in his own palace, after the Streltsii musketeers had risen in rebellion, only to be abandoned by their leader Khovansky. Meanwhile, the prophetess Marfa, who is an Old Believer, seeks to save her lover, Khovansky's son, Prince Andrei, but under the guidance of Dosifei (a figure modelled in part on the Old Believer, Archpriest Avvakum, who was martyred in 1682), she ultimately leads him to the hermitage in the forest where they will all perish in the purifying flames.

Can we call this a 'people's drama'? As Taruskin emphasizes, the protagonists are all aristocrats, even Dosifei; their quarrels are about their own dignity and status, whatever their professions of concern for the fate of Russia. On the other hand, Mussorgsky consulted priests and folklorists for the Old Believer chants, writing to Stasov in July 1873: 'I am gathering folk-honey from all quarters, to make the honeycomb tastier and *more like itself*, because, after all, this is a people's drama.'[22] But what meaning is to be attributed to the phrase 'people's drama', or, for that matter, to Mussorgsky's subtitle to *Khovanshchina, narodnaya muzikal'naya drama*? Does this signify a drama of the people (a popular drama) or a national drama (a musical drama of the nation)? In this case, the context was Mussorgsky's interest in Old Believer chants, but the latter constitute only one part, albeit a vital part for the composer, of his panoramic historical drama, and a part that passes out of 'history' into a world of faith through self-immolation. At the end of the opera, nobody is left alive, and Peter is nowhere to be seen. In this respect, Rimsky-Korsakov's theatrical finale with the advancing trumpets of Peter's troops, while it no doubt reflects the optimism of the 'progressive' Russian

---

[21] Emerson, *The Life of Musorgsky*, p. 100, italics in original; Taruskin, *Musorgsky*, p. 314.

[22] Cited in Emerson, *The Life of Musorgsky*, p. 102, italics in original; Taruskin, *Musorgsky*, p. 323.

state and the forward-looking intelligentsia, is surely misleading and completely at variance with the opera's and the composer's overall pessimism.[23]

There is no doubt that Mussorgsky was deeply interested in Russian history and destiny. 'History is my nocturnal friend, it brings me pleasure and intoxication,' he wrote to Stasov in September 1873.[24] He compiled a considerable list of books and articles for his research on late seventeenth-century Russia, and his operas are rooted in the documents, hymns, rituals and practices of the period. Allied to this fascination was his commitment to authenticity, a commitment that made it impossible for him to embrace the current progressive vision of Russia and its Petrine past. Authenticity, as we have seen, is a hallmark of modern nationalism, the gold standard of culture and politics, and the touchstone of everything national. In this respect, Mussorgsky not only reflected, but contributed to, the growth of nationalism in late nineteenth-century Russia, even more perhaps than Sibelius's contribution to Finnish nationalism. Then there is the question of heroism, or rather lack of it. None of the political leaders in *Khovanshchina* achieve their goals, or transform the course of history. Even Dosifei, the admired leader of the Old Believers, and the closest to a hero, can only lead his followers beyond history and politics. Marfa, too, a heroine in the making, only consummates her passions in self-inflicted death. It would appear that in *Khovanshchina* there are only anti-heroes from whom we, in this world, have nothing to learn.

Finally, there is the question of folk music in Mussorgsky's operas. The real hero of these music dramas is Mother Russia, an almost timeless construct, composed of the Russian people, Russian landscape and Russian traditions, from whom all aliens and alien influences are to be excluded. This helps to account for Mussorgsky's use of folk music, as in the Kromy scene in *Boris Godunov*, and the folk-derived music in the Old Believer chants and the Streltsii prayers in *Khovanshchina*. But, by the time of his last opera, Mussorgsky had abandoned his earlier realism, instead substituting sinuous melodic lines of an increasingly abstract character – the prime example being Marfa's memorable divination scene, when she predicts Golitsyn's downfall and exile. This is in line with Mussorgsky's growing pessimism, which distanced him from Stasov's popular progressivism and encouraged him to embrace an aristocratic conservatism in line with his family background, at a time of increasing political reaction and anti-Semitism in Russia.[25]

Unlike the national voices of Sibelius and Smetana, Mussorgsky's evolved from one pole, of realism and even populism, to another, at once more impersonal and traditional, over the course of a few years. On the other hand, like those of

---

[23] Emerson, *The Life of Musorgsky*, pp. 17–20; Taruskin, *Musorgsky*, pp. 222–3.

[24] Rosamund Bartlett, '"Khovanshchina" in Context', in Batchelor and John (eds), *Khovanshchina*, p. 36.

[25] Gerard McBurney, 'Musorgsky's New Music', in Batchelor and John (eds), *Khovanshchina*, pp. 21–9.

Sibelius and Smetana, Mussorgsky's national voice is always a distinctly personal one. In each case, their personal voices have formed an immediately recognizable national music, with folk-derived elements being transmuted into this personal musical nationalism in line with their vision of the nature and history of their national communities.

## Wagner and German myth

Wagner's colossal music-dramatic projects based on German legends of the medieval era (*Lohengrin, Tannhäuser, Parsifal*) and ancient Germanic myth (*Der Ring des Nibelungen*) were the culmination of the German Romantics' engagement with myth first at a theoretical level and then in practical research. Already in the late eighteenth century, Herder and others had developed the idea of myth as a fusion of poetry and religion that embodied the spirit of a nation and underpinned its literature, religion and customs. In the 1790s the Jena Romantics such as the Schlegel brothers and F. W. J. Schelling called for a 'new mythology' that would overcome the problems of modern culture – the alienation of the individual and the fragmentation and over-rationalization of society – and would help to effect social transformation. Biblical and classical mythologies would be replaced by new symbols and stories that would fuse art and religion and provide the basis for a renewed public life. Schelling thought that this mythology would be the work of an entire people represented by a single poet, as was the case with Homer. He envisaged a new liturgy in the form of rituals and festivals for the people, freeing art from the traditional patronage of court, state, Church and literary market.[26] Wagner revived all these ideas in his music dramas and his writings in what, by the 1840s, were anti-Romantic intellectual times in the universities and public life. In Wagner, myth provides a commentary on political issues of the day: capitalism, industrialization and revolution, Wagner himself having played a part in the latter during the 1849 Dresden uprising. In the writings he undertook while in exile in Zürich after that failed revolution (*Die Kunst und die Revolution*, 1849, *Das Kunstwerk der Zukunft*, 1851, *Oper und Drama*, 1851), Wagner explained his hopes for a regeneration of German culture through an art for the people that would also embody the people's own creativity through the medium of the artist. This art would be guided by human truths and spiritual ideas rather than entertainment or the profit motive. A great summer festival would accomplish the grand historical task of the renewal of art and human culture. What eventually emerged as the Bayreuth Festival reflects these updated Romantic concerns with its ritualistic performance practices and

---

[26] George S. Williamson, *The Longing for Myth in Germany: Religion and Aesthetic Culture from Romanticism to Nietzsche* (Chicago: University of Chicago Press, 2004), pp. 1–13.

amphitheatre-like auditorium, although in practice it rapidly became the preserve of social elites as much as any other opera house.

The period of the French Revolutionary state and the Napoleonic Wars prompted German scholars and writers to search for a specifically national mythology to anchor the newly emerging German national sentiment. This movement was centred on Berlin, at first while under French occupation. In his lectures there, A. W. Schlegel idealized the medieval era for its spirit of chivalry and heroism, and its paternalistic concern for the weak. The Berlin Romantics interested themselves also in the pagan customs of the ancient Germans. They argued that a Germanic religion had been displaced and demolished by Christianity, which they compared implicitly to a foreign power. Although the evidence for a systematic early German religion or a liturgy was distinctly patchy, scholars such as the Grimm brothers aimed to reconstruct it through the interpretation of legends, medieval epics and contemporary folklore. Herder, after all, had argued for the intrinsic connection between art, religion and customs of people of the past. In *Die teutschen Volksbücher* (1807) Joseph Goerres published popular stories from the sixteenth century that, he claimed, formed the written memories of a mythical system. Friedrich de la Motte Fouqué's Wagnerian-sounding *Sigurd, der Schlangentödter* (1808) was the first drama of a trilogy entitled *Der Held des Nordens*. The bleak and bloody thirteenth-century *Nibelungenlied*, despite fitting nationalist theories of German character rather poorly, became a focus of national sentiment in occupied Berlin and was published in numerous competing editions. Finally, Jacob Grimm's monumental *Deutsche Mythologie* (1835) set out to codify the religion of the ancient Germanic peoples, from Icelandic myths of the gods to everyday peasant beliefs. By this time, artists had produced paintings, songs and stories on the subject of German legends. In the 1830s King Ludwig I of Bavaria constructed his own 'Walhalla', a monumental shrine to German heroes over the Danube river near Regensburg.[27]

Wagner's approach to his sources paralleled the Romantics in that he combined and mingled them rather freely. In an essay 'Die Wibelungen: Weltgeschichte aus der Sage' (1848) he maintained that myth and history were intertwined in German legends, as later stories and beliefs overwrote older ones in new forms. The original language was sometimes Old Norse rather than German, but for the Romantics these sources described the same ancient Germanic culture. Wagner was a voracious reader in these areas and drew on medieval and modern German literature for the legends of *Tannhäuser*, *Lohengrin* and *Parsifal* and Celtic legend for *Tristan und Isolde*. The more mythic contents, however, are found in the *Ring*. For his tetralogy Wagner raided the Poetic Edda, the Prose Edda and the Volsunga Saga from Iceland; the *Nibelungenlied*, written in Austria but telling of events of a court on the Rhine and moving briefly to Iceland; the *Thidrek Saga* from Norway; and the sixteenth-century *Lied von hürnen Seyfrid*. Wagner knew the Grimm brothers' work on

---

[27] Ibid., ch. 2.

myths and folk tales, and borrowed many of their fairy-tale motifs such as the woman in an enchanted sleep who is awoken by a hero's kiss, and the youth who leaves home to learn fear.[28]

On the face of it, then, the nationalist dimension of Wagner's use of myths and legends seems indisputable. He realizes the programme set out by A. W. Schlegel: 'Those giant shadows, which appear to us as through a fog, must again acquire firm outlines, and the image of early history [*Vorzeit*] must once more be animated by its own unique soul.' In the figure of Siegfried, Wagner portrays the heroic sacrifice of a great ancestor who has undertaken legendary deeds. The message is underlined by the national homeland imagery in *Tannhäuser*, *Die Meistersinger* and the *Ring*, and the use in Wagner's libretti for the *Ring* of pseudo-antique alliterative *Stabreim* that mimics the style of the ancient epic poetry of northern Europe. The early twentieth-century production traditions of helmets, cloaks and swords conveyed this atmosphere unmistakably to a wide public. Turning to a broader context for Wagner's music, his voluminous prose writings carried chauvinistic messages, and in the early 1840s turned overtly nationalist, and again in the 1860s. In the 1870s that aspect receded in Wagner's own writings on account of his disappointment in the new Reich, but after his death it was intensified by his widow Cosima and the Bayreuth circle. Already in the 1870s and 1880s a stream of books on Wagner and the German nation appeared; thereafter Bayreuth kept them coming. Hitler's love of Wagner, his close association with Bayreuth and the Wagner family, and the Nazis' use of Wagner's works during the Third Reich, are infamous.[29]

But against all this must be set the universalizing tendencies of Wagner's use of myth. The *Ring* is full of Germanic motifs, but is organized as a tetralogy on the model of Aeschylus' *Oresteia* (a trilogy plus a satyr play; Wagner put the equivalent of the latter – *Das Rheingold* – first) and reflects Wagner's hopes for a revival of the (supposedly 'universal') spirit of ancient Greece. The idea that Germany was heir to the spirit of Greece was just as much a part of German intellectual culture since the mid eighteenth century as the theory of myth, and related to it in part. The Hellenic revival – specifically aimed at the culture of Periclean Athens – is found also in Wagner's concept of the *Gesamtkunstwerk*, the layout of the Bayreuth *Festspielhaus* auditorium, his hope for the fusion of art and religion, and the web of orchestral leitmotivs in his later music dramas, which arguably take on the role of the Greek chorus. At the same time, the characters and events of the *Ring* embody grand abstractions (love, necessity, redemption) and play out world-philosophical ideas about human destiny borrowed from revolutionary writers of the early nineteenth century, above all Ludwig Feuerbach. Wagner became a disciple of Feuerbach during his revolutionary phase in the late 1840s, and in his Zürich writings, which paved the way for the

---

[28] Rudolph Sabor, *Richard Wagner, Der Ring Des Nibelungen* (London: Phaidon Press, 1997), pp. 78–107.

[29] Salmi, *Imagined Germany*, p. 178.

*Ring*, he couched the Romantic doctrine of the new mythology in the language of Feuerbachian humanism: it would be 'justified by history' and would replace modern Christian society with a 'social religion of the future'. At this stage, in contrast to his position in 'Die Wibelungen', Wagner separated history from myth, finding 'convention' in the former and 'the human' expressed in the latter. Myth was thus on the side of historical 'necessity', which would erase all historically defined cultural formations, states and legal institutions, including, presumably, nations. In this sense Wagner's approach to myth in the Zürich writings was a return to early Romantic thought of the 1790s, according to which the new myth would arise from processes unfolding within modernity, before their ideas were absorbed by the Berlin nationalist movement of the 1800s.[30]

Wagner's prose writings are full of the binary oppositions characteristic of German *völkisch* thinking: idealism/materialism; culture/civilization; ancient/ modern; interpretation/imitation; monarchy/democracy; and national/ cosmopolitan.[31] All of them tend to map onto German/non-German, in which the non-German is often French and sometimes Jewish. In Wagner's art, these binaries appear occasionally, for instance at the end of *Die Meistersinger*. In the *Ring*, the Wälsungs can be regarded as German heroes, and in Act I of *Siegfried* the protagonist is contrasted with the cringing, deceitful Nibelung Mime, possibly an anti-Semitic stereotype. Yet Siegfried also stands for humanity, not just a single nation. The gods have sinned, and the Gibichungs are highly unattractive, yet these figures are all distinctly Germanic too. Moreover, in his use of myths and legends Wagner did not represent an oppressed people on the stage or portray collective uprisings or the people's will to freedom. For Wagner himself, as opposed to his later official advocates, the national significance of his work lay primarily in what he saw as the destiny of Germany to be the carrier of a universal humanist culture. Subsequent critical interpretations of the meaning of the *Ring* cycle have usually been socialist, psychoanalytical or humanist rather than nationalist.

In his musical style, Wagner conveys a mythic atmosphere through leisurely pacing and epic dimensions, and by setting back the narration and events by means of lengthy orchestral preludes and interludes. He does not draw on folk music or archaic idioms to evoke an historical atmosphere. Indeed, Wagner's progressive musical style in the *Ring* – avoidance of set pieces, use of leitmotivs, chromatic harmony – was part of his critique of 'convention' of which his use of mythic subjects was another aspect. One aspect of his style that does point to a uniquely German past is his extensive and innovative use of the brass instruments, including an instrument created by Adolphe Sax to his specification: the 'Wagner tuba'. This was the time when ancient 'lurs' were being discovered in peat bogs across northern Germany and southern Scandinavia, instruments that according to the Icelandic sagas were used in battle. In the

---

[30] Ibid., chs 1 and 3; Williamson, *The Longing for Myth in Germany*, pp. 190–204.

[31] Salmi, *Imagined Germany*, pp. 11–13.

*Ring*, heroism is usually associated with brass instruments, as with the motifs for Siegfried, including his horn call in *Siegfried* and its noble transformation in *Götterdämmerung* for an entire choir of horns, the sword Nothung (a trumpet arpeggio), the Wälsungs (a stately and melancholy fanfare), Valhalla (initially played by a choir of Wagner tubas) and the Valkyries. In fact, the brass instruments, both loud and soft, colour the whole cycle, from the sustained notes in the horns in the Prelude to *Das Rheingold* to the representation of dawn over the Rhine in the interlude between Scenes 1 and 2 of Act II of *Götterdämmerung*.

## Viva Verdi, viva Italia

For the Czechs, the Finns and the Russians, the national community, whatever the social and political problems, was at least an identifiable and relatively united ethno-cultural division of humanity. For nineteenth-century Italians this was a much more doubtful proposition. Granted, Virgil and Horace had sung the praises of 'Italia' and for nearly half a millennium thereafter the peninsula had been united under Roman rule. But that was far in the past. Dante's Italy was a political mosaic, and at most a cultural and linguistic concept of *italianita* (based on the Tuscan language); and Machiavelli's lone call to expel the foreign invaders went unheeded. By the nineteenth century, Italy was divided into papal states, the Kingdom of Naples in the south, and northern duchies under Habsburg Austrian suzerainty. Through the medieval, Renaissance and *ancien régime* periods, the several regions of Italy had run their individual historical courses, and evolved separate cultures and dialects, notably in Venice. True, these entrenched historical developments had mattered little to Napoleon, whose brief rule presaged a vision, if not the reality, of a united Italy. Nevertheless, despite the strong conservative restoration and reaction after 1815 under the auspices of Metternich's Austria, by the 1830s the small, discontented educated classes, particularly in the North, organized around journals or in secret societies, both in Italy and in exile, fomented considerable, if intermittent, sedition against Austrian and papal rule, with the ultimate aim of creating, albeit in different ways, a united and independent Italian state which would encompass and eventually override the cultural and social cleavages in the peninsula.[32]

This was the background against which Italian bel canto opera flourished, and Verdi's early operas were created. Controversy has raged, and continues to rage, over the degree to which Verdi himself participated in, and more particularly how far his early operas became an icon of the nationalist movement

---

[32] Derek Beales and Eugenio Biaggini, *The Risorgimento and the Unification of Italy*, 2nd edn (London: Pearson, 2002), chs 1–2, 4; Christopher Duggan, *The Force of Destiny: A History of Italy since 1796* (London: Penguin, 2008), ch. 4.

of, the Risorgimento. In the traditional picture, the Risorgimento was the central movement in nineteenth-century Italian politics and society, while Verdi, both as man and composer, was seen as a major symbol and active force in its triumphant course. In contrast to this hagiographic tradition, the revisionist historians bypassed the Risorgimento and its symbols, concentrating instead on analysing the social and economic processes at work in the peninsula, while simultaneously arguing for the greater attractions and popularity of the post-Napoleonic Restoration regimes in Italy. But in recent years, a new 'culturalist' interpretation of nineteenth-century Italian politics has restored the centrality of the Risorgimento. Led by the social and cultural historian Alberto Banti, this new historical movement has sought to explore the cultural canon of literary, artistic and musical works which provided the common fare of the leaders and followers of the Risorgimento through the 'deep images' and emotions of kinship, honour and sacrifice that linked these works with older Christian and aristocratic ideals and virtues. For Banti himself, Italian opera played a crucial role in crystallizing and disseminating these images and emotions, and this was especially true of the early operas of Giuseppe Verdi. Indeed, by 1859, for many educated Italians the letters of Verdi's name came to serve as an acronym for the ruler of Piedmont, Vittorio Emmanuele Re D'Italia, seen by many members of the Risorgimento as the best hope of unifying the peninsula, and who in fact became king of a united Italy in 1861.[33]

But why did Verdi become so closely associated with the Risorgimento? For the hagiographic tradition, this is not a problem. From the beginning of his career, at least since the production of *Nabucco* in 1842, Verdi was recognized as a patriot and his operas as trumpet calls to Italian unity and independence. But for some British historians, Verdi's musical role, whatever his personal national sentiments, was minimal; that is to say, we find little support in his pre-1848 operas for a 'nationalist' Verdi. Roger Parker, in particular, points out that there are no contemporary newspaper or journal reports of audience excitement, let alone mass frenzy, during the early performances of the celebrated chorus in his third opera, *Nabucco* (1842), 'Va, pensiero'; and from this and like silences, he concludes that the image of Verdi the Italian patriot is a much later construction – of the late 1850s, in fact, and even of the late 1870s, in Verdi's sanctioned autobiography dictated to Ricordi. Besides, for Verdi and Solera, his librettist, the quatrains of the chorus of Hebrew slaves in *Nabucco* were integrated with those of the immediately following prophecy of the Jewish leader, Zaccaria, and marked as 'Coro e Profezia' in Verdi's autograph score. As for contemporary audience enthusiasm, this appears to have been reserved for other numbers in *Nabucco*, such as the final hymn, 'Immenso Jehova'. Indeed, some critics

---

[33] Alex Körner and Lucy Riall, 'Introduction: The New History of Risorgimento Nationalism', *Nations and Nationalism* 15/3 (2009), pp. 396–401; Lucy Riall, 'Nation, "Deep Images" and the Problem of Emotions', *Nations and Nationalism* 15/3 (2009), pp. 402–9.

complained of the tendency in Verdi and other composers to hide the pressing current political situation in Italy behind medieval or ancient historical facades, whether in ancient Babylon, the Crusades (as in *I Lombardi*, 1843), the barbarian invasions (*Attila*, 1844) or medieval France (*Giovanna d'Arco*, 1845), while failing to compose operas on Italian themes – at least, until Verdi's *La Battaglia di Legnano* (1848–49). But, then, that was composed during a period of uprising and revolution, when censorship had been abolished.[34]

Nevertheless, what marked out these early operas was, first, their forward dramatic thrust and dynamic energy, and second, a vein of direct, grandiose writing that appealed to the public, and was most clearly exemplified by Verdi's largely unison, patriotic choruses. These start with 'Va, pensiero' in *Nabucco*, and continue with 'O Signore dal tetto natio' in *I Lombardi*, in which the Lombard crusaders, dying of thirst before the walls of Jerusalem, sing nostalgically of the streams of their native Lombardy; 'Si ridesti il leon di Castiglia' in Act III of *Ernani* (1844), a battle hymn of the Venetian Republic under the guise of Castile; and 'Viva Italia!, sacro un patto' at the beginning of *La Battaglia di Legnano*, the hymn of the Lombard League whose forces assemble to confront the invasion of Barbarossa, not to mention the victory march at the end of the work.[35]

The nationalist dimension in Verdi's œuvre did not disappear after 1849 and the return of Austrian rule. We find it in *I Vespri Siciliani* (1855), despite the fact that the Sicilian rising of 1282 against the French occupation was also aimed at fellow Italian Neapolitans; in *Don Carlo* (1867), with its background of the revolt in Flanders against Spanish Habsburg rule under Philip II; in *Aida* (1871), in which the conflict between love and patriotism is most clearly expressed, especially in the Nile scene in Act III; and in the additional Council chamber scene in the revised version of *Simon Boccanegra* (1881). Nor did Verdi's own commitment to a free, united and liberal Italy wane, even after an Italian national state had been finally established in 1870, with the accession of Rome.[36]

But how far do Verdi's commitments matter to an assessment of the national impact of his operas, especially the earlier ones? In recent years, to be sure, authorial intention has been downgraded as against audience reception, in the eyes of many historians, at least as far as national music is concerned. Indeed, for Axel Körner,

> If historians want to establish what an opera meant in its original context of reception, they should not read the libretto or listen to the opera. In order to reconstruct the work's original reception, historians should attempt to forget everything they know about the work and about its transmitted

---

[34] Roger Parker, *Leonora's Last Act: Essays in Verdian Discourse* (Princeton: Princeton University Press, 1997), ch. 2, esp. pp. 23, 24.

[35] Julian Budden, *The Operas of Verdi*, vol. 1, rev. edn (Oxford: Clarendon Press, 1992), pp. 27, 107, 132, 163, 397.

[36] Charles Osborne, *The Complete Operas of Verdi* (London: Indigo, 1997), 389–91, 307–9.

tradition. The historians' only concern should be to find sources revealing the work's original reading at the time.[37]

This applies particularly to the initial reception of the chorus 'Va, pensiero', in *Nabucco*, Körner points out, for which, as we saw, there were no records of any particular audience excitement or resonance. The topic of the opera was not new, and the chorus was perhaps overshadowed by Zaccaria's *Profezia* which followed it immediately. Only after 1848 did it become a symbol of a resurgent Italy.

There are several rejoinders to these claims, specific and general. Linking the chorus with Zaccaria's prophecy rousing the captive Jews to action against their oppressors may also be seen as enhancing, rather than diminishing, its importance. Second, audience familiarity with the theme did not prevent *Nabucco*, and *I Lombardi*, as well as others of Verdi's early operas, from becoming immensely popular in the 1840s. Third and perhaps most important, one might also question the significance of a delay of six years in audience reaction to 'Va, pensiero', seen in the longer term and against the overall political background.[38]

On the broader question of audience reception, the focus on initial audience reading seems rather restrictive, and the argument circular. One could equally well argue that the later reactions are just as important as those of initial audiences. One has only to think of the many 'failures' of literary and musical works, not to mention paintings, at first reading, sight or hearing, works which later became canonical. (A good example in art is Constable's painting *The Hay Wain* of 1821, which only later became an icon of (southern) English landscape over the course of the nineteenth century.) In the case of *La Battaglia di Legnano*, for example, the opera was a great success in Rome in 1849, a failure in Bologna in 1861 and a success in Parma in 1862. Nor can we so completely discount authorial intention, as Körner wants us to do. In Verdi's case, at least, there is a consistency about his national ideals which finds expression in many of his operas, and which seems to have matched his audience's expectations, and this despite constant interference from censorship and the need to use 'period disguise' to circumvent it. In this he was at one with the many artists of the period whose 'historical mobility' enhanced, rather than detracted from, their moral message and dramatic force. For Verdi, what mattered was to compose operas based on real dramatic situations, historical situations, if possible, but at all costs authentic ones in the eyes of himself and his audiences. Moreover, his characteristic themes of kinship, especially father–daughter relationships, honour and patriotic sacrifice, are peculiarly suited to, if not a part of, the overall nationalist ideologies of the period throughout Europe. Hence, the frequent superimposition of romantic love with patriotic devotion, both in Rossini's *Guillaume Tell* and in Verdi's operas

---

[37] Axel Körner, 'The Risorgimento's Literary Canon and the Aesthetics of Reception: Some Methodological Considerations', *Nations and Nationalism* 15/3 (2009), p. 412.

[38] Philip Gossett, 'Giuseppe Verdi and the Italian Risorgimento', *Studia Musicologica* 52/1–4 (2011), pp. 241–57.

(though not in the case of *Aida*), something well understood by Italian audiences of the period.[39] Verdi undoubtedly created in his early operas a national music, which exerted, and continues to exert, a powerful resonance within and beyond the Risorgimento and Italy.

## Conclusion

The musical realization of national myths and legends clearly held immense appeal for both nationalists and composers. The logic of *exempla virtutis* is plain in compositions based on figures such as Lohengrin and Siegfried (Wagner), Libuše and Dalibor (Smetana), Olaf Trygvason (Grieg), Caractacus (Elgar) and Alexander Nevsky (Prokofiev), whose heroism and sacrifice are presented as national attributes for modern-day citizens to emulate. These musical projects served the purpose of vernacular mobilization of citizens either directly, as with the fund-raising activities in Prague and Finland, or indirectly, in the political reception of the operas of Wagner and Verdi. But, as our case studies show, in the work of some of the best-known composers the connections between myth and legend and national music are diverse and intricate, resisting overarching patterns of interpretation, and overlaid with philosophical and aesthetic concerns besides nationalism. Mussorgsky is concerned with anti-heroism and fatalism. Wagner gives his German myths a strong dose of universalism: Siegfried may be a German hero in origin, but his purpose in the *Ring* is to redeem the world. In Verdi, national sentiment and historical and legendary heroes run parallel without explicitly overlapping, their connection being clear to a sympathetic listener or one familiar with a tradition of interpretation. Sibelius's legendary world of the *Kalevala* is primitive and full of violence, enchantment and the amoral forces of nature; although looking back to a golden age of Finnish culture it also distinctly resonates with *fin-de-siècle* European anxieties. These musicians realized the symbolic materials of cultural nationalism in their own individual and extraordinary visions.

---

[39] Alberto Mario Banti, 'Reply', *Nations and Nationalism* 15/3 (2009), pp. 449–53; Gossett, 'Giuseppe Verdi and the Italian Risorgimento'; see also Rosenblum, *Transformations in Late Eighteenth Century Art*, chs 1 and 2.

# 5

# The Music of Commemoration

AT the outset of the period of national music, and near its conclusion, two
choral works stand out as examples of biblical drama around the cycle of
celebration, commemoration and regeneration. Handel's oratorio *Israel in Egypt*
(1738–39) recounts the sufferings of the Israelites in Egypt and their miraculous
deliverance by the hand of God. Part I, entitled 'The Lamentation of the Israelites
for the death of Joseph', reuses an anthem for the funeral of Queen Caroline in
1737 – 'The Ways of Zion do mourn' – which was now set to different words: 'The
sons of Israel do mourn'. Commemoration is followed in Part II by the dramatic
narrative of deliverance of the Israelites, vividly detailing the ten plagues visited
by God on the Egyptians; while Part III, entitled 'Moses' Song' (from Exodus 15:
i–xxi), is a celebration of the deliverance and victory over the Egyptians at the
Red Sea and of the new-found freedom of the Israelites. The drama is carried by
the Chorus, who also comment on it, conveying the character, tribulations and
triumph of the people of Israel. It is difficult to know how far audiences identified
the deliverance of the Israelites with providence for Britain, because many
objected to the predominance of the chorus and to the use of a sacred text as a
secular entertainment.[1]

The other choral work on a biblical theme is Walton's *Belshazzar's Feast*
(1931), composed almost two centuries later. In a sense, commemoration frames
the work through the use of a narrator. However, Walton also highlights the
commemorative aspect in the first part, which commences with Isaiah's prophecy
of Babylon's doom, and then recalls the lament of the Israelites in Psalm 137, in
which the children of Israel hang up their harps by the rivers of Babylon and
mourn for their ancestral land and above all Jerusalem, their chief joy. A second
part provides vivid descriptions of the great city of Babylon, its wealth, its varied
goods and many gods, with apposite 'barbaric' colours and rhythms. Equally
dramatic is the vivid account based on Daniel ch. 5 of Belshazzar's feast, when
he orders the ransacked treasures of the Temple in Jerusalem to be brought. A
sudden pause has the narrator relating the Writing on the Wall and its prophecy
of imminent doom, ending with 'And in that night was Belshazzar the king slain'.
This is followed by the chorus singing the Israelite paean of triumph and freedom,
based on Psalm 81.

---

[1] Anthony Hicks, 'Handel and the Idea of an Oratorio', in Burrows (ed.), *The
Cambridge Companion to Handel*, pp. 161–2.

## Memory and commemoration

In these works and many others, memory plays an important part. Here we are dealing with shared memories rather than aggregated individual memories, that is, shared by an historical community as essential elements of its traditions. While parts of these compositions describe immediate experiences – the plagues, the feast of Belshazzar – others are oriented to a shared past. In *Israel in Egypt*, the Israelites mourn Joseph's death and the good times in his lifetime, now irretrievably lost, in a funereal lament; in *Belshazzar's Feast*, they intone a dirge in remembrance of Zion, the Israelites' land from which they had been ejected by Nebuchadnezzar, and above all of Jerusalem, in answer to the plaintive question, 'How shall we sing the Lord's song in a strange land?' In both cases, the memories narrate past and better times, thereby building up a picture of the generations of a temporal and historical community, enclosing space and traversing time. Of course, memories fade or become distorted; hence the often divergent and sometimes conflicting myths and traditions based on alternative memories of a shared past. But the overall effect of shared memories is to strengthen the bonds of a community, indeed sometimes to forge that community out of memories of oppression, as happened with the Israelites in Egyptian slavery and their subsequent counterparts in Babylonian captivity. Indeed, some would argue that these dramatic narratives provided the template of the idea and the shape of the nation as it emerged across the Western world.[2]

As immediate, experiential memories recede, they are often replaced by recorded memories, encoded in epics, hymns and chronicles, as well as in more elaborated, impersonal and integrated histories, such as were produced by Herodotus and Thucydides in ancient Greece, and by Elishe and Moses Korenatsi in first-millennium Armenia.[3] But, as important as these records are, for our purposes their communal influence is less than the public rites and ceremonies which rehearse the recorded memories of the nation. When fully developed, these recorded memories become integrated in an accepted and often official version of the national narrative from its origins to the present day, which are then presented and choreographed through group and individual movement, and by symbols and traditions, in the carefully staged public rites of the nation. The grand *fêtes* of the French Revolution set the pattern (Fig. 5.1). These rites, as we saw when discussing the music accompanying the *fêtes* in Chapter 1, are both celebratory and commemorative, in the narrower sense of mournful reflection on the life and death of an exemplar of the nation. In fact, the public rites of national celebration and commemoration are often juxtaposed, if not woven together into a single narrative drama, leading ultimately to a vindication of the meaning of sacrifice on behalf of a nation which in turn is symbolically regenerated

---

[2] Hastings, *The Construction of Nationhood*, ch. 8.

[3] Anne Elizabeth Redgate, *The Armenians* (Oxford: Blackwell, 2000), pp. 159–60, 22–4.

Fig. 5.1 Festival of the Federation, 14 July 1790, at the Champ de Mars, late eighteenth century, engraved by Isidore Stanislas Helman (1743–1809) (engraving), Charles Monnet (1732–1808) (after)

through participation of its members in the rites of the nation. So it is necessary to bear in mind when considering the music of commemoration that the latter is often part of a cycle of celebration, commemoration and regeneration, even when in one or other case the order may be inverted, or one or other of these recurring dimensions of national symbolism may be truncated. As we shall see, commemoration, in its narrower sense of sorrow and respectful mourning in musical elegies, funeral marches and lamentations, often comes as part of the wider cycle of celebration and regeneration.[4]

---

[4] Anthony D. Smith, 'The Rites of Nations: Elites, Masses and the Re-Enactment of the "National Past"', in *The Politics of Cultural Nationalism and Nation Building*, ed. Rachel Tsang and Eric Taylor Woods (London: Routledge, 2013), pp. 21–37.

## Musical elements of ritual commemoration

Commemorative rituals, as we have seen, refer back to a national narrative, and more especially to the aspect of mourning and reflection upon the national sacrifices of generations which Ernest Renan had highlighted. To this end, the musical elements which are integral to the ritual drama and symbolism must also mirror the various facets and phases of the drama. Here we can distinguish three kinds of musical elements which, separately or together, give expression to the mass participation, which, in the last two centuries, has come to be a central feature of the rites of nations.

1 *Marches*, or marching songs, have, since the ancient Spartans, when the poet Tyrtaeus is said to have roused and regimented its soldiers, played a key role also in public rituals of commemoration. In fact, marches are normally found in the celebratory or regenerative phases of the cycle; hence the frequency of massed military bands and the predominance of brass instruments and drums, which are widely felt to encourage a spirit of solidarity and purposive action, such as were emphasized not only in military march pasts but in mass spectacles by, for example, the Nazis. But marches, and songs with marching rhythms or associations, have also become necessary components of shared public rituals of remembrance. Solemn marches often accompanied monarchs or great public figures to their final consecration and interment, especially when these public figures were also military commanders. Hence the importance of funeral marches which express by their slow and steady beat the marching tread of soldiers or mourners in a procession, as well as the general atmosphere of sorrow which the authorities wish to encourage.

2 *Choral works*, choirs and massed singing are felt to reflect the spirit of the commemorative event, and give ritual form to the national drama. In this sense, they are more than simply accompaniments to the rituals. In hymns, anthems and choruses, whether sung by professionals or the audience, their function is to elicit both personal and shared memories, and to comment on and point up the meaning of the event in the national salvation drama. Alternatively, they may celebrate great events in the life of the nation, such as the independence of the nation (Independence Day), the giving of a new constitution (Constitution Day), or a revolution such as Bastille Day or the October Revolution. Though these events may be avowedly secular, the musical elements often hark back to religious rituals, especially the hymns and processions of priests. This follows from the meanings attributed to the events as part of a national salvation drama, where the nation has replaced the congregation as the

political communion of citizens with its own rites, symbols, feasts and martyrs.[5]

3  Finally, we must speak of *funereal laments and elegies*, which are peculiar to the commemorative phase of the cycle. These are both individual and shared laments, commemorating the passing of great personages in the life of the nation, or of a multitude of citizens who have made the 'supreme sacrifice' in wars on behalf of the nation, especially the two world wars. Annual remembrance-day ceremonies often incorporate funeral music intended for other occasions and for quite secular purposes, mythological or abstract, elements of which are then re-used in the context of 'rites of remembrance' for the fallen soldiers. We would expect commemorative music to be generally slow, weighty and stately, and to express the pathos of this part of the national ceremony. The performance of such music is also designed to reflect, or create, the ideas of national unity and the equality of the citizens, as they each confront the reality of loss and death. In many ways this is the heart of the public ritual, even when the musical laments occur near the outset of the ceremony, in order to create the appropriate atmosphere of dignified sorrow.

This raises the interesting and important question of how far such public rituals are simply designs by elites or others, or whether they reflect mass participation and a genuine outpouring of national sentiment. There is no doubt that in some cases the ceremonies are the outcome of elite initiatives and designs, especially in new states, mainly outside Europe, though even here a responsive audience is required. But, in the old-established states, the ceremonies have tended to evolve, often over decades or centuries, though we also find newly minted public rituals of commemoration. The cases of self-organizing mass ritual dramas are few and far between: for example, the Soviet workers' dramas after the Russian Revolution or the *Thingspiel* in pre-Nazi Germany. In most cases, organized groups, from veterans to the state or Church, have laid the ground rules for these public rituals.[6]

## The glorious dead

This is borne out by a consideration of the annual British Remembrance Day ceremony. It was established in 1920 by the government of the day and the British Legion, representing the ex-servicemen of the First World War. The year before, both in Paris and in London, ceremonies were held for the interment of the Unknown Warrior, and at the hastily erected catafalques for the victory

---

[5] Smith, *Chosen Peoples*, ch. 2.

[6] Erika Fischer-Lichte, *Theatre, Sacrifice, Ritual: Exploring Forms of Political Theatre* (London and New York: Routledge, 2005), chs 4 and 5.

parades, in response to a massive demand fuelled by a surge of grief on the part of the families of citizens at the huge losses sustained on the Western front and elsewhere. Unlike the British ceremony, the French rites were combined with the annual Bastille Day festivities; hence celebration took precedence over mournful commemoration. The ceremony commences in Paris with the lighting of the torch over the grave of the Unknown Warrior under the Arc de Triomphe, before the grand procession of soldiers and notables down the Champs Élysées to the Place de la Concorde, where the President addresses the citizens, and a military march past is held, the rest of the day being given over to joyful festivities up and down the land.[7] The British Remembrance Day ceremony is held in the wide thoroughfare of Whitehall at the heart of government, chosen for its spacious capacity, in view of the expected crowds of citizens. The ceremony takes place on the Sunday nearest to Armistice Day (11 November) and is attended by the Queen and royalty, as well as political and other notables, all of whom lay wreaths of poppies on the steps of Lutyens's Cenotaph, an abstract geometrical monument in the centre of Whitehall. This reflects the dual nature of the public ritual: official and popular. The ceremony itself is divided into three parts: laments and marches by the brass bands; a service before the notables; and a march past of ex-servicemen in their regiments.[8]

In the first part, massed brass bands play marches such as 'Heart of Oak' and 'Men of Harlech', but they also include laments and elegies, excerpts from classical compositions, among them Arne's 'Rule, Britannia'. Perhaps the most moving of the elegies are Dido's lament from the end of Purcell's opera *Dido and Aeneas*, and Elgar's 'Nimrod', a portrait of A. J. Jaeger, an employee of his publisher Novello, plucked from his *Enigma Variations* (1899), a slow, stately and eloquent section which has come to seem a natural part of this day and is often played on its own. (Ironically Jaeger was German and very much alive at the time Elgar wrote the piece. Yet the simplicity of the melody and texture lends itself to arrangement for brass band and open-air performance, and even in its original orchestral guise it may be taken as an allusion to solemn choral or brass idioms.) Taken as a whole, the generally sombre and dignified music sets the scene for the central official part of the ceremony. Once the notables and royalty have taken their positions around the Cenotaph, a brief traditional Christian service is held by the bishop of London, and the Queen, royalty and notables lay their wreaths on the Cenotaph steps. The musical element is confined to the singing of a hymn, 'O God, our help in ages past', the 'Old Hundredth Psalm', with the spectators joining in with the choir. The official parties then leave the Cenotaph, and the third part, devoted to the people, commences. This takes the form of a march past, but not of soldiers in military uniforms and with weapons, but of members of the wide range of regiments and services that took part in the two

---

[7] Mosse, *Fallen Soldiers*, p. 95.

[8] Jay Winter, *Sites of Memory, Sites of Mourning: The Great War in European Cultural History* (Cambridge: Cambridge University Press, 1995), pp. 103–4.

world wars, as well as more recent ones. The brass bands start up again, playing the marching song 'A Long Way to Tipperary' and other world war favourites, as each regiment marches past the Cenotaph, salutes it and hands in its wreath. This is the democratic part of the ceremony, complementing but also countering the official section. The music of this part meanwhile unfolds the spirit of camaraderie of the men and women who fought and served in the wars, and the pride in their achievements. In the British example, we may regard the first part as commemorative of loss and grief, the second as an act of regeneration through the Christian service and hymn for all, while the third part is more celebratory of the binding solidarity of the nation, the whole symbolizing a narrative that moves from darkness to light, in the hope of national renewal and regeneration by means of so great a sacrifice.

## Musical precursors

It was not only in annual rites of remembrance that music could commemorate the nation and its heroes. But, for the most part, until the early nineteenth century the music of commemoration, and the lamentations it often enclosed, were found mainly in ecclesiastical contexts. Ritual mourning tended to be confined to the Catholic liturgy, especially the Requiem Masses, well into the late nineteenth and early twentieth centuries; in the Requiems of Brahms, Verdi and Fauré, the commemoration of individual loved ones is subsumed in a wider Christian narrative drama. Alternatively, we find individual laments in operatic settings, laments which have, as we saw in the British case, been taken out of their original setting and transposed to another, quite different context. This is the case with Dido's celebrated lament in Purcell's *Dido and Aeneas*; from a lament for an individual (herself), it has on Remembrance Day become an elegy for the British nation, with Dido standing in for the embodied female nation. All these examples of commemorative music have as their object either an individual or humanity as a whole; they have no civic, let alone national, overtones. Handel apart, this holds for almost all eighteenth-century music. Even where one might begin to speak of a civic element, as in, for example, Haydn's *Nelson Mass*, it is largely celebratory, not funerary and not particularly national.

Beethoven's music of the 1800s, probably under the influence of the composers of the French Revolution, takes an important step towards a specifically national music of commemoration in the concert hall. Like many German intellectuals who had hailed the French Revolution and been influenced by its ideals, Beethoven accepted the new French civic republicanism, even if he saw it as pertaining ultimately to humanity at large. He adapted its commemorative and celebratory rituals as the natural setting for his own meditations on the liberated hero (in his opera *Leonore*) and the deceased hero (in the 'Eroica' Symphony), and in the Fifth Symphony, the 'Egmont' Overture and other works.

The 'Egmont' Overture (1808), part of his incidental music for Goethe's play on the subject, is in his heroic and tragic mode, and in the key of F minor associated in the eighteenth century with tragedy and lamentation. Its subject was the exemplary death of Count Egmont in the first stage of the Dutch Revolt against the oppressive rule of the Spanish Habsburgs under Philip II. The Revolt was fuelled in part by Calvinist biblical ideals, and in the course of the next few decades it acquired strong national overtones. On the other hand, Egmont died within the fold of the Catholic Church, as even the Count of Alba, the Spanish commander, admitted, and as a loyal subject of the Spanish king. Nevertheless, the very public spectacle of his beheading made him a martyr for the Netherlands' cause and later an apostle of liberty and resistance. It was this image, captured in Goethe's *Sturm und Drang* drama, rather than the more prosaic reality, that inspired Beethoven's stormy and defiant overture, and Vienna in the Napoleonic era was fertile ground for these messages to be received. Goethe gives Egmont a transcendent vision of freedom in his prison cell just before his execution. Beethoven's overture is remarkable for its formal structure. It is the first sonata-form composition by a major composer to abandon the most basic principle of classical sonata style: the return in the recapitulation section of material first presented outside the tonic key, now in the tonic. In the 'Egmont' Overture, the second theme returns in a non-tonic key, before a subdued section and a pause that Beethoven said represented Egmont's death. The tonic is then regained in a coda, now a transfigured F major, with the music of the 'Symphony of Victory' from the end of the incidental music, representing the ultimate triumph of the Dutch forces and the realization of Egmont's ideals. The overture thus replaces classical formal symmetry and tonal resolution with effects of drama and narrative. Its message of transcendence of death and projection of resolution into the future anticipates later music of commemoration in symphonic genres.[9]

Quite as tragic and heroic, and even more pertinent and influential, is the case of Beethoven's Symphony No. 3 in E flat ('Eroica', 1804). If the long but tightly constructed first movement has an epic character, its second movement, a grand funeral march entitled 'Marcia funèbre', is an essay in tragic heroism, whose model may have been Cherubini's *Hymne funèbre sur la mort du Général Hoche* (1797); Beethoven greatly admired the works of Cherubini. He may also have been influenced by the funeral march in C minor, the key of this movement, from Ferdinando Paer's opera *Achille*, performed in Vienna in 1801. Moreover, Beethoven had already composed a 'Marcia funèbre per la morte d'un eroe', in his Piano Sonata in A flat Op. 26 (1801–2) The 'Eroica's second movement

---

[9] Lewis Lockwood, *Beethoven: The Music and the Life* (New York and London: W. W. Norton, 2003), pp. 266–8; James A. Hepokoski, 'Back and Forth from *Egmont*: Beethoven, Mozart and the Nonresolving Recapitulation', *19th-Century Music* 25 (2002), pp. 127–53. On the Dutch Revolt, see Peter J.Arnade, *Beggars, Iconoclasts, and Civic Patriots: The Political Culture of the Dutch Revolt*. Ithaca and London: Cornell University Press, 2008, p. 185; Philip S. Gorski, 'The Mosaic Moment: An Early Modernist Critique of Modernist Theories of Nationalism', *American Journal of Sociology* 105/5 (2000), pp. 1428–68; Smith, *The Cultural Foundations of Nations*, ch. 5.

suggests a funeral procession for a dead hero, with drum-like dotted rhythms throughout and brass fanfares in places. The music gradually evolves into an intensely powerful and tragic climax, before the almost paroxysmal expression of overwhelming grief ebbs away, and dies with fragmentary snatches of the theme and whispered sounds.[10]

The 'Eroica' Symphony is dedicated, according to the title-page, to the memory of a great man, a 'hero'. We need to recall that the 'hero' (usually but not always a man) and the heroic ideal was a staple of the arts in the late eighteenth and early nineteenth centuries; from the 1750s, if not earlier, Greek and Roman, but also increasingly modern, heroes were depicted performing their *exempla virtutis*, be it of courage or generosity, piety or clemency, but, above all, of self-sacrifice in battle on behalf of their city-state or country. We have only to think of the funeral rites for Voltaire in Paris in 1791 and of Marat in 1793 (see Chapter 1), and of Jacques-Louis David's bold classical series of paintings, from his *Hector and Andromache* (1783) and *The Oath of the Horatii* (1785) to *The Death of Socrates* (1787) and the *Brutus* of 1789. Subsequently, under Napoleon, this heroic and classicizing style reached an imperial climax in the arts and fashion, providing the ideological context for Beethoven's heroic works of the period.[11]

The 'Eroica' Symphony, and especially its second movement, is very much in this mould. We are asked to participate in the commemoration and last rites of a 'great man' in an elegy of great breadth and nobility. At the outset, the great man in question was none other than Napoleon Bonaparte, whose name was inscribed on the first page of Beethoven's copy of the score. But when in late 1804 the First Consul of France crowned himself Emperor of the French – a scene memorably recorded by David – Beethoven is reported to have flown into a rage and erased Bonaparte's name from the first page. The published version in 1806, 'composed to celebrate the memory of a great man', does not mention Bonaparte, and is dedicated to Prince Lobkowitz. Whatever the truth in this account, commemoration here is individual and universal; in true Romantic fashion, the 'great man' is a man for all humanity. But we can also detect another note: the patriotism of a civic republicanism. This is far from being the same as a French nationalism, let alone the emerging German *völkisch* version of nationalism; there is no ethno-cultural element here, at least not for Beethoven. (It was different with French revolutionaries themselves; their civic republican patriotism did contain a strong cultural element, namely, the French language and, later, selected parts of its history. Theirs was a mission for liberty and French civilization.) In the same way, Beethoven's only opera, *Leonore* (1806), based on a libretto entitled *Leonore, ou L'Amour Conjugale* by Jean Nicholas Bouilly, and particularly its

---

[10] Lockwood, *Beethoven*, pp. 204–9.

[11] Rosenblum, *Transformations in Late Eighteenth Century Art*, ch. 2; Joseph Clarke, *Commemorating the Dead in Revolutionary France: Revolution and Remembrance, 1789–1799* (Cambridge: Cambridge University Press, 2007), esp. chs 2 and 3; Smith, *The Nation Made Real*, chs 3 and 6.

final revised version, *Fidelio* (1814), is about the individual and humanity, and the mutual love and heroism of both the innocent victim Florestan enduring the injustice of oppression in his dungeon and his courageous, self-sacrificing wife and rescuer Leonore, and not about a particular national community.[12]

In the next generation the notion of the funeral march became more popular with composers. Chopin's C minor *Prélude* Op. 28 and the slow introduction to the *Fantasy* in F minor Op. 49 are funeral marches; and so is the central third movement of his Sonata No. 2 in B flat minor (1839), whose plan owes something to Beethoven's Op. 26, with its 'Marcia funèbre'. But these are abstract works, unrelated, it would appear, to any community. Berlioz's dramatic *Grande Symphonie funèbre et triomphale* (1840), commissioned by the Minister of the Interior for the inauguration of the Bastille column during the celebrations commemorating the tenth anniversary of the July Revolution, has a funeral march, which is followed by a funeral oration and concludes with a triumphant apotheosis. The work is scored for a vast wind band and revives the open-air monumental style of the French Revolutionary era.[13]

One of the best-known and influential early examples of the collective lament is that of the Egyptians in the opening scene of Rossini's *Mosé in Egitto* (revised 1827). Here they cry out because of the darkness that Moses, at God's command, has called down and that has enveloped the land, and which compels Pharaoh to summon Moses and release the Israelites. This is matched by the celebrated Prayer, when the chorus of Israelites, miraculously delivered from the Red Sea, join Moses, Aaron and Elcia to beseech God to have mercy on His people. It became one of Rossini's most popular collective numbers, its simple, swaying melody a prototype for similar choruses of Verdi.[14] None proved ultimately so famous as the chorus of Hebrew Slaves in Act III of Verdi's *Nabucco* (1842), where Solera's verses follow the biblical model (Psalm 137, again). The largely unison chorus responds, as we saw in the last chapter, to the sentiments expressed in these verses with a direct simplicity that continued to move generations of Italians, and they were spontaneously taken up by the thousands of people who attended Verdi's funeral in 1901:

> Va, pensiero, sull' ali dorate;
> va, ti posa sui clivi, sui colli,
> ove olezzano tepide e molli
> l'aure dolci del suolo natal.

---

[12] Lockwood, *Beethoven*, pp. 209–14; Arblaster, *Viva La Libertà!*, pp. 51–62; David Galliver, 'Leonore, ou l'amour conjugal: A Celebrated Offspring of the Revolution', in Boyd (ed.), *Music and the French Revolution*, pp. 157–68.

[13] Johnson, *Berlioz and the Romantic Imagination*, p. 79; Arblaster, *Viva La Libertà!*, pp. 70–2; Anatole Leikin, 'The Sonatas', in Samson (ed.), *The Cambridge Companion to Chopin*, pp. 160–87.

[14] Arblaster, *Viva La Libertà!*, pp. 70–6.

> Del Giordano le rive saluta,
> di Sionne le torri atterrate;
> o mia patria si bella e perduta,
> o membranza si cara e fatal.

(Fly, o thought, on wings of gold, rest upon those hills, that sand where the air is soft and mild in my dearest native land.

Greet the fallen towers of Zion and the Jordan's shimmering heat. O my country, fair and lost, O remembrance, fatal, sweet.)

The last two lines, above all, with Verdi's sudden crescendo at the beginning of the phrase, which expressed the plight of a people that had lost its land and independence, was to strike a powerful chord over the long term with Italians oppressed in their own land.[15]

The funeral march in Wagner's *Götterdämmerung* that accompanies Siegfried's funeral procession resumes the symphonic commemorative tradition established by Beethoven's transformation of French Revolutionary traditions. Like early nineteenth-century funeral marches it begins and ends in sombre vein but has a brighter middle section in the tonic major key. But this is more than a march: it is an elaborately shaped orchestral interlude between scenes that draws on all thematic, harmonic and orchestral techniques of the *Ring* cycle. Wagner undertakes an extreme heightening of the minor/major contrast, effected by monumental and very brassy scoring, the mood turning from catastrophe and despair to exultation within a few minutes. The turn to major now stands for transcendence, and the death of the hero is unmistakably portrayed as a redemptive sacrifice. Siegfried's funeral march is in C minor, the same key as the funeral march from Beethoven's 'Eroica' Symphony, and the turn to the tonic major (C major) recalls not only that movement but the celebratory finale of Beethoven's Fifth Symphony and also the turn to F major in the 'Egmont' Overture, a precursor of Siegfried's march in its emphasis on transcendence of death and future triumph. The funeral march begins with a 'death' motif – a harsh, repeated chord of C minor on the brass – followed by the sorrowful 'Wälsungs' motif to recall Siegfried's lineage. After a gradual crescendo, the transformation into C major is heralded by the motif for Siegfried's sword, Nothung, before a monumental, transfigured version of 'death' enters in C major. It is followed by Siegfried's original motif and the transformation of his horn call in C major, punctuated by reiterations of transfigured 'death'. The climax fades away and the march ends in sombre mood as the listener is brought back to the drama's present reality. But the music conveys a positive and idealistic message; the death of the hero is a sacrifice that has a meaning for the community, as his ideals transcend his demise and live on in the people assembled around the body. Because of its formal, symphonic shaping and purely orchestral scoring,

---

[15] Osborne, *The Complete Operas of Verdi*, pp. 57–9; Roger Parker, *Leonora's Last Act: Essays in Verdian Discourse* (Princeton: Princeton University Press, 1997), ch. 2.

Siegfried's funeral march functions well as a separate concert-hall piece, and it soon acquired an iconic status. It was used by the Nazis for memorial celebrations and commemorative broadcasts on radio, including the announcement of Hitler's death in 1945, and had a life in New German Cinema of the 1970s in nationally commemorative, if less patriotic, contexts.[16]

Commemoration is also the hallmark of some of Liszt's works, starting with his *Funérailles*, subtitled 'October 1849', the year of Chopin's death and of the execution by the Austrians of thirteen Hungarian generals after the failed 1848 Hungarian uprising, events that deeply affected Liszt. The work opens with the clangour of funeral bells, but its main theme uses a 'gypsy scale' – Liszt regarded the music of the Roma as the genuine folk music of Hungary – and martial triplets in the left hand to recall Chopin's 'Heroic' Polonaise Op. 53.[17] (The Chopin Polonaises, especially those in minor keys, heroic and tragic, constitute a commemorative keyboard tradition of their own.) There is also a commemorative funeral march, entitled 'Marche funèbre: en memoire de Maximilian I, Empereur de Mexique', one of the pieces in the third book of Liszt's *Années de pèleriage, troisième année* (published 1883). Liszt was distressed by the execution of Maximilian by the revolutionary forces, and this is expressed in the sombre opening funeral march, and is only later dispelled by a hopeful fanfare-like melody which ends the work on a note of triumph. It follows another piece, 'Sunt lacrimae rerum: en mode hongrois' (1872), a threnody for the defeat of the Hungarians, his own countrymen, in 1849, after the rising of 1848, the title being taken from Virgil's *Aeneid*, and employing a Hungarian mode emphasizing the chromatic interval of the tritone.[18]

From the perspective of commemoration, the most significant of Liszt's national works are not the popular *Hungarian Rhapsodies* of the early 1850s (as well as some later ones in the 1880s), but the *Historical Hungarian Portraits* (completed 1885). These commemorated four Hungarian statesmen, two Hungarian poets, and one composer and critic, Michael Mosonyi. Stephan Szechenyi was the founder of the Hungarian Academy of Sciences, and served as a minister in 1848; his music suggests a man of determination. Joseph

---

[16] Reinhold Brinckmann, 'Wagners Aktualität für den Nationalsozialismus: Fragmente einer Bestandsaufnahme', in *Richard Wagner im Dritten Reich: Ein Schloß-Elmau-Symposion*, ed. Saul Friedländer and Jörn Rüsen (Munich: C. H. Beck, 2000), p. 127; Jens Malte Fischer, 'Wagner-Interpretation im Dritten Reich: Musik und Szene zwischen Politisierung und Kunstanspruch', in *Richard Wagner im Dritten Reich: Ein Schloß-Elmau-Symposion*, ed. Saul Friedländer and Jörn Rüsen (Munich: C. H. Beck, 2000), p. 146; Roger Hillman, *Unsettling Scores: German Film, Music, and Ideology* (Bloomington: Indiana University Press, 2005), pp. 74–6.

[17] Kenneth Hamilton, 'Liszt's Early and Weimar Piano Works', in Hamilton (ed.), *The Cambridge Companion to Liszt*, pp. 71–2.

[18] James Baker, 'Liszt's Late Piano Works: Larger Forms', in Hamilton (ed.), *The Cambridge Companion to Liszt*, pp. 142–3.

Eotvos, writer and politician, also served as a minister, and Liszt conveys the contemplative and heroic sides of his character. Michael Vorosmarty, a poet and author of the patriotic poem 'Szozat', is given a slowly evolving main theme which leads towards a belligerent ending, depicting a subtle mind with strong conviction. Unrelenting dissonance is the hallmark of the music for Ladislaus Telecki, a member of Kossuth's party who later committed suicide, a shortened version of a 'Trauermarsch'. Franz Deak, also a minister in 1848, helped to formulate the settlement of 1867 between Hungary and Franz Joseph's Austria; and he is given a swaggering march, the piece ending with a triumphant fanfare. Alexander Petofi, a celebrated poet and leader of the March youth movement in 1848, has music that is both elegiac and lyrical, but also moves towards a tragic grandeur. Finally, Michael Mosonyi's funeral procession, with its great climax and peaceful solemnity at the close, rounds off these commemorative musical portraits from the composer's native land, expressing his love and admiration for its leading figures.[19] Bartók's early symphonic poem *Kossuth*, about the revolutionary Hungarian politician, harks back to Liszt's pieces, describing Kossuth's leadership and ending with a funeral march.

## Sacrifice and triumph in Russia

Ideals of resistance and sacrifice, and the accompanying loss and grief, have had a long history in Russia. This is evident in Mussorgsky's operas and his *Songs and Dances of Death* (1875–77). The Holy Fool's lament in the final forest scene near Kromy in the second version of *Boris Godunov* (1872–74) is perhaps the most explicit dirge for the Russian motherland, paralleled only by the self-pitying laments of the Streltsii musketeers in *Khovanshchina* (1874–81), but there is a sense in which the whole of that opera is a litany of the woes of Holy Mother Russia, which can be terminated only by a collective exit from history itself. There were other commemorative pieces of the late nineteenth century, such as Tchaikovsky's elegiac *Piano Trio in A minor* (1882) in memory of Nikolai Rubinstein, and the last movement of his final work, the Symphony No. 6 in B minor ('Pathetique', 1893), that were elegies for individuals or for humanity, and in no way national in orientation.

In Russia, for commemoration and elegies that combine individual with national grief and loss with celebration, we have to wait for the events leading up to and during the Second World War. In the 1930s, that is, until the Soviet–Nazi non-aggression treaty of 1939, Communist Russia under Stalin was bitterly opposed to Hitler's fascism. It was in this political climate that Sergei Eisenstein, to rebuild his career, opted to film the subject of *Alexander Nevsky* (1938), the celebrated episode in Russian history in which the heroic Prince of Novgorod, despite its subjection to the Tatar Golden Horde, was able to mount an iconic

---

[19] Ibid., pp. 126–35.

resistance to the invasion of the Teutonic Knights in 1242. The sparseness of the Russian Chronicle and other records left considerable latitude in the interpretation of these events, but this was counterbalanced by the ideological constraints of the 1930s. In the event, the line between Russian and Soviet history had to be blurred and Alexander made to appear as an exemplary proto-communist and nationalist Russian. Conversely, nobody could be left in any doubt about the links between the cruelty of the medieval Teutonic Knights and that of the Nazis. Eisenstein gave the latter costumes with animal features and made them act in bestial ways to emphasize their barbarism and underline their radical difference from the individual faces and human actions of the Russians; this was heightened by Prokofiev's music, at once fearsome and menacing for the Teutons, heroic and joyous for the Russians. The centrepiece was the extraordinary battle on the ice on Lake Peipus, a perfect fusion of film and music, shot in the middle of a heatwave on a field outside Moscow on crushed asphalt, glass and white sand. In this sequence, we see the familiar charge in wedge formation of the German knights held and surrounded by the defending Russians, the Grand Master of the knights defeated in single combat by Alexander, and the ice subsequently crack under the weight of the knights fleeing in their heavy armour. The battle won, the heroine Olga searches for her Russian beloved among the dead and dying, as she intones a lament for the slain, 'Respond, Bright Falcons', on the field of the dead, commemorating their heroism and sacrifice for the nation, with echoes of Yaroslavna's lament for her husband in Act IV of Borodin's *Prince Igor*. Her lone act of sorrowful commemoration takes place within the usual cycle, with the battle itself standing for regeneration and the Russian victory hymn after the lament for celebration. The result pleased Stalin, and the film, on general release, proved a huge success across the Soviet Union. Shortly thereafter, Prokofiev assembled the music into a cantata for separate performance, and when it was revived in 1942 it proved to be a rallying cry during the Great Patriotic War, with a special complete performance being given on 5 April, the seven-hundredth anniversary of the battle on the ice.[20]

Similar treatment was accorded to Shostakovich's Symphony No. 5 (1937) and Symphony No. 7 ('Leningrad'; 1941). After the official criticism of his work in 1936, Shostakovich adopted the heroic classical form of socialist realism demanded by the Party. His overall conception in the Fifth Symphony was that of the formation of a personality in the context of society, but the conception was tragic as well as optimistic. During the Largo, at the first performance on 21 November 1937, members of the audience wept, apparently for the sufferings of the people. The mournful music contained disguised echoes of the Russian Orthodox requiem and of symphonic preludes written in memory of the dead. In the final movement, the outburst of rejoicing demanded by official arts policy is undercut by dissonant

---

[20] Simon Morrison, *The People's Artist: Prokofiev's Soviet Years* (New York and Oxford: Oxford University Press, 2009), pp. 218–33; Daniel Jaffé, *Sergey Prokofiev* (London: Phaidon Press, 1998), pp. 152–5, 172.

passages, as if to say that progress is inevitably accompanied by human suffering. It is usually accepted that Shostakovich at some level ironizes his triumphant conclusion, inviting us to hear brutality rather than, or as well as, celebration. The heroic classicism of the traditional, four-movement, minor-to-major symphonic form that he uses here – the D minor to D major scheme echoing Beethoven's Ninth Symphony – inevitably unfolds a process of regeneration, but whether the composer fully invests in its truth is questionable.[21]

For the Seventh Symphony, Shostakovich again revived the four-movement classical format, this time with the C minor/C major tonal complex of Beethoven's other minor-key symphony, his Fifth, and at first gave each movement a title: 'War', 'Remembrance', 'The vastness of the Fatherland' and 'Victory'. He later dropped them from the score but allowed them to be known to audiences. The well-known march theme and its eleven variations in the first movement, gradually growing in force and accompanied by repetitive side-drum rhythms, has usually been interpreted as depicting the advance of the German army and its destructive terror, though much of the symphony was conceived before the German invasion of Russia and only completed during the long German siege of Leningrad. Shostakovich said that the heart of the first movement was not the march itself but what he called the 'funeral march' or 'requiem' section that followed it, in which the main theme of the movement returns in a monumental C minor tutti, in contrast to its initial C major presentation, leading to a series of mournful woodwind solos that end with a strange, subdued section featuring a solo bassoon over a septuple-metre ostinato accompaniment that suggests a weary lament (Ex. 5.1). The symphony uses fanfares, folk and pastoral motifs, as well as aggressive timpani to differentiate Russians from their enemies, with the slow movement reflecting on the suffering of the besieged in Leningrad. Here, the classical schema of commemoration and celebration is given symphonic form, and the work was soon received with acclaim by the Russian people and international audiences alike. However, Shostakovich's genuine investment in the outward triumph of the finale and its ostensibly celebratory C major conclusion is again moot.[22]

The same reaction greeted the slow movement of Prokofiev's Piano Sonata No. 7 (1942). Though first performed by Sviatoslav Richter in early 1943, many of its themes had been sketched in 1939. Nevertheless, in the context of the suffering and anguish of the Purges and the Great Patriotic War, the slow movement, with its opening melody derived from Schumann's 'Wehmuth' ('Sadness') in his *Liederkreis* Op. 39, a song telling of the secret sorrow of the heart, proved immensely popular with the public, as did the exhilarating finale, another piece in septuple metre.[23]

---

[21] Maes, *A History of Russian Music*, pp. 353–6; see Taruskin, *Defining Russia Musically*, pp. 511–44 for different interpretations.

[22] Maes, *A History of Russian Music*, pp. 356–7; Jaffé, *Sergey Prokofiev*, p. 172.

[23] Jaffé, *Sergey Prokofiev*, pp. 171–2.

Ex. 5.1  Shostakovich, Symphony No. 7 ('Leningrad'),
first movement (reduction), fig. 60+3–fig. 61+6

# Celebration and commemoration in Britain

In the case of eighteenth- and nineteenth-century Britain, commemoration was closely bound up musically with celebration through regeneration, although one or other predominated, depending on the nature of the event or events, and the source of commemoration, public or private. The causes lay mainly in the domains of religion and politics. The need to bolster the Anglican state religion against a perceived Catholic, and Stuart, threat was crucial for forging a Protestant identity which cast the newly formed 'British' (after the union with Scotland in 1707) as latter-day Israelites resisting Egyptian enslavement. Even more important was the central role of the monarchy in the capital city; commemorative funeral rites on the death of the monarch gave way automatically to the rituals of celebration at the coronation of his or her successor, seen as the renewal and regeneration of the kingdom and nation. Given the close links between monarchy, state and nation in Britain, we should not be surprised at the relatively early date of the music for these rituals or their continued use, especially in view of the prestige of composers like Purcell and Handel; the four anthems which Handel composed for the coronation ceremony of George II in 1727 are among the composer's best-known works, and one of them, *Zadok the Priest*, has been performed at every coronation since that time.[24]

Over time, Handel's music, celebratory and commemorative, was employed on other state occasions: the 'Dead March' from his oratorio *Saul* was played at the Handel Commemoration in 1784, marking the twenty-fifth anniversary of the composer's death, and again at Nelson's funeral procession to St Paul's Cathedral in January 1806. Later celebratory compositions in the sacred mould include Hubert Parry's 'I was glad', as well as his setting of Blake's ecstatic poem known popularly as 'Jerusalem', which has attained the status of an informal second national anthem. It is rivalled in popular appeal only by the triumphant stanzas of 'Land of Hope and Glory', the text by A. C. Benson from Elgar's *Coronation Ode* (1902) for Edward VII's coronation, the tune having first appeared in his 'Pomp and Circumstance' March No. 1 (1901). Elgar's orchestral marches were central to the modern British tradition, starting with the Imperial March for Queen Victoria's Diamond Jubilee, followed by the 'Triumphal March' from *Caractacus*, the five *Pomp and Circumstance* marches (1901–30) and the darker *Coronation March* (1911). This tradition of secular royal celebration continued well into the twentieth century with Walton's dignified march *Crown Imperial* (1937) for the coronation of George VI, as well as his brighter, more exuberant *Orb and Sceptre* for the coronation of Elizabeth II (1953), the titles of the marches, so the composer claimed, recalling the lines from Shakespeare's *Henry V*:

---

[24] Graydon Beeks, 'Handel's Sacred Music', in Burrows (ed.), *The Cambridge Companion to Handel*, p. 177.

> 'Tis not the balm, the sceptre and the ball,
> The sword, the mace, the crown imperial,
> The intertissued robe of gold and pearl …

Elgar, more than any other composer of classical music, built a personal style around the musical vocabulary of the commemorative cycle: quick marches, funeral marches, elegies, laments and choral affirmation. With only a little exaggeration one might say that much of his œuvre approximates a series of fragments, of varying degrees of completeness, from the commemorative cycle. These range from explicitly patriotic statements such as the cantata *The Banner of St George*, written for the celebrations of Queen Victoria's Diamond Jubilee in 1897, to subtler, more abstract concert-hall realizations in his symphonic works. *Caractacus* (1898) has a 'triumphal march' for the victorious legions on their parade through Rome; Caractacus's lament 'O my warriors' for his fallen kinsmen; the patriotic final chorus hymning the British Empire; along with prominent elements of pastoral, homeland landscape and national history. The synthesis of British patriotism and Roman might in the modern British Empire confirms the regeneration of the nation through the sacrifice of the ancient warriors. In later works, Elgar added to his noble idioms a note of sorrow that W. B. Yeats called 'heroic melancholy'. An early instance of this approach is the fragment of the 'Land of Hope and Glory' melody that appears at the end of the first movement of the Coronation Ode, introduced slowly and softly, as if from afar, and gradually swelling with emotion before dying away again. In Elgar's Symphony No. 1 (1908), the opening motto theme is a diatonic march tune in his ceremonial style, which reappears throughout the work and eventually in triumph at the end. The second movement is a quick march and the Adagio third movement strikes a noble but deeply elegiac note. Quick march, elegy and lament are also present in the valedictory Cello Concerto (1919), Elgar's final major composition.

Among his symphonic music, Elgar's most compelling reworking of the commemorative cycle is found in his Symphony No. 2 in E flat (1911). The second-movement Larghetto is a grand and sombre funeral march, while the finale has celebratory marches and long passages of ceremonial grandeur. This symphony has achieved semi-mythic status in English music as an elegy for the Edwardian age and a vision of the darkness of the future, uttered even before war was inevitable or widely expected; its combination of grandeur and nervous energy are heard to convey the submerged doubts and anxieties of Elgar himself and the age as a whole. The symphony is dedicated to the memory of King Edward VII, who had died during its conception, although Elgar denied that the funeral march commemorated the king or (unconvincingly) even that it was a funeral march. As a late-Romantic E flat major symphony in the tradition of Beethoven's 'Eroica' – right down to the C minor funeral march – along with Schumann's 'Rhenish' Symphony, to which it alludes at the opening and elsewhere, and Bruckner's 'Romantic' Symphony, it stands in a tradition of German national symphonic music that references commemoration, homeland landscape and national history (see Chapter 2). The second movement echoes Schumann's solemn Cologne

Cathedral movement as well as Beethoven's 'Eroica', although its most immediate model is another C minor piece: Siegfried's funeral march from Wagner's *Götterdämmerung*. Elgar's main theme recalls the Siegfried motif, and the movement twice works itself to a transfigured major-key climax, where the brassy scoring and especially the rising trumpet motif recall the C major appearance of the 'sword' motif in Wagner's march. The scale and scoring are Wagnerian, and the extreme contrast between the sombre opening and the climax recalls that in *Götterdämmerung*. The reprise of the main theme is accompanied by a sinuous oboe melody that stands for the individual voice of a lamenting mourner: the final distinctive element in the commemorative vocabulary. If *Caractacus* realizes the commemorative cycle in a highly concrete way, Symphony No. 2 could be deemed a dream-like fantasia on some of its elements, highly subjectivized and even overwrought at times.

A more explicitly commemorative work, which draws on and develops Elgar's vocabulary, is the cantata *The Spirit of England* (1917). In January 1915, five months after the start of World War I, Elgar's friend Sidney Colvin suggested that he should write a 'Requiem for the slain', and mentioned Laurence Binyon's poem 'For the Fallen'. Elgar selected this and two further poems by Binyon, 'The Fourth of August' and 'To Women', all published in August 1914 just after the outbreak of war and later incorporated into a collection entitled *The Winnowing-Fan*. 'For the Fallen' includes Binyon's famous quatrain 'They shall not grow old …', which was later to be recited at countless Armistice and Remembrance Day services and carved on British war memorials. For popular and official use, Elgar made a slimmed-down and reworked arrangement of 'For the Fallen', without the solo soprano part, entitled 'With Proud Thanksgiving', at first scored for military or brass band, and intended for performance at the unveiling of the Whitehall Cenotaph in 1919 and at the entombment of the Unknown Warrior in Westminster Abbey in 1920. In the event it was not used, but the original 'For the Fallen' became a staple of the BBC's Armistice Day broadcasts in its early years. In 1933 Elgar's biographer Basil Maine wrote that 'for many, [*The Spirit of England*] has become a national memorial to which they instinctively turn each year on Remembrance Day'.[25]

The 'Fourth of August' begins with idealism and patriotism, but soon moves to religious analogies at the end of the first stanza and in the last:

> Now in thy splendour go before us,
> Spirit of England, ardent-eyed,
> Enkindle this dear earth that bore us,
> In the hour of peril purified.

[25] Rachel Cowgill, 'Elgar's War Requiem', in *Edward Elgar and his World*, ed. Byron Adams (Princeton and Oxford: Princeton University Press, 2007), p. 320.

> Endure, O Earth! And thou, awaken,
> Purged by this dreadful winnowing-fan,
> O wronged, untameable, unshaken
> Soul of divinely suffering man.

The spirit of England is 'purged' and 'purified' in imagery that the Catholic Elgar would recognize as purgatorial; indeed his setting alludes to a number of passages from his oratorio *The Dream of Gerontius* (1900) to a text by Cardinal Newman on the subject of death, judgement and purgatory, confirming the tendency of commemorative compositions to draw on the idioms of sacred music. In Binyon's verses, as Rachel Cowgill points out, 'war is presented not only as a fight for good against evil, but as a purgation of the spirit of the English, from whom self-sacrifice is required to secure the cleansing, revivification, and salvation of Europe'.[26] Binyon captures this notion in the image of the winnowing-fan, the tool in traditional harvest that separates the wheat from the chaff. Elgar's setting of the final verse alludes to the moment of death in *Gerontius* ('Novissima hora est') and transforms the original patriotic mood of the 'Spirit of England' theme into something reflective and even transcendent, suggesting a moment of communion. Although it ends with affirmation, this communion is tender and sorrowful rather than triumphalist.

The grand climax near the end of 'For the Fallen' stands in a tradition of transcendent and regenerative gestures found in Wagner and in Elgar's earlier music and in a general tradition of nineteenth-century symphonic apotheosis. But the movement relies on unstable, highly chromatic harmony and avoids direct affirmation. At the line 'They shall not grow old as we that are left grow old', Elgar's chromaticism intensifies and the music avoids any clear sense of harmonic direction (Ex. 5.2). Even the apotheosis is undercut by chromaticism and the downward drift of Elgar's sequences, and the soft alternation of A major and A minor triads in the final bars brings the work to an emotionally ambiguous conclusion. For early audiences, listening to 'For the Fallen' may have been a cathartic experience, but it offers an elusive communion and it is questionable whether the Spirit of England has been successfully reimplanted in the community. Yet Elgar created a work that for a while in the post-war years spoke to the grief of thousands of people as they tried to continue their lives.[27]

The pastoral and mystical aspects of the British commemorative tradition, beginning with Housman and the Georgian poets in literature and Elgar in music, and continuing with the symbolism of the poppy on Remembrance Day, find a new synthesis in music in two works by Vaughan Williams: *A Pastoral Symphony* (1922) and Symphony No. 5 in D (1943). Neither is explicitly commemorative,

---

[26] Ibid., p. 331.

[27] Ibid., pp. 348–50; Daniel M. Grimley, '"Music in the Midst of Desolation": Structures of Mourning in Elgar's *The Spirit of England*', in *Elgar Studies*, ed. J. P. E. Harper-Scott and Julian Rushton (Cambridge: Cambridge University Press, 2007), pp. 220–37.

Ex. 5.2 Elgar, 'For the Fallen' (*The Spirit of England*) (reduction), fig. 19–fig. 22

Ex. 5.2 *continued*

Ex. 5.2 *continued*

and both scrupulously avoid direct expression of the assertiveness, triumph and violence that one might associate with war, but both draw on the commemorative vocabulary and have always been heard by sympathetic critics as commentary on wartime experiences. In 1938 Vaughan Williams claimed that *A Pastoral Symphony* had less to do with picturesque English fields than the French landscapes remembered from his time in France as a medical orderly. Both symphonies share their expressive world with music for Vaughan Williams's later quasi-operatic 'morality play' on John Bunyan's *The Pilgrim's Progress*, which deals with spiritual endeavour, suffering, death and resurrection.

With his *Pastoral Symphony*, Vaughan Williams gives the genre of the symphony a radical overhaul: the pastoral mode no longer suffices merely for an interlude, a *locus amoenus* within a larger journey, or an idyllic setting for a short piece or tone poem, but permeates the whole of a four-movement work of a type normally associated with the epic and heroic modes. The decision makes sense, though, if we accept that, for Vaughan Williams, wartime experience and its meaning could be authentically conveyed only through this pastoral code, not directly stated. Three of the movements are slow, including both outer movements, normally the locations where symphonic 'action' takes place. Woodwind solos are prominent; the melodies are mainly modal, sometimes pentatonic, folksong stylizations; the harmony relies greatly on parallel triads and avoids the 'directional' harmony of 'leading notes' and the Romantic type of chromaticism. In these respects the *Pastoral Symphony* continues and intensifies the tradition of folksong-influenced symphonic music, just as in its avoidance of motivic development (sequence, fragmentation) in favour of a series of complete, interrelated melodies. The form is fluid: structural boundaries are often obscured. A combination of English and French stylistic influences (English folksong stylizations and Fauré, Debussy and Ravel) parallels the implicit linkage of French and English landscapes.

The commemorative vocabulary appears fleetingly but unmistakably at important points in the *Pastoral Symphony*. Near the end of the first movement the opening motif of the main theme is transformed into a harmonically stable, major-key march tune, with the suggestion of tolling bells, with the most forceful orchestration of the whole movement. This passage sounds in some performances like a projected heroic ending: the conventional goal at the end of a fast symphonic movement. In the event it is broken off and dissolves into nothing. At the heart of the slow movement there is an atmospheric solo for natural (valveless) E flat trumpet that hits the acoustic (out-of-tune) flattened seventh note, which Vaughan Williams said was inspired by the memory of a military bugler during the war who repeatedly missed the octave (Ex. 5.3). The finale begins with a long wordless cantilena for offstage solo soprano over a soft timpani roll: a distant lament. This theme returns in the middle section of the movement, finally reaching a terrible orchestral unison outburst. The symphony ends with the offstage soprano version once again, fading to nothing. If the associations here between death and pastoral were in any doubt, they could be confirmed by the operatic scene entitled *The Shepherds of the Delectable Mountains* (1922) that Vaughan Williams completed soon after the symphony, an early stage in his larger project *The Pilgrim's Progress*. This pastoral scene from Bunyan describes the Pilgrim's preparation for the final stage of his journey and his death and resurrection as he crosses the river to the Celestial City. The quiet atmosphere, modality and parallel triads are shared with the symphony, and the melodic shapes are similar throughout; in particular the opening viola solo recalls the soprano cantilena in the symphony's finale. The Pilgrim's fall into the waters is followed by trumpet calls offstage, alleluias and repetitive bells tolling for his resurrection, a passage that distinctly parallels the climax near the end of the *Pastoral Symphony*'s first movement, where, however, in characteristic fashion, it fades before achieving full presence. In the symphony, national regeneration is again elusive.[28]

For its first audiences, Vaughan Williams's Symphony No. 5 in D was felt to be a kind of uplifting exaltation in a time of war, notably in the haunting opening D major call by the two horns and the turn from uncertainty to assurance, when the music soars out of C minor to E major, and again, later in the movement, when

---

[28] Kennedy, *The Works of Ralph Vaughan Williams*, pp. 168–72; Daniel M. Grimley, 'Landscape and Distance: Vaughan Williams, Modernism and the Symphonic Pastoral', in *British Music and Modernism 1895–1960*, ed. Matthew Riley (Farnham: Ashgate, 2010), pp. 160–74.

Ex. 5.3  Vaughan Williams, *A Pastoral Symphony*,
second movement (reduction), F+5–G+5

the horn call reappears and the full orchestra dominated by the brass makes its great affirmation. After a swiftly moving Scherzo, the beautiful Romanza, which draws on the composer's music for *The Pilgrim's Progress*, suggests in the rich restatement of the cor anglais theme by the strings the serene reassurance for which so many yearned in those dark days. The agitated passage at the centre of the movement corresponds to Pilgrim's 'Save me Lord! My burden is greater than I can bear'; yet this crisis leads again to blessing and redemption. Similarly, in the concluding Passacaglia, there is a sense of journeying to an appointed goal, which is reached with the return of the affirmatory D major horn call, before the final benedictory coda based on the counter-melody of the passacaglia theme. Along the way, that theme is treated to variations that allude to stylized folksong, fanfare and bell tolling, evoking again an atmosphere of national celebration. Symphony No. 5 illustrates the close linkage between the elegiac and regenerative phases of the commemorative cycle, offering in visionary manner the hope of personal and national regeneration.[29]

Commemorative art music was abundant in early twentieth-century Britain, even if few works have resonated with listeners as strongly as those of Elgar and Vaughan Williams. Charles Villiers Stanford's six *Irish Rhapsodies* are dense with commemorative allusions. No. 2 (1903) is subtitled 'The Lament for the Son of Ossian', No. 5 (1917) is dedicated to the Irish Guards and their commander, Lord Roberts, and No. 4 ('The fisherman of Lough Neagh and what he saw'; 1913), the most powerful and dramatic of the series, features Ulster marching band music and appears to reflect Stanford's passionately Unionist views on the Irish Home Rule Bill, which was passing through Parliament at the time.[30] George Butterworth's orchestral rhapsody *A Shropshire Lad* (1913) brings the mystical melancholy of the Severnside tradition and the Housman song cycles by Butterworth himself and others into a synthesis with the orchestral traditions of the Russian *kuchka* and Sibelius. Arthur Bliss's choral symphony with narrator, *Morning Heroes* (1930), sets Hector's farewell to his wife Andromache from the *Iliad*, along with the words of Li Tai Po, Walt Whitman and Wilfred Owen. This symphony draws on the conventional tragic rhetoric and realistic effects (timpani imitating distant gunfire) that Vaughan Williams so scrupulously eschewed in his *Pastoral Symphony*. The British commemorative tradition took on a pacifist character in the late 1930s with Vaughan Williams's *Dona Nobis Pacem* (1936), which sets texts from the Latin Mass, the Bible and Whitman, and John Ireland's coronation cantata *These Things Shall Be* (1937), which includes a march in the British ceremonial style but also quotes the 'Internationale'. This strand later culminates in Benjamin Britten's *War Requiem* (1962).

---

[29] Kennedy, *The Works of Ralph Vaughan Williams*, pp. 279–83; Hugh Ottaway, *Vaughan Williams Symphonies* (London: British Broadcasting Corporations, 1972), pp. 35–40.

[30] Paul Rodmell, *Charles Villiers Stanford* (Aldershot: Ashgate, 2002), pp. 229, 237, 281, 284, 311.

## 'The Voice of the People Again Arose': American commemoration

The music of commemoration assumes a personal and democratic guise in the wartime compositions of Charles Ives. Elements of the commemorative cycle surface everywhere in his music; its central themes include memory, personal and collective; popular local community celebrations and holidays; marching bands; hymn tunes; and, in the spirit of the New England Transcendentalists, the sacredness of everyday experiences. The vernacular music played at parades in his home town of Danbury, Connecticut made a deep impression on Ives in his childhood, as did the ideas of his father, who as a teenager had been a band leader in the Union army during the Civil War. In Danbury George Ives continued to direct bands and play cornet. For war veterans, the marches and hymn tunes of the era carried extraordinary power. Their themes were death, mourning, remembrance, victory and the democratic ideals of the Republic. This milieu left Charles with a sense of the spiritual significance of quotation, a hallmark of his later style. George Ives was also an important influence on his son through his musical experiments such as singing a melody in one key while accompanying it in another, providing the grounding for Charles's unorthodoxy, love of dissonance, extensions of tonality and rhythm, and innovative spatial effects. George Ives's death at the age of forty-nine in 1894 gave his son's recollections of childhood a personally commemorative dimension. In his art Charles returned time and again to the local festivities of his youth, in which the ideals of the Revolutionary War, legends of the Civil War and the memory of his father blended.[31]

Four orchestral pieces composed around 1914–15 realize the commemorative cycle especially well, even if, like most of Ives's music, they were unknown to audiences at the time. In these years, although still militarily neutral, the United States was reflecting deeply on its stance towards the European conflict. The first two are from the Orchestral Set No. 1 (*Three Places in New England*): The *'Saint-Gaudens' in Boston Common (Col. Shaw and his Colored Regiment)* and *Putnam's Camp, Redding, Connecticut*. Although planned before the war, substantial composition took place only after the outbreak of hostilities in Europe. Ives explored even more profound sentiments in two of his masterpieces: *Decoration Day*, the second movement of his *Holidays Symphony*, and *From Hannover Square North, at the End of a Tragic Day, the Voice of the People Again Arose* (1915) from the Orchestral Set No. 2. These pieces are crammed with allusions to the two great conflicts that defined the American nation – the Revolutionary

---

[31] Michael Broyles, 'Charles Ives and the American Democratic Tradition', in *Charles Ives and his World*, ed. J. Peter Burkholder (Princeton: Princeton University Press, 1996), p. 149; Jan Swafford, *Charles Ives: A Life with Music* (New York and London: W. W. Norton, 1996), chs 2 and 3.

War and the Civil War – and with quotations from military music associated with them.[32]

*'Saint-Gaudens'*, which Ives referred to as his 'Black March', is a tribute to the pioneering 54th Massachusetts Volunteer Infantry – the Union army's black regiment – its white commander, Colonel Robert Gould Shaw, and their assault on Fort Wagner in 1863. It records Ives's response to Augustus Saint-Gaudens's memorial sculpture to the regiment on Boston Common. The monument rapidly became a theme of commentary on American values and identity, and several poems were written on the subject, one by Ives himself, with which he prefaced his score. The piece is contemplative and subdued throughout, and entirely eschews conventional heroics. Soft drum beats sound a weary, trudging march that touches on tunes by Stephen Foster, Civil War marching songs and Plantation songs. *Putnam's Camp*, by contrast, is ostensibly comic – unusual for a commemorative piece. It is the result of Ives's splicing together of two earlier pieces (from 1903 or 1904): *Country Band March* and the conspicuously national *Overture & March: 1776*. Ives's programme describes a Fourth-of-July picnic some years previously, held at the camp ground of the Revolutionary War general and rugged citizen-farmer Israel Putnam at Redding, Connecticut, near Danbury. By the 1900s the site was a focus for the preservationist movement, as it was the best-surviving military camp of the Revolutionary War. One child wanders away from the picnic, hoping for a glimpse of the soldiers, and, in a dream, he catches sight of the Goddess Liberty pleading with deserters to remember their great cause and the sacrifices they have made for it. They start to march out of camp nonetheless, but Putnam returns from Redding and they turn back, cheering. The child awakens and runs past a war monument to rejoin the festivities. *Putnam's Camp* is constructed as a march and trio, the contrasted sections corresponding to the two earlier works. It is full of affectionate jokes at the expense of amateur bands, and ends with the first notes of 'The Star-Spangled Banner' emerging through chaos before breaking off. But, beneath the comedy, its serious message is the intertwining of different eras and generations, and the enduring meaning of Revolutionary ideals and sacrifices for early twentieth-century America. National ideals are absorbed into everyday life and existence in all its roughness and uproar.[33]

*Decoration Day* is the second movement of Ives's *Holidays Symphony*, the others being *Washington's Birthday*, *The Fourth of July* and *Thanksgiving*. All these holidays are annual and national, and together they make a seasonal

---

[32] On the dating of these compositions see Gayle Sherwood Magee, *Charles Ives Reconsidered* (Urbana and Chicago: University of Illinois Press, 2008, pp. 125–6), and on the broader historical context, ch. 5.

[33] Swafford, *Charles Ives*, pp. 218–19, 243–5; Denise Von Glahn, 'New Sources for the "St. Gaudens" in Boston Common (Colonel Robert Gould Shaw and his Colored Regiment)', *Musical Quarterly* 81/1 (1997), pp. 13–50; Denise Von Glahn, 'A Sense of Place: Charles Ives and "Putnam's Camp, Redding, Connecticut"', *American Music* 14/3 (1996), pp. 276–312; Magee, *Charles Ives Reconsidered*, p. 125.

cycle. Decoration Day at the end of May (later Memorial Day) served for the commemoration of the Civil War dead. Ives could recall the celebrations in Danbury in precise detail. An elaborate parade moved from Main Street to the cemetery, where the war graves were decorated, hymns were sung and George Ives's playing of 'Taps' – a famous bugle call from the Civil War that told the soldiers to extinguish lights at the end of the day – rang out across the graves. Then the parade formed again and everyone marched back to town to the sound of the band. *Decoration Day* is in two parts. The lengthy, harmonically complex first part is reflective, hesitant and mournful, alluding to fragments of Civil War songs, whereas the shorter second part is raucous and celebratory, based on Reeves's *Second Regiment* march. The music of the first part then returns for a few moments at the end, as though the graveside memories cannot be wholly expunged by the festivities. Between the two parts, just before the band music bursts in, is the quotation of 'Taps', the crux of the piece. A distant trumpet sounds the call softly against a rustling accompaniment, musically symbolizing communion and transcendence and the felt unity of survivors, their families and the war dead. The ghost of George Ives is heard playing across what was by 1912 his own grave, and where Charles knew he too would one day lie. There is here an uncanny similarity of sonority and texture with the trumpet solo from the second movement of Vaughan Williams's *Pastoral Symphony* (1922) which recalls a real battlefield experience that took place a few years later.[34]

*Hannover Square* records an extraordinary experience that Ives had on 7 May 1915, the day a German submarine sank the passenger ship *Lusitania*. When the news reached New York, Ives recalled, everyone in the street that morning and evening was apprehensive, sensing that war was imminent. On the way home from work at his insurance office, Ives reached Hannover Square North station on the Elevated Railway, where he heard a street organist below playing an old hymn, 'In the Sweet By and By', a favourite of his father. Everyone on the platform joined in with singing and humming, from workers to Wall Street bankers. Ives sensed a collective release of tension and an expression of dignity and unity, as well as a strong religious effect: when the hymn was finished, no-one spoke, as though they were in church. In his piece, the hymn gradually emerges out of the uneasy sounds of city background noise and harmonic ambiguity, finally forming the climax and ending with a harmonically pure cadence, before the murmuring sounds of the city resume and then fade away. Ives unexpectedly begins the piece with an offstage chorus and instruments intoning the Te Deum chant, which is gradually transformed into 'In the Sweet By and By', the people's spontaneous spirituality replacing the official forms of the old church. As Jan Swafford observes, 'The carefully shaped illusion of serendipity [was] a defining feature of Ives's maturity.'[35] This is another moment of collective communion, a spontaneous memorial service, conspicuously unofficial and unguided, occurring

---

[34] Swafford, *Charles Ives*, pp. 20–1, 29–30, 252–3.

[35] Ibid., p. 99.

in a mundane setting amongst commuters and labourers together. The composer revives the spirit of the nineteenth-century camp meeting, here in modern, secular and urban guise.[36]

Ives's commemorative pieces are compositionally and aesthetically sophisticated, but, on account of their elusive musical idiom, their message has been available to relatively few listeners. By contrast, the best-known American composition with national commemorative associations is undoubtedly Samuel Barber's elegiac *Adagio for Strings* (1938), even though its original conception was entirely independent of such associations. In its initial guise the piece was a movement from Barber's String Quartet (1937), a work without any programme. It was arranged for string orchestra the following year, when it was first performed in a broadcast by Arturo Toscanini and the NBC Symphony Orchestra. Its national and commemorative status was established when it was chosen for radio broadcast on the announcement of the death of President Franklin D. Roosevelt, and then for memorials to other political and cultural figures, culminating in 1963 in the media coverage of John F. Kennedy's death and burial. After these associations had accumulated, Barber arranged the movement for chorus, setting the Agnus Dei from the Latin Mass, adding a connection with religious sacrifice that matches the Gregorian chant-like rhythms and contours of the phrases and the archaic consecutive fourths and fifths. The *Adagio* was later used in countless films, television programmes and commercials, most famously and intensively in Oliver Stone's harrowing Vietnam war film *Platoon* (1986). In 2001 the *Adagio* was a centrepiece of musical memorial concerts after the September 11 attacks. In the UK it was substituted in the programme of the Last Night of the Proms on 15 September, conducted by the American Leonard Slatkin. Barber's *Adagio* is thus very much a part of American national life, even though nothing in the piece specifies anything about the American nation or even 'the nation' in the abstract.[37]

## Conclusion

In the music of national commemoration we find an especially close and complex interplay between nationalist programmes and classical music. Marches, laments, elegies and choral affirmation were all to be found in the eighteenth-century musical language, but they did not come together for the purpose of

---

[36] Leon Botstein, 'Innovation and Nostalgia: Ives, Mahler, and the Origins of Modernism', in Burkholder (ed.), *Charles Ives and his World*, p. 50; Swafford, *Charles Ives*, pp. 270–1; Magee, *Charles Ives Reconsidered*, pp. 118–20; Von Glahn, *The Sounds of Place*, pp. 90–105.

[37] Barbara B. Heyman, *Samuel Barber: The Composer and his Music* (New York: Oxford University Press, 1992), pp. 173–4; Luke B. Howard, 'The Popular Reception of Samuel Barber's "Adagio for Strings"', *American Music* 25/1 (2007), pp. 50–80.

national commemoration until after the French Revolution, first in music for outdoor ceremonies, and later in the concert hall and opera house. The national commemorative cycle is most strongly realized in art music of the early twentieth century by composers from Russia and Britain, most often in the genre of the symphony. Here the familiar Beethovenian themes of struggle, suffering and victory and Romantic notions of transcendence and the triumph of idealism over material reality, all inherited from nineteenth-century musical traditions, are transferred to national historical experiences. Modern communications technology often played a role in spreading the message of these works in semi-ritualized form to a wide audience: radio for Elgar's *The Spirit of England*, Vaughan Williams's Symphony No. 5 and Shostakovich's 'Leningrad' Symphony, and cinema for Prokofiev's *Alexander Nevsky*. From an aesthetic point of view – and arguably from a moral point of view as well – the most successful of these realizations are incomplete, allusive or partially ironized. Complete and concrete realizations, such as *Caractacus* (dedicated to Queen Victoria) and *Alexander Nevsky*, are national*ist* in our terminology and tend to the propagandistic. Here one could count also, in Russia, Tchaikovsky's Overture *The Year 1812* (1882) and Shostakovich's programmatic, and arguably cinematic, post-war Symphonies No. 11 (*The Year 1905*) and No. 12 (*The Year 1917*, dedicated to the memory of Lenin).

# 6

# The Canonization of National Music

A CANON in art music is a repertoire of high-status music from the past, set apart from everyday entertainment, and regularly and reverentially performed in an ongoing tradition. The rapid growth of ephemeral popular music in the early nineteenth century brought forth a reaction from the elites and those who aspired to join them, for whom concert halls were reconceived as places of solemn attentiveness. In the second half of the century, solo recitals and subscription concerts required a prestigious repertoire that stood outside the changing fashions of commerce and consumption. It was made up of instrumental music by 'master' composers from the eighteenth and early nineteenth centuries. The most important canonic genres were the symphony in orchestral music and the string quartet in chamber music. Opera maintained its traditional prestige in the nineteenth century, but most houses performed a repertoire in a more neutral sense. Canon in its original ecclesiastical context means 'rule' or 'law', and the musical canon gave a rule or set of rules for responding to certain music and for understanding musical culture and its meaning. The canonization of music was part of the great nineteenth-century projects of monumentalization and historicism, which in themselves appealed strongly to nationalists. They took steps – with mixed success – to establish canons of national music comprising works by native composers. These efforts went hand in hand with the foundation of national theatres and conservatories and the winning of state patronage for those institutions and stipends for figurehead composers such as Grieg and Sibelius. The canonic repertories mainly comprised public, large-scale music in traditional genres. But, especially in the twentieth century, smaller pieces such as the Chopin mazurkas could serve as well if they were performed or recorded in large cycles. A complicating factor in the development of canons of national music was the fact that the primary canon was made up almost exclusively of works by composers from Germany and Austria: Bach, Handel, Haydn, Mozart, Beethoven, Schubert, Schumann and Mendelssohn, later joined by Wagner and Brahms. This contrasted with the situation in the eighteenth century, when Italian opera and Italian composers dominated European musical life. Although the new canon was presented as a universal tradition, it was regarded with national pride by Germans, a fact not lost on nationalists from other countries.

For this reason the canonization of national music outside the German-speaking world often reveals two opposed tendencies. On the one hand, nationalists wanted native musicians to write works of similar value and prestige to those of the German masters. Smaller nations that lacked political independence hoped to join an elite club and achieve international validation and acceptance for the national art, showing that members of their nation too could produce art of universal value, despite lacking long-established pedagogical traditions and institutions. Nations thus entered musical competition for international attention, just as they did in more concrete terms with their pavilions at the Paris *Exposition Universelle*. In 1880 Smetana wrote that the goal of his career had been to prove that the musical talent of Czechs lay not just in performance, as had long been recognized across Europe, but in 'creative force', and that Czechs have 'our own and characteristic music'. Not he but the world, he said, would judge whether he had succeeded.[1] His aim, in other words, was to shift international perceptions of Czech musicianship from a reproductive capacity to a productive one at the same level as French, German or Italian composition. In the 1930s and 1940s American critics searched for the 'great American symphony' – a remarkably traditionalist programme that indicates the endurance of the logic of universality and the need for international validation. The establishment of institutions of national music, or the nationalization of existing ones, supported the goals of universality and cultural prestige. The Czech campaign for a national theatre in Prague gave a small nation an opera house of international quality. Grieg's festival of Norwegian music in Bergen in 1898 was meant to showcase Norwegian composers to the world and help them to conquer its concert halls. Rutland Boughton's Glastonbury Festival was an English answer to Wagner's Bayreuth with a strongly Celtic tinge.[2]

On the other hand, the German dominance of the universal canon meant that nationalists outside Germany partly defined their project in opposition to the musical style that they associated with that compositional tradition. This could mean embracing particular genres and avoiding others, or it could mean the inflection of standard musical syntax to create a different and recognizable dialect. Modality and characteristic dance rhythms become important for this purpose. Some musicians – not always composers – strove to create national schools of composition in the late nineteenth and early twentieth centuries, sometimes retrospectively, and those schools later offered convenient schemata for music history textbooks that needed to impose order on the heterogeneous musical styles and developments of the period. These notions can guide our reactions to the musical experience, encouraging us to hear internal consistency or logical development within a repertoire – a consistency that, as modern scholars often point out, may be only partially justified, if at all. The most successful attempts at forming a national school were probably those of Balakirev and Stasov. Although surviving as a coherent group for little more than a decade, the *kuchka* made stylistic innovations that were remembered by Russian musicians of later generations and helped to create a Russian sound in music. That said, their contribution was mythologized in the writings of Stasov, whose views then guided the reactions of Western

---

[1] Curtis, *Music Makes the Nation*, p. 197.

[2] Ibid., ch. 5.

listeners, most significantly the social elites of Paris, for whom Russian national culture packaged by Diaghilev offered an acceptable anti-German exoticism in the years before and after World War I. Stasov's legacy in Russia and the West alike meant that, for much of the twentieth century, critics and musicologists told an oversimplified story about 'Russian music' shaped by binary oppositions and essentialism.[3]

The establishment of national compositional dialects amounts to the practical realization of Herder's *Volksgeist* theory – that each national art contains the 'spirit of the people' and that the spirit is communicated to and understood by audiences of co-nationals. At first, in the early nineteenth century, such notions were vague and enthusiastic; now nationalists attempted to train composers in how to express national spirit and audiences in how to listen for it. This is the 'rule' that canon gives to musical culture, and its legacy is the Czechness, Russianness or Englishness that musicians sometimes speak of to this day. It is a phenomenon of the secondary national canons: musicians do not usually speak of the 'Germanness' of the primary canon, perhaps because the composers did not use conspicuous inflections of standard syntax. Again the process is often retrospective, imposing consistency on things that were not perceived as similar at the time they were produced. English musicians might have been proud of new English compositions around 1900, but, as explained later in this chapter, they did not hear English*ness* in English music as a repertoire until at least the interwar period. The process may be prospective too, however. Stalin's cultural policies of the 1930s revived the by-then-moribund nationalism of the *kuchka* for the sake of building loyalty to the Soviet Union among Russians and the affiliated republics. Russian composers were sent to the provinces to train composers how to write their own national music according to the stylistic traits of the *kuchka*, suitably inflected with native folksong and dance. Since Russian music was said to have begun with Glinka's two operas, the national republics were expected to produce operas of the same two types – heroic drama and national epic – and these were judged against the standard of Glinka.[4] The canonization of national music was thus a messy and prolonged process that included prospective and retrospective efforts to bestow internal consistency, distinctiveness and prestige on repertories that in reality were shaped by a number of cultural and economic forces besides nationalism.

---

[3] Taruskin, *Defining Russia Musically*, pp. xi–xviii; *On Russian Music*, ch. 1; Frolova-Walker, *Russian Music and Nationalism*, pp. 45–8.

[4] Frolova-Walker, *Russian Music and Nationalism*, pp. 320–38.

## The first canons of national music

Canons arrived relatively late in the history of music. William Weber has traced their emergence over the eighteenth century, first in England, along with the related notions of musical 'classics' and 'ancient music'. Music lacked the living classical traditions of literature, poetry, architecture and sculpture, for which the great works of antiquity were well known and preserved. For those arts, humanist scholars could establish standards for criticism and practice that were presented as timeless. It was known that the ancients had music, but they did not notate it, and no names of musicians were known save for mythic figures such as Apollo, Orpheus and Amphion. There were no ancient models for modern compositional practice and only a limited tradition of written criticism of specific musical works. The process of canonization thus required a new sense of the musical past. In England models were provided by the programmes of the annual music festivals held in provincial centres and the liturgical musical traditions of the Anglican Church. These practices were secularized in organizations such as the Concert for Antient Music, which refused to programme music less than twenty years old. The new discipline of music history, to which three important contributions were made in quick succession by Charles Burney (1776), John Hawkins (1776) and Johann Nikolaus Forkel (1788, 1801), also contributed. The English canonic repertoire came to be centred on Handel, but Corelli and Purcell loomed large too, along with other Italian and English composers of the seventeenth and early eighteenth centuries. In France the Académie Royale de Musique (the 'Opéra') preserved an old repertoire until the 1780s, known as 'la musique ancienne'. At the Opéra the elite classes of society came together regularly and conspicuously, and the old repertoire, above all the works of Lully, came to stand for the state, evoking the glory of the reign of Louis XIV. Elsewhere the musical past persisted in modern life through practices connected with certain institutions, festivals or holy days, such as the cult of Allegri's *Miserere*, which was performed in the Sistine Chapel during Holy Week in the seventeenth and eighteenth centuries. The canonization of music involved the expansion and ritualization of such practices in a public context.[5]

An early example of the intersection of musical canon and nation was the 1784 Handel Commemoration, a series of concerts in Westminster Abbey sponsored by the court and the royal family, which established Handel as a national institution and presented his works with vast choral forces. Ostensibly a celebration of the twenty-fifth anniversary of Handel's death, this was an exercise in monumentalization and historicism, and, according to Weber,

---

[5] William Weber, 'La Musique Ancienne in the Waning of the Ancien Régime', *The Journal of Modern History* 56/1 (1984), pp. 58–88; 'The Eighteenth-Century Origins of the Musical Canon', *Journal of the Royal Musical Association* 114/1 (1989), pp. 6–17; *The Rise of Musical Classics in Eighteenth-Century England: A Study in Canon, Ritual, and Ideology* (Oxford: Clarendon Press, 1992).

the establishment of a political ritual, creating a new authority in difficult times following the American War, a constitutional crisis, and the turbulent Parliamentary election of 1784. The Handel Festival celebrated the end of the crisis and the reconfiguration of the British political elites into a new Establishment. Although repeated in five of the next seven years, it did not endure in that form in London, but returned to its origins in provincial festivals through the work of local choral societies, where Handel's oratorios continued to be central to the repertoire for the next century and more.[6]

The first true canon of national music was German, and emerged over the first half of the nineteenth century, founded on Bach and Handel and the Viennese 'Classics' – a term that was first applied to them in the 1830s – Haydn, Mozart and Beethoven. This was mainly a canon of abstract instrumental music based around the genres of symphony and string quartet. The values attached to the German canon were high seriousness and the great artist, the idea of genius and an idealist concept of transcendent creativity. The canon coalesced around historical conceptions of German music with a Hegelian tinge and something of the universal humanism that appealed to German intellectuals around 1800. In 1801 the theologian Johann Karl Friedrich Triest published a treatise on the development of music in Germany in the eighteenth century in the *Allgemeine Musikalische Zeitung*. He conceived the music of the Viennese masters from 1780 to 1800 as a synthesis of the 'learned style' of the early eighteenth century, epitomized by Bach, and the popular 'galant style' of the intervening period. In 1852, another widely read historian, Franz Brendel, argued for a 'special path' (*Sonderweg*) for German music, which expressed German *Kultur* rather than the Western (chiefly French) *Zivilization* (a pejorative term in *völkisch* German thought).[7] Brendel saw the tradition extending into the future; it was he who coined the phrase 'New German School' for Liszt and Wagner. These historians presented a logical internal development in German music, a unity of past, present and future, and a sense of lineage for German musicians. The differences in religion, patronage and musical taste between north and south Germany in the eighteenth century were downplayed, as were Mozart's and Haydn's debts to the specifically Viennese and Italian traditions of their Habsburg milieu. The conceptual convergence of several traditions into a single German music is represented by Mendelssohn's 'Lobgesang' Symphony (1840), written to celebrate the four-hundredth anniversary of the printing press for a midsummer Gutenberg Festival in Leipzig, a celebration of German culture that included processions of guilds and civic associations and a performance of Albert Lorzing's opera *Hans Sachs*, a precursor of Wagner's *Die Meistersinger*. The symphony sets words from the Bible and combines formal models from Beethoven's Ninth Symphony (three instrumental movements followed by choral sections) and eighteenth-

---

[6] Weber, *The Rise of Musical Classics*, ch. 8.

[7] Bernd Spondheuer, 'Reconstructing Ideal Types of the "German" in Music', in Applegate and Potter (eds), *Music and German National Identity*, pp. 52–6.

century oratorio, including chorales that recall Bach's *St Matthew Passion*, the modern premiere of which Mendelssohn had directed. The opening of the first movement alludes to that of Schubert's 'Great C major' Symphony, another work that Mendelssohn had recently premiered, and the first choral section echoes Handel's coronation anthem 'Zadok the Priest'. A later section recalls the creation of light from Haydn's oratorio *The Creation*. The symphony thus gathers together some monuments of German music, past and present, mingles sacred and secular genres, invites a solemn response to concert music, and combines optimistic themes of enlightenment and progress with retrospective musical idioms. Finally, the chorus stands for the German people itself, celebrating its unique cultural heritage in choral affirmation.[8]

The music of J. S. Bach had fallen into neglect in the second half of the eighteenth century almost everywhere except Leipzig and Berlin, and the canonization of German music went hand in hand with the early nineteenth-century Bach revival. In his 1802 biography of Bach, Forkel brought his great history of music as far as the eighteenth century and couched his appeals for financial support in nationalist rhetoric. The title-page dedicates the book to 'patriotic admirers of true musical art'. Bach's works are a national treasure to which those of other nations cannot compare, and Forkel urges his readers to 'be proud' of him. Forkel furthermore argues that Bach is the musical equivalent of the literary classics of ancient Greece and Rome and should be taught in schools as part of a rounded education, establishing for the first time a link between the new idea of musical classics and a German national music. The landmark of the Bach movement was Mendelssohn's 1829 Berlin revival of the *St Matthew Passion*, a crucial step in the definition of the German canon, turning Bach into a national composer by means of the performance of one of his largest, and thus most monumental, works, with a tone of high seriousness and sacredness. Adolf Bernhard Marx, the theorist and editor of the *Berliner Allgemeine Musikalische Zeitung*, predicted that the performance would 'open the gates of a temple long shut down', and would amount 'not to a festival but to a most solemn religious celebration'. At the same time Handel too was reclaimed by Germans, down to the original spelling of his name as Händel, and became a staple of choral festivals in Germany just as much as in England. In 1851 the Bach Gesellschaft embarked on a monumental complete edition of Bach's works, accomplished by the new, historically oriented discipline of musicology. A series of complete editions followed, starting predictably with Handel before moving on to Mozart, Schubert and Beethoven.[9]

If Bach and Handel were the foundation stones of the German canon, then Beethoven was the centrepiece. Whereas they were understood as great craftsmen, playing into a German self-image of skill and industriousness,

---

[8] Bonds, *After Beethoven*, pp. 80–96; Minor, *Choral Fantasies*, ch. 2.

[9] Applegate and Potter, 'Germans as the "People of Music"', pp. 5, 10, 14; Applegate, *Bach in Berlin*, esp. p. 78.

Beethoven was a great individual for the modern age, the epitome of the 'original genius'. Images of heroic struggle, suffering, overcoming and triumph grew up around Beethoven's life and music. The works that best fitted this picture were those of Beethoven's so-called 'heroic style' from the 1800s such as the Third and Fifth Symphonies, the 'Leonore' and 'Egmont' Overtures, and the Piano Sonata Op. 53 ('Waldstein'). The style is characterized by grand, public gestures, highly dramatic effects implying a narrative, driving energy and triumphant conclusions. These pieces become the gold standards for compositional emulation, especially as regards the genre of the symphony, which, in the nineteenth century, was the main vehicle for the sublime in instrumental music. As Robert Schumann remarked in 1839: 'As Italy has its Naples, France its Revolution, England its Navy, etc., so the Germans have their Beethoven symphonies. The German forgets in his Beethoven that he has no school of painting; with Beethoven he imagines that he has reversed the fortunes of the battles that he lost to Napoleon; he even dares to place him on the same level with Shakespeare.'[10] In the nineteenth and twentieth centuries, in Germany and beyond, Beethoven was monumentalized in statues, iconography, editions, performance style, criticism and biography. Furthermore, over the history of his reception, Beethoven acquired a deep connection with German political culture. From the unification of Germany in 1871 to its reunification in 1989 and beyond, the works of the heroic style were used and evoked by German politicians of all stripes.[11]

By the later nineteenth century, as the idea of the composer as original genius took a firm hold, historicism, universalism and German nationalism mingled in manifold ways. In his treatise *Oper und Drama* (1851), Wagner positioned himself as heir to Beethoven's legacy in pioneering the 'necessary' developments in music history. In his centenary essay *Beethoven* (1870), he conceived Beethoven in the terms of his own philosophical hero Arthur Schopenhauer, the deaf composer gaining metaphysical insight into the very essence of the world through his dream-like visions. Yet Beethoven was also portrayed as a characteristically German musician, and the essay was coloured by anti-French chauvinism heightened by the recent Prussian military victory. Wagner's music dramas extend the principle of the German musical canon to the stage: his works aspire to do more than merely enter a repertoire; each aims to be a monumental, transcendent experience. Brahms felt the legacy of Beethoven equally strongly, although, owing to the nature of his classicizing project, more oppressively. His long-delayed series of four symphonies address the sense of a crisis of continuation in the genre and attempt to carry forward a tradition and hold the centre ground in an era of rapid musical change and diversification. No less than Brahms, the modernist Schoenberg was profoundly committed to the

[10] Robert Schumann, *On Music and Musicians*, ed. Konrad Wolff, trans. Paul Rosenfeld (Berkeley: University of California Press, 1983), p. 61.

[11] For a survey, see David B. Dennis, *Beethoven in German Politics, 1870–1989* (New Haven and London: Yale University Press, 1996).

continuation of the German musical tradition, and famously called his twelve-note 'serial' technique, not entirely in jest, 'a discovery which will ensure the supremacy of German music for the next hundred years'.[12]

## Secondary canons of national music

Non-German nationalists of the late nineteenth and twentieth centuries were no less concerned about shaping the future of music, but they had less in the way of past repertoire to work with, at least a recent past that could form the basis for a school of modern composition. The production of secondary canons required the conceptualization of some kind of national musical past on which they could rest.

One useful concept in this kind of project is an earlier golden age of national culture, which nationalists hope can be revived, in spirit if not directly in musical style. In this way modern composers bypass international currents and draw inspiration from the pure spring of an indigenous tradition. Thus the 'English Musical Renaissance' of the early twentieth century presented itself as a 'rebirth' of the great English musical achievements of the Tudor and Jacobean periods; after 1920 Falla conceived neoclassicism as a revival of the great Spanish musical traditions of the sixteenth and seventeenth centuries; and in the years before and during World War I Debussy looked back to the eighteenth-century glory of Couperin and Rameau for a polished classicism and an alternative to the German associations of musical late Romanticism. The Karelian movement in Finland posited a golden age of sorts, even if its musical legacy remained obscure. By reconnecting with the legacies of these eras, musicians sought to redeem a more recent, inglorious past. A compositional golden age was not a prerequisite, though: Smetana aimed to establish a Czech school of composition, but looked to Mozart, Wagner and Liszt for his inspiration, not the rich eighteenth- and early nineteenth-century legacy of Bohemian-born composers such as Stamitz (father and son), Gassmann, Vaňhal, Mysliveček, the Benda and Wranitzky brothers, Dussek, Tomašek, Vořišek and even Gluck.

Not unrelated to the theme of golden ages is the identification of a threatening Other or even an 'enemy within' as objects of resentment, which can serve as rallying points and can give a sense of purpose to movements that might otherwise be diffuse. For secondary canons the obvious Other was German, although musical nationalists seldom directed their ire against German composers and their music as such. The Russian *kuchka* had a threatening Other in Anton Rubinstein, but their objections were to the hiring of German musicians to teach the curriculum at his St Petersburg Conservatory, its conservative

---

[12] K. N. Knittel, 'Wagner, Deafness, and the Reception of Beethoven's Late Style', *Journal of the American Musicological Society* 51/1 (1998), pp. 49–82; Hans Heinz Stuckenschmidt, *Schoenberg: His Life, World, and Work*, trans. Humphrey Searle (New York: Schirmer, 1978), p. 277.

compositional programme and the aristocratic patronage of the Russian Musical Society rather than German music *tout court*. Grieg and Sibelius resented the disdainful reception they sometimes met with in Germany, even as they longed for acceptance there. But Balakirev nevertheless recommended Beethoven and Schumann as models; Sibelius adored Wagner and Bruckner, Smetana, d'Indy and Elgar were Wagnerians, while Vaughan Williams idolized Bach. The German canon itself, being perceived as universal, was not generally defined against an Other, notwithstanding Wagner's demonization of the French in his prose writings and Hans Sachs's warning of foreign domination at the end of *Die Meistersinger*.

Another way to ground a canon of national music was to find a great precursor: a prophet who could provide models for imitation, the foundation stone of the canon and an object of veneration and commemoration. For the *kuchka* the precursor was Glinka, an unlikely figure in some ways, a nonchalant aristocrat with little interest in cultural nationalism, who was nevertheless mythologized as the founder of a Russian school, and whose meeting with the young Balakirev was made to symbolize the passing on of a torch. During Stalin's renationalization of Russian music, Glinka was given a Soviet makeover in books and films to turn him into a progressive, and *A Life for the Tsar* was retitled *Ivan Susanin* after its peasant hero and given a new libretto.[13] After defeat in the Franco-Prussian War, French efforts to renew the national culture included a revival of interest in the master of eighteenth-century French opera, Jean-Philippe Rameau. A centenary Rameau festival was mounted in his home town of Dijon in 1876, and later an edition of his works was produced with editorial contributions from Saint-Saëns, d'Indy, Debussy and Dukas in a notable show of unity. By creating their own classical figure, the French could construct a genealogy for modern French national music that bypassed the German classics. A powerful way to celebrate and 'nationalize' a precursor, and thus the ensuing tradition, was through the repatriation and reinterment of his remains, if they were first buried abroad. In Germany, Wagner pulled off a publicity coup when the remains of Weber, who had died in London in 1826, were returned to Dresden where he had worked as Kapellmeister for the last decade of his life. Wagner composed funeral music on themes from Weber's *Euryanthe* for a torchlight parade and a hymn for male chorus for the burial. He delivered a highly romanticized eulogy at the graveside ('There never lived a more German composer than you ...'), and later reported the events to his own glory and national credit, claiming that the reburial was his own initiative. Wagner thereby established Weber as a musical John the Baptist to himself and helped to establish the notion of German Romantic opera as a national tradition.[14]

[13] Taruskin, *Defining Russia Musically*, pp. 113–15; Frolova-Walker, *Russian Music and Nationalism*, pp. 61–73.

[14] Charles B. Paul, 'Rameau, d'Indy, and French Nationalism', *Musical Quarterly* 58/1 (1972), pp. 46–56; Katharine Ellis, 'Rameau in Late Nineteenth-Century Dijon:

Fig. 6.1 The tomb of composer Carl Maria von Weber (1786–1826) in Dresden, Germany (engraving, nineteenth century)

A nineteenth-century engraving of Weber's tomb presents it as austere and monumental (Fig. 6.1).

The genres selected by composers determined the routes their works might take to canonic status. Symphonists such as Balakirev, Rimsky-Korsakov, Borodin, Tchaikovsky, Glazunov, Dvořák, Sibelius, Elgar, Vaughan Williams, Harris and Copland measured themselves against the heroic legacy of Beethoven; with their symphonies they aimed to join the universal canon and reach for the sublime in a traditional way, albeit usually with some national inflection. However, the main themes of national music surveyed in previous chapters, such as the incorporation of folksong, the representation of the homeland and allusion to myths and legends, found their strongest realizations in the genres of rhapsody, short piano dance piece, opera, symphonic poem and cantata. These genres built up their own modern traditions, and cross-currents could develop between composers from different countries (Chopin influenced the *kuchka* composers,

Memorial, Festival, Fiasco', in Kelly (ed.), *French Music, Culture, and National Identity*, pp. 197–214; Nicholas Vazsonyi, *Richard Wagner: Self-Promotion and the Making of a Brand* (Cambridge: Cambridge University Press, 2010), pp. 50–62.

who in turn influenced Sibelius, who had an effect on Butterworth, Vaughan Williams and Harris). Piano music of virtuoso difficulty and heroic character such as Liszt's Hungarian Rhapsodies and Chopin's mature Polonaises could match the symphony for a sense of heroism, now represented through the physical task of the solo performer, and could encode the struggle of a people for sovereignty and statehood. Short pieces by composers such as Chopin and Grieg could be built into grand collections, especially in complete editions, that seem to encompass the whole life of the nation, an entire folklore for the concert hall. Symphonic poems too were sometimes grouped together as sets. The six pieces from Smetana's *Má vlast* is the obvious example, but national symphonic poems more often come in sets of four, as though aspiring to traditional symphonic status with alternating tempi and contrasts of character: Rimsky-Korsakov's Orientalist *Sheherazade* and *Antar*, Sibelius's *Four Lemminkäinen Legends*, Delius's *North Country Sketches*, and, in a looser sense, Dvořák's four symphonic poems on gruesome ballads from Karel Jaromír Erben's collection *Kytice*, all composed in 1896 (*The Water Goblin*, *The Noonday Witch*, *The Golden Spinning-Wheel* and *The Wild Dove*).

In Chopin's case, his output consisted almost entirely of piano pieces, most of them quite short. In the 1830s and 1840s opera was the main route to national status for a composer, and Chopin's friends in occupied Warsaw urged him – in vain – to write a national opera for the Polish cause. In the nineteenth century the reception of Chopin's music in Poland was dominated by the perception and celebration of national qualities, regardless of genre, although its dissemination was restricted and the early works were heavily favoured.[15] Chopin's music became a centrepiece of the concert pianist's repertoire, and a Chopin complete edition was brought out by Breitkopf & Härtel in 1878–80, an honour up to that time accorded almost exclusively to German and Austrian composers. Chopin thus gained entry to the universal canon, although, since no great Polish composers emerged in the second half of the nineteenth century, he did not provide the foundation for a Polish canon. The era of recording and broadcasting worked in Chopin's favour, as modes of musical consumption changed and his preference for short pieces mattered less. In 1938–39, on the eve of the Nazi invasion of Poland, the great Polish pianist Arthur Rubinstein recorded the complete mazurkas, an exhaustive survey of pieces originally intended for private, amateur performance and published only in sets of three or four. Technology had facilitated and monumentalized what nationalists understood as the communication of the *Volksgeist*. Over the twentieth century the intimate mazurkas came to be regarded as a more authentic Polish expression than the heroic polonaises. The Communist regime in Poland after World War II used Chopin's music for state ceremonies, official concerts and artistic events. Politicians, including the President, participated in the celebration of the centenary of Chopin's death in 1949, while 1960, the one-hundredth-

---

[15] Chechlińska, 'Chopin Reception in Nineteenth-Century Poland', pp. 208, 214–17.

and-fiftieth anniversary of his birth, was officially declared the 'Year of Chopin'.[16]

The complexities of secondary canon-formation are highlighted by the Czech case. Here a distinctive compositional tradition emerged in which certain stylistic traits and subject matter were shared by composers who knew one another, taught one another or even married into one another's families (Josef Suk, for instance, was Dvořák's pupil and then son-in-law). Czech composers and critics spoke freely of 'Czechness' in music, and a way of hearing the repertoire in this way has grown up around it for both Czechs and non-Czechs alike. However, a closer look at the two 'great composers' of nineteenth-century Czech music, Smetana and Dvořák, reveals deep cultural differences. Smetana was a middle-class German speaker who grew up in southern Bohemian towns, and an ideological nationalist with a deep investment in a notion of Czech national culture. He chose to return to his homeland from Sweden and struggle to realize his vision, ultimately at great personal cost – he died in poverty – when he could have continued in secure positions abroad. Dvořák, by contrast, was a Czech speaker of peasant stock from a rural village, whose career after 1878 took on an international dimension after Brahms recommended his *Moravian Duets* to the publisher Simrock, who then commissioned the first set of *Slavonic Dances*. He wrote chamber music for the Viennese and Germans, oratorios and a symphony for the English, and invented a national style for America. Dvořák could write in the 'Czech style' as well as Smetana, and he brought it into his abstract instrumental music in the *furiant* scherzos of Symphony No. 6 and the Piano Quintet Op. 81. His *Hussite Overture* (1883) follows the example of Smetana's *Tábor*, *Blaník* and *Libuše* in quoting the Hussite chorale. But Dvořák himself told his fellow composer Oskar Nedbal that whereas Smetana's music was Czech, his own was really 'Slavic'.[17] He wrote three *Slavonic Rhapsodies* and two sets of *Slavonic Dances*. The latter include a Serbian round dance, a Polish polonaise and a Slovak odzemek, a veritable survey of Slavic musical folklore within the Habsburg empire. As well as the *Moravian Duets* (not very authentic in their references to ethnic music) he produced two sets of Polish mazurkas. A number of his instrumental movements are entitled 'Dumka', a term that refers to a Ukrainian elegy, but in Dvořák's usage means a sectional piece with sharply contrasted slow and fast sections, moving from melancholy to frenzy and back. His operas *Vanda* and *Dimitrij* are based on Polish and Russian subjects respectively, and he did not follow Smetana in writing operas

---

[16] Jim Samson, 'Chopin Reception: Theory, History, Analysis', in *Chopin Studies 2*, ed. John Rink and Jim Samson (Cambridge: Cambridge University Press, 1994), pp. 5–8; Zdzislaw Mach, 'National Anthems: The Case of Chopin as a National Composer', in *Ethnicity, Identity and Music: The Musical Construction of Place*, ed. Martin Stokes (Berg: Oxford and Providence, RI, 1994), pp. 61–70.

[17] Michael Beckerman, 'The Master's Little Joke: Antonin Dvořák and the Mask of the Nation', in *Dvořák and his World*, ed. Michael Beckerman (Princeton: Princeton University Press, 1993), p. 146.

on heroic episodes in Czech history or legend.[18] Dvořák was attracted to the Viennese traditions of abstract instrumental music (sonata, symphony, string quartet, concerto) much more than Smetana, who favoured the 'New German School' of Liszt and Wagner. In terms of Czech politics, Smetana saw himself as part of the free-thinking 'Young Czech' party, which comprised intellectuals, artists and journalists, whereas Dvořák, he said, was from the 'Old Czech' party, associated with the Church and the landed classes. At first Czech intellectuals clearly favoured Smetana. The two great critics and opinion formers in Czech music whose writings spanned almost a century, Otakar Hostinský and Zdeněk Nejedlý, were both Smetana partisans. Nejedlý used his journal *Smetana* to attack Dvořák, and the debates from the 1870s over 'progressive' music and Wagnerism rumbled on through the first two decades of the twentieth century. For Nejedlý, Smetana's successor was Zdeněk Fibich, who was followed in turn by Josef Foerster and Otakar Ostrčil, names today largely unknown outside the Czech lands.[19]

But for the canonization of 'Czech music' as such, these divergences turned out to be if anything a strength. While Smetana represents an ideological programme of national self-realization, contributing the monumental operas and symphonic poems that portray the homeland landscape, recount national myths and legends, and celebrate Czech sovereignty, Dvořák contributed fine works in the abstract instrumental tradition that enables Czech music to join the universal canon. Whereas the ceremonial and occasional status of some of Smetana's explicitly national compositions such as *Libuše* have limited his opportunities for performance, Dvořák has had a major international impact and has spread the reputation of Czech music far more widely. Through Smetana and Dvořák together, Czech music has thus taken two complementary routes to canonic status, while maintaining a degree of stylistic consistency. As with Chopin in Poland, the formation of the Czech musical canon has been shaped by the international reception of Czech music and the prestige thereby bestowed on it as much as by the efforts of indigenous nationalists such as Nejedlý.

The Russian case is similar to the Czech in certain ways. For all the noise made about the *kuchka* by musicologists and intellectuals, in the concert hall Tchaikovsky has been more prominent, especially in England and the United States, on account of his success in symphonic genres. The last three of his six symphonies, the Piano Concerto No. 1, the Violin Concerto and his overtures and symphonic poems have thus joined the regular concert repertoire. This applies also to Rachmaninov with his piano concertos and symphonies. Meanwhile Mussorgsky contributed the 'great Russian opera' (*Boris Godunov*); Balakirev and

---

[18] Ibid., pp. 145–7; Beckerman, *New Worlds of Dvořák*, p. 14.

[19] Tyrrell, *Czech Opera*, pp. 10–11; Marta Ottlová and Milan Pospíšil, 'Motive der tschechischen Dvořák-Kritik am Anfang des 20. Jahrhunderts', in *Dvořák-Studien*, ed. Klaus Döge and Peter Just (Mainz: Schott, 1994), pp. 211–26.

Stasov outlined a nationalist ideology; and Rimsky-Korsakov illustrated it with his polished technique and brilliant orchestral showpieces. One of the tasks of musicologists in recent decades has been to separate the rather heterogeneous repertoire of Russian music from the all-encompassing nationalist conceptions that have been called on to make sense of it. In performance the Russian canon has proved resilient both in the West and in the former Soviet Union. Lenin was in favour of high culture and wanted to build on the great works of aristocratic and bourgeois art and educate the masses in appreciation of them, while Stalin tried to isolate the Soviet Union from modern Western developments in the arts and found indigenous musical traditions a useful political tool. In the mid twentieth century Shostakovich added to the Russian symphonic canon with works that were, from No. 5 onwards, more or less officially approved. Seven of his symphonies were premiered by the Leningrad Philharmonic Orchestra under the legendary directorship of Yevgeny Mravinsky, who occupied the post for half a century between 1938 and 1988. The orchestra became a Soviet showcase for virtuosity and discipline, and a certain cult developed around its renditions, which were felt to carry special authenticity in the Russian symphonic repertoire.

For instance, d'Indy thought the universal tradition was that of the symphony, and that French composers should continue its evolution. At his Schola Cantorum he taught that the greatest symphonist was Beethoven, but that later German composers had not lived up to his standard and the mantle had been taken up by d'Indy's teacher César Franck, whose development of the cyclic principle d'Indy called 'new and *exclusively French*'. D'Indy's allies even put forward François-Joseph Gossec as a rival to Haydn as the father of the symphony, implying that the French in fact owned the symphonic tradition as much as the Germans and could challenge them with superior compositions. By contrast, opponents of the symphony, first Debussy and then others who identified themselves with his stance such as Maurice Ravel and Charles Koechlin,

Canons preoccupied musicians in early twentieth-century France, as the national rivalry with Germany grew intense, Wagner dominated the musical scene, and the Dreyfus affair exposed deep divisions in French society. Most agreed that new French music should express French national identity and increase the nation's pride in its culture, and most brought a universalist perspective to the question, as the French saw themselves as the true bearers of European culture as such, and upholders of 'classical' values in art. Critics often pointed to the poised and polished music of Gabriel Fauré – not himself a nationalist, musically or politically – as an exemplar of French art and national character. But in general, unlike the Germans, French musicians could not agree on what the universal tradition to which they were heirs and that they were to uphold and revive actually was. This led to bitter quarrels.[20]

---

[20] Carlo Caballero, 'Patriotism or Nationalism? Fauré and the Great War', *Journal of the American Musicological Society* 52/3 (1999), pp. 598–9.

argued that the Schola version of the symphony was an imported genre and that it stifled the true French virtues of clarity, simplicity and rootedness in the objective world. The government of the Third Republic came down in favour of the symphony, stipulating in 1904 that the two orchestral concert series in Paris should programme at least three hours of new French music each year, much of it symphonic, and in 1906 instigating a competition for new symphonies with financial rewards and the promise of performances.[21]

Debussy and his followers conceived an alternative national lineage from eighteenth-century French composers: the *clavecinistes*, especially François Couperin 'Le grand' (1668–1733), and the operatic composer and music theorist Jean-Philippe Rameau (1683–1764). As Debussy put it in 1915:

> For many years now I have not ceased to repeat the fact: we have been unfaithful to the musical tradition of our people for a century and a half … In fact, since Rameau, we no longer have had a distinctly French tradition. His death broke the Ariadne's thread that guided us into the labyrinth of the past. Then we ceased to cultivate our garden and instead shook hands with traveling salesmen from all around the world. We listened respectfully to their claptrap and bought their rubbish.[22]

In some of his compositions, mainly works composed during World War I, he memorialized great precursors with classicizing gestures. Debussy's *Hommage à Rameau* (1905), from the first book of his *Images* for piano, is a sarabande in the style of Rameau based on a melody from his opera *Castor et Pollux*. In 1915 Debussy's compositional career took a new direction as he moved away from pictorial and text-based pieces to abstract instrumental works with generic titles. His twelve *Études* for piano (1915) are dedicated to the memory of Chopin, whose complete works Debussy was then editing for the publisher Durand. From Debussy's point of view, Chopin was a non-German composer with a French father who spent most of his adult life in France. Debussy refers in the Foreword to the *clavecinistes*, thus creating a keyboard lineage stretching back through the nineteenth century to the eighteenth, to which he adds his own monumental work, a conspectus of modern keyboard technique in a modern style. Another surprise, given Debussy's earlier aesthetic views, is the planned series of six abstract instrumental sonatas, of which three were completed: those for cello and piano; flute, viola and harp; and violin and piano. Although Debussy had earlier written a string quartet, these were his first pieces entitled 'sonata'. On the published scores he names himself 'Claude Debussy, Musicien Français', and he was concerned that the publisher should have a title-page design that recalled the editions of Couperin or Rameau, not, as was initially proposed, one that he regarded as a plagiarism of a modern Breitkopf design. Nevertheless the German

[21] Brian Hart, 'The Symphony and National Identity in Early Twentieth-Century France', in Kelly (ed.), *French Music, Culture and National Identity*, pp. 131–48.

[22] 11 March 1915, cited in Caballero, 'Patriotism or Nationalism?', p. 605.

associations of the genre were undeniable, and Debussy even incorporated cyclic processes in the manner of Franck and d'Indy, without drawing attention to them. In contrast to the strident anti-German sentiments in his critical writings, then, Debussy's musical canon-formation was an ambiguous process. Another classicizing piece of the time, Ravel's piano suite *Le tombeau de Couperin*, composed between 1914 and 1917, comprises six movements in the form of a French Baroque keyboard suite, each dedicated to the memory of one of Ravel's friends killed in the war, thus directly linking a great French musical precursor to the contemporary national struggle.[23]

## Englishness in music

The concept of Englishness in music, which emerged strongly in the interwar period, is an excellent case study in the canonization of national music. A modern English canon in music was formed in two respects, partly by accident, partly by design: similarities between major composers were emphasized so that they seemed to form a single 'school', and certain ways of hearing and extra-musical associations were applied to each of them. Although there had been notions of 'English music' before this time, the idea that the music of English composers had a particular national quality that distinguished its effect from other music was new. The position that was negotiated in this period shaped responses to English music for the rest of the twentieth century and even down to the present. The significant stylistic and ideological differences between major figures such as Elgar, Delius and Vaughan Williams were downplayed and old quarrels buried, at least in public. The role of the newly founded BBC was crucial, not just in shaping and disseminating this canon of English music, but in creating a context in which it was needed by giving a platform to both popular music and continental ultra-modernism. Faced with this pair of challenges, the English art-music establishment needed to consolidate. Its methods included selection from the major composers' œuvre to emphasize points of overlap; an emollient and lyrical critical tone that dwelled on associations with the English countryside; celebrations, memorials, BBC broadcasts and festivals; and in particular BBC broadcasts of Armistice Day programmes. The responses learned by listeners during this period are reinforced today on CD covers and television images that accompany the music.

The central ideological structure of English music of the late nineteenth and the first half of the twentieth century has been termed the 'English Musical Renaissance', a phrase first used by musicians themselves in the 1880s to refer to compositional developments in England and later elaborated into a story of compositional reconnection with a golden age of the Elizabethan and Jacobean

---

[23] Marianne Wheeldon, *Debussy's Late Style* (Bloomington: Indiana University Press, 2009), pp. 6–7, 10–14; ch. 4.

composers, which had been followed by decline and decay in the eighteenth and nineteenth centuries. More recently historians have used it to refer to a specific programme and a network that attempted to create a centralized English musical establishment.[24] The institutions of the Renaissance in this sense were the Royal College of Music (RCM), Grove's *Dictionary of Music and Musicians*, *The Times* newspaper, the journal *Music & Letters*, and Cambridge University to some extent. The movement later received support from the journal *Scrutiny*. The same personnel were to be found in leading positions at these institutions; they dedicated books to one another and broadly shared one another's views of English music and what should become of it. They included George Grove himself, Victorian musical campaigner, first Director of the RCM and first editor of his *Dictionary*; Hubert Parry, the RCM's second Director, prolific composer and Oxford Professor; Charles Villiers Stanford, composer, Professor at the RCM and Cambridge; W. H. Hadow, Dean of Worcester College Oxford, Vice-Chancellor of Sheffield University, editor of the *Oxford History of Music* and author of *English Music* (1931); Francis Hueffer, music critic of *The Times*; J. A. Fuller Maitland, Groves's successor as editor of the *Dictionary* and Hueffer's successor at *The Times*; Ralph Vaughan Williams, a pupil of Parry and Stanford and himself later a professor at the RCM; H. C. Colles, Professor at the RCM and Fuller-Maitland's successor at the *Dictionary* and *The Times*; and Frank Howes, Colles's deputy at *The Times* and eventually his successor, and author of *The English Musical Renaissance* (1966). All were broadly sympathetic to the Austro-German tradition of the eighteenth and nineteenth centuries, though not its continuation in the twentieth, yet most saw English music as something separate from it, and most took an active interest in English folksong. In Vaughan Williams's generation, as a compositional movement the Renaissance took on the character of a typical nineteenth- or early twentieth-century folklore-based national movement, with folksong, modality and other archaisms of technique to the fore, along with the poetry of Housman and the Georgians and an emphasis on the English homeland landscape. There were stylistic links to Grieg, Sibelius and Russian composers, even if these were underplayed by English musicians themselves in writing. At this stage, the aims of the Renaissance shifted from Parry and Stanford's aspiration to join the universal canon with their symphonies and chamber music to the hope for a national school with a distinctive dialect that would express a unique national spirit.[25]

The 'Renaissance' movement aimed to create a central establishment that would spread its musical values throughout the nation. In terms of composition, its figurehead was Vaughan Williams, whose blend of folksong, modality and interest in Radical politics and literary traditions was easily assimilated. Vaughan Williams himself was born into the 'English intellectual aristocracy', a loose network of mainly Nonconformist families whose high-minded contributions

---

[24] Hughes and Stradling, *The English Musical Renaissance*.

[25] Ibid., pp. 31–51, 97–8.

to culture and public life extended over many generations. These families were an aristocracy not in being blue-blooded but in the way they intermarried. Famous names like Keynes, Trevelyan, Darwin and Macauley can be traced back and forward through the generations.[26] Vaughan Williams was Charles Darwin's nephew, and his sister-in-law married a Maitland, in whose memory the composer wrote his early choral work *Toward the Unknown Region*. Such people shared a heritage in values, religious traditions and literature. There was no question that the fellow clan-member J. A. Fuller Maitland would later recognize in Vaughan Williams a kindred spirit and support his cause.

Elgar and Delius stood outside this network. Through the 1890s, 1900s and 1910s, the names of their associates and patrons almost never overlap with the tight-knit circle of the Renaissance. Vaughan Williams's favourite literary sources from the Puritan and Radical traditions – Bunyan, Blake, Skelton, Whitman, Bright – evidently held little appeal for the Catholic and politically Conservative Elgar, who preferred Shakespeare, the English Romantics and Longfellow and made an oratorio (*The Dream of Gerontius*) from a poem by Cardinal Newman. Delius, in turn, favoured modern continental literature such as Friedrich Nietzsche, Jens Peter Jacobsen and Gottfried Keller. Elgar issued a direct challenge to the Renaissance in his lectures at Birmingham University in 1905–7, implicitly disparaging its achievements and some of its main figures. He showed no interest in folk music and avoided modality. Despite his famous orchestral marches and ceremonial pieces for royal occasions, Elgar's career was driven by aspiration to join the universal canon. Delius, by contrast, the amoral, atheist aesthete, affected to his friends a lifelong contempt for England and everything English, including its music, which he regarded as another aspect of English religiosity and hypocritical moralism. Born in Bradford to German parents, he spoke German as a native and was more at home in Florida, Norway, Paris, Germany and eventually Grez-sur-Loing than in England. The main – arguably pervasive – ethnic influence in his music is African American Plantation singing (pentatonicism, rhythmic snaps), while Grieg's Norwegian idiom was a strong influence too. Both Elgar and Delius stand more in a post-Wagnerian tradition than Vaughan Williams, and thus on the other side of a technical and aesthetic fault line in modern European music and culture. Neither had any investment in an Elizabethan golden age and were not in this sense part of a conscious 'Renaissance' of English music.

This is not to say that there were no points of contact between the three composers' styles or objectives. The mid-century view that all three shared a certain Englishness required some distortion and selectivity, but was not a figment of the imagination. Elgar and Vaughan Williams shared an interest in passages of 'pure' diatonicism, an idiom that can be traced back through Parry to nineteenth-century English church musicians such as Samuel Sebastian Wesley and ultimately through the oratorio tradition to Handel. Of special importance

---

[26] Annan, 'The Intellectual Aristocracy'.

was the idiom of 'English diatonic dissonance', in which complex dissonances are used intensively but always resolved in orthodox fashion in a diatonic context.[27] The opening of Parry's well-known choral ode *Blest Pair of Sirens* (1887) exemplifies the idiom, while its text (Milton's *At a Solemn Musick*) strikes the note of 'English nobility'. Elgar built systematically on this idiom, drawing also on the characteristic textures of the English glee and part-song traditions, and at the same time absorbing Lisztian and Wagnerian influences and deploying brilliant orchestral scoring to create his own highly wrought version of a pre-existent 'English' idiom. Vaughan Williams adopted the style of English diatonic dissonance occasionally in his early works, such as the Parry-like opening pages of *A Sea Symphony* (1910) and the opening of 'Easter', the first of the *Five Mystical Songs* (1911). At these moments, an affinity with Elgar's style is distinctly audible. In later works, however, Vaughan Williams took the diatonic style in other directions, emphasizing modality and the influences of folksong and old English church music. The Elgarian version of the diatonic idiom survived in the occasional and commemorative works of Walton, Bliss and Ireland, but Vaughan Williams had a wider and deeper impact. His modal diatonicism distinguished an 'English pastoral school' in the mid twentieth century, influencing the styles of Herbert Howells, Gerald Finzi and others. Further connection between Elgar and Vaughan Williams include a liking for the medium of the string orchestra – perhaps a legacy of the English Corelli performance tradition – and for the viola as a solo instrument.

Delius meanwhile did not completely shun England during his adult life. His occasional visits to promote his music included one in 1907 when a change in his compositional style can be discerned. The post-Wagnerian chromaticism is diluted, diatonicism and lyricism emerge more strongly, short orchestral tone poems and clear forms replace vast orchestral/choral works or operas on modernist texts. In *Brigg Fair: An English Rhapsody* (1907) Delius wrote variations on an English folksong in a way that placed him at the vanguard of the English folksong movement in composition. Folksong and variation form was a standard format to anyone at the time who knew Russian national music. In *North Country Sketches* (1915), premiered in London, Delius wrote a four-movement orchestral work that resembles a landscape symphony with classical proportions, including a roistering folksy scherzo. Delius had connections with England and the folksong movement through his friends Percy Grainger and Philip Heseltine, and the style can sometimes be heard in pieces such as *A Song before Sunrise* (1919). So, although Delius continued to excoriate the English in private, his own actions prepared his repatriation, including his change of name from Fritz to Frederick at the age of 40.[28]

[27] Jeremy Dibble, 'Parry and English Diatonic Dissonance', *Journal of the British Music Society* 5 (1983), pp. 58–71.

[28] Robert Stradling, 'On Shearing the Black Sheep in Spring: The Repatriation of Frederick Delius', in *Music and the Politics of Culture*, ed. Christopher Norris

In the interwar period, the reception of these three composers converged on a perception of shared Englishness based on an association with landscape, chiefly rolling hills, sometimes described in ecstatic prose and presenting itself as incorrigible. At the same time, however, it is sometimes claimed that the music is as reticent as the English character. In 1947, for instance, the Oxford Professor of Music J. A. Westrup wrote:

> We recognize a quality in English music that makes us appear different. English music is inclined to be romantic yet reserved. Much of it avoids expansive gestures not from a lack of feeling but from a habit of restraint ... What is particularly noticeable in English music is a nostalgic quality that defies precise analysis. It is present in folk-song ... There is in our music something that recalls the English countryside, where there is often no challenge to the eye but a pervading tenderness of harmony and outline.[29]

As Edwardian disputes receded into memory, even the Wagnerian critic, Elgar friend and biographer and sometime Vaughan Williams enemy Ernest Newman eventually made conciliatory noises of this kind:

> For my part I find much of Vaughan Williams's music absolutely English. These things appeal to me profoundly as they do because the English fields and streams and the English poetry that have gone into the making of them have also gone into the making of part of myself. When I muse in the lovely green and quiet English fields in summertime I do so with a host of greatly loved English poets from Chaucer onwards; and when Vaughan Williams joins the company with certain compositions of his I find that this music is English to its very marrow.[30]

Newman's is a powerful nationalist sentiment, positing a transcendent English countryside spirit that finds manifestations in distant historical periods and different artistic media.

From the late 1920s onwards Elgar and Delius were re-evaluated in England through the media of journalism, biography, criticism, concert programming, record production and the policies of the BBC. In both cases selectivity was vital. Elgar's ceremonial works were downplayed; in the post-war era they came to be regarded by many as an embarrassing legacy of Edwardian jingoism and imperialism. The true Elgar was the composer of the abstract orchestral works – the symphonies, concertos, overtures and the *Introduction and Allegro* – and *The Dream of Gerontius*. At the same time this music was felt to breathe the air of the English countryside. At the end of his life Elgar reinforced the countryside link by asking that the cottage near the hamlet of Broadheath in Worcestershire where he was born and lived for the first year of his life should be made into an

(London: Lawrence & Wishart, 1989), pp. 69–105, esp. p. 103, n. 43.

[29] Quoted in Hughes and Stradling, *The English Musical Renaissance*, pp. 166–7.

[30] Quoted in ibid., p. 169.

Elgar Birthplace Museum, suggesting to the visitor that his origins were rural rather than urban petit bourgeois. On the occasions of his seventy-fifth birthday in 1932 and his death in 1934, Elgar was celebrated in books, periodical issues and concerts that reinforced these images.[31]

There was much documentary evidence to support the countryside association: the compositional origins and semi-programmes of the *Introduction and Allegro* and the chamber music; the scenario of *Caractacus*; the second 'dream interlude' from *Falstaff*; and Elgar's own remarks about the sources of his inspiration in the natural landscape of Worcestershire and Herefordshire. However, most of his major orchestral works do not claim to represent or portray the English landscape directly, and most of Elgar's remarks about the natural environment are allusions to Romantic literary sources that he liked to swap with friends. In the late twentieth century a tourist and heritage industry was built around 'Elgar country', where Elgar was literally monumentalized by statues in Worcester, Malvern, Broadheath and Hereford. The identification of Elgar with the Worcestershire landscape culminated in Ken Russell's popular BBC Monitor film *Elgar* (1962); the famous opening sequence of Elgar as a boy riding a white pony along the central ridge of the Malvern Hills is however a fiction. After the composer's death an Elgar memorial issue of *Music & Letters* carried a short article by Vaughan Williams entitled 'What have we learned from Elgar?' He argued that Elgar's inspiration was exclusively English. 'Elgar's music gives us, his fellow-countrymen, a sense of something familiar – the intimate and personal beauty of our own fields and lanes.' But in the end Vaughan Williams came up with surprisingly little that he 'learned from Elgar' in compositional terms, apart from the odd borrowing of a snatch of melody and the general sense that an Englishman could write music of the highest quality. The article is primarily a document of canonization, assimilating the deceased composer to the programme of the Renaissance, turning him into a precursor figure, and closing the great post-Wagnerian divide.[32]

The repatriation of Delius in the 1920s and early 1930s, culturally and then physically with his eventual reinterment, has been called by Robert Stradling a 'study in cultural assimilation and national recuperation'. It was undertaken by supporters such as the critic Cecil Gray, the composer Philip Heseltine and the conductor Sir Thomas Beecham, who wanted to replace Elgar with Delius as the great modern English composer, although their actions led in the end to his incorporation within a 'big tent'. Gray even made a bizarre bid for Renaissance status by claiming that Delius revived an English spirit found in the Elizabethans, Dowland and Purcell. Their efforts culminated in a Delius Festival in London in

---

[31] Jeremy Crump, 'The Identity of English Music: The Reception of Elgar 1898–1935', in *Englishness: Politics and Culture 1880–1920*, ed. Robert Colls and Philip Dodd (London: Croom Helm, 1986), pp. 179–85.

[32] Riley, *Edward Elgar and the Nostalgic Imagination*, pp. 81–5 and 114–15; Hughes and Stradling, *The English Musical Renaissance*, pp. 198–9.

1929, by far the best exposure in England of Delius's entire career. Beecham wrote an article in the *Daily Mail* to coincide with it entitled 'The Composer who stands for England'. The composer himself was in attendance, despite being largely paralysed and confined to a wheelchair, having braved the Channel crossing. Performances of Delius's music in Germany had fallen away after the war, so he lapped up the adulation, keeping his real views on England to himself. The six concerts of the festival were made up mainly of short pieces, with an emphasis on the orchestral tone poems. *A Mass of Life* (originally *Ein Messe des Lebens*, setting Nietzsche's *Also sprach Zarathustra*) was the only large-scale work.[33]

Beecham, Gray and Heseltine introduced the connection with the English countryside that later became a centrepiece of the English reception of Delius; Heseltine and Gray also stressing Delius's folk tunes and modality. Arthur Hutchings's 1948 monograph on the composer dwells on feelings of the English countryside, tenderly enumerating its sights and sounds and comparing Delius's music to the literature of Keats, Jeffries and Hardy. According to Hutchings, *In a Summer Garden* (1908), inspired by Delius's wife's garden at Grez, in fact expresses England instead: 'The lazy Loing is taken as some native Avon, Ouse or Medway.'[34] On 25 May 1935 this idea was given physical realization when Delius's remains were brought back to England from Grez – in line with his stated wishes, admittedly – and reinterred in the churchyard of St Peter's Limpsfield in Surrey, a region with which Delius had no connection during his lifetime. Beecham delivered a graveside oration. Even Vaughan Williams felt he had to attend, despite his deep distaste for Delius and the 'cosmopolitanism' he stood for; this had evidently become a national ceremony that demanded a display of unity. In the later twentieth century Delius's music was neglected on the Continent but was regularly broadcast, performed and recorded in Britain, especially by British musicians. A Delius Trust and a Delius Society were established, and many of Delius's manuscripts are now held by the British Library. Delius was commemorated in 1984 alongside Elgar and Holst on a limited series of stamps issued by the Post Office on the theme of British composers.[35]

In the 1920s the new BBC, founded as a private company in 1922 and nationalized in 1927 under the directorship of the high-minded John Reith, was creating national ritual and ceremony through music. In the years after World War I, such occasions played an important role in cementing national unity and healing the nation's wounds. The development of radio meant a revolution in technology and communication that could spread national events to the widest audience and consolidate national sentiment. In this process, according to Rachel Cowgill, 'certain works came to be sanctioned and elevated above all others as quasi-liturgical emblems of remembrance', above all Elgar's *The Spirit*

---

[33] Stradling, 'On Shearing the Black Sheep in Spring', pp. 75–83.

[34] Arthur Hutchings, *Delius* (London: Macmillan, 1948), p. 82; see also pp. 81–3 and 153–4, cited in Stradling, 'On Shearing the Black Sheep in Spring', pp. 80–1.

[35] Ibid., pp. 75–6.

*of England.* The choices were not inevitable and were much debated within the BBC, as broadcasters worked out how to balance patriotism, militarism and remembrance.[36] The evening concert in 1924 was in hindsight a landmark on account of its linkage of commemoration and pastoral, and for its inclusion of composers who died in the war. After the National Anthem came Sullivan's Overture *In Memoriam*, the now-unknown Julian Clifford's cantata *Meditation* and his symphonic poem *Lights Out*, Elgar's 'For the Fallen' from *The Spirit of England*, and then two pastoral pieces by recently deceased composers, Ernest Farrar's *English Pastoral Impressions* and George Butterworth's *Orchestral Rhapsody: A Shropshire Lad*. At this point the paths of commemoration and English landscape seem to converge, just as they had done recently, even if largely unnoticed at the time, in Vaughan Williams's *Pastoral Symphony* (1922). In 1925 an extensive Armistice Day programme included an all-Elgar concert entitled 'Peace' conducted by Elgar himself. The programme for 1927 was subject to considerable negotiation and planning; it eventually came down to Stanford (*The Last Post*), Elgar ('Meditation') and Parry (*The Glories of our Blood and State*), with Elgar's *The Spirit of England* the centrepiece as usual, but the programme ended tellingly with the choral finale of Beethoven's Ninth Symphony. Here a selection of English national music of the kind familiar from the later ritual of the Last Night of the Proms was placed alongside Beethoven's hymn of universal brotherhood, the classical and the national being mingled. In the 1920s a suitable repertoire of English music for commemoration and celebration was found, some composers or works being tried and dropped, while others became fixtures.[37]

## Conclusion

For much of this book we have been concerned with the inner world of cultural nationalism as realized in music, its signs and symbols in the works of individual composers and the cultural contexts from which they emerged. This symbolism, and the dialects of national music to which it gave rise, provided the materials for the sense of national identity – Frenchness, Russianness, Englishness and so on – that emerged at certain times in these repertories. However, the terms on which the 'contract' of national music was concluded at any given time were not only set by composers but were negotiated partly by critics, performers and opinion-formers through processes of reception, reinterpretation, revival, selection, exclusion and monumentalization. Institutions such as conservatoires, festivals, journals, complete editions and state broadcasters mediated the musical experience to citizens and could be set to a nationalist agenda. At the same time,

---

[36] Rachel Cowgill, 'Canonizing Remembrance: Music for Armistice Day at the BBC, 1922–7', *First World War Studies* 2/1 (2011), p. 76.

[37] Ibid., pp. 78–84.

nationalist goals could be achieved through abstract compositions in traditional genres such as symphony and oratorio, insofar as these demonstrated that the nation's musicians could compete on the international stage and produce music of the highest quality.

# CONCLUSION

# Nations, Nationalism and Classical Music

To return to the questions raised at the outset of this study, what was classical music's contribution to the potency and dissemination of the national ideal, and to what extent did that ideal generate a special category of national music within the art-music repertoire? The foregoing chapters have demonstrated that classical music composers were deeply involved in nation-making work, from the French Revolution (and in England even before) down to World War II, whether directly, through collaboration with nationalist intellectuals, or more indirectly at the level of compositional style and genre. In this period, almost everywhere that musicians possessed literacy in European art-music traditions and training in compositional techniques, repertories of national music emerged. Indeed we could offer here only a selective survey. This was an exceptionally widespread phenomenon, which stretched across Europe, and, in the twentieth century, was found in America too.

How is national music – a music that arouses positive ideas of the nation and national sentiments in its audience – to be defined more concretely? To some extent it is a matter of musical style and syntax, especially in repertoires of the later nineteenth century that draw on ethnic vernacular idioms or develop shared stylistic dialects relative to common-practice harmonic and melodic syntax. But not all national music is like this, and conversely, as we saw in Chapter 2, not all music that draws on ethnical vernacular idioms, especially in the early twentieth century, is well understood as national music. National music implies something more: it is a music that, one way or another, activates the symbolism of the nation through connections with literature and the visual arts, pre-existing national imagery, and in particular concepts of citizenship and community, the homeland, myths, legends, heroic historical episodes, and public commemorative rituals of the nation. Sometimes this symbolism is latent or even unintended by the composer, and the music develops its national significance only belatedly, as nationalists mediate it to its audience through selection, critical interpretation or reinterpretation, revival or monumentalization. National music typically arises from various combinations of these factors: style, cultural themes and reception. In this way classical music develops its own capacity to mobilize citizens to the national cause.

Early phases of national music can be found in the eighteenth century, with the portrayal of the national community in Handel's oratorios and in the massed choral unisonance of the French Revolutionary *fêtes*. Guided by the ideas of Herder and folklore research, nineteenth-century composers developed ethnic-vernacular idioms of varying authenticity, which they incorporated into their high-status art music. These idioms served national music from the 1820s until the early twentieth century, when, in the era of modernism, their national significance was diluted. Under the influence of the Rousseauian return to nature, composers transformed the pastoral style into a diverse vocabulary for national homeland landscapes, first, in the 1840s, as picturesque representations of scenes familiar from visual-art traditions, and then, with deeper identification, moving to wilder and more characteristic regions. With these strategies, especially in the genre of the symphonic poem, they portrayed the naturalization of history and invited a sense of ancestral belonging within the landscape. A vast repertoire of operas, symphonic poems, cantatas and other compositions drew on national myth and legend to promote the virtues of ancient heroes and heroines for modern citizens to emulate. The sacrifices of the ancestors were further mourned and celebrated in the music of national commemoration, beginning in the era of the French Revolution. The nationalization of commemorative idioms continued in nineteenth-century art music, reaching its culmination in symphonic music in early twentieth-century Britain and Russia. The coherence of ethnic vernacular idioms and the unity of national compositional traditions were enhanced by processes of canonization from the mid nineteenth century onwards. Nationalists celebrated great musical figures of the past as national heroes, founded and published complete editions of their works, revived lost golden ages and downplayed differences amongst composers from their own countries.

In eighteenth-century manifestations of national music and in compositions for public performance such as Beethoven's 'Egmont' Overture and Third and Fifth Symphonies, 'the nation' is a rather abstract formation, devoid of specific identity. This is the nation as a type of community as opposed to other forms of community. These works present themselves as utterances in the 'universal language' that music was sometimes said to be at the time, not in a stylistic dialect. The more concrete theme of national identity comes to the fore with later vernacular idioms, landscapes and local colour, as we have shown in Chapters 2 and 3. In places national schools emerged that generated their own symbolic systems in which listeners could acquire literacy and through which sophisticated communication could take place. This approach was especially favoured by musicians from countries without long-standing traditions of musical pedagogy and aristocratic or state patronage of indigenous composition, or where those traditions had lapsed. In Germany, France and Italy it appeared less frequently and was developed less elaborately.

How far back can we push the terms of the 'contracts' of national music? Some recent scholarship has looked to the medieval period for the sources of 'nationhood' and 'national thought'.[1] In the nineteenth century, national music undoubtedly drew on medieval myths, legends and images of the homeland that elite groups had used for their self-definition in centuries past, even if these were often rediscoveries that lacked continuous dissemination over the

---

[1] Hastings, *The Construction of Nationhood*; Leerssen, *National Thought in Europe*.

intervening centuries. But the question really concerns the level of musical style and idiom. To what extent did nineteenth-century composers draw on indigenous musical traditions and national styles in pieces that participated in cultural nationalism and the project of vernacular mobilization? We might look to eighteenth-century theorists' style classifications ('French', 'Italian' and 'German'), the 'French Overture' idiom and the grand style of Lully, the brilliant manner of the Italian instrumental concerto, and the contrapuntal mastery of the Lutheran *Kantor* tradition in north Germany. Were these idioms transformed or built on and then infused with nationalist ideology? The answer is that this occurred only to a limited extent. The polonaise was recognized across eighteenth-century Europe as an emblem of the ancient Polish aristocracy; in his mature polonaises of the 1830s and 1840s Chopin transformed the dance into a virtuoso piano piece with touches of morbidity and militarism that recall the Messianic nationalism of his fellow Parisian exile Adam Mickiewicz and his followers. The style of noble diatonicism cultivated variously by Parry, Elgar, Vaughan Williams, Finzi and other English composers in the decades around 1900 had antecedents in the music of nineteenth-century English cathedral organists, and ultimately in Handel, yet was applied anew in contexts of national commemoration and for the representation of the homeland. But these are isolated instances. More frequently, stylistic links with past compositional traditions were presented as rediscoveries within golden-age revivals, as with Debussy, Falla and, in other respects, Vaughan Williams. In these cases, discontinuity with the recent past, not the renegotiation of an agreed contract with listeners, is the main concern at the level of musical style. The sound of national identity in music was a product of cultural nationalism rather than anything older. It was that movement that encouraged the absorption of folk music into art music and later alerted listeners to distinctive soundscapes that often originated in a single influential work or in the style of one composer.

A good example of how late nineteenth-century national music coalesced around various earlier themes, old and recent, authentic and inauthentic, can be found in Siegfried's funeral march from Wagner's *Götterdämmerung*. The scenario of the *Ring* cycle is based on medieval German literature and north European mythology as rediscovered and reinterpreted by nineteenth-century nationalists and reimagined by Wagner, while the march's musical style and tonality recall post-Revolutionary national commemorative traditions, above all their instrumental abstraction and sublimation in Beethoven's Third and Fifth Symphonies. At the same time certain German musical signifiers are present, such as the emphasis on brass instruments, which reflects the recent discovery of ancient lurs in north German peat-bog burial sites. Finally there is an element of pure contemporary fabrication in the horned helmets produced by Wagner's costume designer for the first Bayreuth *Ring*, Carl Emil Doepler. This was pseudo-historicism for which there was no evidence at all, even though the helmets later became a clichéd image of Wagnerian opera and of popular conceptions of the Vikings.

On the other hand, how long did 'contracts' of national music last in the history of classical music composition? The type of music that specifies a national identity can often be understood as the mixing of genres, modes or stylistic registers: part of a much wider practice of the Romantic era in music, but less characteristic of twentieth-century modernism. An extra-musical or textual label or other association is supplied to prompt the listener as to the national significance of this mixture. For instance, in Dvořák's Symphony No. 6 a *furiant* – a folk dance with a professional compositional legacy on the popular stage and in short piano pieces – functions as a scherzo movement in a genre associated with universal humanism, the sublime, and epic dimensions. In many of Chopin's mazurkas the rhythms, melodic contours, short phrases and repetitive structures of a peasant dance are filtered through saturated chromatic harmonies that in European art music were once associated with the lamentation of an aristocratic character in a Baroque *opera seria* or with settings of the *Stabat Mater* or the *Crucifixus* section of the Mass text. The rustling sound-sheets that specify the homeland soundscapes of Wagner and Sibelius derive, within the history of professional composition, from the piano introductions to German *Lieder* with Romantic nature themes. But whereas this technique originally served the poetic enhancement of subtle lyric verse in domestic performance, in a piece such as Sibelius's *En Saga* it is monumentalized in an elaborate orchestral texture as the backdrop for bardic-style intonations that suggest a gruesome epic tale.

Central, then, to the sense of national identity in art music in the nineteenth and early twentieth centuries – and a distinctive contribution of classical as opposed to popular music to the project of cultural nationalism – is the merging of the local, the familiar and the homely with the universal and the heroic. This applies also at the extra-musical level with the mixture of local homelands and heroic myths and legends of the nation. A mixture of landscape and history – the two genres again occupying different positions in the traditional aesthetic hierarchy – is found implicitly in Mendelssohn's 'Scottish' Symphony, Smetana's *Vyšehrad* and Elgar's *Caractacus*. Moreover the landscapes of national music – aside perhaps from those of Mendelssohn's 'Italian' Symphony – are usually not 'classical' in the sense of Claude Lorraine but may specify some little-known corner of Europe such as the mountains of western Norway, the hills of the English west midlands or the Finnish forests. This mingling of local European cultures and landscapes with classical values stands in a long tradition of primitivist national thought in Europe dating back to the Renaissance reception of Tacitus' *Germania*, in which the author commended the virtuous, republican, if savage, lifestyle of the northern tribes to his fellow countrymen as an antidote to Roman decadence.[2]

In the twentieth century, the onset of modernism in art music worked against the practice of modal, generic or stylistic mixing and thus against national music too. With modernism, inherited ways of writing – compositional rules of

---

[2] Leerssen, *National Thought in Europe*, pp. 36–51.

thumb – became increasingly distasteful, as the composer tried to invent some or all of the constructive principles of each work from scratch. Musical modernism downgraded even generic composition titles, especially in its second phase after World War II. While some modernists incorporated ethnic vernacular idioms deeply into their stylistic experiments, these pointed to supranational, rather than national, conceptions. In the twentieth century, national music lived on more strongly in conservative compositional styles and movements: the symphonic schools in England, the United States and Russia, Copland's 'imposed simplicity', graduates of d'Indy's Schola Cantorum and official Soviet cultural programmes. While it is impossible to specify a single *terminus ad quem* for national music, it is certainly true that since World War II few works of Western art music with national themes have entered the internationally performed and recorded repertoire.

# Bibliography

Abraham, Gerald. *Slavonic and Romantic Music: Essays and Studies*. London: Faber & Faber, 1968.

Adams, Byron, and Robin Wells (eds). *Vaughan Williams Essays*. Aldershot: Ashgate, 2003.

Annan, Noel. 'The Intellectual Aristocracy', in *Studies in Social History: A Tribute to G. M. Trevelyan*, ed. J. H. Plumb. London: Longman, Green & Co., 1955, pp. 241–87.

Antlöv, Hans, and Stein Tønnesson. *Asian Forms of the Nation*. Richmond: Curzon, 1996.

Antokoletz, Elliott. *The Music of Béla Bartók: A Study of Tonality and Progression in Twentieth-Century Music*. Berkeley and London: University of California Press, 1984.

Applegate, Celia. 'What is German Music? Reflections on the Role of Art in the Creation of the Nation'. *German Studies Review* 15 (1992), pp. 21–32.

—— 'How German is It? Nationalism and the Idea of Serious Music in the Early Nineteenth Century'. *19th-Century Music* 21/3 (1998), pp. 274–96.

—— *Bach in Berlin: Nation and Culture in Mendelssohn's Revival of the St. Matthew Passion*. Ithaca and London: Cornell University Press, 2005.

Applegate, Celia, and Pamela M. Potter. (eds) *Music and German National Identity*. Chicago: University of Chicago Press, 2002.

—— 'Germans as the "People of Music": Genealogy of an Identity', in Applegate and Potter (eds), *Music and German National Identity*, pp. 1–35.

Arblaster, Anthony. *Viva La Libertà!: Politics in Opera*. New York and London: Verso, 1992.

Armstrong, John Alexander. *Nations before Nationalism*. Chapel Hill: University of North Carolina Press, 1982.

Arnade, Peter J. *Beggars, Iconoclasts, and Civic Patriots: The Political Culture of the Dutch Revolt*. Ithaca and London: Cornell University Press, 2008.

Baker, James. 'Liszt's Late Piano Works: Larger Forms', in Hamilton (ed.), *The Cambridge Companion to Liszt*, pp. 120–51.

Banti, Alberto Mario. 'Reply'. *Nations and Nationalism* 15/3 (2009), pp. 446–54.

Barlow, Michael. *Whom the Gods Love: The Life and Music of George Butterworth*. London: Toccata Press, 1997.

Barnard, F. M. 'Culture and Political Development: Herder's Suggestive Insights'. *American Political Science Review* 62 (1969), pp. 379–97.

Bartlet, M. Elisabeth C. 'The New Repertory at the Opera During the Reign of Terror: Revolutionary Rhetoric and Operatic Consequences', in Boyd (ed.), *Music and the French Revolution*, pp. 107–56.

Bartlett, Rosamund. '"Khovanshchina" in Context', in Batchelor and John (eds), *Khovanshchina*, pp. 31–7.

Bartók, Béla. *Essays*, ed. Benjamin Suchoff. London: Faber & Faber, 1976.

Batchelor, Jennifer, and Nicholas John (eds). *Khovanshchina: The Khovansky Affair*. Paris, London and New York: Calder Publications, with ENO, 1994.

Beales, Derek, and Eugenio Biaggini. *The Risorgimento and the Unification of Italy*, 2nd edn. London: Pearson, 2002.

Bearman, C. J. 'Percy Grainger, the Phonograph, and the Folk Song Society'. *Music & Letters* 84/3 (2003), pp. 434–55.

Beckerman, Michael. 'In Search of Czechness in Music'. *19th-Century Music* 10/1 (1986), pp. 61–73.

—— (ed.). *Dvořák and his World*. Princeton: Princeton University Press, 1993.

—— 'The Master's Little Joke: Antonin Dvořák and the Mask of the Nation', in Beckerman (ed.), *Dvořák and his World*, pp. 134–54.

—— *New Worlds of Dvořák: Searching in America for the Composer's Inner Life*. New York and London: Norton, 2003.

Beeks, Graydon. 'Handel's Sacred Music', in Burrows (ed.), *The Cambridge Companion to Handel*, pp. 164–81.

Bellman, Jonathan. *The Style Hongrois in the Music of Western Europe*. Boston: Northeastern University Press, 1993.

Berlin, Isaiah. *Vico and Herder: Two Studies in the History of Ideas*. London: Hogarth Press, 1976.

Beveridge, David R. (ed.). *Rethinking Dvořák: Views from Five Countries*. Oxford: Clarendon Press, 1996.

Bhabha, Homi K. *Nation and Narration*. London and New York: Routledge, 1990.

Blakeman, Edward. *The Faber Pocket Guide to Handel*. London: Faber & Faber, 2009.

Blanning, T. C. W. *The Triumph of Music: Composers, Musicians and Their Audiences, 1700 to the Present*. London: Penguin, 2008.

Bohlman, Philip V. *The Study of Folk Music in the Modern World*. Bloomington: Indiana University Press, 1988.

—— 'Landscape-Region-Nation-Reich: German Folk Song in the Nexus of National Identity', in Applegate and Potter (eds), *Music and German National Identity*, pp. 105–27.

—— *Focus: Music, Nationalism, and the Making of the New Europe*, 2nd edn. New York and London: Routledge, 2011.

Bonds, Mark Evan. *After Beethoven: Imperatives of Originality in the Symphony*. Cambridge, Mass.: Harvard University Press, 1996.

Bonehill, John and Geoff Quilley. *Conflicting Visions: War and Visual Culture in Britain and France, c. 1700–1830*. Aldershot: Ashgate, 2005.

Botstein, Leon. 'Innovation and Nostalgia: Ives, Mahler, and the Origins of Modernism', in Burkholder (ed.), *Charles Ives and his World*, pp. 35–74.

Boyd, Malcolm. *Music and the French Revolution*. Cambridge: Cambridge University Press, 1992.

Boyes, Georgina. *The Imagined Village: Culture, Ideology, and the English Folk Revival*. Manchester: Manchester University Press, 1993.

Branch, Michael (ed.). *The Kalevala: The Land of Heroes*. Trans. W. F. Kirby. London: Athlone Press, 1985.

Brincker, Benedikte, and Jens Brincker. 'Musical Constructions of Nationalism: A Comparative Study of Bartók and Stravinsky'. *Nations and Nationalism* 10/4 (2004), pp. 579–97.

—— 'The Role of Classical Music in the Construction of Nationalism: An Analysis of Danish Consensus Nationalism and the Reception of Carl Nielsen'. *Nations and Nationalism* 14/4 (2008), pp. 684–99.

—— 'The Role of Classical Music in the Construction of Nationalism: A Cross-National Perspective'. *Nations and Nationalism* 20/4 (2014), pp. 664–82.

Brinckmann, Reinhold. 'Wagners Aktualität für den Nationalsozialismus: Fragmente einer Bestandsaufnahme', in *Richard Wagner im Dritten Reich: Ein Schloß-Elmau-Symposion*, ed. Saul Friedländer and Jörn Rüsen. Munich: C. H. Beck, 2000, pp. 109–41.

Brockmann, Stephen. *Nuremberg: The Imaginary Capital*. Columbia, SC: Camden House, 2006.

Brody, Martin. 'Founding Sons: Copland, Sessions and Berger on Genealogy and Hybridity', in *Aaron Copland and his World*, ed. Carol J. Oja and Judith Tick. Princeton and Oxford: Princeton University Press, 2005, pp. 15–43.

Brown, A. Peter. *The Symphonic Repertoire*, vol. 3, *The European Symphony from ca. 1800 to ca. 1930, Part A, Germany and the Nordic Countries*. Bloomington: Indiana University Press, 2007.

—— *The Symphonic Repertoire*, vol. 3, *The European Symphony from ca. 1800 to ca. 1930, Part B, Great Britain, Russia and France*. Bloomington: Indiana University Press, 2008.

Brown, Julie. 'Bartók, the Gypsies and Hybridity in Music', in *Western Music and its Others: Difference, Representation and Appropriation in Music*, ed. Georgina Born and David Hesmondhalgh. Berkeley: University of California Press, 2000, pp. 119–42.

—— (ed.). *Western Music and Race*. Cambridge: Cambridge University Press, 2007.

Broyles, Michael. 'Charles Ives and the American Democratic Tradition', in Burkholder (ed.), *Charles Ives and his World*, pp. 118–60.

Budden, Julian. *The Operas of Verdi*, vol. 1, rev. edn. Oxford: Clarendon Press, 1992.

Bullock, Philip Ross. 'Sibelius and the Russian Traditions', in Grimley (ed.), *Sibelius and his World*, pp. 3–57.

Burkholder, J. Peter (ed.). *Charles Ives and his World*. Princeton: Princeton University Press, 1996.

Burrows, Donald (ed.). *The Cambridge Companion to Handel*. Cambridge: Cambridge University Press, 1997.

Caballero, Carlo. 'Patriotism or Nationalism? Fauré and the Great War'. *Journal of the American Musicological Society* 52/3 (1999), pp. 593–625.

Cannadine, David. 'Orchestrating his Own Life: Sir Edward Elgar as a Historical Personality', in Kenyon (ed.), *Elgar*, pp. 1–35.

Celenza, Anna Harwell. *The Early Works of Niels W. Gade: In Search of the Poetic*. Aldershot: Ashgate, 2001.

Charlton, David. 'Introduction: Exploring the Revolution', in Boyd (ed.), *Music and the French Revolution*, pp. 1–11.

Chechlińska, Zofia. 'Chopin Reception in Nineteenth-Century Poland', in Samson (ed.), *The Cambridge Companion to Chopin*, pp. 206–21.

Christoforidis, Michael. 'Manuel de Falla, Flamenco and Spanish Identity', in Brown (ed.), *Western Music and Race*, pp. 230–43.

Clapham, John. *Smetana*. London: Dent, 1972.

Clark, Walter Aaron. *Isaac Albéniz: Portrait of a Romantic*. New York and Oxford: Oxford University Press, 1998.

Clarke, Joseph. *Commemorating the Dead in Revolutionary France: Revolution and Remembrance, 1789–1799*. Cambridge: Cambridge University Press, 2007.

Colley, Linda. *Britons: Forging the Nation, 1707–1837*. New Haven: Yale University Press, 1992.

Colls, Robert, and Philip Dodd (eds). *Englishness: Politics and Culture, 1880–1920*. London: Croom Helm, 1986.

Connor, Walker. *Ethnonationalism: The Quest for Understanding*. Princeton: Princeton University Press, 1994.

Cooper, Barry. *Beethoven's Folksong Settings: Chronology, Sources, Style*. Oxford: Clarendon Press, 1994.

Cooper, David. 'Béla Bartók and the Question of Race Purity in Music', in Murphy and White (eds), *Musical Constructions of Nationalism*, pp. 16–32.

Cowgill, Rachel. 'Elgar's War Requiem', in *Edward Elgar and his World*, ed. Byron Adams. Princeton and Oxford: Princeton University Press, 2007, pp. 317–62.

—— 'Canonizing Remembrance: Music for Armistice Day at the BBC, 1922–7'. *First World War Studies* 2/1 (2011), pp. 75–107.

Crist, Elizabeth Bergman. *Music for the Common Man: Aaron Copland during the Depression and War*. New York: Oxford University Press, 2005.

Crump, Jeremy. 'The Identity of English Music: The Reception of Elgar, 1898–1935', in Colls and Dodd (eds), *Englishness*, pp. 164–90.

Curtis, Benjamin W. *Music Makes the Nation: Nationalist Composers and Nation Building in Nineteenth-Century Europe*. Amherst: Cambria, 2008.

Dahlhaus, Carl. *Between Romanticism and Modernism: Four Studies in the Music of the Later Nineteenth Century*. Trans. Mary Whittall. Berkeley and Los Angeles: University of California Press, 1980.

—— *Nineteenth-Century Music*. Trans. J. Bradford Robinson. Berkeley and Los Angeles: University of California Press, 1989.

Daniels, Stephen. *Fields of Vision: Landscape Imagery and National Identity in England and the United States*. Princeton: Princeton University Press, 1993.

Daverio, John. 'Einheit-Freiheit-Vaterland: Intimations of Utopia in Robert Schumann's Late Choral Music', in Applegate and Potter (eds), *Music and German National Identity*, pp. 59–77.

Dennis, David B. *Beethoven in German Politics, 1870–1989*. New Haven and London: Yale University Press, 1996.

De Val, Dorothy. 'The Transformed Village: Lucy Broadwood and Folksong', in *Music and British Culture, 1785–1914: Essays in Honour of Cyril Ehrlich*, ed. Christina Bashford and Leanne Langley. Oxford: Oxford University Press, 2000, pp. 341–66.

Dibble, Jeremy. 'Parry and English Diatonic Dissonance'. *Journal of the British Music Society* 5 (1983), pp. 58–71.

—— *Charles Villiers Stanford: Man and Musician*. Oxford: Oxford University Press, 2002.

Doge, Klaus. 'Dvořák, Antonín', in Sadie (ed.), *New Grove*, vol. 7, pp. 777–814.

Downes, Stephen. 'Pastoral Idylls, Erotic Anxieties and Heroic Subjectivities in Sibelius' *Lemminkäinen and the Maidens of the Island* and First Two Symphonies', in Grimley (ed.), *The Cambridge Companion to Sibelius*, pp. 35–48.

Duggan, Christopher. *The Force of Destiny: A History of Italy since 1796*. London: Penguin, 2008.

Durkheim, Émile. *The Elementary Forms of the Religious Life*. Trans. J. Swain. London: Allen and Unwin, 1915.

Earle, Ben. *Luigi Dallapiccola and Musical Modernism in Fascist Italy*. Cambridge: Cambridge University Press, 2013.

Eichner, Barbara. *History in Mighty Sounds: Musical Constructions of German National Identity, 1848–1914*. Woodbridge: Boydell Press, 2013.

Ellis, Katharine. *Interpreting the Musical Past: Early Music in Nineteenth-Century France*. New York: Oxford University Press, 2005.

—— 'Rameau in Late Nineteenth-Century Dijon: Memorial, Festival, Fiasco', in Kelly (ed.), *French Music, Culture, and National Identity*, pp. 197–214.

Emerson, Caryl. 'Apocalypse Then, Now and (For Us) Never: Reflections on Musorgsky's Other Historical Opera', in Batchelor and John (eds), *Khovanshchina*, pp. 7–20.

—— *The Life of Musorgsky*. Cambridge: Cambridge University Press, 1999.

Finscher, Ludwig. 'Weber's "Freischütz": Conceptions and Misconceptions'. *Proceedings of the Royal Musical Association* 110 (1983–84), pp. 79–90.

Fischer, Jens Malte. 'Wagner-Interpretation im Dritten Reich: Musik und Szene zwischen Politisierung und Kunstanspruch', in *Richard Wagner im Dritten Reich: Ein Schloß-Elmau-Symposion*, ed. Saul Friedländer and Jörn Rüsen. Munich: C. H. Beck, 2000, pp. 142–64.

Fischer-Lichte, Erika. *Theatre, Sacrifice, Ritual: Exploring Forms of Political Theatre*. London and New York: Routledge, 2005.

Francfort, Didier. *Le chant des nations: Musiques et culture en Europe, 1870–1914*. Paris: Hachette, 2004.

Freeman, Graham. '"It Wants All the Creases Ironing Out": Percy Grainger, the Folk Song Society, and the Ideology of the Archive'. *Music & Letters* 92/3 (2011), pp. 410–36.

Frogley, Alain (ed.). *Vaughan Williams Studies*. Cambridge: Cambridge University Press, 1996.

—— 'Constructing Englishness in Music: National Character and the Reception of Ralph Vaughan Williams', in Frogley (ed.), *Vaughan Williams Studies*, pp. 1–22.

Frogley, Alain, and Aidan J. Thomson (eds). *The Cambridge Companion to Vaughan Williams*. Cambridge: Cambridge University Press, 2013.

Frolova-Walker, Marina. *Russian Music and Nationalism: From Glinka to Stalin*. New Haven and London: Yale University Press, 2007.

Fulcher, Jane. *French Cultural Politics and Music: From the Dreyfus Affair to the First World War*. New York: Oxford University Press, 1999.

—— *The Composer as Intellectual: Music and Ideology in France, 1914–1940*. New York: Oxford University Press, 2005.

Galliver, David. '*Leonore, ou l'amour conjugal*: A Celebrated Offspring of the Revolution', in Boyd (ed.), *Music and the French Revolution*, pp. 157–68.

Gammon, Vic. 'Folk Song Collecting in Sussex and Surrey, 1843–1914'. *History Workshop Journal* 10/1 (1980), pp. 61–89.

Garagola, Lynn. 'Making an American Dance: *Billy the Kid*, *Rodeo*, and *Appalachian Spring*', in *Aaron Copland and his World*, ed. Carol J. Oja and Judith Tick. Princeton and Oxford: Princeton University Press, 2005, pp. 121–47.

Gelbart, Matthew. *The Invention of 'Folk Music' and 'Art Music': Emerging Categories from Ossian to Wagner*. Cambridge: Cambridge University Press, 2007.

Gilliam, Bryan. 'Strauss, Richard', in Sadie (ed.), *New Grove*, vol. 24, pp. 497–527

Gillies, Malcolm (ed.). *The Bartók Companion*. London: Faber & Faber, 1993.

—— 'Bartók, Béla', in Sadie (ed.), *New Grove*, vol. 2, pp. 787–818.

Gillies, Malcolm, and David Pear. 'Percy Grainger and American Nordicism', in Brown (ed.), *Western Music and Race*, pp. 115–24.

Gorski, Philip S. 'The Mosaic Moment: An Early Modernist Critique of Modernist Theories of Nationalism'. *American Journal of Sociology* 105/5 (2000), pp. 1428–68.

Goss, Glenda Dawn. 'Vienna and the Genesis of *Kullervo*: "Durchführung zum Teufel!"', in Grimley (ed.), *The Cambridge Companion to Sibelius*, pp. 22–31.

—— *Sibelius: A Composer's Life and the Awakening of Finland*. Chicago and London: University of Chicago Press, 2009.

Gossett, Philip. 'Giuseppe Verdi and the Italian Risorgimento'. *Studia Musicologica* 52/1–4 (2011), pp. 241–57.

Gray, Camilla. *The Russian Experiment in Art, 1863–1922*. London: Thames and Hudson, 1971.

Grey, Thomas S. 'Tableaux Vivants: Landscape, History Painting, and the Visual Imagination in Mendelssohn's Orchestral Music'. *19th-Century Music* 21/1 (1997), pp. 38–76.

—— 'Wagner's Die Meistersinger as National Opera (1868–1945)', in Applegate and Potter (eds), *German Music and National Identity*, pp. 78–104.

Grimley, Daniel M. 'Horn Calls and Flattened Sevenths: Nielsen and Danish Musical Style', in Murphy and White (eds), *Musical Constructions of Nationalism*, pp. 123–41.

—— (ed.) *The Cambridge Companion to Sibelius*. Cambridge: Cambridge University Press, 2004.

—— 'The Tone Poems: Genre, Landscape and Structural Perspective', in Grimley (ed.), *The Cambridge Companion to Sibelius*, pp. 95–116.

—— *Grieg: Music, Landscape and Norwegian Identity*. Woodbridge: Boydell Press, 2006.

—— '"Music in the Midst of Desolation": Structures of Mourning in Elgar's *The Spirit of England*', in *Elgar Studies*, ed. J. P. E. Harper-Scott and Julian Rushton. Cambridge: Cambridge University Press, 2007, pp. 220–37.

—— *Carl Nielsen and the Idea of Modernism*. Woodbridge: Boydell Press, 2010.

—— 'Landscape and Distance: Vaughan Williams, Modernism and the Symphonic Pastoral', in *British Music and Modernism 1895–1960*, ed. Matthew Riley. Farnham: Ashgate, 2010, pp. 147–74.

—— (ed.). *Sibelius and his World*. Princeton: Princeton University Press, 2011.

Grinde, Nils, and John Horton. 'Grieg, Edvard', in Sadie (ed.), *New Grove*, vol. 10, pp. 396–411.

Groos, Arthur. 'Constructing Nuremberg: Typological and Proleptic Communities in *Die Meistersinger*'. *19th-Century Music* 16/1 (1992), pp. 18–34.

Grosby, Steven. 'Religion and Nationality in Antiquity: The Worship of Yahweh and Ancient Israel'. *European Journal of Sociology* 32/2 (1991), pp. 229–65.

Guibernau, Montserrat. *Nations without States: Political Communities in a Global Age*. Malden, Mass.: Blackwell, 1999.

Hamilton, James. *Turner's Britain*. London: Merrell, 2003.

Hamilton, Kenneth (ed.). *The Cambridge Companion to Liszt*. Cambridge: Cambridge University Press, 2005.

—— 'Liszt's Early and Weimar Piano Works', in Hamilton (ed.), *The Cambridge Companion to Liszt*, pp. 57–85.

Harker, David. *Fakesong: The Manufacture of British 'Folksong' 1700 to the Present Day*. Milton Keynes: Open University Press, 1985.

Harrington, Paul. 'Holst and Vaughan Williams: Radical Pastoral', in *Music and the Politics of Culture*, ed. Christopher Norris. London: Lawrence & Wishart, 1989, pp. 106–27.

Hart, Brian. 'The Symphony and National Identity in Early Twentieth-Century France', in Kelly (ed.), *French Music, Culture and National Identity*, pp. 131–48.

Hastings, Adrian. *The Construction of Nationhood: Ethnicity, Religion, and Nationalism*. Cambridge: Cambridge University Press, 1997.

Helmers, Rutger. *Not Russian Enough?: Nationalism and Cosmopolitanism in Nineteenth-Century Russian Opera*. Rochester: University of Rochester Press, 2014.

Hepokoski, James A. *Sibelius, Symphony No. 5*. Cambridge: Cambridge University Press, 1993.

—— 'The Essence of Sibelius: Creation Myths and Rotational Cycles in *Luonnotar*', in *The Sibelius Companion*, ed. Glenda Dawn Goss. Westport, Conn. and London, 1996, pp. 121–46.

—— 'Beethoven Reception', in Samson (ed.), *The Cambridge History of Nineteenth-Century Music*, pp. 424–59.

—— 'Sibelius, Jean', in Sadie (ed.), *New Grove*, vol. 23, pp. 319–47.

—— 'Back and Forth from *Egmont*: Beethoven, Mozart and the Nonresolving Recapitulation'. *19th-Century Music* 25 (2002), pp. 127–53.

—— '*Finlandia* Awakens', in Grimley (ed.), *The Cambridge Companion to Sibelius*, pp. 81–94.

—— 'Modalities of National Identity: Sibelius Builds a First Symphony', in *The Oxford Handbook of the New Cultural History of Music*, ed. Jane F. Fulcher. New York: Oxford University Press, 2011, pp. 452–83.

Herbert, Robert. *David, Voltaire, 'Brutus' and the French Revolution: An Essay in Art and Politics*. London: Allen Lane, 1972.

Hess, Carol A. *Manuel de Falla and Modernism in Spain, 1898–1936*. Chicago: University of Chicago Press, 2001.

—— *Sacred Passions: The Life and Music of Manuel de Falla*. Oxford: Oxford University Press, 2005.

Heyman, Barbara B. *Samuel Barber: The Composer and his Music*. New York: Oxford University Press, 1992.

Hicks, Anthony. 'Handel and the Idea of an Oratorio', in Burrows (ed.), *The Cambridge Companion to Handel*, pp. 147–63.

Hillman, Roger. *Unsettling Scores: German Film, Music, and Ideology*. Bloomington: Indiana University Press, 2005.

Hirschi, Caspar. *The Origins of Nationalism: An Alternative History from Ancient Rome to Early Modern Germany*. Cambridge: Cambridge University Press, 2012.

Hobsbawm, Eric J. *Nations and Nationalism since 1780: Programme, Myth, Reality*. Cambridge: Cambridge University Press, 1990.

Honko, Lauri. 'The *Kalevala* Process'. *Books from Finland* 19/1 (1985), pp. 16–23.

Hooker, Lynn M. *Redefining Hungarian Music from Liszt to Bartók*. New York: Oxford University Press, 2013.

Hooson, David J. (ed.). *Geography and National Identity*. Oxford: Blackwell, 1994.

Hously, Geoffrey. 'Holy Land or Holy Lands? Palestine and the Catholic West in the Late Middle Ages and the Renaissance', in *The Holy Land, Holy Lands and Christian History*, ed. Robert Swanson. Ecclesiastical History Society, Woodbridge: Boydell Press, 2002, pp. 234–49.

Howard, Luke B. 'Pan-Slavic Parallels in the Music of Stravinsky and Szymanowski'. *Context* 13 (1997), pp. 15–24.

—— 'The Popular Reception of Samuel Barber's "Adagio for Strings"'. *American Music* 25/1 (2007), pp. 50–80.

Howkins, Alun. 'The Discovery of Rural England', in Colls and Dodd (eds), *Englishness*, pp. 62–88.

Huebner, Steven. *French Opera at the fin de siècle: Wagnerism, Nationalism, and Style*. Oxford: Oxford University Press, 1999.

Hughes, Meirion, and Robert Stradling. *The English Musical Renaissance, 1840–1940: Constructing a National Music*, 2nd edn. Manchester: Manchester University Press, 2001.

Hutchings, Arthur. *Delius*. London: Macmillan, 1948.

Hutchinson, John. *The Dynamics of Cultural Nationalism: The Gaelic Revival and the Creation of the Irish Nation State*. London: Allen & Unwin, 1987.

Hutchinson, John, and Anthony D. Smith. *Nationalism*. Oxford and New York: Oxford University Press, 1994.

Huttunen, Matti. 'The National Composer and the Idea of Finnishness: Sibelius and the Formation of Finnish Musical Style', in Grimley (ed.), *The Cambridge Companion to Sibelius*, pp. 7–21

Im Hof, Ulrich. *Mythos Schweiz: Identität, Nation, Geschichte, 1291–1991*. Zürich: Neue Zürcher Zeitung, 1991.

Jaffé, Daniel. *Sergey Prokofiev*. London: Phaidon Press, 1998.

Jam, Jean-Louis. 'Marie-Joseph Chénier and François-Joseph Gossec: Two Artists in the Service of Revolutionary Propaganda', in Boyd (ed.), *Music and the French Revolution*, pp. 221–35.

James, Burnett. *The Music of Jean Sibelius*. East Brunswick and London: Associated University Presses, 1983.

Johns, Keith T. *The Symphonic Poems of Franz Liszt*, ed. Michael Saffle. Stuyvesant: Pendragon Press, 1996.

Johnson, David. *Scottish Fiddle Music in the Eighteenth Century: A Music Collection and Historical Study*. Edinburgh: John Donald, 1984.

Johnson, Graham. *Berlioz and the Romantic Imagination*. London: Arts Council, 1969.

Kallberg, Jeffrey. 'Hearing Poland: Chopin and Nationalism', in *Nineteenth-Century Piano Music*, 2nd edn, ed. R. Larry Todd. New York and London: Routledge, 2004, pp. 221–57.

Karlinsky, Simon. 'Stravinsky and Russian Pre-Literate Theater'. *19th-Century Music* 6/3 (1983), pp. 232–40.

Kelly, Barbara L. (ed.). *French Music, Culture, and National Identity, 1870–1939*. Woodbridge: Boydell Press, 2008.

Kennedy, Emmet. *A Cultural History of the French Revolution*. New Haven and London: Yale University Press, 1989.

Kennedy, Michael. *Portrait of Elgar*. London: Oxford University Press, 1968.

—— *The Works of Ralph Vaughan Williams*, 2nd edn. Oxford: Oxford University Press, 1980.

Kenyon, Nicholas (ed.). *Elgar: An Anniversary Portrait*. London and New York: Continuum, 2007.

Kleiberg, Ståle. 'Grieg's "Slåtter", Op. 72: Change of Musical Style or New Concept of Nationality?' *Journal of the Royal Musical Association* 121/1 (1996), pp. 46–57.

Klinge, Matti. '"Let us be Finns": The Birth of Finland's National Culture', in *The Roots of Nationalism: Studies in Northern Europe*, ed. Rosalind Mitchison. Edinburgh: John Donald Publishers, 1980.

Knittel, K. N. 'Wagner, Deafness, and the Reception of Beethoven's Late Style'. *Journal of the American Musicological Society* 51/1 (1998), pp. 49–82.

Koldau, Linda Maria. 'Monotonie und Dynamik: Smetanas Symphonische Dichtung *Tábor*'. *Die Musikforschung* 59/4 (2006), pp. 328–45.

Körner, Axel. 'The Risorgimento's Literary Canon and the Aesthetics of Reception: Some Methodological Considerations'. *Nations and Nationalism* 15/3 (2009), pp. 410–18.

Körner, Axel, and Lucy Riall. 'Introduction: The New History of Risorgimento Nationalism'. *Nations and Nationalism* 15/3 (2009), pp. 396–401.

Kraus, Beate Angelika. 'Beethoven and the Revolution: The View of the French Musical Press', in Boyd (ed.), *Music and the French Revolution*, pp. 300–14.

Kumar, Krishan. *The Making of English National Identity*. Cambridge: Cambridge University Press, 2003.

Lajosi, Krisztina. 'National Stereotypes and Music'. *Nations and Nationalism* 20/4 (2014), pp. 628–45.

Lambert, Constant. *Music Ho! A Study of Music in Decline*. London: Faber & Faber, 1934.

Large, Brian. *Smetana*. London: Duckworth, 1970.

Laufer, Edward. 'Continuity in the Fourth Symphony (First Movement)', in *Perspectives on Anton Bruckner*, ed. Crawford Howie, Paul Hawkshaw and Timothy Jackson. Aldershot: Ashgate, 2001, pp. 114–44.

Leerssen, Joep. *National Thought in Europe: A Cultural History*. Amsterdam: Amsterdam University Press, 2006.

—— 'Romanticism, Music, Nationalism'. *Nations and Nationalism* 20/4 (2014), pp. 606–27.

Leikin, Anatole. 'The Sonatas', in Samson (ed.), *The Cambridge Companion to Chopin*, pp. 160–87.

Lerner, Neil. 'Copland's Music of Wide Open Spaces: Surveying the Pastoral Trope in Hollywood'. *The Musical Quarterly* 85/3 (2001), pp. 477–515.

Levy, Beth E. *Frontier Figures: American Music and the Mythology of the American West*. Berkeley: University of California Press, 2012.

Leyshon, Andrew, David Matless and George Revill (eds). *The Place of Music*. New York and London: Guilford Press, 1998.

Ling, Jan. *A History of European Folk Music*. Rochester: University of Rochester Press, 1997.

Llano, Samuel. *Whose Spain? Negotiating 'Spanish Music' in Paris, 1908–1929*. New York: Oxford University Press, 2013.

Locke, Ralph P. *Musical Exoticism: Images and Reflections*. Cambridge: Cambridge University Press, 2009.

—— *Music and the Exotic from the Renaissance to Mozart*. Cambridge: Cambridge University Press, 2015.

Lockwood, Lewis. *Beethoven: The Music and the Life*. New York and London: W. W. Norton, 2003.

Loges, Natasha. 'How to Make a "Volkslied": Early Models in the Songs of Johannes Brahms'. *Music & Letters* 93/3 (2012), pp. 316–49.

Loos, Helmut, and Stefan Keym (eds). *Nationale Musik im 20. Jahrhundert: kompositorische und soziokulturelle Aspekte der Musikgeschichte zwischen Ost- und Westeuropa: Konferenzbericht Leipzig 2002*. Leipzig: Gundrun Schröder, 2004.

Loya, Shay. *Liszt's Transcultural Modernism and the Hungarian-Gypsy Tradition*. Rochester: University of Rochester Press, 2011.

McBurney, Gerard. 'Musorgsky's New Music', in Batchelor and John (eds), *Khovanshchina*, pp. 21–9.

McClatchie, Stephen C. 'Performing Germany in Wagner's *Die Meistersinger von Nürnberg*', in *The Cambridge Companion to Wagner*, ed. Thomas S. Grey. Cambridge: Cambridge University Press, 2008, pp. 134–50.

Mach, Zdzislaw. 'National Anthems: The Case of Chopin as a National Composer', in *Ethnicity, Identity and Music: The Musical Construction of Place*, ed. Martin Stokes. Berg: Oxford and Providence, RI, 1994, pp. 61–70.

Madrid, Alejandro L. *Sounds of the Modern Nation: Music, Culture, and Ideas in Post-Revolutionary Mexico*. Philadelphia: Temple University Press, 2008.

Maes, Francis. *A History of Russian Music: From Kamarinskaya to Babi Yar*. Berkeley and London: University of California Press, 2002.

Magee, Gayle Sherwood. *Charles Ives Reconsidered*. Urbana and Chicago: University of Illinois Press, 2008.

Mäkelä, Tomi (ed.). *Music and Nationalism in 20th-Century Great Britain and Finland*. Hamburg: Bockel, 1997.

——*Jean Sibelius*. Trans. Steven Lindberg. Woodbridge: Boydell Press, 2011.

Mann, Michael. *The Sources of Social Power*, vol. 2, *The Rise of Classes and Nation-States 1760–1914*. Cambridge: Cambridge University Press, 1993.

Martin, David. 'The Sound of England', in *Nationalism and Ethnosymbolism: History, Culture and Ethnicity in the Formation of Nations*, ed. Athena S. Leoussi and Steven Grosby. Edinburgh: Edinburgh University Press, 2007, pp. 68–83.

Mellers, Wilfrid. *Vaughan Williams and the Vision of Albion*. London: Pimlico, 1991.

Mercer-Taylor, Peter (ed.). *The Cambridge Companion to Mendelssohn*. Cambridge: Cambridge University Press, 2004.

Meyer, Michael. *The Politics of Music in the Third Reich*. New York: Peter Lang, 1991.

Meyer, Stephen C. *Carl Maria von Weber and the Search for a German Opera*. Bloomington: Indiana University Press, 2003.

Milewski, Barbara. 'Chopin's Mazurkas and the Myth of the Folk'. *19th-Century Music* 23/2 (1999), pp. 113–35.

Minor, Ryan. *Choral Fantasies: Music, Festivity, and Nationhood in Nineteenth-Century Germany*. Cambridge: Cambridge University Press, 2012.

Morrison, Simon. *The People's Artist: Prokofiev's Soviet Years*. New York and Oxford: Oxford University Press, 2009.

Mosse, George L. *The Nationalization of the Masses: Political Symbolism and Mass Movements in Germany from the Napoleonic Wars through the Third Reich*. Ithaca and London: Cornell University Press, 1975.

——*Fallen Soldiers: Reshaping the Memory of the World Wars*. New York: Oxford University Press, 1990.

Murphy, Michael. 'Moniuszko and Musical Nationalism in Poland', in Murphy and White (eds), *Musical Constructions of Nationalism*, pp. 163–80.

Murphy, Michael, and Harry White (eds). *Musical Constructions of Nationalism: Essays on the History and Ideology of European Musical Culture, 1800–1945*. Cork: Cork University Press, 2001.

Newman, Gerald. *The Rise of English Nationalism: A Cultural History, 1740–1830*. London: Weidenfeld & Nicolson, 1987.

Noa, Miriam. *Volkstümlichkeit und Nationbuilding: zum Einfluss der Musik auf den Einigungsprozess der deutschen Nation im 19. Jahrhundert*. Münster and New York: Waxmann, 2013.

Onderdonk, Julian. 'Ralph Vaughan Williams' Folksong Collecting: English Nationalism and the Rise of Professional Society'. Ph.D. dissertation, New York University, 1998.

—— 'Hymn Tunes from Folk-Songs: Vaughan Williams and English Hymnody', in Adams and Wells (eds), *Vaughan Williams Essays*, pp. 103–28.

—— 'The Composer and Society: Family, Politics, Nation', in Frogley and Thomson (eds), *The Cambridge Companion to Vaughan Williams*, pp. 9–28.

Osborne, Charles. *The Complete Operas of Richard Wagner*. London: Da Capo Press, 1993.

—— *The Complete Operas of Verdi*. London: Indigo, 1997.

Ottaway, Hugh. *Vaughan Williams Symphonies*. London: British Broadcasting Corporation, 1972.

Ottlová, Marta and Milan Pospíšil. 'Motive der tschechischen Dvořák-Kritik am Anfang des 20. Jahrhunderts', in *Dvořák-Studien*, ed. Klaus Döge and Peter Just. Mainz: Schott, 1994, pp. 211–26.

Ottlová, Marta, Milan Pospíšil and John Tyrrell. 'Smetana, Bedřich', in Sadie (ed.), *New Grove*, vol. 23, pp. 537–58.

Parakilas, James. 'How Spain Got a Soul', in *The Exotic in Western Music*, ed. Jonathan Bellman. Boston: Northeastern University Press, 1998, pp. 137–93.

Parker, Robert. 'Chávez (y Ramírez), Carlos (Antonio de Padua)', in Sadie (ed.), *New Grove*, vol. 5, pp. 544–8.

Parker, Roger. *Leonora's Last Act: Essays in Verdian Discourse*. Princeton: Princeton University Press, 1997.

Parry, Hubert. 'Inaugural Address'. *Journal of the Folksong Society* 1/1 (1889), pp. 1–3.

Paul, Charles B. 'Rameau, d'Indy, and French Nationalism'. *Musical Quarterly* 58/1 (1972), pp. 46–56.

Paul, David C. *Charles Ives in the Mirror: American Histories of an Iconic Composer*. Urbana, Chicago and Springfield, University of Illinois Press, 2013.

Paulin, Scott D. 'Piercing Wagner: The *Ring* in *Golden Earrings*', in *Wagner and Cinema*, ed. Jeongwon Joe and Sander L. Gilman. Bloomington: Indiana University Press, 2010, pp. 225–50.

Pekacz, Jolanta T. 'Deconstructing a "National Composer": Chopin and Polish Exiles in Paris, 1831–49'. *19th-Century Music* 24/2 (2000), pp. 161–72.

Pople, Anthony. 'Vaughan Williams, Tallis, and the Phantasy Principle', in Frogley (ed.), *Vaughan Williams Studies*, pp. 47–80.

Porter, Cecelia Hopkins. *The Rhine as Musical Metaphor: Cultural Identity in German Romantic Music*. Boston: Northeastern University Press, 1996.

Redgate, Anne Elizabeth. *The Armenians*. Oxford: Blackwell, 2000.

Renan, Ernest. *Qu'est-ce qu'une nation?* Paris: Calmann-Levy, 1882. English translation in Bhabha, *Nation and Narration*, pp. 8–22.

Riall, Lucy. 'Nation, "Deep Images" and the Problem of Emotions'. *Nations and Nationalism* 15/3 (2009), pp. 402–9.

Riasanovsky, Nicolas. *A History of Russia*. Oxford: Oxford University Press, 1963.

Rigby, Kate E. *Topographies of the Sacred: The Poetics of Place in European Romanticism*. Charlottesville: University of Virginia Press, 2004.

Riley, Matthew. *Edward Elgar and the Nostalgic Imagination*. Cambridge: Cambridge University Press, 2007.

Rink, John. *Chopin, the Piano Concertos*. Cambridge: Cambridge University Press, 1997.

—— 'Rhapsody', in Sadie (ed.), *New Grove*, vol. 21, pp. 254–5.

Robson-Scott, W. D. *The Literary Background of the Gothic Revival in Germany*. Oxford: Clarendon Press, 1965.

Rodmell, Paul. *Charles Villiers Stanford*. Aldershot: Ashgate, 2002.

Rosen, Charles. *The Romantic Generation*. Cambridge, Mass.: Harvard University Press, 1995.

Rosenblum, Robert. *Transformations in Late Eighteenth Century Art*. Princeton: Princeton University Press, 1967.

Rosenthal, Michael. *Constable: The Painter and his Landscape*. New Haven: Yale University Press, 1989.

Roshwald, Aviel. *The Endurance of Nationalism: Ancient Roots and Modern Dilemmas*. Cambridge: Cambridge University Press, 2006.

Russ, Michael. *Musorgsky: Pictures at an Exhibition*. Cambridge: Cambridge University Press, 1992.

Sabor, Rudolph. *Richard Wagner, Der Ring Des Nibelungen*. London: Phaidon Press, 1997.

Sadie, Stanley (ed.). *The New Grove Dictionary of Music and Musicians*, 29 vols, 2nd edn. London: Macmillan, 2001.

Salmi, Hannu. *Imagined Germany: Richard Wagner's National Utopia*. New York: Peter Lang, 1999.

Samson, Jim. *The Music of Szymanowski*. London: White Plains and New York: Kahn & Averill, 1980.

—— *The Cambridge Companion to Chopin*. Cambridge: Cambridge University Press, 1994.

—— 'Chopin Reception: Theory, History, Analysis', in *Chopin Studies 2*, ed. John Rink and Jim Samson. Cambridge: Cambridge University Press, 1994, pp. 1–17.

—— *Chopin*. Oxford and New York: Oxford University Press, 1996.

—— 'Nations and Nationalism', in Samson (ed.), *The Cambridge History of Nineteenth-Century Music*, pp. 568–600.

—— (ed.). *The Cambridge History of Nineteenth-Century Music*. Cambridge and New York: Cambridge University Press, 2001.

—— 'Music and Nationalism: Five Historical Moments', in *Nationalism and Ethnosymbolism: History, Culture and Ethnicity in the Formation of Nations*, ed. Athena S. Leoussi and Steven Grosby. Edinburgh: Edinburgh University Press, 2007, pp. 55–67.

—— 'The Story of Koula: Music and Nationhood in Greece'. *Nations and Nationalism* 20/4, (2014), pp. 646–63.

Saylor, Eric. '"It's Not Lambkins Frisking At All": English Pastoral Music and the Great War'. *Musical Quarterly* 91/1–2 (2009), pp. 39–59.

Scales, Leonard. 'Identifying "France" and "Germany": Medieval Nation-Making in Some Recent Publications'. *Bulletin of International Medieval Research* 6 (2000), pp. 23–46.

—— 'Late Medieval Germany: An Under-Stated Nation?', in *Power and the Nation in European History*, ed. Leonard Scales and Oliver Zimmer. Cambridge: Cambridge University Press, 2005, pp. 166–91.

Schama, Simon. *Citizens: A Chronicle of the French Revolution*. New York and London: Knopf and Penguin, 1989.

—— *Landscape and Memory*. London: Fontana, 1996.

Schneider, David E. *Bartók, Hungary, and the Renewal of Tradition: Case Studies in the Intersection of Modernity and Nationality*. Berkeley: University of California Press, 2006.

Schumann, Robert. *On Music and Musicians*, ed. Konrad Wolff. Trans. Paul Rosenfeld. Berkeley: University of California Press, 1983.

Seaton, Douglas. 'Symphony and Overture', in Mercer-Taylor (ed.), *The Cambridge Companion to Mendelssohn*, pp. 91–111.

Seton-Watson, Hugh. *Nations and States: An Enquiry into the Origins of Nations and the Politics of Nationalism*. London: Methuen, 1977.

Smith, Anthony D. *The Ethnic Origins of Nations*. Oxford: Blackwell, 1986.

—— *National Identity*. London: Penguin, 1991.

—— *Nationalism and Modernism: A Critical Survey of Recent Theories of Nations and Nationalism*. London: Routledge, 1998.

—— *Myths and Memories of the Nation*. Oxford: Oxford University Press, 1999.

—— *Chosen Peoples: Sacred Sources of National Identity*. Oxford: Oxford University Press, 2003.

—— *The Cultural Foundations of Nations: Hierarchy, Covenant, and Republic*. Oxford: Blackwell, 2008.

—— *Nationalism: Theory, Ideology, History*. Cambridge: Polity, 2010.

—— 'National Identity and Vernacular Mobilisation in Europe'. *Nations and Nationalism* 17/2 (2011), pp. 223–56.

—— *The Nation Made Real: Art and National Identity in Western Europe, 1600–1815*. Oxford: Oxford University Press, 2013.

—— 'The Rites of Nations: Elites, Masses and the Re-Enactment of the "National Past"', in *The Politics of Cultural Nationalism and Nation Building*, ed. Rachel Tsang and Eric Taylor Woods. London: Routledge, 2013, pp. 21–37.

Sørensen, Øystein (ed.). *Nordic Paths to National Identity in the Nineteenth Century*. Oslo: Research Council of Norway, 1994.

—— 'The Development of a Norwegian National Identity during the Nineteenth Century', in Sørensen (ed.), *Nordic Paths to National Identity*, pp. 15–35.

Spencer, Stewart. 'Wagner's Nuremberg'. *Cambridge Opera Journal* 4/1 (1992), pp. 21–41.

Spondheuer, Bernd. 'Reconstructing Ideal Types of the "German" in Music', in Applegate and Potter (eds), *Music and German National Identity*, pp. 36–58.

Steinberg, Michael P. *Listening to Reason: Culture, Subjectivity, and Nineteenth-Century Music*. Princeton: Princeton University Press, 2004.

Stradling, Robert. 'On Shearing the Black Sheep in Spring: The Repatriation of Frederick Delius', in *Music and the Politics of Culture*, ed. Christopher Norris. London: Lawrence & Wishart, 1989, pp. 69–105.

—— 'England's Glory: Sensibilities of Place in English Music, 1900–1950', in *The Place of Music*, ed. Andrew Leyshon, David Matless and George Revill. New York and London: Guilford Press, 1998, pp. 176–96.

Strath, Bo. 'The Swedish Path to National Identity in the Nineteenth Century', in Sørensen (ed.), *Nordic Paths to National Identity*, pp. 55–63.

Stuckenschmidt, Hans Heinz. *Schoenberg: His Life, World, and Work*. Trans. Humphrey Searle. New York: Schirmer, 1978.

Suchoff, Benjamin. 'Fusion of National Styles: Piano Literature, 1908–11', in Gillies (ed.), *The Bartók Companion*, pp. 124–45.

Sugar, Peter F. *Ethnic Diversity and Conflict in Eastern Europe*. Santa Barbara: ABC-Clio, 1980.

Sutcliffe, W. Dean. 'Grieg's Fifth: The Linguistic Battleground of "Klokkeklang"'. *Musical Quarterly* 80/1 (1996), pp. 161–81.

Swafford, Jan. *Charles Ives: A Life with Music*. New York and London: W. W. Norton, 1996.

Taruskin, Richard. *Musorgsky: Eight Essays and an Epilogue*. Princeton and Chichester: Princeton University Press, 1993.

—— *Stravinsky and the Russian Traditions: A Biography of the Works through Mavra*, 2 vols. Berkeley: University of California Press, 1996.

—— *Defining Russia Musically: Historical and Hermeneutical Essays*. Princeton and Chichester: Princeton University Press, 1997.

—— 'Nationalism', in Sadie (ed.), *New Grove*, vol. 17, pp. 689–706

—— *On Russian Music*. Berkeley and Los Angeles: University of California Press, 2009.

—— *The Oxford History of Western Music*, vol. 3, *Music in the Nineteenth Century*, 2nd edn. New York and Oxford: Oxford University Press, 2010.

Tawaststjerna, Erik. *Sibelius*. London: Faber & Faber, 1976.

Taylor, Benedict. 'Nostalgia and Cultural Memory in Barber's *Knoxville: Summer of 1915*'. *Journal of Musicology* 25/3 (2008), pp. 211–29.

—— 'Temporality in Nineteenth-Century Russian Music and the Notion of Development'. *Music & Letters* 94/1 (2013), pp. 78–118.

Thaden, Edward C. *Conservative Nationalism in Nineteenth-Century Russia*. Seattle: University of Washington Press, 1964.

Ther, Philipp. *Center Stage: Operatic Culture and Nation Building in Nineteenth-Century Central Europe*. Trans. Charlotte Hughes-Kreutzmüller. West Lafayette: Purdue University Press, 2014.

Thomson, Andrew. *Vincent d'Indy and his World*. Oxford: Clarendon Press, 1996.

Tilly, Charles. *The Formation of National States in Western Europe*. Princeton: Princeton University Press, 1975.

Tischler, Barbara L. *An American Music: The Search for an American Musical Identity*. New York and Oxford: Oxford University Press, 1986.

Todd, R. Larry. 'On Mendelssohn's Sacred Music, Real and Imaginary', in Mercer-Taylor (ed.), *The Cambridge Companion to Mendelssohn*, pp. 167–88.

Toftgaard, Anders. 'Letters and Arms: Literary Language, Power and Nation in Renaissance Italy and France, 1300–1600'. Ph.D. thesis, University of Copenhagen, 2005.

Tonnesson, Stein and Hans Antlov. *Asian Forms of the Nation*. Richmond: Curzon Press, 1996.

Trumpener, Katie. 'Béla Bartók and the Rise of Comparative Ethnomusicology: Nationalism, Race Purity and the Legacy of the Austro-Hungarian Empire', in *Music and the Racial Imagination*, ed. Ronald Radano and Philip V. Bohlman. Chicago: University of Chicago Press, 2000, pp. 403–34.

Tyrrell, John. *Czech Opera*. Cambridge: Cambridge University Press, 1988.

—— 'Janáček, Leoš', in Sadie (ed.), *New Grove*, vol. 12, pp. 769–92.

Vaget, Hans Rudolf. 'The "Metapolitics" of *Die Meistersinger*: Wagner's Nuremberg as Imagined Community', in *Searching for Common Ground: Diskurse zur deutschen Identität, 1750–1871*, ed. Nicholas Vazsonyi. Cologne: Böhlau, 2000, pp. 269–82.

Vaillancourt, Michael. 'Modal and Thematic Coherence in Vaughan Williams's *Pastoral Symphony*'. *Music Review* 52 (1991), pp. 203–17.

Vaughan, William. *German Romantic Painting*. New Haven: Yale University Press, 1994.

Vaughan Williams, Ralph. *National Music and Other Essays*. Oxford: Oxford University Press, 1987.

Vazsonyi, Nicholas. *Richard Wagner: Self-Promotion and the Making of a Brand*. Cambridge: Cambridge University Press, 2010.

Von Glahn, Denise. 'A Sense of Place: Charles Ives and "Putnam's Camp, Redding, Connecticut"'. *American Music* 14/3 (1996), pp. 276–312.

—— 'New Sources for the "St. Gaudens" in Boston Common (Colonel Robert Gould Shaw and his Colored Regiment)'. *Musical Quarterly* 81/1 (1997), pp. 13–50.

—— *The Sounds of Place: Music and the American Cultural Landscape*. Boston: Northeastern University Press, 2003.

Vovelle, Michel. 'La Marseillaise: War or Peace', in *Realms of Memory: the Construction of the French Past under the Direction of Pierre Nora*, ed. Lawrence D. Kritzman, trans. Arthur Goldhammer, vol. 3, *Symbols*. New York and Chichester: Columbia University Press, 1998, pp. 29–74.

Warrack, John. *Carl Maria von Weber*. Cambridge: Cambridge University Press, 1976.

Weber, Max. *From Max Weber: Essays in Sociology*, ed. H. Gerth and C. W. Mills. London: Routledge and Kegan Paul, 1948.

Weber, William. 'La Musique Ancienne in the Waning of the Ancien Régime'. *The Journal of Modern History* 56/1 (1984), pp. 58–88.

—— 'The Eighteenth-Century Origins of the Musical Canon'. *Journal of the Royal Musical Association* 114/1 (1989), pp. 6–17.

—— *The Rise of Musical Classics in Eighteenth-Century England: A Study in Canon, Ritual, and Ideology*. Oxford: Clarendon Press, 1992.

Wheeldon, Marianne. *Debussy's Late Style*. Bloomington: Indiana University Press, 2009.

Whittall, Arnold. *Romantic Music: A Concise History from Schubert to Sibelius*. London: Thames and Hudson, 1987.

—— 'The Later Symphonies', in Grimley (ed.), *The Cambridge Companion to Sibelius*, pp. 49–65.

Will, Richard. *The Characteristic Symphony in the Age of Haydn and Beethoven.* Cambridge: Cambridge University Press, 2002.

—— 'Haydn Invents Scotland', in *Engaging Haydn: Culture, Context and Criticism,* ed. Mary Hunter and Richard Will. Cambridge: Cambridge University Press, 2012, pp. 44–74.

Williamson, George S. *The Longing for Myth in Germany: Religion and Aesthetic Culture from Romanticism to Nietzsche.* Chicago: University of Chicago Press, 2004.

Wilson, Alexandra. *The Puccini Problem: Opera, Nationalism and Modernity.* Cambridge: Cambridge University Press, 2007.

Winter, Jay. *Sites of Memory, Sites of Mourning: The Great War in European Cultural History.* Cambridge: Cambridge University Press, 1995.

Wood, Caroline. 'Orchestra and Spectacle in the *Tragédie en musique*, 1673–1715: Oracle, Sommeil and Tempête'. *Proceedings of the Royal Musical Association* 108 (1981–82), pp. 25–45.

Wortman, Richard. 'The Coronation of Alexander III', in *Tchaikovsky and his World*, ed. Leslie Kearney. Princeton: Princeton University Press, 1998.

# Index

# Music in Society and Culture

*Volumes already published*

*History in Mighty Sounds:*
*Musical Constructions of German National Identity, 1848–1914*
Barbara Eichner

*Music and Ultra-Modernism in France: A Fragile Consensus, 1913–1939*
Barbara L. Kelly

*The Idea of Art Music in a Commercial World, 1800–1930*
edited by Christina Bashford and Roberta Montemorra Marvin